Life Settlements and Longevity
Structures

For other titles in the Wiley Finance Series
please see www.wiley.com/finance

About the authors

JIM ASPINWALL is Adjunct Professor of Mathematics at Florida Southern University, and on the board of a private equity firm, an investment bank and managing member of a hedge fund. With over 30 years in the business, Jim has a wide range of experience. At Chase Manhattan Bank he was the prime developer of Chase's REALM system, a risk management and derivatives pricing system, which was used, by Chase Manhattan Bank and over 200 clients around the world. While at Chase Jim was involved in Project Cloud, which was a state of the art Artificial Intelligence system that could forecast changes in credit rating 2 years out with a 95% accuracy rate. He has also had experience at other major Investment Banks, including Banc One and Nomura, Japan's largest Brokerage house, where he was involved in credit arbitrage trading and the creation of large credit structures. While head of quantitative research and development at Abbey National Jim oversaw the development, pricing and risk management of multiple structured products such as trigger swaps and power reverse dual currency bonds and was involved in the start up of Abbey's Credit Derivatives desk. Jim was in the undergraduate Liberal Arts program at The Ohio State University and studied Theoretical Math at the University of Cincinnati's graduate Mathematics program and quantitative finance in the MBA program also at the University of Cincinnati.

GEOFF CHAPLIN studied mathematics at Cambridge (MA 1972) and Oxford (MSc 1973, DPhil 1975) and trained as an actuary (FFA 1978) while working in a life insurance company. He moved to the City in 1980 and has worked for major banks (including HSBC, Nomura International, and ABN AMRO). As a partner in Reoch Credit he has consulted to law firms, hedge funds, corporate treasurers, institutional investment funds and risk control departments of major banks in the areas of credit and mortality risk. He has been involved in the credit derivatives market since 1996 and life settlements structures since 2003. Geoff has also maintained strong academic interests – he was a visiting (emeritus) professor at the University of Waterloo, Canada, from 1987 until 1999. He has also published many articles in Risk, the Journal of the Institute and Faculty of Actuaries, and others, speaks regularly at conferences and is the author of *Credit Derivatives: Risk Management, Trading and Investing* published by John Wiley & Sons Ltd, 2005.
(continued on back flap)

MARK VENN is Managing Director and Chief Executive Officer of ClearLife, a service provider which uses advanced data security and workflow management to support its customers in the life settlement and premium finance markets. Through its secure end-to-end business management system, ClariNet™, ClearLife assists its customers in all aspects of their business, from policy evaluation and risk analysis all the way to portfolio servicing and performance tracking. ClearLife has offices in Alexandria, VA and in London, United Kingdom.

Prior to founding ClearLife, in 2005 Mark established Mizuho International plc's Asset Finance Group, a principal investment team formed to focus on the life settlements market. Mark recruited and managed a team of six front office professionals and worked with Mizuho's support teams to build a dedicated legal, information technology and operations infrastructure for life settlements. Through this process, Mark gained invaluable experience in designing and developing business procedures, information technology and risk management systems, tailored to the specific requirements of longevity and mortality risk. He also initiated and maintained relationships with key service providers and counterparties in the life settlements market.

Over two years, Mark grew Mizuho's life settlements portfolio to over US$1.2 billion in face amount. While at Mizuho, Mark also founded the Institutional Life Markets Association ("ILMA"), which has become the leading trade association for institutional participants in the life settlements and premium finance markets.

Mark holds a master's degree in law from Cambridge University and qualified as a barrister in 1990.

Life Settlements and Longevity Structures

Pricing and Risk Management

Jim Aspinwall

Geoff Chaplin

Mark Venn

A John Wiley and Sons, Ltd., Publication

Library of Congress Cataloging-in-Publication Data

Aspinwall, Jim.
  Life settlements and longevity structures : pricing and risk management / Jim Aspinwall,
Geoff Chaplin, and Mark Venn.
    p. cm.
  Includes bibliographical references and index.
  ISBN 978-0-470-74194-8 (alk. paper)
1. Life insurance.   2. Viatical settlements.   3. Longevity.   I. Chaplin, Geoff.
II. Venn, Mark.   III. Title.
  HG8771.A7 2009
    368.32–dc22   2009015949

A catalogue record for this book is available from the British Library.

Set in 10/12pt Times by Aptara Inc., New Delhi, India

Contents

Introduction

by Con Keating

The proverb usually attributed to Benjamin Franklin that "*In this world nothing can be said to be certain, except death and taxes*" is apposite in the context of life assurance and offers some cold comfort from the uncertainty and financial market turmoil of recent times. As trust broke down, the very role of bank "inside money", in resolving the questions of uncertainty central to exchange in financial markets, came to be questioned. With volatility in financial markets surging to unprecedented levels, financial risk management for most assets became more black art than quantitative science. The mutual dependence of so many financial asset prices upon a common international liquidity became painfully evident with prices moving in near total lock-step; diversification, the workhorse of sound risk and investment management, has recently proved to be a very elusive concept in practice – and its value all the higher.

The search for investment assets that are not highly dependent upon the vagaries of the "animal spirits" evident in traditional financial markets is now more important than ever. Unfortunately the alternative investment world of hedge funds and private equity has proved disappointing to many; perhaps this should not have been a surprise given their dependence on credit from their prime brokers and bankers when executing their chosen investment strategies.

The essential risk process in any individual's life assurance policy is, of course, independent of the course of financial events. People live and die according to the natural rhythms of their life-cycles, unrelated to the performance of financial markets. Life settlements satisfy *the* primary requirement for risk diversification to be present and enduring.

It is important to realize, however, that some elements of the life assurance contract are affected by financial conditions more generally, and that complete independence of performance in consequence is not to be expected. For example, there is the obvious role of interest rates in discounting cash flows – as rates decline, this discount process results in higher present values for the cash flows expected under the policy, and vice versa. Indeed, as returns available elsewhere in financial markets vary, so the relative attraction of life settlements will co-vary and with that their quoted and traded prices.

The credit standing of the insurance company that has written the policy is a central issue, and of course also not entirely independent of the state of other financial markets. But it should nevertheless be noted that the recent much publicised difficulties of a few companies in the insurance world do seem to have arisen more from their forays into financial engineering than from their traditional insurance activities. The principal liquidity route to bank insolvency, the depositor run, is of course not a relevant concern for insurance companies.

There has always been a strange ambivalence evident to the development of secondary markets in life assurance policies. Often precisely those people who advocate the use of life assurance in personal life-cycle financial management resist inchoately the development of secondary markets. For some this may cynically be viewed as preservation of the status quo and their profitability; poor surrender value and uncompetitive markets go far in enhancing insurance company profits and the remuneration of their managements. For others, however, it appears little more than some social taboo associated with death. Notwithstanding that resistance, the life settlements market in the USA is hardly recognizable when compared to the mid-1990s; the growth is quite remarkable, and seems likely to continue.

A particular problem for this market, and one that has delayed or slowed its development, has been the absence of a single authoritative source of description and analysis. The life settlements market has also widely adopted and adapted techniques more familiar in capital markets and actuarial science; the diverse professional backgrounds of the authors of this book are particularly relevant in this context. The ambition of the book is to provide that single authoritative introductory source to life settlements, together with an elementary explanation of the financial techniques in use in this market, while remaining accessible to a broad readership.

The US insurance market has a unique character which arises in part from its state by state authorization, regulation and supervision. Against this background it is most useful to have the historic development of these products and markets outlined, together with some discussion of the principal issues surrounding this development. Chapter 1 addresses this history and the practices that have developed over time, and ends with a synopsis of the principal legal issues; this sets the institutional and contractual scene within which the modelling and analysis of subsequent chapters is framed.

Readers are introduced in Chapter 2 to the elementary mathematics of mortality and survival. The analogous relationship between credit, default and corporate survival is exploited supplying motivation for many of the models subsequently discussed. Somewhat irreverently, the difference between human and corporate mortality was once described to me as being "largely the extent to which resurrection is possible and credible". Certainly one of the more intriguing analytical aspects of credit risk insurance is the extent to which the likelihood of default and/or the magnitude of recovery post-default can be influenced by the active intervention of the insurer. This, of course, is largely a question of the corporate insolvency laws applicable within a particular jurisdiction to life settlements which is outside the scope of this book. However, it should be remembered that their legal status is not identical: both have the rights of individuals but their responsibilities differ, which some argue was a contributing factor to the incentive distortions that inflated the credit crunch.

Chapter 2 ends with a discussion of transaction rating. The role and relevance of ratings agencies, or statistical ratings organizations (SROs) as they are more formally known, has been the subject of much debate recently and indeed there are proposals extant from, among many others, the European Commission (EC) to introduce regulation. The urge to regulate in the wake of any series of financial problems is entirely understandable, but of course the history of the world has long been littered with instances of regulation written in haste which subsequently caused mayhem themselves. The financial economists' roundtable (FER) has recently produced a considered paper which sees the need for three types of reform and whose proposals are worth reproducing here in their entirety as this blueprint for regulation is clearly superior to that advanced by the EC:

> *First, FER supports strategies designed to improve SRO incentives by increasing the transparency of their modelling practices and holding their managements accountable for negligent ratings errors.*
>
> *Second, the FER challenges the wisdom of incorporating SRO ratings in securities and banking regulations issued by governmental entities. By outsourcing public authority to private firms, this practice intensifies the conflicts of interest that SRO personnel must resolve.*
>
> *Finally, to acknowledge differences in the degree of leverage that is embedded in different issues of securitized debt, FER recommends that SROs be required to state an express margin for error in their ratings for every tranche of securitized instruments.*

If nothing else, these proposals may serve as useful measures and metrics for the likely efficacy of any regulations ultimately adopted.

Chapter 3 is most ambitious in scope and complexity, but introduces complex subjects with simple vanilla products and models. The distinction between securitizations and structured products is important, and is often overlooked by other commentators. The need for error estimates associated with model forecasts, contained also in the last sentence of the above FER statement on ratings, should be a salutary caution for all when journeying into the land of financial models. Rather more generally, George Box offered the observation that: *"Essentially, all models are wrong, but some are useful."* The November 2008 Financial Reporting Council consultation paper entitled *Modelling* is recommended to those interested in the broader detail of the evaluation of model construction, robustness and fitness for purpose.

It is refreshing to see the introduction of complex and newer areas of financial modelling such as neural networks and levy processes, although, in the spirit of William of Ockham, it should be recognized that complexity is not usually a virtue in a model. Indeed with many models, one should be questioning in the formal mathematical sense the very existence of the statistic or parameter being estimated; never more was this true than with the recent major market equity index volatilities of 60%, 70% and 80%. Put rather simplistically, with volatility this high and unstable, it is reasonable to question whether the variance of the distributions is well defined. We should not lose sight of one of the overarching principles of stochastic control systems: simplicity is a virtue and is often a prerequisite for effective control – something that does not yet appear to have percolated through broadly to the financial risk regulatory authorities.

Chapter 4 illustrates some commonly utilized investment structures for life settlements and focuses attention upon differences in their financial risk aspects. In offering this introduction I feel that I can use this opportunity to make a few brief but general points about risk and risk management in a financial context. Many commentators have recently compared financial risk management to gambling, although this is badly misguided. With a game of chance we can specify ahead of the gamble all possible outcomes and assign probabilities to them. This is the mathematics of closed systems and the principal theorems of academic finance – Arrow-Debreu and Lucas's rational expectations – are of this fixed point closed system form. The reality is that we cannot specify all future possible outcomes, let alone assign probabilities to them; this is the land of open systems with far greater complexity than a casino. In only too many cases in financial risk management are closed system models applied in the wrong circumstances, but with life settlements or mortality risk more generally we are not faced by such open system risk management concerns – unless immortality becomes a realistic prospect. Indeed the effect of the time value of money is to limit the effect of mortality risk on current values.

The discussions of Chapters 5 and 6 – which are centred respectively on capital market mechanisms for the limitation of the risks of life settlements portfolios and the use of life settlement portfolios in mitigating the risks of traditional capital market instruments – are some of the strengths of this book. More often than not life settlements are first encountered in one of these settings.

The newest area of development in mortality and longevity analysis and risk management has been the development of derivatives which have, as their underlying, these risk factors. While there has undoubtedly been much discussion of these techniques and instruments, there is, to date, little evidence of their use in the execution of commercial business. However, going forward, if the obvious counterparty credit exposure concerns can be remedied, it is clear that these techniques have applications far broader than just life settlements.

The final chapter is concerned with hedging and risk management and includes methods for the evaluation of hedging effectiveness. This latter aspect is rather important. If we take nothing else away from the credit crisis, it should be that credit risk did not diversify as the rating agency models implied – and of course the similarity between credit "risk" and longevity "risk" is more than passing.

1
Life Insurance: Primary and Secondary Markets

INTRODUCTION

This chapter explores the background to the development of the market for life settlements – the sale of life insurance policies to financial investors. It describes the parties involved in a typical life settlement transaction and the associated process. It concludes with a review of some of the legal and practical issues associated with life settlements.

1.1 HISTORY, APPLICATION AND TERMINATION OF LIFE INSURANCE POLICIES

1.1.1 History: Early Life Insurance

Risk protection has been a primary goal of humans and institutions throughout history. Protecting against risk is the reason for insurance. One of the first records of life insurance was in Rome, where burial clubs were formed, known as *Fratres*. These clubs were set up by the poor to pay for the funerals of their members and to help the surviving family members financially.

Following the fall of Rome most types of insurance were abandoned. Around 450 AD, guilds began to be established for the various types of highly skilled trades. Accounts from that date suggest that these guilds helped their members with various types of insurance, including life and disability.

Insurance in Asia can be traced back to the Vedas, the oldest sacred texts of Hinduism. For instance, Yogakshema, the name of Life Insurance Corporation of India's corporate headquarters, is derived from references within the Rigveda, one of the texts. It is suggested that a form of "community insurance" was prevalent in India around 1000 BC, practised by the Aryans.

1.1.2 Modern Insurance

Illegal almost everywhere else in Europe, life insurance came into its own in England, where it was vigorously promoted in the late seventeenth century. During this time, insurance began to be transacted at Edward Lloyd's Coffee House in Tower Street, London, where ship owners and underwriters (known as "backers") met to put together insurance contracts and other shipping and merchant-related business.

While serving as a means of risk avoidance, life insurance also appealed strongly to the gambling instincts of England's burgeoning middle class. Gambling was so rampant that when newspapers published names of prominent people who were seriously ill, bets were placed at Lloyd's Coffee House on their anticipated dates of death. Reacting against such practices, 79 merchant underwriters broke away in 1769 and two years later formed a "New Lloyd's Coffee House" that became known as the "real Lloyd's". Making wagers on people's deaths ceased in 1774 when Parliament forbade the practice in the Life Insurance Act of that same year.

Slightly more tolerably – as one assumes they had at least some vested interest in the survival of the individuals in question – those same gamblers had made use of mortality information drawn from John Graunt's *Observations on the Bills of Mortality*[1] (published in 1662) to bet on the survival rates of those captains to whom they entrusted their ships. The tables published in Graunt's book are often cited as the first recorded example of a population mortality table and his work led to his election as a Fellow of the Royal Society – no mean feat for a haberdasher, at a time when those engaged in trade were largely ignored by this august body.

Life insurance is not gambling, but its development has spurred the growth of the mathematical science of probability. Today this science has been refined through actuarial studies and has become the foundation of pricing technology for credit default swaps (CDSs).

1.1.3 Insurance Moves to America

The US insurance industry was built on the British model. The year 1732 saw the birth of the first insurance company in the American colonies in Charleston, South Carolina, providing fire insurance. In 1759, the Presbyterian Synods in Philadelphia and New York sponsored the creation of the Corporation for Relief of Poor and Distressed Widows and Children of Presbyterian Ministers – the first life insurance corporation in America established for the benefit of ministers and their dependents. The first recorded issue of a life insurance policy for the general public in the United States occurred in Philadelphia, on 22 May 1761.

1.1.4 Summary

Life insurance was originally dominated by the mutual life insurance companies – companies owned by their policyholders, who therefore received a pro rata share of the company's profits from underwriting life insurance. Similar to the mutual life insurance companies were fraternal life insurance companies, which were started by the various trade associations and fraternal orders to assist their members, the first example being the Ancient Order of United Workmen, organized in 1868 in Meadville, Pennsylvania (Zelizer, 1983). These should be distinguished from stock life insurance companies where the profits are made for the benefit of the stockholders.

Today life insurance has become a major industry across the globe, with many different types of policies available for the consumer and offered by a multitude of insurance carriers. However, most development of structured life insurance products has been driven by the US market, primarily owing to its size. By the end of 2007, total life insurance coverage in the USA reached US$19.5 trillion, including corporate and individual cover (ACLI, 2008).

Companies such as Lloyd's have been keeping statistics on life expectancies since the late nineteenth century. Actuarial estimation of life expectancies in the general population has therefore become a very exact science. The challenge for an investor is to apply this science to the much smaller populations involved in life settlements.

---

[1] The full title being "Natural and Political OBSERVATIONS Mentioned in a following INDEX, and made upon the Bills of Mortality". The Bills of Mortality published a list of deaths in London and surrounding areas, including cause of death. They were created by Charles II and his civil servants to provide an early warning system for the onset and spread of bubonic plague – Graunt used them to generate a statistically based estimation of the population of London.

1.1.5 Applications of Life Insurance

An individual might have several reasons for taking out a life insurance policy on his or her life. Examples of these reasons include:

(1) to provide financial support to dependents in the event of the early death of the breadwinner;
(2) to pay for funeral expenses, death and/or inheritance taxes;
(3) to facilitate other financial contracts – for example, many mortgage lenders require that a life insurance policy be taken out as a precondition to a mortgage loan;
(4) to provide compensation for the disruption to a business in the event of the death of a senior employee or director (known as "key man" insurance); and
(5) as a means of saving (often tied to retirement).

The reason for taking out life insurance will often drive the selection of the type of policy. Some policy types will be appropriate for one situation but not for another. For example, a policy that pays out only on death is appropriate for (2) above whereas a policy that pays out at a certain age, if the insured survives to that age, is appropriate for (5) above. Similarly, a term life policy (under which the policy terminates with no payment if the insured lives longer than the specified term) might be appropriate for (3) above but is unlikely to provide appropriate cover for (1) or (4).

With the spread of company-sponsored and private pension schemes, insurance to provide coverage for dependents (item (1) above) is now often part of a pension scheme and may also be included in the benefits package offered by some employers.

1.1.6 The Parties Involved in a Life Insurance Policy

Several parties are involved in the issue and maintenance of a life insurance policy and each has different roles, responsibilities and interests in the process.

The *owner* of a life insurance policy (also described as the *policyholder*) is the person responsible for making premium payments under that policy. This person is often – but not always – the same as the *insured*, the individual whose life is the subject of the life insurance policy. On occasion, the owner of a life insurance policy may be a trust or a corporation (a so-called "non-natural person"), which is typically the case in policies issued for retirement or tax planning and, of course, for "key man" policies which are usually owned by the employer company.

There may be more than one person insured under a life insurance policy (see "Life Insurance Products and Underwriting" below for a discussion of "first-to-die" and "second-to-die" policies). There will also be at least one (and potentially more than one) *beneficiary*. The beneficiary receives the payout on the policy if it matures through the death of the insured(s) during the prescribed term. The owner has the right to designate the beneficiary of the policy and to change the beneficiary at any time. The company that has issued the life insurance policy is referred to as the *carrier* or the *insurer*. As life insurance is heavily regulated in most jurisdictions, the carrier will need to be licensed to issue life insurance in the relevant territory. In the United States, a carrier wishing to underwrite life insurance throughout the nation will require licensing in each of the fifty states and Washington DC as well as territories such as Puerto Rico.

In many cases – certainly in the case of "traditional" life insurance policies – the owner and the insured will be the same person and the beneficiary or beneficiaries will be dependents of the owner/insured. It is also possible for the owner and the beneficiary to be the same person – for example, where the dependent son takes out a life insurance policy on his parent in order to meet funeral expenses or where a company takes out a life insurance policy on several of its key employees. It is theoretically possible for the same person to be owner, insured and beneficiary under a life insurance policy, but this is rarely seen. It is, however, important to remember that the same person may play two roles in respect of a life insurance policy, as will be seen when considering the process involved in a life settlement.

1.1.7 Life Insurance and Life Assurance

In the United Kingdom, insurance market participants may refer to "life assurance" – not a term that exists in the United States. *Assurance* policies are designed to provide a payout upon the occurrence of an event which is certain, but where the timing is uncertain – hence the term "life assurance", as death is a certainty but the timing of death is uncertain. By contrast, *insurance* policies are designed to provide a payout upon the occurrence of an event which is uncertain, for example, buildings insurance or contents insurance where it is not certain that your house will collapse or that you will suffer a loss as a result of fire, flood or burglary. In this book we will refer to insurance policies throughout – the distinction between assurance and insurance being irrelevant to life settlements, securitization and/or derivatives.

1.1.8 Termination and Surrender of Life Insurance Policies

There are many reasons why the owner of a life insurance policy may find that policy surplus to requirements. The owner may have taken out insurance in relation to a house purchase or his or her own business. At a later date the policy may no longer be required: the house may have been sold, or the related mortgage loan paid down as the owner's income rose; dependents may have grown up or the insured's marriage may have broken down; a company may have evolved to a point where "key man" insurance is no longer appropriate; or the owner may be seriously ill and may need to realize investments to pay for medical expenses. A variety of reasons can exist for selling an asset and – except to the extent that the insured's state of health affects the value – these reasons should be irrelevant to the calculation of that sale price.

Until recently (the late 1980s), the only option was to surrender the policy to the life insurance company. This involves returning the policy to the carrier – literally, surrendering the right to receive payments under the policy – in exchange for a cash payment, known as the *cash surrender value*. Calculation of this cash surrender value is based upon the specific terms of the policy, but it will certainly depend upon the total amount of premiums paid into that policy since inception (among other factors). The cash surrender value may, in some cases, be zero (if, for example, the policy has only recently been issued and it is therefore subject to high surrender penalties). The cash surrender value will **not** take account of the health status of the insured; its calculation is prescribed in the policy document and the carrier is required to treat all owners of the same policy equally. This goes some way towards explaining why cash surrender values are low. Because the carrier cannot take into account the health status of the insured in calculating the cash surrender value, it must be conservative and therefore assume that it has given up a significant asset – the right to receive ongoing premium payments for many years to come – in exchange for being released from an insignificant liability such as the obligation to pay out the net death benefit at some date, potentially many years in the future. Simply discounting the respective asset and liability flows will show why it is rational for the carrier to be reluctant to surrender the right to receive those ongoing premium payments.

While the carrier is proscribed from incorporating current insured health status in the calculation of its cash surrender values, third parties are not so proscribed. Accordingly, in the late 1980s early 1990s, investors began to consider the risks and rewards of owning life insurance policies and found the returns to be highly significant, even on a risk-adjusted basis – as we will see when we look at the development of the viatical and life settlements markets later.

1.2   LIFE INSURANCE POLICY TYPES AND UNDERWRITING

There are several types of life insurance products that may feature in a secondary market transaction. The type of product is usually more relevant to physical transactions (such as the sale of legal and beneficial interest in a policy through a life settlement) rather than a derivative transaction (such as the assumption of longevity risk through an index swap, of which more later). The purchase of a physical policy exposes the buyer to all of the terms and conditions of ownership of that policy (including, for example, the risk that the carrier defaults upon its obligations under the policy), whereas the majority of derivative contracts focus more on the transfer of longevity risk as we will see in later chapters. It is important to note that very rarely are any two life insurance products created equally. Carriers have a vast range of policy options available, and as the design of a life insurance product is not usually based upon ease of access to the secondary market, it is vital to review the terms of each policy in detail before making a buying decision.

Policies can be divided into *permanent insurance* and *term insurance*. Permanent insurance policies continue for the duration of the insured's life (subject to a contractual maturity date, generally after what would be the insured's 100th birthday). Permanent insurance policies generally accrue a cash value. Payout of the accumulated cash value is assured at the end of the policy, and as long as the policy is kept in force the carrier pays out the contractual death benefit upon the death of the insured and retains the accumulated cash value. Term insurance, by contrast, only pays out the death benefit in the event that the insured dies during the specified term of the policy, and no cash value accrues to the owner. It is often possible to convert term insurance into permanent insurance, by following a procedure laid out in the policy document.

Policies can also be divided into *participating* and *non-participating*. A participating policy allows the policyholder to share in the carrier's surplus – the policy owner receives a dividend representing that portion of the carrier's premium income that is not needed to cover death benefit payments, additions to reserves or administrative expenses. It is very similar to participating in the carrier's investment returns. The vast majority of individual life policies purchased today are non-participating policies.[2]

1.2.1   Universal Life

Universal life policies are a type of permanent life insurance and are usually, but not always, non-participating. Universal life policies account for over 95% of the life insurance policies transacted in the life settlements markets and represent the majority of in-force life insurance policies in the United States (ACLI, 2008). Universal life policies can be described as combining a savings account (which we refer to here as the *cash account*) with a life insurance policy.

---

[2] 79% of individual life policies purchased in 2007 were non-participating (see Life Insurers Fact Book, 2008).

At this time, we should introduce a concept that may be new to those not experienced with life insurance terms – the *cost of insurance*, or "COI". Generally, the owner of a life insurance policy will describe the cost of that policy in terms of the amount of premium that he or she pays to the carrier, be it annual, semi-annual, quarterly or monthly. The uninitiated might assume, with some justification, that this premium is to compensate the carrier for agreeing to pay the net death benefit upon the death of the insured – indeed, the amount of the first year's premium payment is often the deciding factor when it comes to selecting the carrier for a new life insurance policy. In the case of a universal life policy, however, the premium is paid into the cash account and that cash account balance (the *account value*) then attracts interest at a given rate (the *current crediting rate*). The current crediting rate is set by the carrier based upon the performance of its investments, which, in the case of universal life policies, are usually long-term fixed interest assets, e.g., higher rated corporate and government debt instruments. The carrier then debits the cash account to meet expenses, typically an administrative charge on each premium payment and further monthly charges to meet the cost of maintaining and administering the policy. The carrier also debits the cash account with the COI – a specified amount of money that reflects the mortality risk assumed by the carrier (i.e. the risk that the insured dies earlier than the carrier expected, causing the carrier to lose money on the policy). For this reason, in calculating required premium payments, the carrier will apply the COI to the *net amount at risk* – the amount by which the contractual death benefit payment exceeds the account value that has been built up in the policy. The higher the account value, the less the carrier has at risk (as the carrier retains all of the account value upon the death of the insured). The distinction between premium payments and the cost of insurance is critical to the correct evaluation and pricing of a policy for a prospective life settlement, for reasons that will be explained in subsequent chapters.

We referred earlier to the cash surrender value of the policy, being the amount that a carrier will typically pay out were the owner to surrender the policy. The cash surrender value of a universal life policy is always less than or equal to the account value (it may be reduced by the amount of any *surrender charges* that are applied to the policy). Carriers typically impose surrender charges on newly issued policies during the first few years of issue (potentially as long as 15 years, depending upon the product). These surrender charges are imposed to offset the costs incurred by the carrier in issuing the policy – processing the application, underwriting the insured(s) and paying commission to the *producer* (the life insurance agent who introduced the new owner/insured to the carrier).

Universal life policies typically have a *policy maturity date*, which is defined by reference to the date on which the policy was first issued (the *policy issue date*). The policy maturity date is typically the first anniversary of the policy issue date (a *policy anniversary*) after the insured's 100th birthday. Policies issued before 2001 will occasionally have an earlier maturity date – for example, the policy anniversary after the insured's 99th, 97th, 95th or even 90th birthday.[3] If the insured survives beyond the policy maturity date, coverage under a universal life policy typically ceases, and after this time the carrier may be obliged to make no payment on the death of the insured, or may only pay out the cash surrender value.

The amount paid by the carrier upon the death of the insured depends on the terms of the policy. It may be a fixed amount (referred to as *level death benefit*) or a variable amount. If

---

[3] Insurance carriers have gradually migrated from the 1956 mortality tables to the 2001 mortality tables. The 1956 tables have much higher levels of expected mortality in earlier durations than the 2001 tables, so policies issued before the introduction of the 2001 tables generally set a maturity date well before the insured's 100th birthday as the tables assumed that the probability of living to age 100 was statistically insignificant.

variable, it may be described as *increasing death benefit* (in which case it usually equals the fixed amount stated on the policy plus the then current account value) or in the case of policies issued recently, as *return of premium* (ROP), in which case the death benefit payable at any time is a function of a stated amount plus the total amount of premium payments made up to that date. Policies with a ROP component typically have a limit on the total amount to be paid out, such that the ROP component stops within a few years of issue, with the policy usually reverting to a level death benefit payout.

Accrual of interest on the account value for a universal life policy is generally tax free in the United States, making this a good policy for estate planning.

1.2.2   Variable Universal Life

Variable universal life policies – also a type of permanent life insurance – have many of the same characteristics as universal life policies. The difference arises in the management of money in the cash account. As mentioned, cash account balances in universal life policies are typically invested by the carrier in long-term, fixed rate instruments with minimal credit risk. Accordingly, the current crediting rate on those policies tends to be reasonably low albeit – it is to be hoped – relatively stable. Variable universal life policies introduce an element of discretion for the owner as it is possible to invest the balance in the cash account across a number of different sub-accounts, managed by the carrier. These sub-accounts will have exposure to different investment strategies and asset classes, potentially including short-, medium- and long-term fixed rate instruments, equities, commodities and corporate credit. The opportunity to vary the mix of investments creates a greater potential rate of return, albeit with higher volatility.

Universal life and variable universal life policies have flexible premiums and for that reason are often described as *flexible premium adjustable life policies*.

1.2.3   Term Insurance

Term insurance is frequently used for "key man" policies and for policies purchased to support a fixed term mortgage loan. The phrase describes a policy with a fixed term, which pays out a prescribed amount to the beneficiary following the death of the insured within that term. There is no accumulated account value for term insurance and the insurance coverage is terminated at a specific date with no further payment if the insured survives beyond this date. Owners of term policies pay premiums based solely on what the carrier determines is required to cover the risk of the insured's death during the term, given the insured's age and medical history (as underwritten just prior to issue of the policy) based upon a fixed death benefit amount. As a result, younger persons and shorter terms will generally attract lower insurance premiums.

1.2.4   Endowment Insurance

An endowment policy has a fixed term, like a term policy, but unlike a term policy it pays a defined amount in the event that the insured survives to the end of the fixed term. Premiums are higher – often substantially higher – than term insurance contracts, as there is certainty that an amount will be paid out by the carrier. However, the amount to be paid is frequently uncertain, as it is usually dependent upon the performance of investments made by the carrier.

Endowment policies were commonly issued in the UK to support interest-only mortgage loans. Such policies were often sold to UK homeowners during the 1990s on the basis that the endowment would increase in value over the term of 15, 20 or 25 years such that it would repay the principal amount due on the mortgage loan at its maturity. Poor performance of the underlying investments and a litany of mis-selling complaints, as well as a change in the tax treatment, caused endowment policies to fall out of fashion and very few have been issued in the UK in the last five years (ABI, 2008).

The widespread use of endowment policies in the UK created one of the first secondary markets for insurance instruments – the traded endowment policies, or "TEPs" market. TEPs were bought and sold at auctions conducted by specialist endowment brokers. Such auctions continue today, although compared to the US life settlements market, the value and number of the endowment policies traded is very low.

1.2.5   Whole Life

Whole life insurance is the generic name for a policy that continues until the death of the life assured. Such policies have increasing accumulated value as the insured ages. The premium payments are structured to "overpay", such that the account value will build up to the contractual death benefit amount by a defined age (usually 100), progressively reducing the carrier's net amount at risk.

The most common type of policy sold in the USA is the whole life policy. Here the policy holder pays a fixed annual premium over his or her life in exchange for a whole life policy with specific death benefits or face amount as stated on the policy. The beneficiary of the policy receives full benefit from the policy regardless of the date of death. Premiums are usually constant, based upon the average actuarial premium amount needed to cover claims for the policy holder's entire life – as a result premiums are larger than needed to cover the mortality risk in the early years. The excess premium is invested at a pre-stated rate and as this cash surrender value grows it can be used for other possibilities.

Whole life insurance combines features of both term insurance (where the premiums are fixed) and permanent life insurance (where a cash value accrues within the policy and payout of the cash value is assured at expiration of the policy). In the life settlements market, participating policies are most often whole life policies rather than universal life policies.

1.2.6   Policy Riders

Carriers will frequently offer extra options with their insurance products, to be added at issue. These are commonly known as "riders", such as:

- *Extended Death Benefit Rider:* In this case, if the insured lives past a certain date (typically the first policy anniversary after he or she has attained the age of 100), no further premium payments are due but the carrier remains obliged to pay the net death benefit (or some other amount, depending on the terms of the rider) if the insured dies before a later policy anniversary date, e.g. age 105, 100, 115 or 125.
- *Term Rider:* If the insured dies within a short time after issue of the policy (say 5 or 10 years), the death benefit payment is increased by a fixed amount, equivalent to owning a separate term life insurance policy on the insured.

	Insurance Type	Premium	Death Benefit	Cash Accumulation	Investment Choice
Term	Level Term Insurance	Relatively low, fixed	Fixed during the term, then zero	No	No
	Renewable Term Insurance	Relatively low, increasing	Fixed	No	No
	Decreasing Term Insurance	Relatively low, decreasing	Decreasing during the term, then zero	No	No
Permanent	Whole Life Insurance	Relatively high, fixed	Fixed minimum amount, some upside	Yes	No
	Universal Life Insurance	Relatively high, flexible	Variable	Yes	No
	Variable Whole Life Insurance	Relatively high, fixed	Fluctuates with the performance of the investment	Yes	Yes
	Variable Universal Life Insurance	Relatively high, flexible	Fluctuates with the performance of the investment	Yes	Yes
Endowments	Level Term Insurance	Relatively high, fixed	Fixed during the term, then zero	Yes	No

Figure 1.1   A comparison of insurance products

Riders may be offered as incentives to purchase insurance from a particular carrier or offered as a "bolt-on" to a policy when first issued. We will look in later chapters at how riders can affect policy pricing. Figure 1.1 compares some characteristics of the different policy types.

1.3   DEVELOPMENT OF THE VIATICAL SETTLEMENT AND LIFE SETTLEMENT MARKETS

1.3.1   History and Inception

Although the secondary market for life insurance is relatively new, the judicial ruling in the Supreme Court case of Grigsby v. Russell in 1911 declared the policy owner's right to transfer legal ownership and beneficial interest to a third party at his or her own discretion.

The first of such transactions occurred amidst the devastating impact of the AIDS epidemic in the mid-to-late 1980s, when life insurance policies were purchased from terminally ill individuals, for an amount made up of a percentage of the policy face value. A key driver for this change was the requirement of vast sums of capital by terminally ill AIDS patients to primarily finance expensive health care fees. Subsequently, this type of transaction was given the term "viatical" and the viatical settlements industry was born.

However, it was only after the Health Insurance Portability and Accountability Act (HIPAA) was signed into law in 1996 that the life settlements market emerged. Aside from imposing a series of administrative, physical and technical safeguards on the storage and use of protected health information, HIPAA essentially confirmed the right of the owner of the life policy to transfer ownership/beneficial interest to a third party having no insurable interest in the life of the originally insured party, while determining the tax treatment of the corresponding gain. This effectively allows third party investors to freely purchase life insurance policies at the discretion of the policy owner and beneficiary, hence, creating a market for life settlements.

1.3.2 Negative Sentiments

The life settlements industry has had more than its fair share of negative sentiment. Early transactions in viatical settlements involved the sale of policies insuring the lives of AIDS patients to some retail investors, with the promise that the returns would be extremely high and realized in a very short period as long as the investors continued to pay the required premiums over this period. The "magic bullet" effect caused by the availability of highly active antiretroviral therapy (Palella *et al.*, 1998) to combat AIDS resulted in the insured individuals living much longer than the investors had been led to expect, leading to losses and the inevitable lawsuits from state and federal regulators.[4] Increasing regulation – as insurance is regulated at state level in the USA one is transacting in 50 separate markets rather than one – and the cross-over of insurance methodologies and experience has led to most of the bad apples being weeded out. However, the "headline risk" continues, with an enforcement action against a significant market participant brought by Eliot Spitzer[5] in 2006, resulted in a claim for $2.1 billion in triple damages under the federal RICO statute (Racketeer Influenced and Corrupt Organizations Act of 1970).[6]

The life insurance lobby has used these "bad apples" in support of its campaign to promote regulation that will effectively eliminate the life settlements industry, through the implementation of legislation at state level and via the National Association of Insurance Commissioners (NAIC) Model Act drafting process.[7] The life settlements industry has responded to this pressure through lobbying for appropriate regulation at state level – supporting consumer choice through maintaining the availability of life settlements in as many markets as possible.

---

[4] SEC v. Mutual Benefits Corp *et al.*, Case No. 04-60573-CIV-MORENO: a widely reported lawsuit against Mutual Benefits Corp., its directors and affiliates over the mis-selling of viatical settlements to investors.

[5] The People of the State of New York by Eliot Spitzer v. Coventry First LLC, Montgomery Capital Inc. *et al.*, index no. 404620/06 (New York State Supreme Court).

[6] Ritchie Capital Management, LLC *et al.* v. Coventry First LLC *et al.*, ECF Case 07 Civ. 3493 (DLC) (USDC Southern District of New York).

[7] See the press release at: http://www.naic.org/Releases/2007_docs/viatical_settlements_model.htm. The NAIC treats the Model Act as under continuing development.

1.3.3   Market Size

Two recent surveys have estimated that the available market size will grow from an estimated $13 billion in 2004 to $161 billion over the next few decades; through a combination of population ageing and increasing market penetration (penetration is currently estimated at around 3% – see Bernstein Research (2005, 2006)). The face amount that cleared through the market grew from around $10 billion in 2005 to $12 billion in 2007.[8] In common with other asset classes, the life settlements market contracted significantly during 2008, as institutional investors fight to repair the damage to their balance sheets. However, life settlements is attracting a much wider audience within the investor community than was the case even two years ago, and once investor activity picks up again, growth in life settlements activity should be much more rapid than in other, more traditional, asset classes.

1.3.4   Institutional Involvement

The bad press dealt to the life settlements industry might explain the historical lack of capital markets interest in what should be an attractive asset class – after all, credit derivative swap (CDS) pricing was derived from life insurance underwriting methodologies, so credit traders should feel that they understand the risks extremely well. Intensive regulatory and compliance requirements, the lack of market transparency and efficiency and extremely high barriers to entry have historically tended to turn most investors away from the product. In March 2007, the Institutional Life Markets Association (ILMA) was formed by six leading investment banks (Bear Stearns, Credit Suisse, Goldman Sachs, Mizuho International, UBS and West LB) to promote legislative initiatives and best practices in the life settlements and premium finance industry. ILMA is endeavouring to develop and agree higher standards of market practice and to enhance transparency in the industry through fee disclosure and standardized documents.

1.4   THE PARTIES INVOLVED IN A LIFE SETTLEMENT TRANSACTION

We will review the process associated with a typical life settlement transaction later in this chapter. First, let us introduce the parties involved in the transaction. For this purpose we assume that the transaction is a "traditional" life settlement, i.e. that the life insurance policy has not been originated through a premium finance programme. We divide the parties into *direct* participants (those directly involved with the movement of the policy and the transfer of title) and *indirect* participants (those who provide services that are associated with the transaction).

Direct participants in the transaction include:

- *Policy owner:* Also known as the "policy holder" and in the context of a life settlement transaction as the "seller", this person is the owner of the policy immediately prior to the transaction. The policy owner may be a natural or a non-natural person. Once the policy has been sold, this person has no further interest in the policy.
- *Agent:* This is usually the life insurance agent (often referred to by insurance companies as a "producer") who sold the policy to the policy owner, or with whom the policy owner has

---

[8] The 2007 figure was taken from Conning Research (October 8, 2008) Life Settlements: New Challenges to Growth; the 2005 figure was estimated on the basis of a poll of market participants.

an existing relationship. The agent's role is to introduce the seller to a broker and then to liaise between the seller and the broker as necessary to ensure successful completion of the transaction.

- *Broker:* A life settlements broker. If the policy owner is located in a state which regulates life settlements and/or viatical settlements, the broker will be required to be licensed in that state in order to participate in the transaction. The broker's role is to represent the interests of the seller in dealing with the provider. This includes soliciting the best offer for the policy by submitting the policy to as many providers as possible, in order to create a wide market for that policy.
- *Provider:* A life settlements provider. As for the broker, the provider may be required to be registered in the state in which the policy owner is located. The provider's role is to act as the buyer of the policy (with respect to the policy owner). It is the provider's responsibility to ensure that sale and transfer documentation conform to relevant state regulations relating to life settlement practice and procedure. The provider may also have an ongoing role in the transaction, as state regulation may require the provider to retain records and to assume responsibility for servicing the policy after completion of the transaction.
- *Investor:* Sometimes referred to as the "funder", the investor is usually the ultimate owner of the policy. The investor usually acquires the policy in a transaction with the provider which, although legally distinct, is often so close in time as to be virtually simultaneous with the acquisition from the seller. The investor may be a natural person, but more commonly is a bank, a large institutional investor, a hedge fund or an established special purpose vehicle (SPV).
- *Escrow agent:* All transactions in regulated states (i.e. transactions where the policy owner is resident or organized in a regulated state) are required to employ an escrow agent. The escrow agent receives the signed change of ownership (CoOwn) and change of beneficiary (COB) forms from the policy owner and releases these forms to the provider or trustee once the agreed purchase price for the policy has been received from the provider. The escrow agent holds the agreed purchase price until the change of ownership and change of beneficiary has been acknowledged by the carrier and then releases the agreed purchase price to the seller. The escrow agent is usually a bank and will often be affiliated with the trustee.
- *Trustee:* Frequently, an investor that is an institution, a fund or a SPV will engage a third party to act as trustee of the policy. The role of the trustee is to safeguard the documents associated with the policy (the policy form and/or policy certificate). In some structures, the trustee also becomes the legal owner of the policy itself, with the investor becoming the beneficial owner. This is usually done to comply with the financing structure of the investor; for example, debt issued by a SPV may be secured on the policies which the SPV acquires, in which case the trustee will function as trustee of the debt and will hold the policies for the benefit of the debt-holders. In this case, the trustee is responsible for completing and filing the change of ownership and beneficiary form with the carrier. The trustee becomes the owner of record of the policy with respect to the carrier and receives all of the policy correspondence (e.g. premium notices, grace notices and annual statements) from the carrier. In this case, the trustee will be required to work with the tracking agent to complete and submit the claim package in the event of the death of the insured (or both insureds, in the case of a "second to die" joint life policy).
- *Collateral manager:* A transaction which uses a SPV or a fund will usually employ a collateral manager (also referred to as the "investment manager" or "asset manager"). The

collateral manager chooses the policies that will be acquired by the SPV or fund. The duties of the collateral manager with respect to any one policy acquisition may include:

- confirming that the policy satisfies the eligibility criteria for inclusion in the portfolio of policies owned by the SPV or fund;
- monitoring performance of the policy over time; and
- undertaking optimization of the policy to minimize premium payments and maximize actual and/or prospective returns to the investors in the SPV or fund.

The collateral manager will have other duties with respect to the portfolio of policies. We will review these in later chapters.

Indirect participants in the transaction include:

- *Insured(s):* The insured or insureds are natural persons whose lives are insured under the policy. Although the insured will be required to sign documents as part of the closing of the transaction, he or she is not a contractual counterparty as – unless the insured is also the policy owner – he or she has no legal or beneficial interest in the policy.
- *Carrier:* The carrier is the insurance company that has issued the policy. The carrier is critical to the transaction, since it pays the sum assured in the event of the death of the policyholder. The investor therefore assumes the credit risk of the carrier as part of the transaction. The carrier's role in the transaction is to register the change of ownership and beneficiary in its books and records – it is the acknowledgement of this registration that usually triggers the payment of the purchase price and/or broker fees, as will be seen when we review the transaction process itself.
- *Medical underwriter:* Sometimes confusingly referred to as the "life expectancy provider", the medical underwriter uses its knowledge of elder mortality and the medical records of the insured to produce a life expectancy report for each insured. The life expectancy report typically includes an estimation of the life expectancy for the insured (usually expressed as a number of months) and may also include a paragraph describing the salient features of the insured's health, ICD9 codes appropriate to the insured and a mortality curve for the insured. Note that a life expectancy report is not necessarily required for a transaction to close – however, the majority of investors require at least one life expectancy report and, more often than not, two or three life expectancy reports (each from a different medical underwriter) in order to proceed with the transaction.
- *Servicer:* The servicer has no direct role in the completion of the transaction, but rather is responsible for the "care and feeding" of the policy after its acquisition. Its responsibilities may include monitoring correspondence on the policy, undertaking health status tracking (see "Tracking Agent" below), updating medical information and monitoring the premium payments on the policy.
- *Tracking agent:* Like the servicer, the tracking agent has no direct role in the completion of the transaction. Once the transaction has closed, the tracking agent is charged with tracking changes in the health of the insured. The tracking agent typically does this using a combination of direct contact with the insured (e.g. telephone calls, postcards) and public record checks (e.g. the US Social Security Administration Death Master File,[9] which tracks the "return" of social security numbers upon the death of an individual). The tracking agent is usually responsible for obtaining copies of death certificates after the death of an insured.

---

[9] http://www.ntis.gov/products/ssa-dmf.aspx.

Any business investing in life settlements will need advice and assistance from professional advisers. Although rarely directly involved in an individual life settlement transaction, maintaining a relationship with experienced professional advisers is critical to the success of the business as a whole. Actuaries help determine the appropriate mortality tables (successors to John Graunt's work in London in the 1660s, now based upon many millions of observations); assess the reasonableness of the mortality schedule provided by medical examiners; perform an underwriting review of the medical examiners used in the transaction; help in the valuation and structuring of the transaction; and may help to determine the liquidation value of a portfolio of policies. Attorneys help to ensure that documentation is complete and has been prepared in compliance with appropriate regulations, and they may also check compliance with "insurable interest"[10] and other insurance axioms. They may help to verify that brokers and providers (and, in some cases, medical underwriters) are licensed in the relevant states; draft medical disclosure forms complying with privacy laws; and, in the case of a SPV, they will ensure that the bankruptcy remote issuing entity has been created in such a way as to protect the interests of the investors. Finally, accountants will assist in structuring a fund or SPV in order to optimize its withholding tax treatment; address the recognition of income and expenses by the fund or SPV; and advise on the tax treatment appropriate to the acquisition, maintenance and disposal of a portfolio of life settlements.

1.5   THE LIFE SETTLEMENT PROCESS

The process for a life settlement transaction is complex and lengthy. Transactions rarely take less than 90 days to complete and frequently take 120 days or longer, particularly if the bidding process is not successful on the first attempt.

The process below assumes that there is a single broker, a single provider and a single investor involved in the transaction and also assumes that the policy owner is the sole insured on the policy. In reality, there are usually multiple brokers, providers and investors involved in the bidding process – such that the flow of information (at least in the stage up to a purchase price being agreed) looks something like Figure 1.2.

In our perfect world of a single broker, a single provider and a single funder (although two or more medical underwriters!), a typical life settlements transaction works as follows:

1. The policy owner decides to sell his or her policy and contacts the agent to initiate the process. The decision may, in some cases, have been prompted by the agent following research which indicates that the policy owner can reduce the cost of ownership by selling a more expensive (in COI terms) "old" policy and replacing it with a less expensive "new" policy.
2. The agent contacts a broker, licensed in the state of residence of the policy owner. The broker sends to the agent some documents for completion by the policy owner – usually an application form and a HIPAA release form. The HIPAA release authorizes the disclosure of personal health information concerning the policy owner by attending physicians, hospitals and other health care providers. The application form will ask the policy owner to set out his or her recent medical history and to supply information on the policy, including the names of all beneficiaries.

---

[10] The doctrine of insurable interest will be discussed later in this chapter.

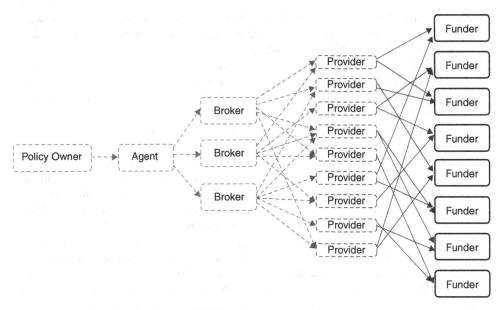

Figure 1.2 Information flow in a typical life settlement transaction

3. The policy owner completes the HIPAA release form and the application form. The agent requests a current policy illustration from the carrier. This illustration usually shows the minimum constant annual premium required to carry the policy to maturity (usually age 100 or later) with a minimal remaining account value at maturity (usually $1 or $1000, depending on the face amount of the policy).

4. Once all of the documents have been completed and the policy illustration received, the agent sends them to the broker.

5. The broker sends the signed, completed HIPAA release form on to one of the companies that retrieves medical records for the insured – a process that can take four to six weeks to complete. The retrieval company will request an APS (attending physician statements) from each doctor identified on the application form. It will also request hospital records and, in some cases, prescription records for the policy owner. A full set of medical records can total between 100 and 250 pages.

6. The broker sends the set of medical records to one or more medical underwriters. The broker will select the underwriters based on its knowledge of the target provider's requirements – typically two or more life expectancy reports are required.

7. The medical underwriters generate a life expectancy report for the insured, based upon the information contained in the medical records. The medical underwriter usually constructs a vector of mortality debits and credits for the insured, which may vary with time (as there is evidence to suggest that some illnesses have a greater effect in the short term than the medium to long term). The medical underwriter applies this vector of debits and credits to a mortality curve appropriate for the insured's gender, smoking status and age and calculates a life expectancy for the insured. The life expectancy report will contain this life expectancy and may also contain a specific mortality curve for the insured, an outline of the vector of mortality debits and credits and commentary on the insured's health and

medical history. The process of producing a life expectancy report typically takes between 10 days and four weeks from receipt of the medical records, assuming that the medical records submitted by the broker are complete.

8. The broker receives the life expectancy reports from each medical underwriter and sends them, together with the illustration and a completed application form (which may be the provider's application form, completed by the broker based on information in the broker's application form) to the provider.

9. The provider receives the package from the broker and reviews the contents. If the policy appears suitable for the provider (i.e. it is likely to be purchased by a funder with which the provider is working), then the provider will set the policy up in its systems for evaluation. Evaluation of the policy typically breaks out into a *qualitative evaluation* (for example: is the policy face amount above the minimum and at or below the maximum amount the funder will accept? Is the age of the insured above the funder's minimum attained age?) and a *quantitative evaluation*. The quantitative evaluation involves entering the characteristics of the policy into a pricing model to calculate an assumed gross purchase price at one or more target IRRs (which will be set by the funder). The quantitative evaluation will be developed using a pricing model that has been developed by the provider and/or the investor, or using one of the third-party models that have been developed for use with life settlements.

10. If so required, the provider will forward the package for the investor's direct evaluation. In this case, the investor will usually communicate to the provider a maximum gross purchase price which the investor will pay to acquire the policy.

11. Prior to making a decision on the policy, the provider may communicate with the investor and with the broker. It may ask the broker for information about other bids that the broker has received for the policy and may seek clarification of information submitted by the broker.

12. Once it has completed the policy evaluation, the provider either advises the broker that it is unwilling to consider a bid for the policy (e.g., because it falls outside the provider's "buying box") or it communicates an initial bid to the broker. Often, the gross purchase price communicated to the broker will be accompanied by restrictions on what proportion of that gross purchase price can be paid to the broker and agent as commission and what proportion must be paid to the seller. It may also require that the compensation earned by the broker and agent be fully disclosed to the policy owner at the time of contract.

13. Assuming that a bid is communicated to the broker, the provider may then become involved in an auction for the policy, in which the broker seeks to ensure that it is obtaining the best possible price for the policy owner, who is the broker's client.

14. Ultimately, the agent and the policy owner will identify a bid that they wish to pursue. Although this should be the highest bid in terms of gross purchase price, it is often difficult for the agent and/or broker to compare "apples with apples" when considering bids. Many fail after a price has been agreed because of incomplete or inconsistent information; others fail because the documentation requirement is too onerous for the policy owner to complete. For these reasons and others, the bid ultimately recommended to the policy owner may not be the best bid economically, but rather the most likely to close (in the experience of the broker and/or agent).

15. Once the bid has been selected, the broker informs the provider. The provider then prepares a closing document package, which includes all of the documentation necessary to close

the transaction – a life settlement contract, consent forms for the policy owner's spouse, any dependents and the current beneficiaries under the policy, plus any disclosure forms required by the funder or mandated by regulation in the policy owner's state of residence. Once complete, the closing document package is sent to the broker, who sends it on to the agent.

16. The agent liaises with the policy owner to complete the closing document package. Many of the documents are required to be notarized upon execution by the policy owner, his or her spouse/dependent(s) and the current beneficiaries under the policy. The agent will also request a written verification of coverage (VOC) from the carrier, which sets out updated information concerning the policy – recent premium payments, account value, cash surrender value, current and future COI and details of any outstanding policy loans or recent withdrawals. The agent will also assemble the original documentation for the policy, including the policy form and the policy schedule, as well as a copy of the carrier's application form completed by the policy owner when the policy was originally issued. The agent will also request a copy of the relevant CoOwn and COB forms from the carrier, which will be signed "in blank" by the policy owner (so that the identity of the new owner can be completed later in the process).

17. Completion of the closing document package usually takes some three to four weeks from receipt by the broker. Once completed, the broker sends the original life settlement contract and the signed CoOwn and COB forms directly to the escrow agent, to be retained pending receipt of the *seller compensation*. This is the portion of the gross purchase price that is to be paid to the seller (as distinct from the portion due to be paid to the agent/broker as commission). The balance of the documents in the closing document package (together with copies of the documents sent to the escrow agent) are sent directly to the provider.

18. Once the closing document package is received by the provider, fully completed, the provider usually sends it on to the investor for review. The investor conducts a document verification process, which compares the contents of the closing document package with the information previously received by the funder on the case, to ensure consistency with what has been received before. The investor may outsource this responsibility to a third party with staff experienced in reviewing closing document packages and with systems designed to administer this process effectively.

19. The document verification process can usually be completed in two to three business days, assuming that no further issues present themselves. Examples of issues that can occur at this stage include pricing issues (e.g. the information on the written VOC discloses that the account value, cash surrender value or net death benefit amount differ significantly from what was assumed during policy evaluation) and compliance issues (e.g. a discrepancy between information on the original policy application and the information provided in the broker's application form or the provider's application form).

20. Assuming that no problems arise in the course of document verification, the provider instructs the escrow agent to send the original CoOwn and COB forms to the trustee for signature and onward transmission to the carrier.

21. The trustee completes the CoOwn and COB forms upon receipt, signs them and sends them on to the carrier.

22. The carrier processes the change forms upon receipt and sends back an acknowledgement of the change of ownership and beneficiary to the trustee, at which point the trustee is confirmed as the legal owner of the policy on the books and records of the carrier. The trustee sends this acknowledgement on to the provider and to the investor. The trustee

updates its own books and records to show the provider as the beneficial owner of the policy. Immediately thereafter, the trustee transfers the beneficial interest in the policy to the investor.

23. The escrow agent then releases the seller compensation to the policy owner. The payment to the policy owner starts the clock on the rescission period – the period during which the policy owner is legally entitled to reverse the sale should he or she choose to do so. This period is usually between five and fifteen business days after payment of the seller compensation and it varies from state to state.

24. After the expiration of the rescission period, the investor transfers the balance of the gross purchase price (i.e., the commission due to the agent and/or broker) to the provider. The provider pays this on to the broker, which pays the agent.

A timeline for the transaction process is shown in Figure 1.3.

1.6   LEGAL ISSUES

The legal issues surrounding life settlements are complex and shifting. Prospective investors in life settlements should take steps to ensure that they seek and obtain legal advice from an attorney with experience of life settlements and life insurance. Nothing set out in the following paragraphs, or elsewhere in the book, should be taken as advice – it represents the authors' opinions as to the scope of some of the more critical legal issues affecting the market at the time of writing.

Although the life settlements market as such does not exist in the UK, a lot of the key legal concepts draw their basis from English law and particularly English insurance law. US insurance law has departed significantly from English law over the last century – English law still treats insurance as an inalienable contract, under which the policy cannot be separated from the risk. The US, by contrast, takes exactly the opposite view and holds that the policy owner has the right to transfer legal ownership and beneficial interest in the policy to a third party at his or her discretion.[11]

Both US law and English law draw upon the doctrine of insurable interest to support their respective positions on transfer of ownership. A person taking out a policy of life insurance is required to have an insurable interest in the life so insured, i.e. an interest in the continuing health of the insured. It is assumed that a person has an insurable interest in his or her own life, as well as in the lives of his or her spouse and/or dependents. An insurable interest can exist between business partners and between a company and its key employees (but not necessarily its non-key employees). It may also exist where there is no more than a financial connection between the parties – e.g. where you stand to suffer a financial loss were the insured to die. English law requires that the insurable interest continue throughout the life of the policy[12] – US law requires that an insurable interest exist at issuance only. In the USA, therefore, the absence of an insurable interest on the part of a subsequent assignee or transferee of the policy does not invalidate that assignment or transfer, nor does it render the policy void or unenforceable against the carrier (assuming that the owner has complied with its other terms).[13]

---

[11] Grigsby v Russell, 222 U.S. 149 (1911) (United States Supreme Court).

[12] Although note that there is currently a proposal before the Law Commission to consider amending the law on insurable interest: Insurance Contract Law Issues Paper 4: Insurable Interest, January 14, 2008.

[13] Grigsby v Russell, 222 U.S. 149 (1911) (United States Supreme Court).

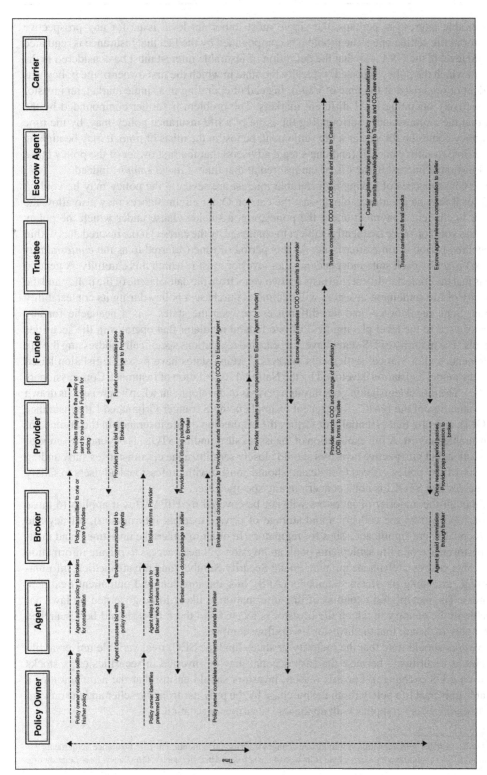

Figure 1.3 Timeline of a life settlement transaction

Insurable interest is, perhaps, the single most important legal issue for any prospective investor in life settlements. The problem is compounded by the fact that insurance is regulated at state level in the USA – so that the definition of insurable interest must be considered in the state in which the policy is issued (typically the state in which the first owner of the policy was resident or organized at the time of issue). Instead of operating in a single market, an investor is effectively operating in 51 different markets. The problem is further compounded by the fact that the circumstances surrounding the issue of a life insurance policy may, by the time the policy comes up for sale as a life settlement, be lost in the mists of time. It may be nigh on impossible to satisfy oneself (and one's legal advisers) that the first owner of the policy had a valid insurable interest in the life of the insured at that time. *Caveat emptor*, indeed.

The consequences of having no insurable interest are severe – the policy may be void *ab initio* or it may be unenforceable against the carrier. Other circumstances may also allow the carrier to challenge payment under the policy, e.g. a suicide clause under which the policy becomes void (or, more frequently, subject to challenge by the carrier) if the insured dies within a specified period of time after issue. As this period of time (referred to as the *contestability period*) is set by each state independently, an investor must research this carefully. A general rule is that the contestability period lasts for two years from the date of issue of the policy and the majority of life settlement investors will decline to purchase a policy during its contestability period. State regulation – and the differences between the states – is a headache for any investor used to the level playing field of one federal regulator that operates in the securities markets. The majority of US states have now enacted regulations specifically addressing the life settlements and/or viatical settlements markets.[14] Many states have passed legislation based upon the model legislation developed by the National Association of Insurance Commissioners (NAIC). The model legislation goes through periods of development when a new issue is drawn to the attention of the NAIC – one recent example being STranger-Originated Life Insurance (STOLI), a phrase that essentially describes the origination of life insurance in the absence of an insurable interest. A full exploration of the issues surrounding STOLI is beyond the scope of this section, but prospective investors should closely scrutinize the circumstances surrounding the issue of any policy offered for sale and should consult with professional advisers to satisfy themselves that STOLI is not a concern in any specific case.

Although the majority of investors will not be covered by HIPAA (as it applies to those whose job involves the collection and storage of private medical information), privacy and confidentiality are significant issues for regulators. In order to undertake investment and monitor performance of a life settlements pool, an investor will need access to private information (e.g. name, address, telephone number, Social Security Number) and private medical information (e.g., attending physician statements (APS), hospital inpatient and outpatient treatment records). The receipt and retention of this information is likely to be governed by laws applicable in the country in which the investor is located and these laws should be researched thoroughly to ensure that the investor's workflow complies.

Investors should note that the majority of states (and the SEC) treat variable universal life policies as securities – because the cash account may be invested in securities (e.g., stocks listed on a US exchange). For this reason, investors should ensure that the acquisition of a variable universal life policy (both the purchase by the provider from the seller and the onward sale to the investor) complies with applicable securities legislation.

---

[14] The list of states with regulations promulgated changes from month to month. The Life Insurance Settlements Association (LISA) maintains a legislative map at its website which is updated frequently: http://www.lisassociation.org.

1.7   OTHER ISSUES

Investing in life settlements is not for the faint of heart. The business and legal issues are significant and the infrastructure required to support a business is complex; but the risk-adjusted returns can be compelling, with little or no correlation to other asset classes and low volatility. An investor wishing to explore participation in the market will have many issues to consider in addition to those already listed above. A few of these issues, and some suggestions as to how to address them, are listed below.

- *Medical underwriting is an inexact science.* A life expectancy report is a statement of opinion, not of fact, and there is no guarantee that the insured dies before, at, or after the number of months specified in the report. Medical underwriters usually draw their life expectancies by reference to an assumed population of 1000 lives, each having the same health characteristics as the insured. The life expectancy is usually expressed as the number of months after which at least 50% of this assumed population has died. By definition, this means that up to 50% of this assumed population has **not** died by this date. Remembering that the insured is as likely to die after the stated life expectancy as before is vital to an appreciation of how longevity risk can affect returns in a pool of life settlements.
- *No two policies are created equal.* When considering acquisitions, it is vital to read the policy form and policy schedule in full, together with the terms of any policy riders. Many policies will have characteristics that may not manifest themselves in the illustration but will be of economic value in the future, even if they cannot easily be factored into the pricing of the policy prior to acquisition.
- *Information has a very short half-life.* Given the speed with which life expectancy under-writers adjust their methodologies, investors should try to refresh medical information and life expectancy assumptions regularly. As this may have an impact on revenue recognition, investors should agree an appropriate policy to address such information updates with senior management, advisers and auditors, when setting up their business.
- *Relationship management is as important as data management.* With so many different parties involved in each transaction, managing all of the associated relationships is a full-time job. Many investors with a banking background will assume that "money talks" and that sellers will not distinguish one offer from another on the basis of anything other than price, but in a market with very limited standardization, nothing could be further from the truth. Life settlements will undoubtedly migrate towards a standardized platform over time, but needing to placate regulators and legislators in 50 different states is a significant time barrier to that process. Soliciting and closing good quality policies therefore depends on having the right relationships and on maintaining those relationships.

In this chapter, we have examined the circumstances that gave rise to the development of the life settlements market. We have discussed the type of policies that an investor might encounter in the life settlements market and identified the direct and indirect participants in a life settlement transaction. We have also outlined the process involved in a typical life settlement transaction and considered some of the legal and practical issues associated with transacting in life settlements. The next two chapters will focus on the pricing of mortality-linked instruments, such as life settlements, before we go on to consider some of the structures in which life settlements can be employed.

2

Mortality and Credit Structures, Valuation and Risk

INTRODUCTION

In investment banking and as investors we are familiar with mortality products in the context of corporate mortality (default). Such products include bonds, loans, default swaps and CDO structures. Later in the book we will be looking at structures built around life settlements portfolios: our aim in this chapter is to explain the relevant human mortality calculations and relate them to calculation methods familiar in finance for the analysis of the instruments mentioned above.

2.1 CDS AND CDO CONTRACTS

2.1.1 CDS

A CDS contract has many similarities with a life insurance contract. A CDS has a reference entity – the entity whose "death" triggers the payment on the contract – and has a maturity date (like a term insurance contract) and an agreed premium payable over the life of the contract. There are some irrelevant (for our purposes) complications in CDS contracts to do with the definition of the death of the reference entity (correctly termed a "credit event"), and the payoff on a credit event is equivalent to a cash payment of the amount "insured" less a proportion, R. This proportion is termed the recovery rate and applies because typically, under corporate defaults, debt does not become worthless – there is often a significant recovery on a credit event. If we assume that recovery is zero then a CDS contract and a term life insurance contract have essentially the same features, and the same modelling approach is appropriate for either. This is covered in more detail below.

A CDS contract has two parties to the deal – a writer of protection (having the same role as a life insurance company for life insurance contracts), and a buyer of protection. Typically for CDS the buyer and the writer are unrelated to the reference entity. The buyer pays the regular agreed premium and the writer pays the "sum insured" (less recovery) in the event of a credit event during the life of the contract.

2.1.2 CDO

CDO is a generic term for a financial structure where a portfolio of risky assets defines a reference pool whose cash flows (particularly related to credit events) are used to define the cash flows on "tranches of risk". The acronym originated from "Collateralized Debt Obligation" but the correct name is now CDO and typically such structures are neither collateralized, nor related to debt or obligations. The underlying assets may be CDS contracts, bonds (CBO), loans (CLO), lease or rental contracts, mortgages, or any other credit risky structure and may be physically backed by such assets (or a mix of such assets) or typically synthetically related to such assets.

For example, there are standardized credit portfolios – iTraxx related to European reference entities, and CDX related to US reference entities. We will look at the example of the CDX IG (investment grade) reference pool which comprises 125 reference entities each equally weighted. The precise names are selected every six months – giving rise to different series related to the date of introduction of that particular reference pool. The rules for selection need not concern us in detail: the names are chosen from liquid (regularly traded) reference entities for CDS contracts to ensure a certain diversification across different industries and – at the time the index is constructed – must be investment grade. The index can be traded in various maturities (3, 5, 7, and 10 years) with a writer of protection paying capital sums if a credit event occurs, and a buyer of protection paying a regular premium (say, 50-bps on a 5-year contract). If such a contract is traded in a notional of $100 million then each of the 125 reference entities is equally weighted, and this amounts to a risk to or protection on $0.8 million for each reference entity. If after, say, 9 months a credit event occurs on one name then assuming zero recovery the writer pays $0.8 million to the buyer and the contract continues on the remaining 124 names ($99.2 million notional); the 50-bp premium continues but is related to this reduced notional. Further credit events give rise to further capital payments and a gradually reducing premium as the notional reduces (although the premium rate of 50-bps remains fixed).

Such standardized index portfolios are used to trade standardized CDO tranches which work as follows, again taking the CDX IG 5-year as an example. Risk is tranched into 0–3%, 3–7%, 7–10%, 10–15%, 15–30% and 30–100% of losses. The former figure in each pair is referred to as the "attachment point", and the latter figure as the "detachment point" and the tranches are often referred to using [3, 7] notation to mean the 3–7% tranche. The 4% difference is known as the tranche thickness, and all the percentages relate to the original size of the portfolio (before the impact of any defaults). We illustrate how this works by considering two 5-year transactions – one on the [0, 3] tranche in $30 million notional (i.e., a $1,000 million reference pool) and one on the [3, 7] tranche in $40 million (again with a $1,000 million reference pool). The agreed premiums might be as follows.

1. On the [0, 3] tranche there will typically be a lump-sum up-front payment from the buyer of protection to the seller and, in addition, a regular ongoing payment of 500-bps per annum (amounting to 5% × $30 million = $1.5 million per annum[1]).
2. On the [3, 7] tranche we will assume a premium of 200-bps.

If a credit event occurs after 9 months – assuming zero recovery – the writer of the [0, 3] tranche protection pays the buyer $8 million and the notional reduces from $30 million to $22 million. The contract continues with the 500-bp premium related to the reduced notional (so reducing from $1.5 million to $1.1 million). There is no impact either in terms of capital flows or changed premium amounts on the [3, 7] tranche.

On a second default – again assuming zero recovery – the writer of the [0, 3] tranche protection again pays the buyer $8 million, the notional reduces to $14 million, the premium amount reduces to $0.7 million, and there is no cash flow impact on the [3, 7] tranche.

---

[1] Actually premium is paid on an "actual/360" day count convention so the amount is slightly higher than this.

A third default (with zero recovery) reduces the tranche notional to $6 million and the premium to $0.3 million.

The fourth default results in a loss of $8 million on the notional reference pool. The writer of the [0, 3] tranche – where only $6 million of protection now remains – pays $6 million to the buyer of protection and that contract is now terminated. Now, for the first time, the writer of the [3, 7] contract will make a capital payment of $2 million to the buyer and the contract continues with a reduced notional of $38 million and the amount of premium reducing from $0.8 million to $0.76 million on an annual basis.

A fifth default will result in a further $8 million payment and a reduction in the remaining notional to $30 million, etc.

It should be realized that a transaction can take place on any one tranche independently of any other tranche – for example, a deal could take place on the [10, 15] tranche with no accompanying deals on any other tranche.

2.1.3   Synthetic and Cash Flow CDOs

The above example is of a market standard "synthetic CDO". Other synthetic CDOs are created by investment banks related to different pools of reference entities and with different tranching structures and maturity dates. For example, to meet a client's need a bank may sell 6-year protection on a [2, 5] tranche of protection on a reference pool of 100 US, European and Asian names. The notional amount associated with each name will not necessarily be equal and may differ for each and every name. Such transactions are referred to as (a tranche of) a bespoke synthetic CDO.

If the CDO is backed by a real portfolio of assets (as opposed to simply a list of reference assets) then the structure can become more complicated with all the cash flows related to the assets – premium/coupon payments, for example – being used to drive both capital and income payments on a CDO structure. Typically in such cases all tranches of protection exist and are traded at the outset (but secondary trading on such tranches is rare) and there may be a variety of other complications such as quality tests on the reference pool to determine whether and how much is paid to certain tranches on certain dates.

Typically "investors" buy risk and receive premium (they are selling protection) and traders take both sides, but bank structuring departments will generally be buying protection from investors on bespoke CDO tranches and hedging risk by buying and selling protection on standard CDO tranches and CDS contracts.

CDS and CDO contracts are covered more fully in Chaplin (see the Bibliography for details).

2.1.4   Life Policy CDOs

The same structuring concepts can be applied to a reference pool of life settlements. The seller of protection will be the owner of individual life insurance policies and the "investor" will be buying protection. Premiums will be paid and capital will be received as the insured individuals die. The first tranche of protection – say the [0, 30] tranche – will receive capital first but at unknown dates and the final tranche – say the [80, 100] tranche – will be the last to be paid off completely. A life policy CDO is closely analogous to the buyer of protection side of a financial CDO but will be a new concept for "investors" who typically take the underlying risk.

2.2 VALUATION APPROACH AND DATA

2.2.1 Approach

Investment banks approach the valuation (mark-to-market) and hedging of their products using mathematical models that operate as an interpolation tool, given known data. A familiar example is the use of the Black-Scholes option pricing model, which is *calibrated* to known data (traded option prices) and an *implied volatility surface* is produced. This surface (defined at certain dates and strikes) is used together with *interpolation rules* to obtain volatilities at intermediate (or extrapolated) dates and strikes, which can then be used to price options on the books – but not trading at these dates and strikes. Another example (which we will explain in more detail below) is the use of the Poisson model to *imply default rates* given an assumed *recovery rate* at future dates for a specific reference entity using the market prices for credit default swaps maturing at those dates. These rates, together with an *interpolation routine*, are then used to price default swaps at intermediate dates.

This valuation approach is variously referred to as "pricing off your hedge" or "risk-neutral pricing".

A different approach to the same assets is usually taken by investors. In valuing a default swap on a specific entity they will first look at the rating of the underlying credit. Other information may also be used, but in the most naive approach this rating, together with historical default and recovery rates obtained from the rating agency studies, is used to calculate default probabilities to future dates (again using an interpolation routine) and these probabilities can then be used to value the asset.

This valuation approach is variously referred to as "historical pricing", "natural measure pricing" or "actuarial pricing".

The reader should note three things.

1. Investment banks also often use natural measure pricing when valuing structures referencing non-traded assets – for example, a CDO based on car lease contracts, rental receipts, Formula-1 racing receipts, etc.
2. The mathematical model used in both approaches may be identical – it is only the data used in the model that differs.
3. The application of the two different approaches to the same asset (where this is possible) will give two different results. The risk-neutral approach may be correct in the context of the calculation of the appropriate hedges to have in place to lock in a certain profit on a deal, while the natural measure approach may be correct in the context of predicting the financial outcome of the deal.

In the context of life settlements the risk-neutral pricing approach is not possible – several maturity policies on a single specific life do not trade actively in the secondary market. Pricing of life insurance contracts therefore follows the natural measure (actuarial) approach.

2.2.2 Data

The reader is assumed to be familiar with the data collected by the rating agencies in their default and recovery studies. In addition there is academic and banking studies and research in these areas (see, for example, Altman *et al.*, 2004)

Actuarial pricing typically uses data collected and analysed by actuarial bodies based on raw data supplied by investment companies and others in prescribed formats. The Valuation Basic Table (VBT) Team collects and analyses data from contributing companies for the Society of Actuaries in the USA, and the Continuous Mortality Investigation (CMI) Committee does likewise for the Institute and Faculty of Actuaries in the UK. In the following paragraphs we briefly describe some of the key components of this data analysis – where relevant including specific approaches for the VBT data – and identify areas of relevance for valuation of current policies.

In analysing data generally, it is important to separate the data into similar sets. In the context of life insurance this might mean collecting data in the first place only for certain types of policies; subsequent subdivision of the data might be by age, sex, smoking status, term since the policy commenced (the *select period*) and underwriting status (for example, some policies might require minimal underwriting, some might follow a standard underwriting procedure and others might have been subject to a much tougher underwriting analysis). Mortality curves are developed separately for these subdivisions. In the case of the VBT data select periods up to 25 years were used and the tables for policies greater than 25 years in force are referred to as ultimate tables.

In analysing the data certain items are typically excluded – policies with very large or small amounts insured, for example – and at high ages where data is sparse, general population mortality data is included. The mortality curves for ultimate rate are derived first and the select period curves are then derived by relating select mortality rates to ultimate rates. In deriving ultimate mortality rates the raw observed rates are not reflected in the tables but attempts are made to remove random irregularities in real data to estimate the true underlying mortality rates. Such a process is referred to as *graduation* and many such smoothing methods are available.

In the case of the "2008 VBT" tables, data used for the analysis related to the years 2002–2004 but tables are produced appropriate to mortality in the specific year 2008: explicit account is taken of secular changes in mortality from 2003 (the history mid-point) to 2008 and is referred to as an "improvement factor". Note in passing that if a valuation is being performed in 2011 using the 2008 table, then explicit account needs to be taken of the following:

1. Expected mortality changes between 2008 and 2011.
2. In valuing expected cash flow in a later year, expected changes in mortality between 2011 and that year.

The VBT data used an annual improvement factor applied to mortality rates (1% improvement per annum for males with ages between 30 and 80; 0.5% per annum for females with ages between 45 and 80).

2.3 THE POISSON PROCESS

The Poisson process is widely used in actuarial science, in the life sciences and in investment. It is the core model behind the pricing of default swaps, and is used in the pricing of many structured products. In fact, it is so widespread it is often used without the user being aware that he or she is applying a Poisson process.

The following definition is taken from Wikipedia:

A Poisson process, named after the French mathematician Siméon-Denis Poisson (1781–1840), is the stochastic process in which events occur continuously and independently of one another (the word event used here is not an instance of the concept of event frequently used in probability theory). A well-known example is radioactive decay of atoms. Many processes are not exactly Poisson processes, but similar enough that for certain types of analysis they can be regarded as such; e.g., telephone calls arriving at a switchboard (if we assume that their frequency doesn't vary with the time of day, but it does), webpage requests to Wikipedia, or rainfall.

We can add the following relevant examples of a Poisson process: the time to a credit event for a specific reference entity; the time to death for a given individual.

Homogeneous Poisson Process

A homogeneous Poisson process is defined by a rate parameter h (also known as the intensity) that can be interpreted as the rate of occurrence of the event, such that the probability that a default occurs in the next moment of time Δt is $h \cdot \Delta t$ and the probability that the name survives from now (time $= 0$) to time t is

$$S(t) = \exp(-h \cdot t)$$

Non-homogeneous or Time-Changed Poisson Process

In general, the rate parameter may change over time. In this case, the generalized rate function is given as $h(t)$. The survival probability becomes

$$S(t) = \exp\left(-\int_0^t h(x)dx\right)$$

A homogeneous Poisson process may be viewed as a special case where $h(t) = h$, a constant rate.

Expected, Median and Modal Life

The above terms have precise mathematical meanings and the concept of expected life is widely used in life insurance. However, it is often misused – instead of expected life, one of the other measures is meant instead. The correct definitions are as follows.

Expected life is the expectation under the Poisson distribution (the "average" life) and is given by

$$EL = \int_0^\infty t \cdot h(t) \cdot \exp\left(-\int_0^t h(x)dx\right)dt$$

The *median life* (or *half-life*) is the point where half the population is expected to have died and is given implicitly by *Me*, where

$$0.5 = \exp\left(-\int_0^{Me} h(x)dx\right)$$

The *modal life* is a less common concept and is the point where the number of mortalities (relative to the initial population) is highest and is given by finding the maximum value of

$$h(t) \cdot \exp\left(-\int_0^t h(x)dx\right)$$

There may be several local modes.

Implementations

This model (and others) may be applied in continuous time (as above) or in discrete time (for example, using end month or end year dates). In the investment banking quant world the continuous time implementation is generally preferred, while investors and the actuarial community often use discrete time implementations. Either approach is possible and capable of giving accurate and, to all intents and purposes, identical results. One advantage of the continuous time approach is that an explicit time interpolation procedure has to be built in at the outset and the accuracy of the implementation can be easily adjusted. On the other hand, the discrete time approach presents problems if a more accurate implementation is required as this necessitates a fundamental rewrite of the implementation, and the discrete time implementation is often rather ad hoc.

In this chapter we follow the continuous time approach.

2.4 SINGLE LIFE MORTALITY CALCULATIONS

In this section we review the pricing of financial products (CDS contracts and life settlements) on a single reference entity.

2.4.1 Corporate Mortality: CDS Contracts and Bond Pricing

We describe the industry standard CDS model as documented in Chaplin (2005). This uses a time-changed or non-homogeneous Poisson process driving the hazard rate and an assumed recovery rate on default.

The benchmark, par or fair market CDS spread for a CDS contract is the fixed fee for CDS protection, such that the present value of the contract is zero and is the premium obtained from the market for a range of different maturities (typically 1–5, 7 and 10 years for active reference entities). Standard CDS contracts have regular fee payments on a 20th March, June, September, December cycle. In addition, any accrued but unpaid fixed fee is paid upon the triggering of a contingent payment after a credit event has occurred (if any).

Valuing a CDS Contract

This uses the same formula as is used for bootstrapping the hazard rate. The only difference is that in the case of a valuation of a deal on the same reference entity, the contractual premium (rather than the fair market premium) is taken into account.

Mathematical Description

The value to a holder of protection of a CDS subject to premium p basis points per annum is given by the following formula:

$$V = \int_{t_0}^{t_n} (1 - R(t)) \cdot h(t) \cdot \exp\left(-\int_{t_0}^{t} h(x)dx\right) \cdot D(t)dt - p \cdot \sum_{i=1}^{n} \frac{t_i - t_{i-1}}{360} \cdot S(t_i) \cdot D(t_i)$$

$$-p \cdot \sum_{i=1}^{n} \int_{t_{i-1}}^{t_i} \frac{t - t_{i-1}}{360} \cdot S(t) \cdot D(t) \cdot h(t)dt \qquad (2.1a)$$

where $R(t) = R$ is the constant assumed recovery rate, $h(t)$ is the hazard rate, $S(t)$ is the survival probability given by

$$S(t) = \exp\left(-\int_{0}^{t} h(x)dx\right) \qquad (2.1b)$$

and $D(t)$ are the discount factors (typically log-linearly interpolated from the input data).

The CDS model is usually implemented as a "closed form" model using fast numerical integration.

General Description

The formula is in three parts. The first part represents the value of the payment to the protection holder of par minus recovery. This payment can occur at any time between the effective and the maturity date and occurs at time t with a probability equal to the probability that the reference entity survives up to time t multiplied by the hazard rate. This payment is then discounted off the discount curve back to today (we typically assume a 30-day delay in the payment of the recovery amount).

The second part calculates the quarterly premium amount (difference in days between payment dates times the premium rate divided by 360), and multiplies this by the probability that the reference entity survives up to the premium payment date, then discounts this back to today.

The third part calculates the accrued to be paid in the event of a credit event at time t (number of days since last coupon date times the premium rate divided by 360), multiplied by the probability that a default occurs at time t (as above – the probability that the reference entity survives up to time t multiplied by the hazard rate), discounted back to today.

Risk-Neutral Pricing: Bootstrapping the Hazard Rate/Survival Probability Curve

A set of fair market premiums for CDS contracts on the underlying reference entity is used to compute a term structure of implied default probabilities assuming a hazard rate curve up to the maturity date. This hazard rate is calculated so that the present value of each CDS contract is zero (using the formula above). This formula requires the effective date, maturity date, premium payment dates, a discounting curve derived from LIBOR/swap rates, the survival probability curve obtained from the hazard rate, and the assumed recovery rate in the event of a credit event. Premiums are calculated on an actual/360 day count convention.

Interpolation of the hazard rate curve to intermediate dates is typically piecewise constant or piecewise linear. Currently piecewise constant is more commonly used because minor irregularities in the CDS curve are magnified by piecewise linear calibration and typically lead to a "sawtooth" shape of hazard rate curve.

Natural Measure Pricing: Calibrating to Historical Data

The above method takes historically derived recovery rates and market-implied hazard rates from traded CDS prices. The alternative approach of using historically derived data for hazard rates is simply applied as follows. Typically the rating for the reference entity is used (or a derived rating may be used). This rating is then used to look up one-, two-, three-, ..., n-year survival probabilities based on historical data. The first is used with formula (2.1b) to derive a one-year hazard rate. The two-year and the one-year survival probabilities are then used to calculate a one-year forward one-year survival probability (the smaller probability divided by the larger) and again formula (2.1b) is used to calculate the one-year forward one-year hazard rate, and so on.

Negative Hazard Rates

Some sets of calibrating data may imply negative forward hazard rates. This is an indication of an arbitrage – the longer-dated contract is cheaper [in capital value] than the shorter-dated contract but offers more protection. In such circumstances the credit modelling theory collapses (it is based on the assumption of arbitrage-free markets). In addition, the time-changed Poisson process no longer works. The presence of negative forward rates should be confirmed by checking the implied hazard rates at each calibrating date and, in the event of a negative value, the calibrating data should be corrected to be consistent with no arbitrage. This is unlikely to apply if historical data is used because, even though the historical data will have been manipulated in some way, negative hazard rates will have been precluded in the derivation of the historical summary data.

Bond Pricing

A similar approach can be used for bond pricing and is useful where bond data but no CDS data is available.

The pricing model is similar to the CDS model and may be used to derive an implied hazard rate curve. In practice bonds are not as liquid as CDS contracts and additionally different bonds may have different features that make one bond (and the implied hazard rate) not directly comparable to another from the same issuer. We describe the case of a single bullet bond without options where we assume a single constant hazard rate curve.

Mathematical Description

The value to a holder of a deterministic bond carrying a coupon g_i paid at time t_i for $i = 0$ to $n - 1$ and where $t_{n-1} = T$ is given by the following formula:

$$V = \int_0^T R(t) \cdot (1 + A(t)) \cdot h(t) \cdot S(t) \cdot D(t)dt + S(T) \cdot D(T) + \sum_{i=0}^{n-1} g_i \cdot S(t_i) \cdot D(t_i)$$

where $R(t) = R$ is the constant assumed recovery rate, $h(t) = h$ is the constant hazard rate, $S(t)$ is the survival probability given by

$$S(t) = \exp\left(-\int_0^t h(x)dx\right) = \exp(-ht)$$

and $D(t)$ are the discount factors.

General Description

The formula is in three parts. The first part represents the value of the recovery amount on a default event. Recovery is based on outstanding capital amounts and also the accrued coupon from the last coupon payment date. This payment can occur at any time between the effective and the maturity date and occurs at time t with a probability equal to the probability that the reference entity survives up to time t multiplied by the hazard rate. This payment is then discounted off the discount curve back to today (we assume a 30-day delay in the payment of the recovery amount).

The second part multiplies the value of promised cash flow at maturity (income and capital) by the probability that the reference entity survives up to the due date, then discounts this back to today. The third part values the expected coupons.

Note that if we assume that the recovery rate is zero then the formula corresponds to valuing the bond off a shifted discount curve where the shift is the bond spread (its "z-spread"). Typically recovery rates for debt are greater than zero – a common mistake is to assume that the bond spread corresponds to the default rate, but this is not the case if $R > 0$.

The model may be extended to contingent cash flow single name structures, but is not needed here.

Risk Analysis in the Corporate CDS Context

The valuation model has two main objectives:

1. To provide a mark-to-model valuation for those deals on the books that do not trade in the marketplace based on information gleaned from deals that do trade.
2. To provide risk numbers to allow the risk of the book of positions to be managed.

Explicitly this latter point means stressing the input data to the model to determine how the value of each deal would change if the input data changed as assumed. These risk numbers include sensitivity to the following.

1. Interest rate levels (a "shift" in the curve) and changes at specific maturities ("bumping" the curve).
2. A shift in the calibrating spread/CDS premium curve.
3. Bumping the calibrating spread/CDS premium curve at each calibrating maturity in turn.
4. Recovery rate sensitivity.
5. Default event sensitivity.
6. For portfolio products there is also sensitivity to correlation.

These risk numbers are then used both in the hedging of individual trades and in the risk control of the entire book. Typically the latter involves a hierarchical view of the book – working up from data at the individual deal level, then aggregating all deals of the same name, then aggregating by (for example) industry and rating, ultimately getting to a single risk number for the entire book. At each level limits are imposed on the maximum risk that will be tolerated. For example, this might mean being prepared to accept a large risk to a single reference entity (if it is investment grade) but relatively small (near zero) interest rate risk across the entire book.

2.4.2   Generic Life Policy Valuation

We have now actually described the model used for valuing life contingencies. It is the same as the "default" model used above – "default" corresponds to death of the life assured and the "recovery" on a life assurance contract is zero. Differences are essentially those of calibration and classification.

A "reference entity" is now a "life assured" and the key parameters defining the survival or hazard rate curve are sex and smoking status (at the time the policy was taken out) instead of rating. The mortality rate is a function of the individual's age and there are other key parameters that actually give rise to a set of mortality curves (a mortality table) rather than a single curve for a given age and smoking status: the age at which the policy was taken out and known medical and other information on the individual. This gives rise to a hazard rate curve appropriate to the (say) male non-smoker who took out his life insurance policy at age (say) 43.

In practice many pricing implementations use an unnecessarily crude implementation – using survival and default probabilities based on age last birthday, or nearest age. This leads to valuation problems as the life assured goes through a birthday and can be improved by interpolating to the age in months (or quarters, etc.). The best solution is to use a continuous time implementation and to interpolate to both

(a) exact age, and
(b) exact period since the policy was taken out.

This process can be improved by calibrating the model (with a continuous time dependent hazard rate) to the mortality rate table. The calibrated model can then directly calculate mortality and survival probabilities to any date directly using inbuilt interpolation functions. The interpolation function over time could be any of the following.

(a) *Piecewise constant:* The hazard rate is assumed constant between birthdays. This is un-realistic but simple and fast to implement; it is typically used in the credit markets where calibrating data is less smooth than human mortality data.

(b) *Piecewise linear:* This is only a little more complicated and nearly as fast. The slope of the hazard rate shows jumps at birthdays but the rate itself is continuous.

(c) *A smooth function:* Some smooth functions also have simple closed form implementations but this is not generally the case.

Two interpolations are required – one over age and the other over select period. It is normal to use the same interpolation function (constant, linear, . . .) for both.

The generic mortality curves are based on historically collected data. These curves may be adjusted on an ongoing basis to reflect secular changes that are believed to have occurred since the data was collected, and to reflect changes which are anticipated to occur in the future. An 'ageing' formula close to that used in the construction of the US VBT tables may be used. For example, males aged under 85 may have 2001 VBT mortality multiplied by $\exp(-0.01)$ per year from July 2001, and females by $\exp(-0.005)$ to allow for secular improvement in mortality rates for younger males and younger females from 2001 up to the valuation date. Further adjustment may be applied after the valuation date.

This "generic table" approach to survival curves is modified for each individual at the time a policy is take out according to the known medical history and lifestyle of the individual. This process is usually undertaken with the help of an "underwriter" whose expertise is in the interpretation of medical and other data into survival curve adjustments, and may also include advice from medical practitioners.

In the following section we discuss ways in which the generic mortality curve may be adjusted for an individual. These adjustment methods are also of potential interest in stress-testing policy values.

2.4.3 Mortality Adjustments

Mortality curves are based on very little specific information about the individual – typically the person's sex, smoking status at the time the policy was taken out, and age when the policy was taken out (the survival rates are obtained using the individual's actual date of birth and the current date). At the time an individual applies for a policy – or at other times if a medical examination or questionnaire is required in relation to a transaction of the policy – more detailed information is available concerning the individual's lifestyle and health status. This information is used to decide the type of adjustment to make and how large that adjustment should be. The main types of adjustment to the generic survival curves are as follows.

Additional Mortality

One of the simplest adjustments is to add a constant additional mortality (hazard) rate C to the rates implied in the survival curve – or, equivalently, multiply the annual survival probabilities by a factor (< 1 if $C > 0$). Such an adjustment is commonly made if the life assured takes part in hazardous pursuits such as hang gliding, bungee jumping without a rope, Russian roulette, etc.

Added (Subtracted Years)

Again this is simple to apply and the life assured is treated as someone born n years earlier, where n is the number of added years. This is often used to handle a wide range of medical conditions.

Mortality Factors

A mortality factor is a multiplier applied to the hazard rate and leads to a lower survival curve if the factor is greater than 1. Again this is a common approach to handling a range of medical conditions.

The above approaches may be combined – for example, a mortality factor M and a constant additional hazard rate C can be combined to give a new hazard rate $C + Mq$, where q is the unadjusted hazard rate (for the age and select period).

Life Expectation

Life expectation and median are defined above, but one definition of life expectancy used in the marketplace is the time period T such that the probability of surviving to T is 50% (i.e. the median, not the expectation). In trying to match the underwriter's "expectation" we must first determine clearly what the underwriter means by the term. An underwriter may have a feel for the impact of certain conditions on the life "expectation" of the individual and may give his opinion in this form – the actuary may then use this information to adjust the mortality curve so that the underwriter's life expectation is produced. This may be done by adjusting the curve by added years, or a mortality factor, or other means.

It is important to remember that all the above adjustments should be made to the hazard (mortality) rate curve and a survival probability curve recreated from the adjusted hazard rates.

2.4.4   Risk Analysis in the Life Assurance Context – Mortality Curve Stresses

Unlike the corporate CDS market it is generally not possible to effect hedges of life insurance contracts. The aim of the risk assessment is therefore to calculate and control the risks on the entire portfolio. This will typically mean hedging out interest rate risk, and also trying to achieve a sufficient level of risk diversity that exposure to regional effects or specific medical conditions is acceptably small. One risk that cannot be diversified away easily (for an investor in life insurance contracts) is a general reduction in mortality rates. An insurance company writing life insurance contracts has the same (opposite in sign) risk – and insurance companies often hedge this risk by writing pension annuities.

The following sections concentrate on the methods of calculating mortality risk.

Adjustments to mortality may be applied to reflect a fear that – at least for life settlement bought in the secondary market – the policies being sold may be being sold by individuals whose health is better than expected.

Various arbitrary adjustments may be made such as the following.

- Using an alternative mortality table.
- Reduce mortality by $x\%$ of the mortality rate in the first year, $y\%$ in the second and $z\%$ in the third. At high ages, or poor health, this may be an unreasonably large reduction in mortality so a reduction in these percentages may be applied if the life expectancy is short. The above

may be applied if the unadjusted life expectation is more than N years, no adjustment is applied if the life expectation is less than M years ($M < N$), and a linear reduction in x, y and z is used in between. For very low life expectancy the anti-selection factors reduce to zero. This approach has the impact of increasing life expectancy slightly and also of compressing the mortality distribution.

- Reduced mortality factor. MF $= 1 + (\text{MF} - 1) *$ (number) – this has no impact if the MF is unity.
- Subtracted years from age (applied before MF is used).
- Rising mortality. The input MF is adjusted to $Ft = 1 + (\text{MF} - 1) * (1 - \text{Math.Exp}(- (\text{years} + 1)))$, where "years" is the number of years into the policy. Again this has no impact if MF is unity.

Additionally, alternative ways of stressing the shape of the mortality distribution, but leaving the life expectation unchanged, may be important – if a specific structure is sensitive to the distribution of mortalities about the mean then this is a stress that should be applied. For example:

- A "regime switching" stress. This takes a blend of two mortality curves – one based on a low mortality factor and the other based on a high factor – and hence a very different distribution of mortality. The mortality curves used are obtained from the standard table and using adjusted mortality factors of $1 + (F - 1) \times A$ and $1 + (F - 1) \times B$, where $B = 1/A$ and $A = 2$. The factor 2 represents a substantial change in the distribution shape from the initial distribution. This approach produces a substantially greater standard deviation of mortality.
- The mortality stress formulae in the above paragraph have the impact of compressing the distribution (about a changed mean). An alternative is to replace the mortality factor MF by a time-increasing factor $F(t)$, where $F(0) = 1$ (no adjustment to standard age related qx), and is subject to the life expectancy being unchanged. One formula achieving this is $F(t) = 1 + A \times (\text{MF} - 1) \times (1 - \exp(-at))$, where $a = -\ln(0.5)/(\text{LE}/2)$, and $A = \int q(t)dt / \int q(t)(1 - \exp(-at))dt$, where integration is over 0 to LE. For large t we have $F(\infty) = A \times F0 - 1$. This approach produces a substantially smaller standard deviation of mortality.

2.5   CORRELATION AND PORTFOLIO CALCULATIONS

We have not defined precisely what we mean by correlation, nor will we do so until later, but we will briefly talk about the source of correlation and develop an intuitive understanding of what is happening.

Corporate entities do not default at a uniform rate (for the same rating) over time. Instead we observe periods of time when defaults generally are low and periods when they rise to very much higher levels. This tendency for defaults to occur in bunches that is the correlation we need to capture. Figure 2.1 shows the historical default rate derived from actual defaults and shows a strong tendency for defaults to bunch in time together with periods of very low numbers of defaults.

In addition to the pattern described above we also observe bunching of defaults in particular industries over time: Airlines, 5 defaults 1989–1990; Hotels/Casinos, 10 defaults 1990; Oil, 22 defaults 1982–1986, Banks 2008.

The source of correlation of default is clear – it is the higher risk of default at certain times because of general economic conditions, industry-related conditions or other causes. We might guess that the best way to implement this is by correlating default rates. In practice

Default rate (%)

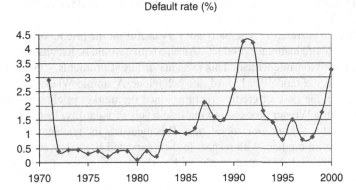

Figure 2.1   Historical default rate

this is not done as it has been found to be an impractical approach; instead, correlation is implemented by correlating default time using Copulas described in detail below. This results in an implementation in which it is simple to calibrate individual risks, and is also faster to execute.

Thinking now about portfolios of life insurance policies there is potentially the same problem. New diseases (e.g. AIDS, bird flu) or medical risks (e.g. chemical hazard) may pose a threat to the general population or to population groups. Poor lifestyle patterns or improving diet may lead to general deterioration or improvement in life expectancy. It is clear looking at the way life expectancy at birth has improved over the last few centuries that correlation in human mortality is indeed present within the population as a whole. Other risks have an impact on certain subsets of the population; for example, war has a greater impact on those (generally males) within the age range eligible to be conscripted into the services. A correlation similar to the correlation that exists within corporate credits also exists within the human population.

There are other examples of correlation of life expectancy which have been addressed within the insurance industry purely for the purposes of quoting certain types of policy. For example, married couples may take out a policy paying on the second death, and here there is likely to be correlation between the two mortalities because of shared lifestyle and environment risks or benefits. Additionally, it is known that twins have correlated mortality partly because of similar genetic make-up.

The reader is probably familiar with the concept of correlated events. If we have two coins that can each come up heads or tails we can estimate the correlation of the occurrence of "heads" by tossing the coins many times and recording heads as $+1$ and tails as -1 for each coin on each trial. If the coins are fair the expected result is 0 for each coin and we would expect no correlation in the tosses, but we could estimate the actual correlation from the average of the product of the $+1$ and -1 results for each pair of tosses.

If we now replace the coins with two lives, and consider a specific time interval – say one year – then (assuming that the lives have the same mortality curve) there is a small chance p that either one of them will die within one year. We could in principle (based on a sample of many pairs of similar lives) estimate the correlation of their mortality within the year. It is important to note that this concept of correlation is dependent on the time interval chosen. If we increase the interval, the probability of death will increase and the chance that they will both die within that period will increase – if we make the period 100 years then p is almost 1 and the correlation will also be almost 1.

Such a concept of correlation is actually not very useful for the pricing of credit structures – including structured life insurance products. An alternative would be to consider the correlation of hazard rates (Poisson intensities). This presents different problems – the main one being the need to introduce a model for hazard rate behaviour. A simple Wiener process is known to be unrealistic in the case of credit structures since the market pricing of such structures is inconsistent with a Wiener process and realistic levels of volatility. Instead the correlation concept that is used is *default time correlation*. This measures the tendency for two (or more) lives to die early, or to die late, with respect to their expected lives. The concept is explained in more detail in the following paragraphs and in the details of the implementation of the correlation model.

If we have a portfolio of risks (whether credit default risks of lives insured) then the expected value of this portfolio is the sum of the value of the individual risks. On the other hand, if we structure the portfolio – for example, creating a CDO style tranche of risk or protection – then we may be at risk not only to the individual event risks but also to the way in which these events are correlated. For example, if we think about the junior and senior tranches of a CDO, and imagine simulating defaults that may occur, then if there is no correlation between default events we would expect a small number of defaults to be simulated time and again – leading to a regular significant proportion of the junior tranche being affected and the senior tranche being unaffected. On the other hand, if there is high correlation among the defaults then (because the total expected number of defaults is unaffected by a change in the correlation) on most simulations we expect to see very few defaults leading to a small impact on the junior tranche and no impact on the senior tranche. However, occasionally we expect to see a large number of defaults wiping out the junior tranche and eating substantially into the senior tranche. Thus correlation will have an impact on the value of individual tranches – and structures generally – although it has no impact on total portfolio value.

Correlation Matrix

One further general point the reader should be familiar with is what constitutes a correlation matrix (being the table of correlations between all pairs of names in a portfolio of n names). A correlation matrix has the following properties.

1. The correlation of a name with itself is always unity, so the correlation matrix has 1s on the diagonal.
2. The correlation of A with B is the same as that between B and A – so the matrix is symmetrical.
3. All correlations lie between -1 and $+1$.

In particular if all the correlations (apart from the diagonal) are equal to the same number c, where $0 <= c < 1$, then the matrix is a correlation matrix. However, the matrix will not be a correlation matrix if c approaches -1. Imagine we have three coins, A, B and C. If A comes up heads and A and B have nearly -1 correlation, then B comes up tails. If B and C also have nearly -1 correlation then C comes up heads. This means A and C have nearly $+1$ correlation and we cannot set the correlation between them to be -1.

The precise (necessary and sufficient) conditions for a matrix to be a correlation matrix are given in Press *et al.* (2002). A matrix which is not a correlation matrix will lead to a breakdown of the calculations at some point.

In addition to the example above, where $1 > c >= 0$ (which forms the basis of many practical applications of the Normal Copula model) it should be realized that a correlation matrix derived from a set of market data (e.g. spreads or equity prices) over the same time period will give rise to a correlation matrix.

2.5.1 Copulas

A Copula is a means of generating a joint statistical distribution given observed partial distributions. Two relevant examples are:

1. The CDS spread curves give information about the default distributions of each entity. A Copula can give us a joint (correlated) default distribution consistent with these CDS curves.
2. The individual mortality curves of a husband and wife have an unknown joint distribution – a Copula can give us a joint distribution consistent with these individual mortality curves.

We will discuss Copulas by examples rather than going into general and largely irrelevant theory. More mathematical detail is given in Nelsen (1988) and *The Encyclopedia of Actuarial Science* (2004) and Chaplin (2005) gives some further examples in the context of credit derivative pricing.

We discuss the following examples in detail:

1. Some Bivariate copulas (uncorrelated case, Frechet)
2. The Gaussian (Normal) Copula
3. Copulas used in joint life pricing.

2.5.2 Bivariate Copulas

A bivariate Copula (a Copula with two parameters) is a cumulative distribution function $C(u, v)$, where u and v are in [0, 1] such that $C(u, 0) = C(0, v) = 0$ and $C(u, 1) = u$, $C(1, v) = v$ – i.e. the marginals are uniform. In addition we require $C(u1, v1) + C(u2, v2) - C(u1, v2) - C(u2, v1) >= 0$ for $u1 <= u2$ and $v1 <= v2$. Four such Copulas are:

1. The independent Copula: $C(u, v) = uv$
2. The Frechet lower bound: $C(u, v) = \max(0, u + v - 1)$
3. The Frechet upper bound: $C(u, v) = \min(u, v)$
4. The Frank Copula: for $a <> 0$,

$$C(u, v) = a^{-1} \log(1 + (\exp(au) - 1)(\exp(av) - 1)(\exp(a) - 1)^{-1})$$

Note that as $a \to 0$ the Frank Copula tends to the independent Copula, as $a \to \infty$ it tends to the Frechet lower bound, and as $a \to -\infty$ it tends to the Frechet upper bound.

The reader will note that a correlation number does not appear explicitly in the above Copulas – although it does in the Normal and some other Copulas. Instead a Copula generally contains one or more parameters (a in the case of the Frank Copula) which imply correlation.

Two "measures of association" are Spearman's rho and Kendall's tau defined as

$$\rho = 12 \int_0^1 \int_0^1 C(u, v)dudv - 3$$

$$\tau = 4 \int_0^1 \int_0^1 C(u, v)dC(u, v) - 1$$

Note that for the above first three Copulas we find both rho and tau are 0, -1, $+1$ respectively.

Also note that there is an infinite choice of different Copulas (and correlation structures) consistent with given partial distributions. In particular we can produce Copulas from a generating function $f: [0, 1] \rightarrow [0, \infty)$ such that $f(0) = 0$, the first derivative is negative, and the second derivative is positive by

$$C(u, v) = f^{-1}(f(u) + f(v))$$

Such Copulas are called Archimedean Copulas (and can be trivially extended to higher dimensions), and there is an infinite choice of generating functions with these properties. In particular the following generators are commonly used.

1. Generator for the Clayton Copula: $t^{-h} - 1$ for $h > 0$
2. Generator for the Gumbel–Hougaard Copula: $(-\log(t))^h$ for $h >= 1$
3. Generator for the Frank Copula: $-\log((\exp(ht) - 1)/(\exp(h) - 1))$ for $h < 0$

Further discussion of Copulas can be found in Nelsen (1998) and *The Encyclopaedia of Actuarial Science* (2004, pp. 375ff).

2.5.3 Gaussian Copula and Correlation in CDO Structures

Typically the Gaussian Copula is used in the pricing and hedging of bespoke tranches by investment banks, and is also used by investors in pricing deals – but the way in which the Copula is driven (the source of the correlations) is different.

First we describe the way the Gaussian Copula is applied and the relevant mathematics – all of which is very straightforward and simple. The application we describe is by simulation. This approach is relatively easy to understand and is applicable to a wide variety of credit and life insurance structures. There are alternative implementations – the "semi-closed form" – which are mathematically more complex but result in a much faster calculation, although these approaches do not have such wide applicability.

Consider a portfolio of n reference entities – typically the reference pool of a CDO. Four steps are involved:

1. Generate n uncorrelated random numbers from a Normal distribution.
2. Correlate these in a way driven by an $n \times n$ correlation matrix.
3. Convert each of these correlated Normal random numbers into correlated default times for each of the n names.
4. Using the generated default time to value the structure.

Generating (Uncorrelated) Normal Random Numbers

This can be done in a variety of ways – two standard approaches are as follows.

1. In Excel use the rand() function which generates a uniformly distributed random number on [0, 1] (with a mean of 0.5 and a variance of 1/12), sum 12 of these and subtract 6.
2. Use the Box–Muller transformation [Numerical Recipes] to convert an uncorrelated pair of uniform random numbers x_1 and x_2 into an uncorrelated pair of Normal random numbers:

$$y_1 = \text{sqrt}(-2\ \ln(x_1))\ \cos(2p\ x_2)$$
$$y_2 = \text{sqrt}(-2\ \ln(x_1))\ \sin(2p\ x_2)$$

Use these methods to generate n Normal random numbers.

Correlating the Normal Random Numbers

Given an $n \times n$ correlation matrix P (we discuss where this comes from below) we can produce Cholesky decomposition using a lower triangular $n \times n$ matrix L such that

$$P = L \times L^T$$

Code to perform this decomposition is given in Press *et al.*

We can now use the matrix L to correlate the random numbers.

For example, given the 2×2 correlation matrix $P = \begin{bmatrix} 1 & r \\ r & 1 \end{bmatrix}$

where $-1 < r < 1$, then

$$Z_k = \sum_{j=1}^{n} L_{k,j} \cdot x_j$$

and we find the matrix $L = \begin{bmatrix} 1 & 0 \\ r & \sqrt{(1-r^2)} \end{bmatrix}$

satisfies the decomposition formula. The correlated normal random numbers are then given by

$$z_1 = x_1$$
$$z_2 = r \cdot x_1 + \sqrt{(1-r^2)} \cdot x_2$$

and it can be verified directly that z_1 and z_2 are Normal(0, 1) and have correlation r.

Converting Correlated Normal Random Numbers into Correlated Default Times

For any given reference name, and its hazard rate curve (derived, for example, from CDS spreads for that name) we can equate the Normal random number z to a survival probability $S(T)$ through

$$z = \exp\left(-\int_0^T h(x)dx\right)$$

and – after solving for T – this gives us a simulated default time T for that reference entity. Doing this for all the reference names produces simulated default times that are correlated through the Copula generation process.

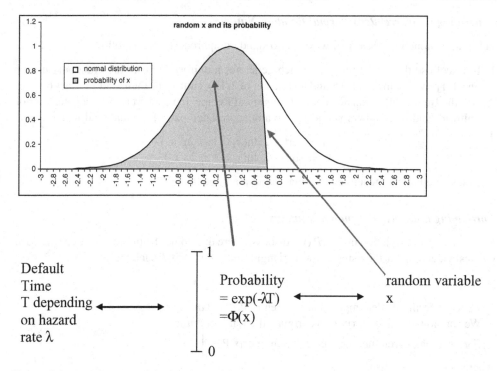

Default
Time
T depending
on hazard
rate λ

Probability
$= \exp(-\lambda T)$
$= \Phi(x)$

random variable
x

Figure 2.2 Development of the copula model

The process so far is summarized in Figure 2.2 where the hazard rate is assumed constant.

Valuing the Structure

As long as the cash flows generated by the structure (for example, a CDO or *n*th to default basket) are defined completely by the default times of the underlying reference entities, then the default times we have generated produce one possible realization of the outcome of the structure. In practice we sort the default times in increasing order, and those that exceed the maturity date of the transaction can be ignored – those names being treated equally as survivors to the end of the transaction. Default times occurring before the maturity date give rise to cash flows defined by the structure. We can calculate all the relevant cash flows that occur under this scenario – generally treating capital and income (premium) items separately – and value all these cash flows to the valuation date by discounting off the (unadjusted) swap rate curve.

This valuation is specific to the simulation performed. We now need to repeat many simulations in order to calculate expected values (and standard deviations are useful to estimate accuracy) and hence the product value derived from these average values. Typically 10,000 to 1,000,000 simulations give rise to usable answers and reasonable run times depending on the structure.

Source of Credit Correlation for CDO Pricing

Investment banks use market data for standard CDO structures (iTraxx, CDX Investment Grade and High Yield) and use the Copula model to calculate an *implied correlation* for the standard structures and tranches. The process is actually more involved than is described below, but is essentially as follows.[2] Knowing the CDS curves for the underlying reference names and the prices at which a tranche trades, the Copula model is used to find the single correlation number (the entire correlation matrix is 1s on the diagonal and the same number everywhere else) consistent with that price. The correlation structure for the tranche is then used to interpolate correlations for bespoke deals (which do not trade in the secondary market).

Investors take a very different – natural measure – approach. Unfortunately the default time correlations in the model are not directly observable. A variety of alternative sources of appropriate correlations are used.

1. It is known (for example, see Chaplin (2005: p 239) that if a CDO tranche is delta hedged (using the hedge ratio from the model and positions in individual CDS contracts) then the hedging strategy is subject to risk from changing spreads and *spread correlation*. Such correlation does not figure in the model explicitly but it turns out that the re-hedging profit or loss is zero if the spread correlation is the same as the default time correlation. This provides some justification for using spread correlation as a proxy for default time correlation.
2. One set of data that is readily available is equity price data and equity correlation. It is common to use equity correlation as a proxy for default time correlation. Theoretically this has little justification – although there is a theoretical argument that default time correlation and *asset correlation* should be the same. Unfortunately the relationship between asset and equity prices (one aspect of the liabilities of a firm) is not a simple one.
3. A third approach is an ad hoc assignment of correlations: if two companies are in the same industry but different countries then a correlation of, say, 0.2 is used, but if they are different industries and countries, and one is investment grade and the other high yield, then a correlation of, say, 0 is used.

2.5.4 Correlation in Life Insurance

Copulas have been used in life insurance in the valuation of joint life and last survivor insurances – these are the life insurance analogy of first and second-to-default credit derivatives. In the credit case the Normal Copula is typically used; in the life insurance case a variety of bivariate copulas, Normal and Student's *t*, have been used.

Correlation will have an impact on the relative values of liabilities supporting a life insurance company (equity and loans) – however, there is little evidence that mortality correlation has been considered in the valuation of these liabilities. It should not be assumed that correlation is zero – we know that life expectation generally has increased substantially over the last few hundred years and the recent VBT analysis assumes a continuing 0.5–1% per annum reduction in mortality rates. However, a chart of mortality rates (for a given age, sex, smoking status) over time will show substantially less variation than the credit default rate chart above. Given that credit correlations are typically in the 20–30% area, we might guess that mortality

---

[2] Current practice is to use "base correlations", which are the correlations applicable to "base tranches" – tranches that have attachment points at 0%. The advantage of this process is that it provides a one-to-one mapping between base correlation and tranche prices. However, this level of detail is not relevant for our purposes in this book.

correlations are in the 2–3% region – but clearly some more detailed research should be undertaken. In addition, at times of war correlation in certain age groups and occupations may rise considerably, and correlations within certain medical condition groups will be higher.

2.6   RATING TRANSACTIONS

This section is a very brief outline of the approach that Moody's Investor Services takes to the rating of structured credit transactions, and the approach A.M. Best takes to rating structured life insurance contracts (neither Standard & Poor's nor Moody's Investor Services currently rate these transactions).

First the aim of the rating process is very different from the aim of the mark-to-model valuation process used by the investment banks, and the analytical aspect is closer to the way investors look at transactions. However, mathematical models are abstractions of reality and are incorrect – in some cases they may be very close to the way the real world works but more often than not such models fail to capture significant elements of risk. The starting point of all the above rating agency approaches is a general review of not only the structure itself but the parties involved in its issue and management and a "common sense" assessment of the risk. Part of the risk assessment of credit transactions includes the use of a mathematical model, but it should be remembered that this is intended to be only one aspect of the risk assessment.

The objective of the mathematical analysis of a CDO structure or tranche is to assess the credit default risk. The models used by the rating agencies are mathematically the same as the Normal Copula model used by the investment banks for marking to market, but the objectives and data used are very different. The key variable in the assessment of risk is the percentage expected loss on the tranche over the life of the deal, and this can be compared to the historical percentage losses over the same life of rated debt. If a tranche has an expected loss percentage over a 5-year period between that of bonds initially rated BBB+ and BBB, then the tranche will be rated BBB. In the calculations of the expected loss for the tranche the following inputs are used.

1. The hazard rate curve associated with each reference entity as defined by its rating (not current CDS spreads). The hazard rates may be stressed by a factor.
2. The historical recovery rate according to the seniority of the debt. The recovery rate may also be stressed.
3. A correlation matrix defined by tags associated with the reference entity. Tags can include such characteristics as industry group, country of registration, rating (investment grade or high yield), and other factors. The actual correlation numbers used for each pair of sets of tags is a fixed number defined by the rating agency not by market data.

Thus while the mathematical model is identical to the investment banks' pricing model, the input data is very different. The objective is to assess the risk of actual loss, not the correct price for that risk.

There is no reason why a similar process cannot be applied to structured life insurance contracts. In this case pricing inputs and rating agency inputs would be likely to be more similar (market prices for life insurance contracts are not available so there is nothing corresponding to market CDS spread data). Stresses can be applied to mortality curves according to the insured's medical condition, for example, and a correlation matrix related to medical conditions, sex, smoking status and the insured's home location for example could be created.

The following is an outline of A.M. Best's approach to rating structured life transactions (A.M. Best, 2008). It begins with a *qualitative review* and general requirements and procedures.

1. *Policies*
   (a) There are restrictions on the types of policy allowed in the structure if a rating is to be given – for example whole life, universal life, convertible term (subject to constraints) are allowed. Policies must be issued by US insurance companies on US citizens, together with a variety of other conditions and requirements.
   (b) There are constraints on the proportion of risk according to primary medical condition. There is also a cap on the mortality factor (the multiple of the mortality rate) assumed to apply to any individual.
2. *Service Providers*
   (a) Requirements on the underwriting process – the skills of those involved, information on their process, data used, rating methodology and historical accuracy (expected versus actual mortalities for lives underwritten in the past). Two independent medical assessments are required (underwriters can differ significantly in their assessment of the average life of a pool of impaired lives).
   (b) An independent review of the underwriting process, methodology and procedures is required.
   (c) The policy providers need to be identified; the terms under which the purchase contracts are written (these must meet various criteria); and the fees paid to the providers must be transparent.
   (d) Legal review of the life insurance sales documentation, in particular looking at the question of insurable interest.
   (e) Tracking agent(s) should be identified and are subject to review by A.M. Best.
   (f) The skills of the collateral manager are assessed.
   (g) Having a backup collateral manager and tracking agent is beneficial.
   (h) A CPA firm should be appointed to perform certain auditing procedures.
   (i) The arrangers of the transaction, their backgrounds, and ongoing financial interest in the transaction are reviewed.
3. *Medical records*
   (a) Recent (under 12 months old) medical reports will reduce the stress applied by A.M. Best in its rating methodology
   (b) Consistency checks on recent and original medical records should be made.
4. *Policy age and transfer*
   (a) Policies should be over 24 months old.
   (b) Checks should be made to ensure transfer to the structure is uncontestable.
5. *Diversity*
   (a) In addition to diversity across medical conditions, maximum exposure to any one insurance company should not exceed 15%.
   (b) Stresses are increased if fewer than 300 lives are in the pool, or if individual policies exceed 1/30th of the exposure.
6. *Longevity risk mitigation*
   Stop loss insurance (the ability to put policies at face value if the life continues a certain period beyond expected) – subject to the insurer – may improve the rating.

7. *Residual portfolio value*

   A conservative approach (based on an unadjusted mortality table) is used to estimate the residual value of the pool at legal maturity. This has increasing impact on shorter transactions.

8. *Liquidity risk*

   The illiquidity of life settlements contracts means a liquidity facility is beneficial to the rating to avoid having to rely on selling policies to meet the structure's cash flow needs.

9. *Pool cost*

   Prior to the establishment of a pool of insurance contracts the rating relies on estimates of fair market prices and expenses for the contracts.

10. *Acquisition schedule*

   Prior to establishment of the pool, the structurer should provide a schedule giving the expected time to purchase of the pool and the required characteristics.

11. *Policy optimization*

   Premiums on policies may deviate from the original premiums (for example they may be minimum premiums to keep the policy in force, increasing over time). Software used to calculate such premiums or optimization will be tested.

12. *Portfolio liquidation*

   For shorter legal maturities (under 20 years) a liquidation plan should be prepared including commencing policy sale two years prior to maturity.

13. *Management expertise*

   The management and their experience in such transactions is reviewed.

14. *Documentation*

   (a) Documentation giving an opinion on the tax implications of the structure should be provided.

   (b) Legal opinion on a wide range of topics should be given.

The following procedures are then used for an *analytical review of the credit risks.*

1. *Life settlement mortality profile*

   A.M. Best uses standard mortality tables for its evaluation taking the ratings given by the medical assessment unless full data and tables are provided by the underwriter. In the former case the worse of the derived life expectancy and the underwriter's given life expectancy are used.

2. *Insurance company risk*

   Insurance company risk is assessed via the (A.M. Best) rating assigned to that company.

3. *Insurance company impairment*

   In the event of insurance company impairment (bankruptcy, etc.) a table of recovery rates on policies is assumed.

4. *Life settlement liquidation value during impairment*

   At legal maturity no value is given to unmatured policies issued by insurance companies below a certain rating.

5. *Cash flow model*

   (a) The issuer's model of the transaction is analysed and compared with Best's own model
   Mortality tables

   (b) Where mortality tables are not provided by the underwriter, Best uses the individual life expectancy to derive a mortality stress applied to the standard mortality table to match the expected life. (i) If the life expectancy of the pool is less than 80% of that for an unimpaired pool then the mortality curves are improved by a constant factor chosen to increase the pool expectancy to the 80% level. (ii) A further stress is then applied according to policy size.

(c) Where mortality tables are provided similar adjustments to those tables are applied as described in (i) and (ii) above.

Modelling

Best uses a simulation model for the lives independently to calculate expected cash flows

6. *Stresses*

Stresses include the following:

(a) mortality rates – particularly in the first three years;

(b) mortality improvements over time;

(c) premium payments;

(d) correlation of medical impairment mortality;

(e) payment delay;

(f) tracking cost;

(g) interest rates;

(h) insurance company impairments and recoveries;

(i) ratings of liquidity providers & longevity cover providers; and

(j) final liquidation value.

7. *Qualitative issues*

The factors in the initial qualitative assessment are reviewed with potential impact on the quantitative evaluation.

In addition there are requirements on the data to be provided to A.M. Best, both initially and on an ongoing basis.

2.7 RISK MANAGEMENT OF A STRUCTURED LIFE SETTLEMENTS PORTFOLIO

We will briefly review the risk management processes for a portfolio of traded financial assets and compare this with the risk management process in an insurance company relating to its pool of mortality risks. We then look at some of the current risk management/policy evaluation solutions in this field.

2.7.1 Risk Managing a Book of Traded Financial Assets

A bank running a book of credit risks – say credit default swaps and CDOs – will measure the risk on each individual transaction. These risks are outlined in Section 2.4 above and are typically calculated using the bank's risk management software – which may be home grown or third party.

Once these risks have been calculated at the individual transaction level, then individual transactions can be aggregated in a variety of ways as described in Section 2.4. The purpose of this aggregation is twofold:

1. *To keep risks in certain areas within limits.* This means defining what those areas are and setting a limit structure. For example, one area (or "bucket") might be 5-year maturity credit spread risk on US investment grade names. A collection of such buckets

(different maturities; sub-investment grade names probably divided into rating bands; other geographical regions) would enable the risk on every transaction to be captured at the bucket level. A maximum risk limit would then be assigned to each bucket. The process would be repeated possibly using a different bucketing structure – perhaps a coarser one (total spread risk across all transactions being one of the coarsest) or a finer one (for example, at the reference name level or at the industry level). In order to apply such a methodology a valuation and risk calculation engine is required for individual transactions and additional risk measures may be applied to the entire portfolio (VaR type analysis).

2. *To enable risks to be hedged by similar (but opposite) transactions.* For example, a high risk in the 5-year US investment grade consumer cyclical bucket may be brought within the defined limit (or reduced further) by an opposing transaction in any representative name within this bucket (subject to individual name limits not being breached).

This process is applied to all risks – spread, default event, interest rate, correlation, etc., as described in Section 2.4.

The purpose is therefore twofold – (1) measurement (and containment) and (2) hedging through opposing transactions.

2.7.2 Risk Managing a Portfolio of Mortality Risks in an Insurance Company

Within an insurance company a similar process can be applied (and some procedures are defined by statutory requirements). Analogous valuation and risk calculations can be performed as described in Section 2.4. However, in the case of a life insurance portfolio there are several differences of emphatic as well as methodology.

(a) With the exception detailed below, the focus is primarily on measurement not hedging since the underlying life insurance contracts are not openly traded.
(b) The underlying portfolio is typically single (and a few joint) life policies so correlation risk does not have a large impact on expected value.
(c) A portfolio of life insurance contracts is typically hedged by having a portfolio of pension annuity contracts – high mortality rates and losses on the former are offset by savings on the latter if the high rates apply to both portfolios.

Within (a) the key risk reduction strategy is diversification – across region, employment area, medical condition, age, etc. – and measurement of the risk with the appropriate buckets is key to being able to diversify as much as possible.

2.7.3 Risk Managing a Life Settlements Portfolio

A life settlements portfolio differs from an insurance company portfolio in that it is owned by a bank or investor rather than an insurance company (and the risks are the other way round) as well as typically having some structured element bringing a significant correlation risk at the expected value level ("direct correlation risk").

In all three cases – bank book of financial risks, life insurance portfolio, and structured life settlements portfolio – there is a correlation risk on the distribution of values (as opposed to expected value – "indirect correlation risk"). This is typically measured by VaR analysis.

The objective in risk managing a life settlement portfolio is measurement and control of risks – similar to a life insurance company – with the added complication of a direct correlation risk.

2.7.4   Current Risk Management Software

Risk management tools have not yet been widely dispersed within the life settlements industry, largely because institutional penetration was extremely limited in the years prior to 2004. There are, however, some companies that have produced pricing and/or valuation models for use with life settlements. The following descriptions give an outline only of the functionality of current software: for current capabilities the reader should contact the vendors directly.

MAPS

Model Actuarial Pricing Systems (MAPS) was formerly a software development team within Milliman, Inc., one of the larger actuarial firms and one which is highly active in the life settlements arena. MAPS was spun out of Milliman in the second half of 2008 and is responsible for maintaining what has become known in the life settlements market as the "Milliman model", which we will refer to here as the "MAPS model". In its current form, the MAPS model is an Excel spreadsheet with a Microsoft Access database containing the policy information. The user is able to enter and store the characteristics of a single policy along with the premium projection and valuation parameters in the Access database. MAPS also offers a portfolio model which performs stochastic analysis of expected cash flows for multiple policies and provides detailed analysis of the distribution of aggregate results. An example of the output available from the portfolio model is included in this book as Appendix A.

The single policy version of the MAPS model is widely used in the market as a *lingua franca* to communicate relative value. It can calculate a current value at a given IRR for the mortality-adjusted cash flows within the policy – it can also calculate prices for a given IRR target. The model uses a combination of Excel forms and spreadsheet entry to submit data and its results are generated within the workbook. The single policy MAPS model has a great deal of flexibility which assists those seeking to price policies with embedded RAP or ROP features.

Lewis & Ellis

Lewis & Ellis (another actuarial firm with significant expertise in life insurance) has developed a spreadsheet-based policy valuation model, entitled LE*SETTLEWARE™. This is easier to manipulate than the MAPS model and, while it has less flexibility than the MAPS model in dealing with more advanced policy features such as RAP and ROP, it is completely spreadsheet based, with all valuation parameters and policy information being entered directly into the spreadsheet. LE*SETTLEWARE™ has some features that are not present in the MAPS model (for example, it better addresses the derivation of mortality factors from life expectancies, as it allows for the difference in information between the different medical underwriters (some offer a mean value for the life expectancy, some offer the median value)), but it is not as well recognized in the market as the MAPS model.

Reoch Credit Model

The functionality of the software is to implement the valuation of single life and structured life products and thereby calculate sensitivities for all the relevant inputs largely as described in 2.4.2–2.4.4 and the correlation methodology of Section 2.5. In addition to valuation (expected value) and valuation sensitivity, the software also allows access to the distribution of values and measures such as standard deviation or, more usefully, percentiles of the distribution (similar to value at risk, or VaR, analysis).

Attention focuses on the "longevity risk" when looking at LSPs. This can be interpreted in a variety of ways:

1. Sensitivity to a shift in the mortality curve (uniform reduction in mortality rate) at the individual name level.
2. A shift in all mortality curves simultaneously.
3. The tail of the value distribution – for an individual policy or for a structure or portfolio.
4. The impact of correlation changes on expected value.

The first is easy to understand, and the second can be thought of as a very crude correlation impact (all names are 100% correlated in mortality rate) but is a rather unrealistic measure. The tail of the distribution gives a better measure of longevity risk on the portfolio, particularly if correlation is embedded in the calculations of portfolio values. The final measure has zero value for single name life settlements but potentially a significant impact for structures. The Reoch Credit software allows access to all these measures.

3
Structured Products and Securitization

3.1 SECURITIZATION

Starting in the late 1970s and progressing until today volatility in the markets has caused practitioners to look for newer and better ways to reduce risk. Interest rates hit all-time highs in the early 1980s and financial institutions and individuals alike were caught up in the interest rate spiral. The equity markets in sync increase in volatility and newer and better ways to measure and manage risk were needed, hence the birth of securitization and structuring.

Any promise to pay by a firm or individual creates a financial instrument. These promises to pay can be of almost infinite variety. The value of the instrument rests to a large extent with the perceived ability of the borrower to repay the funds. The backing of this instrument can range from an individual pledging to repay up to and including a collateral-backing guaranteeing repayment. By issuing a collateral-backing the perceived ability to repay is enhanced. The packaging of this collateral to enhance repayment is the process of securitization.

The securitization market is large and varied. The largest piece of this market is still the Mortgage-Backed Securities (MBS) market. Other securitized assets include Credit Card Loans, Auto loans, Home Equity Loans, Equipment Leasing, Student Loans, etc. Generally any product that throws off a cash flow can be securitized. In 1996 Nomura Securities, one of the largest brokerage firms in the world, sold a very successful bond into the market, securitized by the cash flows of over 5000 English pubs owned by Nomura.

Figure 3.1 is a flow chart of a very simple securitization.

The asset is sold into a trust. The trust pays for the asset either up front in full or over time. The trust then pools assets and sells a bond into the capital markets backed by the cash flows of the pooled assets. Generally the trust breaks up the sale of the bond into tranches with different ratings. The senior tranche will have a higher rating because of a waterfall effect, whereby principal and interest are paid on the senior tranche before any payouts are made on the junior or subordinate tranches.

Figure 3.2 is an example of a more reasonable structure.

We now have expanded the players in the process.

Sponsor

The sponsor is the initiator of the securitization. In most cases this is either a bank or investment bank. Reasons for the securitization are many, but are usually to sell off all or part of an asset into the market for cash. Most of the time the sponsor is not the owner of an asset such as a pool of mortgages from a bank securitized by an investment bank to be sold into the market. To sell a securitization, which can be quite large, you need a distribution channel and most firms do not have large enough distributions. When the asset is an alternative asset such as credit cards or life settlements, the securitization almost always necessitates the services of a large investment bank. In most cases the sponsor and the underwriter (see below) are the same entity.

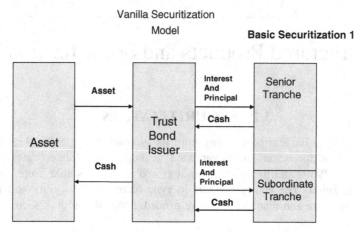

Figure 3.1   Vanilla securitization structure

Originator/Transferor

The owner of the asset is the originator. Many small to medium-sized banks are originators of mortgage loans or credit sensitive assets. Selling the asset off allows the bank to reduce its exposure to credit or interest rate movements while, at the same time, improving the bottom line by keeping the servicing on the loan.

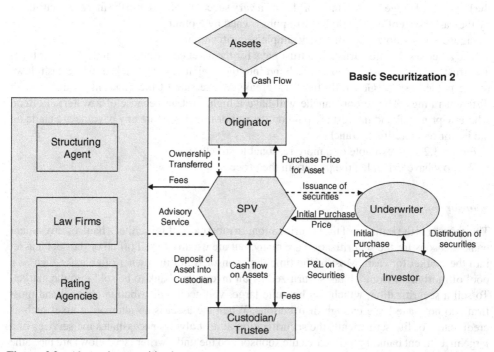

Figure 3.2   Alternative securitization structure

Asset Purchaser/Transferee/Securitized Product Issuer

In most cases in a securitization a new entity is established as a risk-remote Special Purpose Vehicle (SPV) or Special Purpose Entity (SPE). The SPV will purchase the asset for cash up front or payments. It will then establish a security that can be sold off into the market. In most cases a small portion of the SPV is an equity piece. In some cases rather than an SPV a corporation could be established to take possession of the asset, or multiple SPVs could be established transferring ownership of all or part of the asset.

Trustee

The trustee is responsible for looking after the investor, which may mean verifying and valuing the pledged collateral in the SPV. There may be certain conforming standards the assets need to follow. It may mean modelling the value of the asset in cases where there is not a market price.

Custodian and/or Servicer

The custodian will collect cash flows from the assets and disburse cash flows to the security if necessary. This will be especially important in life settlements. Because it is a relatively new product there are only a few custodial departments with the capability of handling life settlements. An important part of the process is identifying when an individual passes away, and because the beneficiary of the policy is now a trust, the immediate family has little incentive to notify the life insurance company of the passing. It therefore falls upon the custodial agent to track life policies and collect payment.

Structurer

The structurer is simply the entity that puts the securitization together and prices the tranches. This entity will model senior/subordinate cash flows and any waterfall effect. The structurer will price and model risks for the selling agency.

Underwriter

The underwriter simply markets and distributes the security. In many incidents there will be a lead underwriter who will set up a syndicate.

Rating Agencies

Rating agencies review the security, determine the likelihood of repayment of principal and interest, and give the security a rating based upon a risk assessment. There are many rating agencies with differing specialties depending upon the type of security.

Legal

Any securitization sold into the market will need a prospectus – a legal representation of the security. It is vitally important to have the services of an experienced legal adviser to steer you through all the legal pitfalls of the capital markets. Qualification of investors, risks, cash flow representations should all be reviewed by legal council.

Regulatory

Any instrument sold into the street or even issued by a regulated entity will have to follow existing laws and regulations. Regulators may even take an active role in the issuance of the security. If, for example, a market price is not available for the security a carve-out procedure may be used. If this is the case regulators will become very involved in the process.

Risk Management

As was discussed above, the issuance of a securitized product will generally not eliminate risk completely but simply rearrange it. It will always be necessary to run risk profiles on any new instrument to identify the stress points of the instruments. Multiple simulation techniques can be used to look for "tails' in a distribution of returns and to answer "what if" scenarios.

3.1.1   Other Examples: Synthetic Securitization

Synthetic securitization can vary widely in nature, structure, design and size. Figure 3.3 shows the securitization of a synthetic structure. Normally the asset is sold into the trust, the trust

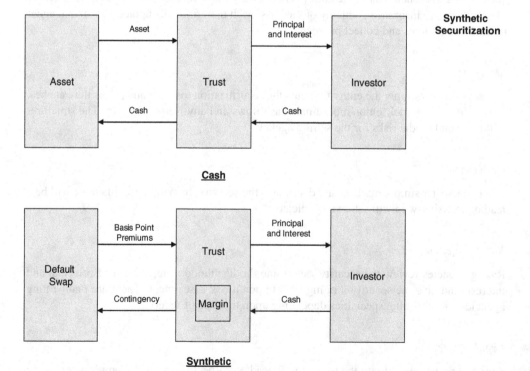

Figure 3.3

structures a capital markets product sold on to the investor and the cash from the sale is placed back into the trust.

With a synthetic structure the derivative is sold and the premiums collected into the trust. It is these premiums that back the payout of principal and interest on the liability. As an example, a synthetic tranche of a CDO might consist of a number of credit default swaps sold with the premiums received from the sale of the default swap going to the trust. The trusts will then have to make good on any default over the life of the investment and, as a result, will require margin or collateral in the trust. If no defaults happen the premiums on the default swaps should be sufficient to cover all liabilities.

This process reduces the need for large up-front funding and can be extremely valuable if and when it appears that the premiums are overpriced. In Chapter 5 we talk about the synthetic LSP. As of this writing, because of the newness of the life settlement indices, the synthetic side of the trade appears to have some value.

3.1.2 Prestructures

It can soon be seen that these structures can become complex. Figure 3.4 shows a Mortgage-Backed Securities structure needed just to securitize the MBS programmes.

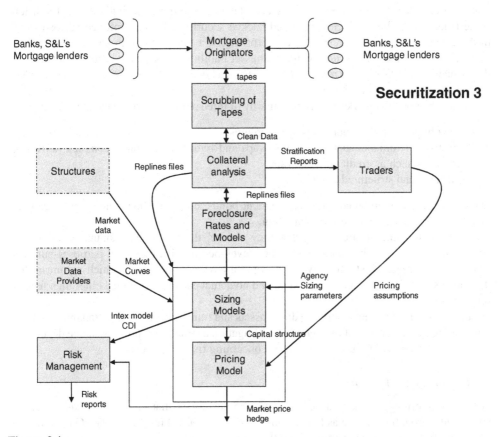

Figure 3.4

All of these structures fall under the heading of Asset-Backed Security and, as mentioned above, the largest of these is the Mortgage-Backed Security. Because of volatile interest rates in the late 1970s banks and Savings and Loans found themselves in a position of holding mortgages issued many years previously at extremely low rates compared to the high costs of borrowing they now faced. One of the solutions was to sell them. Investment banks, Salomon being the largest among them, purchased these mortgages and pooled them. Using a legal pass-through system, the mortgage payments were then used to pay the principal and interest of a bond the investment banks sold. The credit risk of this bond was little because most mortgage-backed securities held conforming mortgages (Ginnie Mae, Freddie Mac, Fannie Mae) which were then guaranteed by the full faith and credit of the federal government. However, these bonds were still subject to the vagaries of interest rates. The pool may end up holding mortgages with low rates paying a bond with higher rates. One of the ways around this was through over-collateralization, holding 120% collateral to guarantee payment on 100% of the asset. This was the introduction of the securitization process that opened a Pandora's Box of securitized or asset-backed products.

3.2 STRUCTURED PRODUCTS

The structured product is simply an extension of securitization. While securitization reduces risk by diversifying it over a pool of assets instead of residing in a single asset, it still left some risks within the product. Mortgaged-backed securities, for example, could lose value in the event of a rise in interest rates or, surprisingly, a fall in rates. In addition, cash flow structure became more important with newer asset liability management requirements within the financial institutions. As a result, such structures as Planned Amortization Classes (PACs – discussed below) were developed.

To date the financial markets consist primarily of three main types of financial instruments:

1. Direct obligations of corporations or sovereigns.
2. Derivative instruments such as vanilla swaps and futures to the more complex derivative instruments such as credit default swaps.
3. Securitized and structured assets.

Direct obligations include equities, government bonds, corporate bonds and any instrument that can be converted into a direct obligation.

Derivative instruments are exactly that, they "derive" their value from an underlying direct obligation. Most derivative instruments were developed for risk reduction purposes but may have large leverage. Most derivatives at inception have zero value, by which we mean that the value is calculated off a notional value and no actual cash is exchanged other than fees or premiums.

Securitization takes the underlying direct assets and transforms them into tradable units. By rearranging the cash flows of the underlying obligation a structuring process can be developed to suit the investor's particular requirement concerning risks and returns.

3.2.1 Mortgage Structures

Within the mortgage market, structures could be developed that guaranteed fixed payment with yields through the curve as long as interest rates remained in a range. The Collateralized Mortgage-Backed Security demonstrated this capability.

A collateralized mortgage obligation (CMO) is a financial debt vehicle. Legally a CMO is a SPE that is wholly separate from the institution that creates it. The entity is the legal owner of a set of mortgages, called a pool. Investors in a CMO buy bonds issued by the entity, and receive payments according to a defined set of rules with the payments backed by the mortgages themselves. The bonds are issued in tranches or classes with each tranche or class having predefined rules as to which class gets paid first and under what situation the rules are to change.

The primary reason for the development of the CMO was to eliminate the risk of interest rate movements in either direction and/or structure cash flows that conformed or matched liability cash flow, thereby hedging the risk of the investment. Investors in CMOs wish to be protected from this risk. Although this risk cannot be removed, it can be reallocated between CMO tranches so that some tranches have some protection against the risk, while other tranches will absorb more of the risk. To facilitate this allocation of prepayment risk, CMOs are structured such that prepayments are allocated between bonds using a fixed set of rules. The most common schemes for prepayment tranching are described below. As can be seen, the extension into structuring from securitization added an additional level of sophistication but also helped to reduce or eliminate risk that securitization alone could not address.

Within the mortgage market alone structuring has exploded to include the following partial list. While these structures relate to a mortgage product it should be noted that these type of structures can be designed for any security that throw off a cash flow. We will look at a number of these products and their relationship to the life settlement market.

From Wikipedia we have the following partial list.

Sequential tranching (or by time)

All of the available principal payments go to the first sequential tranche, until its balance is decremented to zero, then to the second, and so on. There are several reasons that this type of tranching would be done:

The tranches could be expected to mature at very different times and therefore would have different *yields* that correspond to different points on the *yield curve.*

The underlying mortgages could have a great deal of uncertainty as to when the principal will actually be received since home owners have the option to make their scheduled payments or to pay their loan off early at any time. The sequential tranches each have much less uncertainty.

Parallel tranching

This simply means tranches that pay down *pro rata*. The coupons on the tranches would be set so that, in aggregate, the tranches pay the same amount of interest as the underlying mortgages. The tranches could be either fixed rate, or floating rate. If they have floating coupons, they would have formulae that make their total interest equal to the collateral interest. For example, with collateral that pays a coupon of 8%, you could have two tranches that each has half of the principal, one being a floater that pays LIBOR with a cap of 16%, the other being an inverse floater that pays a coupon of 16% minus LIBOR.

A special case of parallel tranching is known as the IO/PO split. IO and PO refer to Interest Only and Principal Only. In this case, one tranche would have a coupon of zero (meaning that it would get no interest at all) and the other would get all of the interest. These bonds could be used to speculate on *prepayments*. A principal-only bond would be sold at a deep discount (a much lower price than the underlying mortgage) and would rise in price rapidly if many of the underlying mortgages were prepaid. The interest-only bond would be very profitable if few of the mortgages prepaid, but could get very little money if many mortgages prepaid.

Z bonds, sometimes called equity bonds

This type of tranche supports other tranches by not receiving an interest payment. The interest payment that would have accrued to the Z tranche is used to pay off the principal of other bonds, and the principal of the Z tranche increases. The Z tranche starts receiving interest and principal payments only after the other tranches in the CMO have been fully paid. This type of tranche is often used to customize sequential tranches, or VADM tranches.

Schedule bonds (also called PAC or TAC bonds)

This type of tranching has a bond (often called a PAC or TAC bond) which has even less uncertainty than a sequential bond by receiving prepayments according to a defined schedule. The schedule is maintained by using support bonds (also called companion bonds) that absorb the excess prepayments.

Planned Amortization Class (PAC) bonds have a principal payment rate determined by two different prepayment rates, which together form a band (also called a collar). Early in the life of the CMO, the prepayment at the lower PSA will yield a lower prepayment. Later in the life, the principal in the higher PSA will have declined enough that it will yield a lower prepayment. The PAC tranche will receive whichever rate is lower, so it will change prepayment at one PSA for the first part of its life, then switch to the other rate. The ability to stay on this schedule is maintained by a support bond, which absorbs excess prepayments, and will receive less prepayments to prevent extension of average life. However, the PAC is only protected from extension to the amount that prepayments are made on the underlying MBSs. When the principal of that bond is exhausted, the CMO is referred to as a "busted PAC" or "busted collar".

Target Amortization Class (TAC) bonds are similar to PAC bonds, but they do not provide protection against extension of average life.

Very Accurately Defined Maturity (VADM) bonds

VADM bonds are similar to PAC bonds in that they protect against both extension and contraction risk, but their payments are supported in a different way. Instead of a support bond, they are supported by accretion of a Z bond. Because of this, a VADM tranche will receive the scheduled prepayments even if no prepayments are made on the underlying.

Non-Accelerating Senior (NAS) bonds

NAS bonds are designed to protect investors from volatility and negative convexity resulting from prepayments. NAS tranches of bonds are fully protected from prepayments for a specified period, after which time prepayments are allocated to the tranche using a specified step down formula. For example, a NAS bond might be protected from prepayments for five years, and then would receive 10% of the prepayments for the first month, then 20%, and so on. Recently, issuers have added features to accelerate the proportion of prepayments flowing to the NAS class of bond in order to create shorter bonds and reduce extension risk. NAS tranches are usually found in deals that also contain short sequentials, Z bonds, and credit subordination.

NASquentials

NASquentials were introduced in mid-2005 and represented an innovative structural twist, combining the standard Non-Accelerated Senior (NAS) and Sequential structures. Similarly to a sequential structure, the NASquentials are tranched sequentially, however, each tranche has a NAS-like hard lockout date associated with it. Unlike with a NAS, no shifting interest mechanism is employed after the initial lockout date. The resulting bonds offer superior stability versus regular sequentials, and yield pickup versus PACs. The support-like cash flows falling out on the other side of NASquentials are sometimes referred to as RUSquentials (Relatively Unstable Sequentials).

Coupon tranching

The coupon stream from the mortgage collateral can also be restructured (analogous to the way the principal stream is structured). This coupon stream allocation is performed after prepayment tranching is complete. If the coupon tranching is done on the collateral without any prepayment tranching, then the resulting tranches are called "strips". The benefit is that the resulting CMO tranches can be targeted to very different sets of investors. In general, coupon tranching will produce a pair (or set) of complementary CMO tranches.

IO/Discount fixed rate pair

A fixed rate CMO tranche can be further restructured into an Interest Only (IO) tranche and a discount coupon fixed rate tranche. An IO pays a coupon only based on a notional principal, it receives no principal payments from amortization or prepayments. Notional principal does not have any cash flows but shadows the principal changes of the original tranche, and it this principal off which the coupon is calculated. For example, a $100 million (mm) PAC tranche off 6% collateral with a 6% coupon ("6 off 6" or "6-squared") can be cut into a $100mm PAC tranche with a 5% coupon (and hence a lower dollar price) called a "5 off 6", and a PAC IO tranche with a notional principal of $16.666667mm and paying a 6% coupon. Note the resulting notional principle of the IO is less than the original principal. Using the example, the IO is created by taking 1% of coupon off the 6% original coupon gives an IO of 1% coupon off $100mm notional principal, but this is by convention 'normalized' to a 6% coupon (as the collateral was originally 6% coupon) by reducing the notional principal to $16.666667mm ($100mm/6).

PO/Premium fixed rate pair

Similarly, if a fixed rate CMO tranche coupon is desired to be increased, then the principal can be removed to form a Principal Only (PO) class and a premium fixed rate tranche. A PO pays no coupon, but receives principal payments from amortization and prepayments. For example a $100mm sequential (SEQ) tranche off 6% collateral with a 6% coupon ("6 off 6") can be cut into a $92.307692mm SEQ tranche with a 6.5% coupon (and hence a higher dollar price) called a "6.5 off 6", and a SEQ PO tranche with a principal of $7.692308mm and paying no coupon. The principal of the premium SEQ is calculated as $(6/6.5) * \$100$mm, the principle of the PO is calculated as balance from $100mm.

IO/PO pair

The simplest coupon tranching is to allocate the coupon stream to an IO, and the principal stream to a PO. This is generally only done on the whole collateral without any prepayment tranching, and generates strip IOs and strip POs. In particular *FNMA* and *FHLMC* both have extensive strip IO/PO programmes (aka Trusts IO/PO or SMBS) which generate very large, liquid strip IO/PO deals at regular intervals.

Floater/inverse pair

The construction of CMO floaters is the most effective means of getting additional market liquidity for CMOs. CMO floaters have a coupon that moves in line with a given index (usually 1 month LIBOR) plus a spread, and is thus seen as a relatively safe investment even though the term of the security may change. One feature of CMO floaters that is somewhat unusual is that they have a coupon cap, usually set well out of the money (e.g. 8% when LIBOR is 5%). In creating a CMO floater, a CMO inverse is generated. The CMO inverse is a more complicated instrument to hedge and analyse, and is usually sold to sophisticated investors.

The construction of a floater/inverse can be seen in two stages. The first stage is to synthetically raise the effective coupon to the target floater cap, in the same way as done for the PO/Premium fixed rate pair. As an example, using $100mm 6% collateral targeting an 8% cap, we generate $25mm of PO and $75mm of "8 off 6". The next stage is to cut up the premium coupon into a floater and inverse coupon, where the floater is a linear function of the index, with unit slope and a given offset or spread. In the example, the 8% coupon of the "8 off 6" is cut into a floater coupon of:

$$1*\text{LIBOR} + 0.40\%$$

(indicating a 0.40%, or 40bps, spread in this example)

The inverse formula is simply the difference of the original premium fixed rate coupon less the floater formula. In the example:

$$8\% - (1*\text{LIBOR} + 0.40\%) = 7.60\% - 1*\text{LIBOR}$$

The floater coupon is allocated to the premium fixed rate tranche principal, in the example the $75mm '8 off 6', giving the floater tranche of '$75mm 8% cap + 40bps LIBOR SEQ floater'. The floater will pay LIBOR + 0.40% each month on an original balance of $75mm, subject to a coupon cap of 8%.

The inverse coupon is to be allocated to the PO principal, but has been generated off the notional principal of the premium fixed rate tranche (in the example the PO principal is $25mm but the inverse coupon is notionalized off $75mm). Therefore the inverse coupon is 're-notionalized' to the smaller principal amount, in the example this is done by multiplying the coupon by ($75mm /$25mm) = 3. Therefore the resulting coupon is:

$$3*(7.60\% - 1*\text{LIBOR}) = 22.8\% - 3*\text{LIBOR}$$

In the example the inverse generated is a '$25mm 3 times levered 7.6 strike LIBOR SEQ inverse'.

As explained above, by pooling the cash flows from a group of assets we can pool those payments and make payments on a structured product. This pooling of assets into one payment can enhance the perception of payment and thus generate a better rating on the secured asset than any of the underlying individual assets. This is the main purpose of this process. Over-collateralization extends this ability to improve the rating by pooling 120% of the underlying 100% of the securitization.

The process of restructuring the cash flow generated by this securitization to conform to risks or returns required by the investor is called the structuring process.

3.2.2   Other Examples

In addition to structuring to reduce interest rate risk or match cash flow, structure can be used to help with currency rate risk and increase yields. Below are just three examples of a plethora of possibilities.

- *Power Reverse Dual Currency Bond*
  In the late 1990s interest rates in Japan were extremely low and in fact at times the real rate was even negative. However many institutional investors in Japan were restricted from investing in any investment that was not Yen denominated. A structure was developed whereby the investor could invest in a trust that paid in yen but invested the funds off shore in Deutsche Marks (still around at that time) or US dollars and then brought the return back to yen. Because of the low interest rates in Japan the yield was "hyped up" through the use of a power option.
- *Yield enhancement bond*
  Sometimes referred to sarcastically as a precipice bond or granny buster bond, structures were designed to give the investor enhanced yields with risks delayed until the term of the bond.
  One such structure was a 5-year fixed rate S&P A-rated bond that would yield 3% higher rates than comparable A-rated bonds. This was done by structuring a bond with an option called a look-back option whereby the issuer of the bond would pay the investor for the option. In this case the option was worth 3% a year for 5 years.
  The problem with the structure was that the issuer of the bond had the right to exercise the look-back option, which was exercisable in the last 6 months of the bond. If the index on which the look-back was written was below its initial level, the issuer of the bond did not have to pay back the full principal, and if the index had fallen far enough the issuer did not have to pay back any of the principal.
- *Synthetic Structure*
  As a final example here, but certainly not exhaustive, in explanation we look at a synthetic bond. Here the structure takes a derivative and uses it as if it were the original structure. Within the CDO market credit bonds are pooled and tranched and the payments from the tranches are made from the payments from the pool of bonds. By selling a pool of credit derivatives we receive the quarterly fee for the sale of the derivative and this payment acts the same as if the underlying bond pool was paying into the tranche. We have created a synthetic cash flow that mirrors the underlying bond pool and has all the risks as the underlying bond pool. In the event of a default the bond pool would be reduced in value. In the synthetic pool the same process would take place in that the default swap would have to make good on the principal of the underlying bond that defaulted.

Securitization By Type

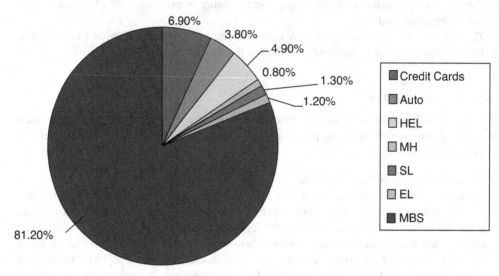

Figure 3.5

In the early 2000s the process expanded to include lower credit assets causing a great deal of excitement. It generated into innovation gone mad as high-risk assets such as sub-prime loans were pooled into MBSs and the MBSs were then pooled into CDO tranches which were then pooled into CDO^{2}s. When the economy started to turn down and the realization that the underlying original sub-prime pools were experiencing a large default rate, panic struck and wholesale selling occurred driving out the credit spreads and causing a reduction in the price of these structures. Further compounding the problem was the fact that the underlying asset somehow got lost in the shuffle and in the case of a default of the sub-prime mortgage no one knew where the loss was to occur.

Figure 3.5 gives a breakout of securitization by type listing, Figure 3.6 gives a breakout by size and Figure 3.7 presents several types of securitizations. As can be seen, the mortgage product still dominates the securitization process.

3.3   THE RISKS OF STRUCTURED PRODUCTS

As can be seen from above, for the last 30 plus years the financial markets have been unbundling risks in an effort to design products to hedge specific market risks. All the latter bonds and CMOs discussed above were an attempt to mitigate risk in one format or another. For the last 20 years financial engineers have gone mad with structured products designed to have specific cash flows timed for specific terms and subject to specific market variables. As seen from the sub-prime markets, risks still exist. Most recently the credit derivative markets evolved out of the insurance surety bond guarantees and credit enhancement policies.

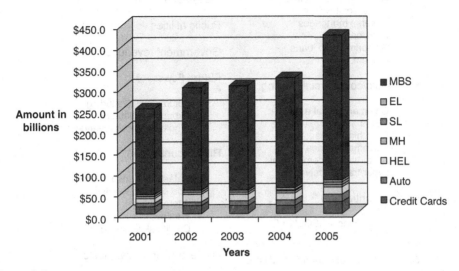

Figure 3.6

The main concern with the underlying securities was found to be the fact that they were stochastic in nature and, by the very definition of stochastic, price movements are not predictable.

By pooling different products into a structure, attempts were made to try to hedge away what was not predictable by replication. If we can match the cash flows of one security with the equal and opposite cash flows of another product, we have hedged the risks and that is the objective of the structured product.

3.3.1   Problems with Correlations and Volatility

This process, however, generated new problems. An analogy would be going to the doctor because you have an illness. The doctor gives you a drug to cure the illness but that drug has side effects. You re-visit the doctor to cure the side effects. The doctor then gives you other drugs to help with the side effects, but each new drug has its own side effects and you need more drugs to cure each new side effect. Eventually you have forgotten what the original illness was and you have a medicine cabinet full of drugs.

Every time you combine two or more stochastic processes you end up with a co-integration problem. Like a drunk man walking a dog, no one knows which direction either will take but they are tied together with a leash. In many cases it is modelling the correlation and volatility of the pieces of the structure that becomes difficult or impossible and causes us to forget the original problem. Look at the mortgage example just discussed. The original problems are the risks with known results of volatility movements. Default on a single mortgage was not an issue on conforming loans. It has now turned into the risk of default on many mortgages with unknown results. In many cases no one even knows where the mortgage is.

Retail Lending:

Residential real estate
Home equity loans
Reverse mortgages
Auto loans
Sub-prime auto loans
Student loans

Wholesale/commercial lending:

Commercial real estate
REITs
Franchise loans
Equipment leases
Asset backed commercial
paper/trade receivables

Bank securitization

Bank loans – CBOs/ CLOs
Credit cards

Collateralized debt obligations/ CDOs

Private equity/ Hedge fund investments

Non performing loans

Re-packaging and structured
product CDOs

Aircraft leases and revenues

Industrial revenues

Public utilities

Government revenues

Future flows:

Future flows (including
Export receivables)
Whole Business revenues

Risk securitization:

Catastrophe Insurance risk
Non catastrophe risk
Alternative risk transfer
Weather risk
Credit risk securitization

Intellectual property, music
royalties etc.

Alternative Asset securitisation

- Fashion industry assets

Miscellaneous

- Small and Medium
  companies/businesses
- Healthcare

Figure 3.7

The problem with modelling the stochastic process then comes down to a problem of parameterizing the stochastic functions, leading to the measure of volatility and correlation.

Volatility and correlation are not directly observable in markets, but are hugely important in the pricing and risk management of these products.

3.3.2   Pricing Structures

Structured products by their very nature are pieced together like Lego building blocks. In many cases there is not an active market trading the end piece of these building blocks. For that reason pricing and risk managing structured products has to be done via a model rather than a market. Boundaries can be established by pricing the individual pieces within the structure but because of a variety of variables (discussed below) some form of pricing model is needed to put all the pieces together.

Data collection and the interrelated movements of that data are the major problem. For example, can we directly investigate the shape of the distribution? To do this we need large amounts of data for the distribution to be accurate and often that data is just non-existent or has huge unmanageable outliers. Using moments of a distribution with inadequate data might be imposing structure on a distribution that is simply not there.

Where do we get our information? Historical data is backward looking and implies that history will repeat itself. This is usually never the case and imposes a stationarity process on the model that is simply not reasonable. If we generate our information from implied data, forward looking data, we may be imposing market bias and market inefficiency on the model.

However, forward looking data is not actually trying to forecast future volatility or correlation but simply pricing in λ, a risk parameter, which will bias the estimate and is difficult to price out.

How much structure do we want? Too much structure will over-parameterize the model and the results will be noise with no predictability. Not enough structure and your model will be simply wrong.

It can be seen from the above that the structure/model you choose will have tremendous impact on the output and the two basic pixies in the whole process are correlation and volatility, driven by the fact that we are looking at a stochastic non-predictable process.

We are going through this process only as a very basic review of structuring and will show later how LSPs can overcome most of these problems.

3.4 MODELLING

3.4.1 Implied Models

Implied Probability

Implied probability does not try to forecast future values but takes those values from what the markets give. In a deterministic world these implied values could be used as fairly exact numbers, but in a stochastic world a bias is priced in to compensate for the fact that we are not sure what the future holds. It is this unknown bias that skews the results and causes error within the model. This would equate to forecasting error found in other methodologies if it were not for the fact that this error can be forward hedged away. As a result, this methodology offers less risk than other forecasting possibilities but takes away excessive returns in the process.

As an extension, model building can be built around an arbitrage approach. This process is especially important in model calibration. As discussed below, the simplest form of this arbitrage modelling would be the implied forward interest rate shown in Figure 3.8.

$$R_f = \frac{R_2 T_2 - R_1 T_1}{T_2 - T_1}$$

Where R_f=Forward Rate

$R_1 \& R_2$ are Rates for times $T_1 \& T_2$ (3.1)

As an example, if the rate is 1% per year the 1-year return on a \$100 bond would be \$1. The second year return, assuming a zero rate of 1.5%, would be \$1.50. This implies a 1-year forward rate of 1.1%. If our model produces different numbers, our implied forwards are wrong or we need to recalibrate our system.

Even in more sophisticated structures like a credit default swap, swapping the fixed bond into an asset swap yielding LIBOR plus or minus, and then backing that bond with a default

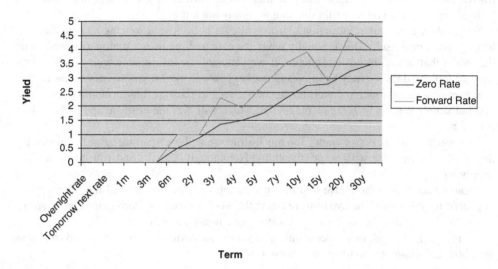

Figure 3.8

swap, should get us close to the treasury rate, given that interest rate risk and default risk have been forward hedged away.

This arbitrage process is generally the backbone of calibration within model constructions and will insure, given our assumption that our model is calculating correctly. The problem then comes back to assumptions.

Implied probability needs market liquidity. These models are basically used with non-linear securities such as implied volatility in options and implied correlation in interest rate derivatives. There are a plethora of models to choose from.

The easiest implied probability model would be that used in the options market. Given that you have complete information we could take the first derivative in the limit of a call option to completely parameterize the volatility distribution. For example:

$$\lim_{h \to 0} \frac{call(S, t; K - h, T) - call(S, t; K, T)}{h}$$

$$= \frac{\partial call(S, t, KT)}{\partial K}$$

$$= v(t, T)\, Q(S(T) > K) = probablility\ distribution\ Q(S(T) \leq K)\ under\ Q \quad (3.2)$$

Where

$S = Strike$

$t = Time$

$K = Price$

$T = Term$

Differentiation of the above yields

$$\lim_{h \to 0} \frac{call(S, t; K - h, T) - 2call(S, t; K, T) + call(S, t; K + h, T)}{h^2}$$

$$= \frac{\partial^2 call(S, t, K, T)}{\partial K^2}$$

$$= v(t, T) \, q(K) = \textit{The density function under } q \qquad (3.3)$$

Where

$S = Strike$

$t = Time$

$K = Price$

$T = Term$

The problem here is the paucity of data and the lack of liquidity. Again, with enough data, the above implied volatility calculations can be used to force out the entire skew in actively traded markets using an implied tree approach to build binomial or trinomial trees trying to recover the stochastic nature of the option surface.

Implied Volatility

One of the measures actively being used in the markets today is the smile. Figure 3.9 shows the smile for an option. Here the X and Y axis represent the option's Delta and Days to Maturity and the Z axis is the implied volatility. As can be seen from the graph the at-the-money (ATM) strikes are priced lower, have a lower implied volatility than the in-the-money (ITM) and out-the-money (OTM) options. Given the volatility of the underlying, volatility of the options should be the same across the spectrum and you would expect a clustering effect rather than a smile.

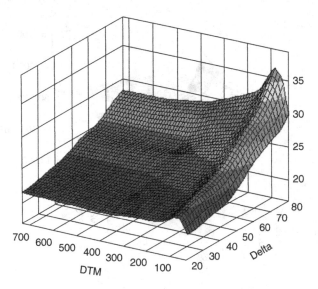

Figure 3.9

The reasons for this effect to date have not been fully explained save the theory that risk protection, or what is an insurance premium, is in reality forcing tails in the distribution and causing the smile effect.

This is not an unusual event within non-linear markets. Equity options markets exhibit the same effect, although not to the same degree and it is sometimes referred to as a smirk.

Fitting curves to the points along the smile or smirk is problematic at best and a number of techniques have been developed from quadratic interpolation to splining techniques to fit the distribution. All have problems and to date most traders use a combination of techniques to fit the curve. Methods that use a "sticky delta" approach, which ties the volatility to the price, seem to work best.

Even more difficult, but generally far more informative, is the volatility surface. This is produced by combining both strike prices and exercise dates to create a 3-D surface. Using historical data and projecting out using implied data will allow the user to see the pattern formed up to the present and the expectations of these patterns into the future. See Figure 3.10.

Again forming this surface only adds a level of complexity to the process and if the fitting methodology is flawed the information drawn from that surface will also be flawed.

Implied Correlation

The easiest way to view implied correlations would be to look at the yield curve of any interest-bearing security although any security with a time series should suffice, the reason being the triangular effect within the time series. For example, there is a relation between the spot and the forward rate within the yield curve that can produce an arbitrage if mis-priced.

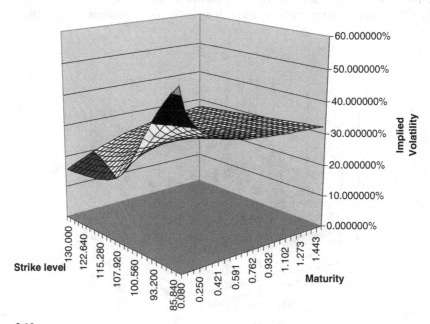

Figure 3.10

Information backed out in this way is much more accurate due to the arbitration effect although it is still subject to market vagaries, incompleteness and noise. Below is the mathematical calculation for the implied correlations in the interest rate, equity and credit markets. Using implied volatilities the implied correlation ρ can be measured and backed out.

Equity markets, while not as complete as interest rate markets, also exhibit a correlation between the σ_M or market volatility and the $\sum_{i=1}^{n} \omega_i \sigma_i$, the sum of the market volatilities. Initially we look at the sum of the $\rho's, \rho_i$.

Averaging all the $\rho's$ yields

$$\sigma_M^2 = \sum_{i=1}^{N} \omega_i \sigma_i^2 + \rho \sum_{i=1}^{N} \sum_{j \neq i} \omega_i \omega_j \sigma_i \sigma_j \qquad (3.4)$$

Using the implied volatility above you can force out the implied correlation ρ

$$\rho = \left[\frac{\sigma_M^2}{\sum_{i=1}^{N} \omega_i \sigma_i} \right] \qquad (3.5)$$

for sufficiently large N.

With the implied volatility and implied correlations the parameters for the implied distributions can be found.

3.4.2 Parametric Models

Parametric models are a slave to estimation parameters. In implied probability λ, the risk measure is backed out of the market but parametric models require you to estimate λ and other risk measures like κ a mean reverting parameter. These measures are extremely difficult to obtain and if their variance and correlations tend to a switching parameter best measured with a bimodal distribution, the mis-specifications could be large. Long Term Capital Management fell foul of this problem in 1998.

Parametric models are mainly used to measure risk and centre around time series evaluations. It is difficult to use parametric models to price a bid/asked spread on a trading desk.

Many times the risk factors are illiquid or non-existent. As a result you need to extend parameterization of the model in order to add more structure. Again parameterization can create a model that produces nothing but noise and it is this trade off that is more of an art than a science in modelling.

Autoregressive Conditional Heteroskedasticity (ARCH) Models

ARCH models focus on non-linear time series that focus on variance or volatility. ARCH relates the error variance to the square of a previous period's error. The models are generally used in time series that exhibit time-varying *volatility* clustering, i.e. periods of swings followed by periods of relative calm.

These are the first of a series of models that lead to a stochastic volatility best represented in the markets today.

Let's look at a time series with trend and seasonality removed. Let $\{X_t\}$ represent a time series of financial price information in a natural log form. This best expresses the random walk series and is expressed as follows:

$$X_t = \sigma_t \varepsilon_t$$

Where

ε_t *is a sequence of iid random variables with a zero mean and unit variance*
σ_t *is a local conditional std*

We should be careful here to define variance as a measure of dispersion around an expected mean of a random variable. Because of the ease of use we most often refer to the standard deviations as the positive square root of the variance. We make this point because further on we talk about instantaneous variance and the variance of the variance. We will define these terms more closely when they appear.

Let us assume further that the square of σ_t depends on the most recent value of the time series

$$\sigma_t^2 = \gamma + \delta x_{t-1}^2 \tag{3.6}$$

where γ and δ are chosen to ensure that σ_t^2 must not be negative. This is an ARCH model. Note that the model has no error term and, as such, has no stochastic term. It depends generally on the last squared value in the time series. These, then, are by definition Martingale processes and produce a white noise.

Generalized Autoregressive Conditional Heteroskedasticity (GARCH) Models

The ARCH model has been generalized to allow dependence on past values of σ_t^2. This new GARCH (p, q) model, where p is the order of the GARCH term σ^2, and q is the order of the ARCH terms ε^2, can then be expressed as follows:

$$\sigma_t^2 = \gamma + \sum_{i=1}^{p} \delta_i x_{t-1}^2 + \sum_{j=1}^{q} \beta_j \sigma_{t-1}^2 \tag{3.7}$$

These models are also Martingales and have a constant finite variance. Identifying the appropriate GARCH model is difficult and it is assumed GARCH $(1, 1)$ is the standard model. Because of specification difficulties, the family of GARCH models has grown to accommodate specific needs in determining the volatility structure or the time series. Below is only a partial list.

IGARCH
EGARCH
GARCH-M
QGARCH
GJR-GARCH
TGARCH
APARCH
FIGARCH
FIEGARCH
FIAPARCH
HYGARCH

Stochastic Volatility Models

In looking at the model above the first problem that jumps out is the constant volatility. Both t and $t - 1$ undergo the same shock. In reality volatility is volatile. An extension to the GARCH family is the stochastic volatility models. In these models the shock to the volatility is separate and distinct to the shock to the pricing.

$$\sigma_t^2 = \gamma + \sum_{i=1}^{p} \delta_i x_{t-1}^2 + \sum_{j=1}^{q} \beta_j \sigma_{t-1}^2 + \sum_{k=1}^{r} \eta_t \qquad (3.8)$$

where the shock to the variance is independent of the shock to the price.

These models lead to the better know uses in option pricing such as the Hull-White model.

Local Volatility Models

Finally, under this class of modelling we have the local volatility models. These models are an extension of the stochastic model where the diffusion or volatility is a function of time. The constant elasticity of variance model would be an example here.

The CEV functions calculate the theoretical price, sensitivities, and implied volatility of options using a valuation technique based on the constant elasticity of variance option pricing model. This model considers the possibility that the volatility of the underlying asset is dependent upon the price of the underlying asset.

This model is a more realistic version of the Black-Scholes model because studies have shown that price variances do change as the asset price changes. The Black-Scholes model assumes a constant asset price volatility regardless of the level of the security price.

The CEV model requires γ as a parameter in the calculation of option values. This value can be derived from the value of sigma (σ). The equation for deriving γ is:

$$\gamma = \sigma \times S(1 - \rho)$$

where: sigma (ρ) = standard deviation of the continuously compounded rate of return of a security per unit of time; S = security price; and ρ = coefficient of elasticity.

3.4.3   Realized Moments

While the implied moments refer to the market's assessment of future moments, the realized moments measure what actually happened in the past. The measurement of the moments depends on the particular situation. For example, one could calculate the realized volatility for the equity market between 2:00 and 3:00 on any specific day by taking the standard deviation of the daily returns within that month, or one could look at the realized volatility between 10:00 am and 11:00 am by calculating the standard deviation of one minute returns.

This is the most recent development and has lead to resurgence in high-frequency testing. The idea being that the realized parameters in higher frequency testing indicate the present parameters and mute any error in sampling historical data while at the same time eliminating the problems with implied testing. The process is moving towards an instantaneous sampling.

The questions being asked have to do with the frequency of sampling needed to best estimate the parameters of the distribution. The problem with this line of modelling is that it is replete with autocorrelation and bid/asked trading assimiles associated with different markets.

Realized Volatility

The volatility of asset returns plays an important role in financial markets. As shown above, volatility modelling and forecasting have received much attention from academics and practitioners. Numerous models have been constructed, among these the most popular formula is the Black-Scholes option price model, in which the key assumption is that the volatility is constant over time. However, empirical evidence shows that constant volatility is not realistic. The other commonly used model discussed above is the ARCH model or its extension, the GARCH process, which allow the volatility to change over time. The ARCH (or GARCH) is commonly used due to the availability of an explicit likelihood function.

Unfortunately, the standard ARCH/GARCH cannot pick up the asymmetric behaviour between asset returns and volatility. In contrast, the stochastic volatility (SV) models allow volatility to follow a stochastic process with its own error source. As a result, the SV models can capture the asymmetric behaviour between asset returns and volatility, in particular, the leverage effect. However, the mixture of distributions makes the estimation difficult. The explicit likelihood function is unavailable.

Most of the studies of stochastic volatility focus on the model with lagged dependence due to its tractability. The stochastic volatility model with dependence is more flexible in its ability to fit into the high kurtosis of asset returns.

The availability of high-frequency intra data make the calculation of realized volatility possible. Studies show that as a consistent, unbiased estimator of actual volatility, the realized volatility is more accurate. Using realized volatility as a proxy of actual volatility, the latent variable in the stochastic volatility models can now be considered observable; consequently, the traditional time series methods can be used for modelling and forecasting.

Realized Correlation

Once you turn your attention to high-frequency correlations you run into massive data problems. The most common approach to the multivariate case is matrix algebra. A major problem to this approach is that the parameters to be estimated can become huge very quickly. Other restrictions imposed to ensure that the matrix is tractable, such as a positive definite structure, become difficult with massive data. Most practitioners and academics simplify the process by compressing the data using factor analysis or principal component analysis, but those processes lead to errors in and of themselves. Using orthogonal matrices with eigenvalues used to reconstruct GARCH models have shown some success, but again the major problems are the tremendous amount of data used in high-frequency modelling, the amount of time needed for computation and the model over-specification.

Copulas

The study of the relationship between two or more random variables remains an important problem in statistical science. Initially it was a problem faced by life insurers where the questions were asked, "Does the death of a spouse on a second to die policy affect the life of the other, or can we look at life expectancies independently of each other?" – the problem being the measure of joint distribution. Interestingly it was the solution to this problem that answered the correlation question in bond portfolio analysis and allowed us to price and risk manage the tranches of large structures like CDOs. There is a need to understand the distribution of several random variables interacting together. Unfortunately, the modelling of many of these problems has often been based on a set of simplified assumptions.

Let us look at two dependent random variables X and Y. The marginal distribution of X and Y is the linear correlation coefficient

$$\rho(X, Y) = \frac{Cov(X, Y)}{\sqrt{Var(X)Var(Y)}} \tag{3.9}$$

where $Cov(X, Y)$ is the covariance of X and Y; $Var(X)$ is the variance of X; and $Var(Y)$ is the variance of Y.

Because of linearity, the joint distribution between two or more variables can most easily be expressed using a copula. A copula separates the joint distribution into two contributions: the marginal distributions of the individual variables and the interdependency of the probabilities.

See Chapter 2 for calculations of some of the better known copulas and examples of their uses.

The major problem among investment banks issuing CDOs and CDO^2s was trying to estimate the likelihood that all the companies in the CDO tranche would go bust at once. Their fates might be tightly intertwined. For instance, if the companies were all in closely related industries, such as auto-parts suppliers, they might fall like dominoes after a catastrophic event. In that case, the riskiest slice of the pool would not offer a return much different from the conservative slices, since anything that would sink two or three companies would probably sink many of them. Such a pool would have a "high default correlation".

But if a pool had a low default correlation – a low chance of all its companies stumbling at once – then the price gap between the riskiest slice and the less-risky slices would be wide.

Interestingly the solution came from the life insurance industry in their quest to solve the interdependency of life expectancies. As will be seen later, the problem with credit interdependency can once again be assuaged by the life insurance industry in the form of LSPs. Copulas can then be used as a way of forcing out both variance and covariance or correlation.

The approach to formulating a *multivariate distribution* using a copula is based on the idea that a simple transformation can be made of each *marginal variable* in such a way that each transformed marginal variable has a *uniform distribution*. When applied in a practical context, such transformations might be fitted as an initial step for each margin, or the parameters of the transformations might be fitted jointly with those of the copula. This marginal transformation allows us to look at the tail distributions, which are really where the risk is, instead of the entire correlation of the distributions.

There are many families of copulas which differ in the detail of the dependence they represent. A family will typically have several parameters that relate to the strength and form of the dependence.

Neural Nets (modality and switching processes)

Neural nets form an entirely new approach to time series analysis. Originally developed to try to replicate the human brain, this approach has been used in a number of different ways to include the financial markets. It is best used when the data indicates a bimodal appearance or when the intention is to identify patterns.

A neural net is a method of connecting a set of inputs with a set of outputs in a non-linear manner. These connections are made by way of layering, which contains neurons or nodes.

The problem with this approach is that the structure or architecture has to be determined by the data available, leading back to the problems of data collection.

Lévy Process

In probability theory, a Lévy process is any continuous-time stochastic process that starts at 0, is a function defined on the real numbers or a subset of them, and is everywhere right-continuous but has left limits. This function has "stationary independent increments" and is best used with Wiener and Poisson processes.

A continuous-time stochastic process assigns a random variable X_t to each point $t \geq 0$ in time. In effect it is a random function of t. The increments of such a process are the differences $X_s - X_t$ between its values at different times $t < s$. To call the increments of a process independent means that increments $X_s - X_t$ and $X_u - X_v$ are independent random variables whenever the two time intervals do not overlap and, more generally, any finite number of increments assigned to pairwise non-overlapping time intervals are mutually (not just pairwise) independent. To call the increments stationary means that the probability distribution of any increment $X_s - X_t$ depends only on the length $s - t$ of the time interval; increments with equally long time intervals are identically distributed.

In the Wiener process, the probability distribution of $X_s - X_t$ is normal with expected value 0 and variance $s - t$.

In the Poisson process, the probability distribution of $X_s - X_t$ is a Poisson distribution with expected value $\lambda(s - t)$, where $\lambda > 0$ is the "intensity" or "rate" of the process.

The probability distributions of the increments of any Lévy process are infinitely divisible. There is a Lévy process for each infinitely divisible probability distribution.

In any Lévy process with finite moments, the nth moment $\mu_n(t) = E(X_t^n)$ is a polynomial function of t; these functions satisfy a binomial identity:

$$\mu_n(t + s) = \sum_{k=0}^{n} \binom{n}{k} u_k(t) \mu_{n-k}(s) \tag{3.10}$$

While not used much in the financial study of life expectancy because of its handling of the Poisson function, it offers new possibilities.

3.5   LIFE SETTLEMENT POOL (LSP)

We have now come full circle, back to the LSP (the purpose of this treatise) and its volatility and correlation measure.

Below we look at a LSP and evaluate its volatility and correlation inter and intra the pool. We show how the LSP itself has very little volatility and merging with other securities can dampen the volatility in a structured product. We also show the correlation within the pools and how there is little if any correlation inter the LSP. LSPs generally do not track any of the external market forces. Stocks can go up or down; interest rates can move (save the change in the discounting factor); business cycles can go up or down; commodities can move; none of this has little if any effect on the value of a LSP.

Having said all that, and going back to our medicine cabinet, while we can eliminate or reduce most of the above modelling problems with LSPs, we do introduce two new risks:

liquidity risk and extension or longevity risk. However, as these risks are much easier to address and hedge, they will be covered in detail in later chapters.

3.5.1   Volatility in LSPs

There are basically two volatility rates that need to be looked at within the LSP. The first is the mark-to-market changes on a day-to-day or month-to-month basis. These changes will be determined by the mortality rates, and the volatility of these mortality rates is very low in comparison to spread volatilities. You may see changes due to plagues or the outbreak of war and, as a result, volatility might rise during these periods but generally volatilities even during these times remain low and are very slow to appear. Daily/weekly volatility should not be affected. As a result changes in the price of a pool of life settlement policies are low and almost deterministic. This volatility centres completely around the life expectancy calculation, which is itself a stochastic process (see Chapter 2).

The volatility of a single life based on the life expectancy calculation is a jump diffusion calculation with a Poisson process. Given that it is an uncertain event, we can calculate the expected time to death (default in a bond) and also a standard deviation of that time (under a constant hazard rate h the time is $1/h$ and the variance of the time is also $1/h$). For a pool of such policies there is a small positive correlation, but let's ignore this for simplicity at the moment. For the pool (of n identical lives) the expected time to default of all lives is still $1/h$, but the variance is now $1/nh$.

As a result, the volatility of a single life calculation can be $+/-$ the life expectancy. As the number of policies in the pool grows, the volatility calculation becomes more stable and tends to

$$\frac{\mu}{\sqrt{\upsilon}}$$

Where

$\mu = $ *the mean of the pool*

$\upsilon = $ *the number of policies*

As the number of policies in the pool grows the volatility is reduced.

The second volatility, the volatility of payout, is non-existent. Generally speaking the payout due to death is guaranteed and is fixed if the life expectancy calculation is accepted.

3.5.2   Correlation in LSPs

If we introduce a correlation then we have to calculate results numerically using numerical methods like the copula calculation described above. Correlation with most variables intra market is almost non-existent, as mentioned above.

Looking again at historical mortality rates (Figure 3.11) for males age 25, there is a crisis – albeit less frequent and less extreme – at times of war or plague, and trends downward over an extended period of time reflecting medical advances and improved living conditions. You can see the rise in deaths of males during the two great wars of the twentieth century. However, for the first time since records have been kept on the US population, life expectancy has gone down. But this is more attributable to life style than anything else and is extremely slow

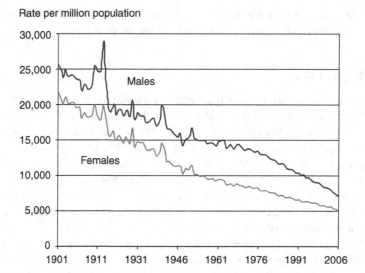

Figure 3.11

moving. Other than that there has been a steady downturn in mortality and any correlation to market variable is almost non-existent.

Correlations inter-market can influence results, but again is not a major factor. An example would be asbestos workers, smokers or those who have hazardous jobs.

As a result, adding LSPs to structured products will improve diversity and reduce exposure to volatility, jump diffusion risk and correlation to cyclical risks.

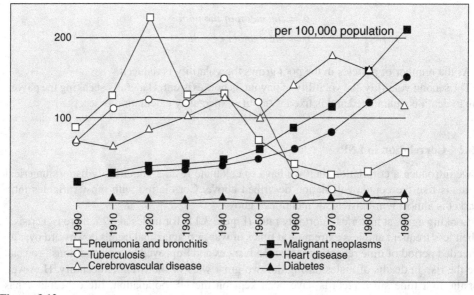

Figure 3.12

Other risks, such as interest rates generally, will not effect the marked-to-market price of a pool of life settlement policies other than the fact that the discount factor will change. Cash surrender values within a whole life policy yield such a low return that changes in interest rates have little effect on the long-term value of cash surrender values.

3.5.3 Credit Risks

Credit ratings from the issuing companies' point of view should also be a non-issue. In addition to the fact that most insurance companies find it difficult to write business with a credit rating of under an investment grade, 46 of the 50 states in the USA have insurance pools guaranteeing payment of insurance. This generally means that there are two reserves standing behind the payment of the life policy: the insurance companies and the states.

3.5.4 LSP: Examples

Figure 3.13 shows a pool of life settlements with a face value of the portfolio being $100 million. Headings across the top lists the issuing company, the ratings of the company issuing the policy, the face value of the policy, the date the policy was issued, the type of policy (usually whole life or universal, but could be other types as discussed below), the age of the insured and the expected life of the insured. Please note that, in this structure, nowhere is the name of the insured listed. Also note that the expected life is an adjusted expected life, by which we mean that, at the time the policy is sold into the trust, a new life expectancy is issued.

Summary statistics are shown at the bottom of the table. There are a total of 57 policies in this pool. The total face value is $100 million, the average age of the policy holder is 77 years and the adjusted life expectancy, the life expectancy recalculated at the sale of the policy into the trust, is 104 months or 8.67 years. Notice also that there are no names and ratings of the issuing life insurance companies are S&P A-rated companies or better.

In effect the policy holder will sell the policy on to a trust which then becomes the beneficiary of the policy. Upon death the death benefit is paid into the trust. In return the trust will pay a settlement fee to the policy holder and continue to keep the policy in force generally by continuing to pay premiums as well as all other expenses.

A detailed explanation of this process is set out in Chapter 1.

Figure 3.14 shows the securitization of this pool and identifies the players. Again Chapter 1 addresses details of this structure.

Advantages of an LSP: to the policy holder

There is an advantage to the policy holder. Generally the policy was taken out while the individual was in his 40s, 50s or 60s and in his peak earning years. Today the kids have left the nest, the house is paid for or he has downsized, pensions, IRAs and other retirement funds have kicked in and the last thing the individual needs is an expensive life insurance policy. They have three choices.

- Take out all the cash surrender value in the policy and lapse the policy.
- Continue to pay on a policy they really don't need.
- Today, sell the policy on to a Trust which will pay substantially more than the cash surrender value.

ISSUER	RATING	FACE VALUE	TYPE	AGE	ADJ EM (2003 IN MONTHS)	FACE VALUE BY PERIOD	PERCENTAGE BY PERIOD
PRUDENTIAL LIFE	AA	$2,000,000.00	WL	85	48		
METLIFE	AA	$1,000,000.00	WL	78	48		
PACIFIC MUTUAL LIFE	AA	$2,000,000.00	WL	76	48	$5,000,000.00	5.00%
JEFFERSON PILOT	AAA	$2,000,000.00	WL	82	60		
UNITED OF OMAHA	AA	$450,000.00	WL	81	60		
PRIMERICA	AA	$3,000,000.00	UNV	80	60	$5,450,000.00	5.00%
MASS MUTUAL	AA	$2,000,000.00	UNV	79	72		
COLUMBUS LIFE	AAA	$750,000.00	UNV	79	72		
COLUMBUS LIFE	AAA	$750,000.00	UNV	77	72		
TRANSAMERICA	AA+	$500,000.00	WL	78	72		
US LIFE OF NYC	A+	$2,000,000.00	WL	82	72		
WEST COAST LIFE	AA	$2,000,000.00	UNV	74	72		
US LIFE NYC	A+	$2,000,000.00	WL	82	72	$9,000,000.00	10.00%
TRAVELERS	AA	$3,000,000.00	UNV	82	84		
TRAVELERS	AA	$5,000,000.00	WL	82	84		
US LIFE NYC	A+	$2,000,000.00	UNV	73	84	$10,000,000.00	10.00%
TRAVELERS	AA	$3,000,000.00	WL	78	96		
TRAVELERS	AA	$2,000,000.00	UNV	79	96		
EQUITABLE LIFE	AA	$2,000,000.00	WL	76	96		
NEW YORK LIFE	AA	$2,000,000.00	UNV	78	96		
JOHN HANCOCK	AA	$1,000,000.00	UNV	76	96	$10,000,000.00	10.00%
CNA	A	$1,750,000.00	UNV	74	108		
JOHN HANCOCK	AA	$1,500,000.00	UNV	74	108		
AETNA LIFE	AA	$1,000,000.00	UNV	70	108		
SOUTHWESTERN LIFE	A+	$1,000,000.00	UNV	78	108		
NEW YORK LIFE	AA	$2,000,000.00	UNV	78	108		
TRANSAMERICA	AA	$1,000,000.00	UNV	80	108		
TRANSAMERICA	AA+	$3,500,000.00	WL	77	108		
MASS MUTUAL	AA	$4,000,000.00	WL	83	108		
CROWN LIFE	A	$2,000,000.00	UNV	79	108		
AMERICAN GEN	AA	$1,200,000.00	WL	81	108		
CHUBB LIFE	AA	$750,000.00	WL	80	108		
MIDLANDS	AA	$300,000.00	WL	83	108	$20,000,000.00	20.00%
US LIFE OF NYC	A+	$3,000,000.00	WL	86	120		
JEFFERSON PILOT	AAA	$2,000,000.00	WL	75	120		
TRANSAMERICA	AA+	$1,500,000.00	UNV	75	120		
SEC LIFE	AA+	$2,000,000.00	UNV	75	120		
US LIFE OF NYC	A+	$3,000,000.00	UNV	81	120		
JEFFERSON PILOT	AAA	$3,000,000.00	WL	79	120		
TRANSAMERICA	AA+	$3,000,000.00	WL	78	120		
THE MIDLAND CO	A+	$500,000.00	WL	82	120		
NEW YORK LIFE	AA	$1,250,000.00	WL	69	120	$19,250,000.00	20.00%
NEW YORK LIFE	AA	$3,000,000.00	WL	69	132		
METLIFE	AA	$2,000,000.00	WL	68	132		
WEST COAST LIFE	AA	$1,600,000.00	WL	84	132		
WEST COAST LIFE	AA	$1,600,000.00	UNV	79	132		
OLD REPUBLIC LIFE	A	$1,000,000.00	UNV	68	132		
THE HARTFORD	AA	$1,000,000.00	WL	76	132		
THE HARTFORD	AA	$1,500,000.00	WL	81	132		
UNITED OF OMAHA	AA	$1,000,000.00	WL	82	132		
WEST COAST LIFE	AA	$600,000.00	WL	81	132		
WEST COAST LIFE	AA	$1,000,000.00	WL	79	132		
UNITED OF OMAHA	AA	$1,000,000.00	WL	79	132		
NEW YORK LIFE	AA	$1,000,000.00	WL	78	132		
SAFECO LIFE	AA	$500,000.00	WL	61	132		
PRINCIPAL LIFE	AAA	$1,500,000.00	WL	60	132		
PRINCIPAL LIFE	AAA	$1,000,000.00	WL	64	132		
THE TRAVELERS	AA	$1,000,000.00	WL	62	132	$21,300,000.00	20.00%
TOTALS		$100,000,000.00		77	104	$100,000,000.00	100.00%

Figure 3.13

Because of the limited alternatives the prices paid by the Trust for policies are substantially higher than other alternatives to the owner of the policy while substantially lower than any theoretical value. Generally speaking, policies with a 10-year life expectancy, a sought after term, can be purchased for anything between 10 and 35 cents to the dollar. There are pressure points within the markets that are building as this asset class becomes more acceptable but it doesn't take rocket science to understand that purchasing something for 25 cents and receiving

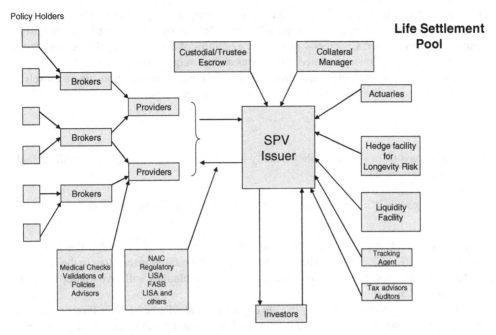

Figure 3.14

1 dollar in 10 years with little risk is a good investment. Contestable policies are cheaper than non-contestable policies, as is variable life and universal life. Lower credit quality will also be less expensive while shorter life expectancies are going to be more expensive.

In the market, not too long ago, a $50 million policy was sold by a well-known business executive in his 90s for approximately 75 cents on the dollar.

The insurance agent will also benefit from this process by standing in the middle of the transaction. While (to date) no fee is generated by the sale of the life policy, the holder of the policy now has a significant amount of cash that needs to be reinvested and the insurance agent will be happy to help.

Advantages of a LSP: to the Investor/Trust

Because of the regulatory environment there exists an arbitrage effect in the life settlement market today. Life insurers would love to be able to purchase their debt back at 10 to 35 cents on the dollar but they are prevented by law from doing so.

As a result, there is generated an almost arbitrage effect to the purchaser of the policies because:

- The credit quality of the policy is usually very good, investment grade or higher and many policies have the backing of the state in which they are issued. This gives the purchaser a double guarantee. Please note that lower credit quality can be offset with credit derivatives yielding a higher return than the high-quality policies alone.
- As stated above, because of the lack of alternatives for the seller and, at present, a wait-and-see attitude by major institutions from entering into this market in a big way, market prices

for these policies is very good. A buy and hold programme can generate a 9% return and a managed pool can generate a few hundred basis points above that. Using leverage pushes that return even higher. Chapters 4 and 5 give examples of a number of different structures along with the cash flows generated, the returns and subsequent risk.

• While this is still an emerging asset class there are a number of firms establishing themselves as market makers, although no one seems to be dominating as yet.

Risks of an LSP

The actuarial payoff for one life policy exactly mirrors that used to calculate a credit default swap with a recovery rate of zero.

$$notional \times \int (mortality\ rate \times survival\ prob \times discount\ factor)$$

Now take a pool of policies that are not independent and you can value the pool as a single tranche [0%, 100%] CDO. The expected value will be fairly insensitive to the assumed correlation but the standard deviation will not. Higher correlations will give higher variation in the capital value of the pay off.

In Chapter 2 we covered more fully the life expectancy calculation because this is where the only real risks to this portfolio lie. Above we used the integral of the mortality rate, survival probability and a discount factor. This calculation implies several things. First, a continuous calculation, which is distinct from mortality rates that can be discrete calculations. Second, the integral is calculating over some distribution. Factor analysis is used in life expectancies as opposed to large data base analysis in mortality calculations.

In general most firms use a factor analysis programme that can have up to 38 different factors all developed from massive data bases collected over many years (see Figure 3.15).

The reason for a factor analysis approach as opposed to a simple mortality table and probability measures is that we can structure our portfolio in such a way that it does not approximate a normal distribution in any way. We can skew the pool dramatically in our favour by the selection process or generate fat tails. Mortality tables assume normal distributions, with the advantage that some tables have billions of data points going back to the late 1800s.

As stated above, a single named portfolio of one life policy will have the statistical appearance of a Poisson process to the time of death, which means, given a number of assumptions that are not necessarily true, that the standard deviation equals the expected life, and is an example of a jump process. As more policies are added, the distribution of life expectancy becomes normal with a standard mean and a standard deviation:

$$\frac{mean}{\sqrt{Number\ of\ policies}}$$

Using the pool figures in Figure 3.13 we have 57 policies with a mean of 104 months and the standard deviation would be

$$\frac{104}{\sqrt{57}} = 13.8\ months$$

Therefore, if the average life of this pool is 10 years (120 months), with 1 standard deviation being 13.8 months or a little over 1 year. Any obligation due in 10 years securitized by a pool

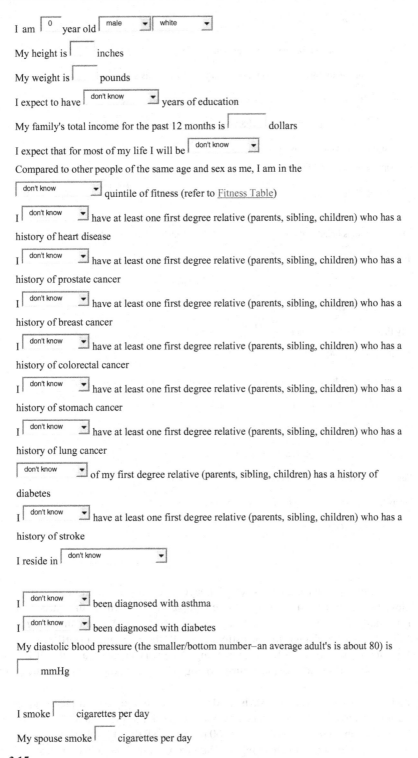

I am [0] year old [male ▼][white ▼]

My height is [   ] inches

My weight is [   ] pounds

I expect to have [don't know ▼] years of education

My family's total income for the past 12 months is [   ] dollars

I expect that for most of my life I will be [don't know ▼]

Compared to other people of the same age and sex as me, I am in the
[don't know ▼] quintile of fitness (refer to Fitness Table)

I [don't know ▼] have at least one first degree relative (parents, sibling, children) who has a history of heart disease

I [don't know ▼] have at least one first degree relative (parents, sibling, children) who has a history of prostate cancer

I [don't know ▼] have at least one first degree relative (parents, sibling, children) who has a history of breast cancer

I [don't know ▼] have at least one first degree relative (parents, sibling, children) who has a history of colorectal cancer

I [don't know ▼] have at least one first degree relative (parents, sibling, children) who has a history of stomach cancer

I [don't know ▼] have at least one first degree relative (parents, sibling, children) who has a history of lung cancer

[don't know ▼] of my first degree relative (parents, sibling, children) has a history of diabetes

I [don't know ▼] have at least one first degree relative (parents, sibling, children) who has a history of stroke

I reside in [don't know ▼]

I [don't know ▼] been diagnosed with asthma

I [don't know ▼] been diagnosed with diabetes

My diastolic blood pressure (the smaller/bottom number–an average adult's is about 80) is

[   ] mmHg

I smoke [   ] cigarettes per day

My spouse smoke [   ] cigarettes per day

Figure 3.15

I have [don't know ▼] drinks per day

I travel [   ] thousand miles per year in an automobile

The driver of the automobile which I most frequently travel in is a [don't know ▼]

The age of the driver of the automobile which I most frequently travel in is [   ] years

I [don't know ▼] regularly wear seat belts when travelling in an automobile

The automobile which I most frequently travel in [don't know ▼] regularly keep to speeds appropriate to road conditions

The driver of the automobile which I most frequently travel in is [don't know ▼] drunk while driving

Of the 10 things listed in the Stress List, [   ] of them happened to me in the past 12 months

I am a [don't know ▼]

I work in the [don't know ▼] industry

My father worked in a [don't know ▼] job

My first regular occupation is a [don't know ▼] job

My current occupation is a [don't know ▼] job

Of the 5 types of food in the Dietary Diversity List, on average I consume [   ] types

[don't know ▼] than 10% of my energy intake comes from fat

I [don't know ▼] among the 15% most depressed of the population

I have had [   ] sexual partners in the past 12 months

For most of my sexual encounters, I [don't know ▼] use condoms

On average, I have [   ] hours of sleep a day

Figure 3.15 (*Continued*)

of life expectancies could have a year's delay in payout causing a default in the structure. The standard deviation of your estimator should be compared to the uncertainty arising from the unknown mortality curve(s). If the mortality curve is wrong by X (we can only guess what X is) and this leads to a change in our estimator of Y, then picking a portfolio size with a statistical accuracy (as above) of 10 years is going to be very accurate and therefore have no significant error in relation to the uncertainty arising from the unknown underlying mortality curve.

It should be noted that factor analysis is used to more accurately determine the place within the distribution. In most cases life expectancy portfolios offer a selection process. This greatly skews the distribution. When assembling a $100 million LSP the purchaser of the pool usually has choices. Under this scenario choosing a policy from an individual who is age 72 but gets up every morning, runs 5 miles, is 6 feet tall and weighs 165 pounds, doesn't smoke, eats a well-balanced diet, has no history of heart trouble or cancer, and goes to bed every night at 9:30 would be eliminated from the portfolio in favour of a policy from a gentleman who is 72 years of age but thinks exercise is moving from the couch to the refrigerator, smokes, is 450 pounds, has had triple by-pass surgery and emphysema. This type of selection process greatly skews the distribution in favour of the holder of the pool and insures the average life of the pool thus eliminating extension risk.

Two points:

1. Generally, life expectancy is used as a descriptive statistic only. Financially we are interested in other variables, which will require other estimators.
2. Your portfolio life expectancy will be a weighted average of the individual ones. The standard deviation of this will be more heavily influenced by the better lives (where the expectancy is greatest), whereas your real risk is that the curve itself has been grossly miscalculated for an unhealthy life which is in fact a healthy life.

For calculation of all the risks, simulation is the simplest and quickest method.

There are a number of ways to hedge this risk, which will be covered in detail in later chapters, but suffice to say if the policies are cheap enough you can over-collateralize the pool, purchase an insurance wrap or purchase an extension swap. Again, all these issues will be covered in later chapters.

3.5.5   Other Risks

There is also liquidity risk in the investment, given that keeping the policy in force requires an insurance premium and fees at a time when little or no cash flow is being generated by the pool. However, reserve accounts or pooling these policies with other types of asset classes can overcome this problem. Liquidity options can be purchased as well as the establishment of liquidity providers.

In addition premium financing is available and many providers like to go out 7 years as this is a break-even calculation. After 7 years the cash surrender value can keep the policy in force for the remainder of the term.

There is also an extension risk. Given that the actuarial projection is estimated at 10 years, the actual life can extend naturally into 13 years or beyond.

Above we went into detail with regard to extension risk. Outliers such as the possibility of a cure for cancer can drastically alter life expectancies: or a natural ageing discovery. But these event risks can work both ways. A terrorist explosion in the heart of New York City, wars or plagues can skew the results.

Generally speaking, these risks are minimal and most actuarial systems have a random death statistic anyway.

For the first time in US history, life expectancy has fallen. Researchers think this has to do with poor life styles. If this continues, expected life calculations will have to be redone.

Correlation risks can be used in the selection process but generally play no part in life expectancies. The probability that I die has no correlation to the expectation of anyone else's death, other than a nuclear attack.

One caveat to correlation risk would be to choose a portfolio of asbestos workers or some other group of workers with statistical life expectancies that are skewed in some way.

Finally, under risk is the possibility of fraud. It is difficult in the best circumstances to determine life expectancy, but if information used to calculate the life expectancy is not altogether correct, this can skew the results. As with any emerging market where profit can be made, charlatans can enter. Physicians, although generally not many, may over-state the severity of an illness of a patient for the express purpose of decreasing the life expectancy calculation and driving up the resale value of the policy.

Also life agents eager for future business and profit can try to obfuscate policy values on both sides of the trade by standing in the middle and reducing the payout to the policy holder selling the policy and to the broker purchasing the policy.

There is even a growing cottage industry generating new business ventures by "flipping" life policies. By that we mean signing up new clients for life policies with the express intention of selling the policies on in x months for a profit. While not illegal, the agent has a fiduciary responsibility to his client. Getting the client into an expensive programme without a clear understanding of the outcome of the process could cause the client to lose money and not be seen as a prudent investment by the regulators. At present, there is not a liquid market for contestable policies with which to generate rational prices, and the client could end up selling the policy for less than the premium paid into it.

As a result a great deal of due diligence has to be done on each and every policy. Below is a 28-step due diligence process that most Trusts follow to verify the legitimacy of the policies in the Trust. At present there are several stock exchange traded actuarial firms and service providers who will validate each life policy before it is placed into the Trust

3.5.6 Due Diligence

Below is a sample listing of the due diligence a firm will have to go through to make sure the policy is in force and in good standing with no liens against it and agreement with all who are involved.

It should be noted that many of the following are the responsibility of the issuing life insurance company. For example a life insurance company can be fined heavily if they fail to pay off the policy upon death within 30 days.

1. *Application for settlement* – The documentation received from the insured and policy owner, which commences the policy purchase transaction, including details about the policy and the insured.
2. *Certification of mental competency* – Statement from the physician of the Insured and the Seller that the individual in question is of sound mind to commence the policy sales transaction. This is not always required in cases where the seller and/or insured is transparently of sound mind – many funders require that certifications be provided when the individual is aged over, for example, 80.
3. *Compliance – HIPAA releases and confidentiality* – Notification that the handling and transfer of all documents will comply with state and federal privacy rules.
4. *Insurance policy original application* – Complete copy of the original application for insurance by the insured as submitted to and received from the insurance company of the policy issue.
5. *Verification of policy authenticity* – Written certification by the insurance company of policy issue that the policy is valid and in full force, with definition of policy type and effect.

6. *Verification of policy premium payments* – Written statement from the issuing insurance company of the policy premium status (these verifications are usually covered by the written Verification of Coverage).

7. *Verification of liens, encumbrances and assignments* – Written verification and indemnification of liens, encumbrances and assignments against policy including UCC-1 search.

8. *Verification of policy ownership* – Written verification of registration of policy ownership from insured, owner and insurance company.

9. *Verification of policy beneficiaries* – Written verification of registration of beneficiaries of the policy from insured, owner and insurance company, and beneficiaries.

10. *Verification of policy ownership release on sale* – Written verification of release of all policy ownership interests on close of asset purchase segment of the escrow, obtained from the policy owner and any other parties in interest.

11. *Verification of beneficial interest transfer on sale* – Written verification of the transfer of all policy beneficiary interests on close of asset purchase escrow, obtained from the policy owner and any other parties in interest.

12. *Verification of life expectancy (medical, actuarial)* – Written verification of the estimated life expectancy of the insured from medical and actuarial reviews.

13. *Verification of medical records from personal physician* – Written verification of and copies of all relevant medical records of the insured.

14. *Verification of third party life term reviewers' opinions* – Written verification by third-party evaluators of insured's medical and actuarial records.

15. *Verification of AVS LE appraisal* – Written verification summary of AVS Life Expectancy estimates.

16. *Certification of purchaser qualification* – Written statement of purchaser qualification per United States Securities Act of 1933 as amended, in compliance with state regulations.

17. *Certification of state regulations compliance* – Written certification of compliance with state insurance regulations governing advance settlements of life policies.

18. *Trust operation instructions verification* – Written instructions for operation of the Trust and escrow related to the settlement process.

19. *Trustee agreements* – Written agreements between the Trustee and all parties to the settlement transaction.

20. *Acquisition broker agreements* – Written agreements between the policy owner, insured, and policy agent.

21. *Escrow agreements* – Written transaction escrow agreements and instruction for the settlement process, accounting and payment disbursements.

22. *Policy transfer agreement* – Asset purchase agreement.

23. *Settlement services and servicing agreement* – Written agreement with servicing entity to monitor and close policy claims at maturity.

24. *Bank Trust agreement* – Written instructions with Bank Trustee regarding all custodial functions related to the Trust.

25. *Funds disbursement agreements* – Written pay orders to escrow and payments processing.

26. *Third-party purchaser funder agreements* – Written agreements with funders, lenders, and/or third-party purchasers.

27. *Offering documents, subscription agreements, indenture agreements.*

28. *Third-party contingency insurance and/or reinsurance.*

3.6 CONCLUSION

Structured products – while suffering from a bad reputation at present – were developed like all derivative products as a means of reducing risk and possibly segmenting cash flow while at the same time maintaining higher yields within the structure.

Problems arose because the structures were simply combining multiple stochastic processes which themselves had risk.

The LSP, as we will see in subsequent chapters, will allow a true arbitrage of sorts that can be used singularly or in combination with other capital markets and structured finance products to truly reduce risk and, at the same time, keep yields high.

As with any true arbitrage process it will not last forever. Life companies are already changing their pricing methodologies and writing in restrictive clauses. But given that there are trillions of dollars of existing life policies in the market today and approximately $10 billion coming on yearly, changes should be slow and offer substantial returns to those who wish to enter into this new asset class.

The remainder of this text simply shows some of the many permutations and combinations of product that can be structured for low-risk high-profit products.

## 4

Examples of LSP Securitization: A Principal Protected Fund

INTRODUCTION

In Chapters 4, 5 and 6 we will look at structures from an expected value perspective; as such, all products will be priced at par at inception. We will then address risk not from the standpoint of a change in price but from the standpoint of a change in cash flows. The major concentration will be the change in residual value which, as we will show, is the major risk in most of these structures. As explained in Chapter 2 and further in Chapters 7 and 8 there are basically three methodologies in pricing life insurance policies and by extension life settlement portfolios; deterministic, probabilistic and stochastic. As shown, they can generate very different numbers for the same policy. Deterministic pricing is based on the end date or life expectancy. For example, if the life expectancy of a policy were 80 months, the policy would have small negative cash flows for 79 months followed by a huge positive cash flow at term. Probability looks at a mortality curve and takes into consideration that deaths may occur before or after the expected date. Stochastic pricing is based on a Monte Carlo simulation of thousands of life expectancies and a mean or median is then used.

For purposes of illustration we will use the deterministic pricing methodology for several reasons. First, it establishes a fixed term. Second, the residual value is the major risk with these products and we will concentrate on how to mitigate that risk in later chapters. Third, we can assign a probabilistic measure to the process by simply calculating a standard deviation around the expected life expectancy. We will generate a mortality curve for the portfolio by simply aggregating the life expectancies. It will be this runoff curve we use over the next few chapters to evaluate the structures.

In Chapters 7 and 8 we will start to look at pricing first from an instantaneous forward expectation construction and then as a stochastic process. We need to make this jump when we talk about derivative products and their use in the life settlement structure.

Life insurance policies when purchased into a trust act like any other security. As such the permutations and combinations of these products are almost endless. We start by looking at simple securitizations of the product and extend this process in Chapter 5 to include structures. We spent a good deal of time in Chapter 3 on MBS, CMO and CDO products. In Chapters 5 and 7 we show that LSPs can be used in place of mortgages and other derivative products with substantial added benefits. For now we concentrate on simple securitizations of LSPs.

Figure 4.1 shows the flow of a simple LSP. As you can see, there are multiple players and multiple functions. Chapter 1 went into detail of exactly what each function does and the problems associated with each area. For now we cover just a very brief review of the functions listed below.

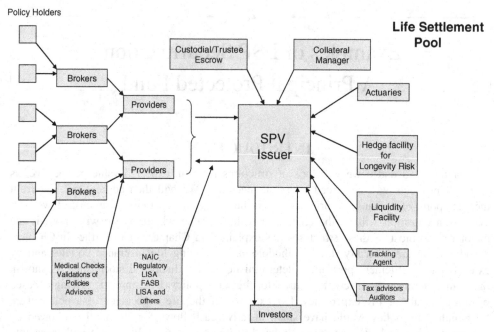

Figure 4.1

Brokers

Brokers are the general agents who sell the policies into the market. We will discuss "STOLI" (STranger Originated Life Insurance) and other regulatory and legal issues in depth later, but at this point we want to stress that we subscribe to LISA rules and are demonstrating products that conform. The life policies described here and throughout the book are life policies sold into the secondary market after a conscious decision has been made that the policies are no longer needed. Brokers who "flip policies" are not part of this discussion.

Providers

Providers collect, clean and perform due diligence on the policies brought to them by the brokers. There are a growing number of providers who act as market makers buying and selling policies and pools of policies over the web and in the open market.

SPV Risk Remote

The trust or corporation will reside in the SPV or SPE. This is a risk-remote entity who will own the asset.

Custodial

The custodial agent is usually a bank or trust company. It takes possession of the security, in this case the life settlement policy, and is responsible for reporting, managing and processing the security, in this case the life policy. In previous years, not many custodial departments had the ability to accept LSPs or policies. They simply did not know how to report or handle them. For example, at death how is the policy holder notified? The family has given up the benefits of the policy and has no incentive to notify the trust about the death. The custodial agent is responsible for tracking the health status of the insured lives, although it may elect to outsource the tracking to a specialist company.

Collateral Manager

Like a CDO, the product has to have a manager. As funds run off they have to be reinvested or paid out. In an active pool the funds are reinvested in new policies. Hedging procedures may need to be in place. The process will need to be ramped up. In a $100 million pool, purchasing policies one by one will take time. All this falls under the collateral manager.

Medical and Actuarial Review

The provider will generally do the due diligence on the policies but in most cases an outside actuarial service will provide an Adjusted Life Expectancy (ALE). If the policy was issued 20 years ago with an expected life (LE) of 20 years, it is unreasonable to expect a zero or negative Life Expectancy. The application is resubmitted and a new medical examination may be needed to provide an ALE. This is usually coordinated by an *actuarial firm.*

Hedge Facility

In many instances an outside hedge facility may need to be put in place if the collateral manager cannot or will not do it. The hedge function can often be sophisticated and need additional expertise or additional functions, and the issuance of a longevity bond or a surety bond may require additional services. The mandate of the SPV will determine this function.

Liquidity Provider

As mentioned many times in this treatise, the two major risks with a LSP are liquidity and longevity. Because no cash flow will be thrown off in the early years of the structure a liquidity provider will need to be put in place. The liquidity provider can come in many different shapes and sizes. For example, in the event that this is a Sharia compliant bond, no interest can be charged. One way around this dilemma is to purchase a put option from a hedge fund or other provider. In the event that cash is needed, the collateral manager simply puts the option to the hedge fund in return for needed cash.

4.1   A SIMPLE EXAMPLE

The simplest example of securitization using LSPs is the originating and or purchasing and holding of contestable pools. As with any security there are "pressure points" within the pricing mechanism. Governments try to keep certain bond issues liquid, such as 10-year and 30-year bonds. These bonds even have a secondary market of derivatives, futures and options, priced off these products. As a result there exists a "tap curve" with most government bond issues priced below the standard curve because of liquidity. Restated, these issues are cheaper.

The reverse exists within the life settlement issues. In today's market everyone is searching for whole life or universal life policies with a life expectancy of around 10 years. Prices in these areas are rich. If, however, you could use 15-year, 20-year or longer life policies these prices would be cheaper by comparison.

The cheapest pools of life settlement policies are the contestable policies. These policies have recently been written and, as a result, the issuing company still can renege on payment if for any of a number of reasons the information given by the policy holder turns out to be false. A patient with terminal cancer could try to falsify documents to obtain an expensive policy. Medical practitioners may falsify medical examinations to try to change the terms of the life policy.

Historically the number of policies failing to make it through the contestability stage has been less than 1% due to the rigorous due diligence the issuing company goes through before issuing the policy. The contestability period is usually 2 years. As a result, a programme to originate or purchase contestable policies in the 10-year life expectancy range, and hold them for $1^1/_2$ to 2 years then resell them, is a huge money-making process. Generally speaking, because there is not a lot of demand for these policies initially the price is 10 to 12 cents on the face value of the dollar. Holding this portfolio for 2 years and then selling it on at the then high-demand non-contestable 10-year basket would result in a sale of 25 to 35 cents on the dollar. That is a 13–15 cent profit in $1^1/_2$ to 2 years, or 43% return. Assuming a 2–3% premium payment and a 5% failure of the contestability portfolio, you would still be left with a return in the 32–35% range.

As with any high-yield investment there are risks with this programme. Many insurance companies are now writing into the policy a contingency that the policy cannot be sold on. Also, the amount of money paid into the policy at the time the contestable policy is to be sold on is an easy number to calculate. A 55-year-old man may have to pay $60,000 a year for a $5 million face value life policy. If the policy is only 6 months old, the purchaser of the policy will know immediately that the seller of the policy has only paid $30,000 in premiums into the programme. In addition, the expected life will be calculated and the premiums that will need to be paid by the trust purchasing the policy can be calculated. The bottom line being that nothing will be hidden in the transaction and it will then be up to the purchasing trust to determine the value of his insurability. It may be that after paying in $30,000 for 6 months and then attempting to sell the policy on (if that is permitted), they may only be offered $35,000 for the policy. The trust could even offer less than the $30,000 if there were a flood of similar policies in the market at the time of sale.

Finally, STOLI is coming under tremendous scrutiny. The process of buy and flip is beyond the scope of life insurance, and trade associations from both sides of the industry have spoken out against this practice. Regulators are looking at the process closely and there are major law suits in the USA that could render such activities unfeasible in the future.

Nevertheless, the returns are substantial, given the risks in place at present, and this is a textbook example of regulatory arbitrage.

4.2   OTHER POOL EXAMPLES

We will use the following assumptions in the next three examples. They are only examples but they closely represent live transactions. Some, if not all, of the assumptions may be challenged but these are only intended to be examples of what can be done by securitizing LSPs. We are of the opinion that many of the assumptions below are very conservative, but it is not the purpose here to debate these assumptions.

4.2.1 Assumptions

- It is assumed that $100 is to be invested in purchasing a LSP.
- The cost of these life policies is 20 cents on the dollar. Therefore, in theory we could purchase $500 worth of face value. But because these pools throw off no cash flow for the first few years a percentage of the $100 will be kept in reserve.
- In this example we purchase only policies from carriers rated at least A by Standard & Poor's or A2 by Moody's Investor Services.
- These policies are only non-contestable policies (using contestable policies and over-collateralizing will greatly improve yields but will not be shown here) and are either whole life or universal life policies (again programmes using term or variable life could be structured to yield better returns, but we defer those examples also).
- The average life of the LSP is 10 years (which has been determined by a well-respected actuarial firm) and the life expectancies are adjusted life expectancies. By that we mean the life expectancies are calculated as of the time of purchase into the trust, not when originally issued.
- The runoff schedule (see Figure 4.3) was taken from the life expectancies of the pool.
- No policy is larger than $5 in death benefit.
- Because the LSP has an average expected life of 10 years, only 80% of the pool matures on or before the 10-year term.
- Any policies still in force at the end of the 10-year term can be sold back into the market at 60% of face value. This should be a very conservative assumption given that there is a secondary market for these policies and it is becoming more and more liquid; the value of the policy grows almost linearly as each day the policy holder lives brings the policies a little closer to term, and time is very much a linear function.
- Insurance premiums (2.9% of face) have to be maintained to keep the policies in force. In addition, a management fee (1% of investment) and custodial fees (0.02% of investment) have to be paid in addition to set-up costs and other miscellaneous fees.
- Any and all excess cash will be invested at a 4% rate.
- Any cash excess over and above the 3-year expense requirement can be invested in money market funds, but is not considered here.
- No insurance carrier will represent more than 20% of the total portfolio.

4.2.2 Statically Managed Fund

Figure 4.2 is an example of a pool of life policies. The pool has 57 policies that total $100 million of face value. This particular pool is a mixture of whole life and universal life issued by A-rated carriers or higher.

Across the top is:

- The issuer of the policy
- The rating of the Insurer
- The face value of the policy
- The type of policy

ISSUER	RATING	FACE VALUE	TYPE	AGE	ADJ EM (2003 IN MONTHS)	FACE VALUE BY PERIOD	PERCENTAGE BY PERIOD
PRUDENTIAL LIFE	AA	$2,000,000.00	WL	85	48		
METLIFE	AA	$1,000,000.00	WL	78	48		
PACIFIC MUTUAL LIFE	AA	$2,000,000.00	WL	76	48	$5,000,000.00	5.00%
JEFFERSON PILOT	AAA	$2,000,000.00	WL	82	60		
UNITED OF OMAHA	AA	$450,000.00	WL	81	60		
PRIMERICA	AA	$3,000,000.00	UNV	80	60	$5,450,000.00	5.00%
MASS MUTUAL	AA	$2,000,000.00	UNV	79	72		
COLUMBUS LIFE	AAA	$750,000.00	UNV	79	72		
COLUMBUS LIFE	AAA	$750,000.00	UNV	77	72		
TRANSAMERICA	AA+	$500,000.00	WL	78	72		
US LIFE OF NYC	A+	$2,000,000.00	WL	82	72		
WEST COAST LIFE	AA	$2,000,000.00	UNV	74	72		
US LIFE NYC	A+	$2,000,000.00	WL	82	72	$9,000,000.00	10.00%
TRAVELERS	AA	$3,000,000.00	UNV	82	84		
TRAVELERS	AA	$5,000,000.00	WL	82	84		
US LIFE NYC	A+	$2,000,000.00	UNV	73	84	$10,000,000.00	10.00%
TRAVELERS	AA	$3,000,000.00	WL	78	96		
TRAVELERS	AA	$2,000,000.00	UNV	79	96		
EQUITABLE LIFE	AA	$2,000,000.00	WL	76	96		
NEW YORK LIFE	AA	$2,000,000.00	UNV	78	96		
JOHN HANCOCK	AA	$1,000,000.00	UNV	76	96	$10,000,000.00	10.00%
CNA	A	$1,750,000.00	UNV	74	108		
JOHN HANCOCK	AA	$1,500,000.00	UNV	74	108		
AETNA LIFE	AA	$1,000,000.00	UNV	70	108		
SOUTHWESTERN LIFE	A+	$1,000,000.00	UNV	78	108		
NEW YORK LIFE	AA	$2,000,000.00	UNV	78	108		
TRANSAMERICA	AA	$1,000,000.00	UNV	80	108		
TRANSAMERICA	AA+	$3,500,000.00	WL	77	108		
MASS MUTUAL	AA	$4,000,000.00	WL	83	108		
CROWN LIFE	A	$2,000,000.00	UNV	79	108		
AMERICAN GEN	AA	$1,200,000.00	WL	81	108		
CHUBB LIFE	AA	$750,000.00	WL	80	108		
MIDLANDS	AA	$300,000.00	WL	83	108	$20,000,000.00	20.00%
US LIFE OF NYC	A+	$3,000,000.00	WL	86	120		
JEFFERSON PILOT	AAA	$2,000,000.00	WL	75	120		
TRANSAMERICA	AA+	$1,500,000.00	UNV	75	120		
SEC LIFE	AA+	$2,000,000.00	UNV	75	120		
US LIFE OF NYC	A+	$3,000,000.00	UNV	81	120		
JEFFERSON PILOT	AAA	$3,000,000.00	WL	79	120		
TRANSAMERICA	AA+	$3,000,000.00	WL	78	120		
THE MIDLAND CO	A+	$500,000.00	WL	82	120		
NEW YORK LIFE	AA	$1,250,000.00	WL	69	120	$19,250,000.00	20.00%
NEW YORK LIFE	AA	$3,000,000.00	WL	69	132		
METLIFE	AA	$2,000,000.00	WL	68	132		
WEST COAST LIFE	AA	$1,600,000.00	WL	84	132		
WEST COAST LIFE	AA	$1,600,000.00	UNV	79	132		
OLD REPUBLIC LIFE	A	$1,000,000.00	UNV	68	132		
THE HARTFORD	AA	$1,000,000.00	WL	76	132		
THE HARTFORD	AA	$1,500,000.00	WL	81	132		
UNITED OF OMAHA	AA	$1,000,000.00	WL	82	132		
WEST COAST LIFE	AA	$600,000.00	WL	81	132		
WEST COAST LIFE	AA	$1,000,000.00	WL	79	132		
UNITED OF OMAHA	AA	$1,000,000.00	WL	79	132		
NEW YORK LIFE	AA	$1,000,000.00	WL	78	132		
SAFECO LIFE	AA	$500,000.00	WL	61	132		
PRINCIPAL LIFE	AAA	$1,500,000.00	WL	60	132		
PRINCIPAL LIFE	AAA	$1,000,000.00	WL	64	132		
THE TRAVELERS	AA	$1,000,000.00	WL	62	132	$21,300,000.00	20.00%
TOTALS		**$100,000,000.00**		**77**	**104**	**$100,000,000.00**	**100.00%**

Figure 4.2

- The age of the insured
- The adjusted expected mortality in months

In the equity markets an example of a statically managed fund would be an index fund. The only trading that would be done in that instance would be to rebalance to the index. Most equity mutual funds would be examples of actively managed funds.

Year	80% runoff Normal	1 std extension	2 std extension
0	0	0	0
1	0	0	0
2	0	0	0
3	0	0	0
4	0.05	0	0
5	0.05	0.05	0
6	0.1	0.05	0.05
7	0.1	0.1	0.05
8	0.1	0.1	0.1
9	0.2	0.1	0.1
10	0.2	0.2	0.1
	0.8	0.6	0.4

Figure 4.3

Fixed income funds can also be actively or passively managed. The manager of an actively managed fund would be allowed to trade fixed income securities if in the opinion of the manager better relative value existed in other instruments. In a statically managed LSP the pool is purchased at inception and held until term. Any runoff (maturity of the policies) is invested in short-term cash instruments only. Figure 4.3 gives the percentage runoff for this pool of life policies as generated from the actuarial life expectancy. As a risk assessment we ran three scenarios, one of which was a "most likely" that would have 80% of the portfolio running off before or at term with 20% of the policies still in force at term. We then looked at 1 standard deviation and 2 standard deviations of the expected life scenario for risk assessment.

As mentioned above (and can be seen more clearly in Figure 4.5, column 10, there is no cash flow for the first 4 years under a most likely scenario, and then only a 5% cash flow. Under a 2 standard deviation errors in the life expectancy there is no cash flow for the first 5 years. It should be reiterated here from the risk assessment above, actuarial science is very exact. They can tell you almost to the person the number of people who will die in a specific time in a specific location. The problem is that they cannot tell you who, and that is exactly what you want to know as an investor in LSPs. However, most of the brokers who specialize in the collection of life policies for the purpose of pooling them and selling them on, give you a selection process as explained in Chapter 3. This selection process allows you to pick and choose policies that skew the results greatly in your favour over a simple mortality table of the population in general. This skewing of the distribution in your favour makes any estimate of the runoff schedule, using mortality tables, very conservative.

Figure 4.4 shows the net cash outflows for this pool using the most likely scenario. Across the top we have the cost of the LSP. At 20 cents on the dollar it will take $20 to purchase a pool with a face value of $100. Premiums have to be paid out in order to keep the policies in force. Other expenses include management fees, custodial fees and set-up costs.

One note: there is in this example a column (column 4) labelled "wrap fees". There are several insurance companies who will write insurance on life settlement portfolios. These insurance policies are in no way standardized and come in many sizes and shapes. For example, if at term the face value of the pool is not realized the insurance company will take the pool and pay off the full face value. Payoffs can be a percentage of the face, for example 80%. Some will take the full portfolio, work off the pool until the full loan value is realized and then return the pool to the fund to collect any further residual value. Some wraps can include

year	(1) Life Policies	(2) Premiums on remaining active policies	(3) Mgt Fee	(4) Wrap fee	(5) Custodial, Trustee, mgt, etc.	(6) Set up costs	(8) Total out flow
0	$20.0	$0.0	$0.0	$0.0	$0.0	$0.25	$20.3
1	$0.0	$2.9	$1.0	$0.0	$2.0	$0.00	$5.9
2	$0.0	$2.9	$1.0	$0.0	$2.0	$0.00	$5.9
3	$0.0	$2.9	$1.0	$0.0	$2.0	$0.00	$5.9
4	$0.0	$2.8	$1.0	$0.0	$2.0	$0.00	$5.8
5	$0.0	$2.6	$1.0	$0.0	$2.0	$0.00	$5.6
6	$0.0	$2.3	$1.0	$0.0	$2.0	$0.00	$5.3
7	$0.0	$2.0	$1.0	$0.0	$2.0	$0.00	$5.0
8	$0.0	$1.7	$1.0	$0.0	$2.0	$0.00	$4.7
9	$0.0	$1.2	$1.0	$0.0	$2.0	$0.00	$4.2
10	$0.0	$0.6	$1.0	$0.0	$2.0	$0.00	$3.6
Totals	$20.0	$21.9	$10.0	$0.0	$20.0	$0.3	$72.1

Figure 4.4

any interest payments. In a structured finance project backed by pools of life settlements (see Chapter 5) the wrap will guarantee the loan with the collateral on the wrap being both the project and the LSPs.

In addition there are several other longevity risk hedges to include a newer index swap, and Chapters 7 and 8 give details of how to hedge the longevity risk.

Insurance companies also come in many sizes and shapes from S&P AAA-rated carriers to A-rated A.M. Best insurance companies.

Many lenders in Europe require a wrap on a LSP simply because they do not want to be stuck with a pool of life insurance policies at term. They feel that they simply do not have the trading experience to work out this type of security pool. US lenders seem more amenable towards the LSP without the wrap and many US banks are becoming more familiar with the products. Their trust and custodial departments manage these types of pools, and these lenders are familiar with the small but growing number of market makers in this field, making it easy enough to sell on the residual value.

At the time of writing, no wrap exists in the market which, in the opinion of the authors, represents a sensible exchange of risk for return. Undoubtedly, the development of the secondary market will drive speciality insurers to improve product offerings and pricing in this space, but it is likely to take some time before a compelling opportunity presents itself.

Figure 4.5 shows the net cash inflows given the runoff assumptions for the life expectancies. Note that the Net Flows (column 12) has a total of $107.9. Referring back to column 10, we see that the first runoff from this investment is not until year 4 and then it is only 5% of the

(9) Investment	(10) Maturities of policies	(11) Total In Flows of cash	(12) Net Flows	(13) Cumulative Reserve	(14) Excess cash reinvested at 4%	(15) Sale of Policies Still in Force
$100.00	$0.0	$100.0	$79.8	$79.8	$0.0	
	$0.0	$0.0	-$5.9	$73.9	$3.2	
	$0.0	$0.0	-$5.9	$68.0	$3.0	
	$0.0	$0.0	-$5.9	$62.1	$2.7	
	$5.0	$5.0	-$0.8	$61.3	$2.5	
	$5.0	$5.0	-$0.6	$60.7	$2.5	
	$10.0	$10.0	$4.7	$65.4	$2.4	
	$10.0	$10.0	$5.0	$70.3	$2.6	
	$10.0	$10.0	$5.3	$75.6	$2.8	
	$20.0	$20.0	$15.8	$91.4	$3.0	
	$20.0	$20.0	$16.4	$107.9	$3.7	$12.0
$100.0	$80.0	$180.0	$107.9	$107.9	$28.3	$12.0

Figure 4.5

face value of the pool . For this reason a reserve requirement is needed and all this goes into the Cumulative Reserve (column 13).

Also note in this example that only 80% of the portfolio matures; 20% remains in force at the end of term and will be sold off at 60% of value.

The calculation of value for a life policy is almost linear in nature, meaning that every day we live the closer to term we get. As a result, policies grow in value daily and really never depreciate. Any policy with a 10-year expectation still in force after 10 years will have greatly appreciated in value and be worth much more than the initial price. A residual value for the policy can be calculated and we cover that in a separate chapter, but for purposes of simplification a 60% residual value was chosen and is in the opinion of the authors very conservative.

The net result after 10 years, paying all expenses, was $148 in return:

- $108 in the cumulative account
- $12 from the initial portfolio still in force ($20) sold at 60%
- $28 in interest earned

This was a 4.3% IRR. Again this is a return totally uncorrelated to any market parameters such as the stock market or the bond market.

The only real risk to this investment is the error in the expectation of mortality within the LSP, or what has been labelled longevity or extension risk. The fact of death is certain – the timing is uncertain.

4.2.3   A Managed Pool

As the life policies in the above example ran off (matured), the funds were invested in a savings account earning 4%. This is a static approach. An extension of this would be to allow the manager to reinvest the cash runoffs into new LSPs, which would generate added returns given the 5 times leverage in the pricing of the life insurance policies. This 5 times leverage and added return comes with little or no added risk.

We use the same LSP used in the buy and hold strategy and the same assumptions as set out in section 4.2.1, save as cash builds up in the reserve account we sweep the account and purchase more life policies initially leaving 3 years of expenses.

Figures 4.6 and 4.7 show the cash outflows and cash inflows for this investment.

year	(1) Life Policies	(2) Premiums on remaining active policies	(3) Mgt Fee	(4) Wrap fee	(5) Custodial, Trustee, mgt. etc.	(6) Set up costs	(8) Total out flow
0	$20.0	$0.0	$0.0	$0.0	$0.0	$0.25	$20.3
1	$0.0	$2.9	$1.0	$0.0	$2.0	$0.00	$5.9
2	$0.0	$2.9	$1.0	$0.0	$2.0	$0.00	$5.9
3	$0.0	$2.9	$1.0	$0.0	$2.0	$0.00	$5.9
4	$0.0	$2.8	$1.0	$0.0	$2.0	$0.00	$5.8
5	$0.0	$2.6	$1.0	$0.0	$2.0	$0.00	$5.6
6	$0.0	$2.3	$1.0	$0.0	$2.0	$0.00	$5.3
7	$0.0	$2.0	$1.0	$0.0	$2.0	$0.00	$5.0
8	$0.0	$1.7	$1.0	$0.0	$2.0	$0.00	$4.7
9	$0.0	$1.2	$1.0	$0.0	$2.0	$0.00	$4.2
10	$0.0	$0.6	$1.0	$0.0	$2.0	$0.00	$3.6
Totals	$20.0	$21.9	$10.0	$0.0	$20.0	$0.3	$72.1

Figure 4.6

(9) Investment	(10) Maturities of policies	(11) Total In Flows of cash	(12) Net Flows	(13) Cumulative Reserve	(14) Available for Reinvestment	(15) Life Expectancies Purchased
$100.00	$0.0	$100.0	$79.8	$79.8	$0.0	$0.0
	$0.0	$0.0	-$5.9	$73.9	$62.2	$310.8
	$0.0	$0.0	-$5.9	$5.8	$0.0	$0.0
	$0.0	$0.0	-$5.9	-$0.1	$0.0	$0.0
	$5.0	$5.0	-$0.8	-$0.9	$0.0	$0.0
	$5.0	$5.0	-$0.6	-$1.5	$0.0	$0.0
	$10.0	$10.0	$4.7	$3.2	$0.0	$0.0
	$10.0	$10.0	$5.0	$8.2	$0.0	$0.0
	$10.0	$10.0	$5.3	$13.4	$1.7	$8.7
	$20.0	$20.0	$15.8	$27.5	$15.8	$79.2
	$20.0	$20.0	$16.4	$28.1	$16.4	$82.1
$100.0	$80.0	$180.0	$107.9	$28.1	$96.2	$480.8

Figure 4.7

There are only two differences between the static portfolio and the actively managed strategy. With the static portfolio all cash flows are invested in a cash account. Here we allow the manager to invest the excess cash into new policies. However, because of liquidity provisions we have to establish a reserve account. Here we use 3 years of expenses as a minimal initial reserve requirement. Any and all excess cash above the reserve requirement is "swept". If at the end of the first period there are at least 3 years of expenses in the reserve account, the excess cash is swept off and used to purchase more life policies. The only other requirement is that the cumulative account can never be allowed to become too negative. This is not a great concern as the cumulative reserve is earning interest which is not taken into consideration here, and the life settlement policies can always be sold off if liquidity is needed. Further, a liquidity provider that will lend against the market value of the pool can be established at the inception of the fund, and this will be discussed more fully in Chapter 8.

As can be seen above the excess cash allows us to purchase $480 of additional life policies. The runoff of these new policies is shown below in Figure 4.8.

Again because the bulk of the new policies were purchased in the latter years a blended price was used between the initial 20 cents and the term price of 60 cents used for the initial still in force policies.

An alternative to selling reinvested policies which were purchased close to the term of the project is to cut off the repurchase of new life policies at 7 or 8 years into the programme.

It is assumed here that the new policies can be purchased at the same price as the old policies. While this assumption, and many others used here, are subject to debate this is just an example and not an actual trade.

Of the $480 additional policies purchased, only $247 matured.

year	1	2	3	4	5	6	7	8	9	10	Total
0	$0.0										$0.0
1	$0.0										$0.0
2	$0.0	$0.0									$0.0
3	$0.0	$0.0	$0.0								$0.0
4	$15.5	$0.0	$0.0	$0.0							$15.5
5	$15.5	$0.0	$0.0	$0.0	$0.0						$15.5
6	$30.9	$0.0	$0.0	$0.0	$0.0	$0.0					$30.9
7	$30.9	$0.0	$0.0	$0.0	$0.0	$0.0	$0.0				$30.9
8	$30.9	$0.0	$0.0	$0.0	$0.0	$0.0	$0.0	$0.0			$30.9
9	$61.9	$0.0	$0.0	$0.0	$0.0	$0.0	$0.0	$0.0	$0.0		$61.9
10	$61.9	$0.0	$0.0	$0.0	$0.0	$0.0	$0.0	$0.0	$0.0	$0.0	$61.9
Totals	$247.4	$0.0	$0.0	$0.0	$0.0	$0.0	$0.0	$0.0	$0.0	$0.0	$247.4

Figure 4.8

The net result after 10 years, paying all expenses to include a management fee of 1%, was $392 in return:

- $28 in the cumulative account
- $12 from the initial portfolio still in force ($20) sold at 60%
- $247 in reinvested life policies that matured
- $104 in reinvested life policies that were still in force and sold at 45 cents on the dollar.

This equates to a 14% IRR.

4.2.4 Looking at Risks

Below are the results if we assume that the life expectancies provided by the actuaries are off by 1 standard deviation. Again, if the average life is 10 years and there are 57 policies in the pool, the standard deviation would be

$$\frac{\mu}{\sqrt{57}}$$

Or

$$\frac{10}{7.55} = 1.32 \, Years$$

That would push the first cash flow out approximately one year until year 5 instead of year 4 (see Figure 4.9)

Figures 4.10–4.12 show the cash flows with the delayed payouts.

The net result after 10 years of a 1 standard deviation error in life expectancies, paying all expenses, was $315.8 in return or a difference from expectation of $66.2:

- $23 in the cumulative account
- $24 from the initial portfolio still in force ($40) sold at 60%
- $186.5 in reinvested life policies that matured
- $82.3 in reinvested life policies that were still in force and sold at 45 cents on the dollar.

Year	80% runoff Normal	1 std extension	2 std extension
0	0	0	0
1	0	0	0
2	0	0	0
3	0	0	0
4	0.05	0	0
5	0.05	0.05	0
6	0.1	0.05	0.05
7	0.1	0.1	0.05
8	0.1	0.1	0.1
9	0.2	0.1	0.1
10	0.2	0.2	0.1
	0.8	0.6	0.4

Figure 4.9

year	(1) Life Policies	(2) Premiums on remaining active policies	(3) Mgt Fee	(4) Wrap fee	(5) Custodial, Trustee, mgt, etc.	(6) Set up costs	(8) Total out flow
0	$20.0	$0.0	$0.0	$0.0	$0.0	$0.25	$20.3
1	$0.0	$2.9	$1.0	$0.0	$2.0	$0.00	$5.9
2	$0.0	$2.9	$1.0	$0.0	$2.0	$0.00	$5.9
3	$0.0	$2.9	$1.0	$0.0	$2.0	$0.00	$5.9
4	$0.0	$2.9	$1.0	$0.0	$2.0	$0.00	$5.9
5	$0.0	$2.8	$1.0	$0.0	$2.0	$0.00	$5.8
6	$0.0	$2.6	$1.0	$0.0	$2.0	$0.00	$5.6
7	$0.0	$2.3	$1.0	$0.0	$2.0	$0.00	$5.3
8	$0.0	$2.0	$1.0	$0.0	$2.0	$0.00	$5.0
9	$0.0	$1.7	$1.0	$0.0	$2.0	$0.00	$4.7
10	$0.0	$1.2	$1.0	$0.0	$2.0	$0.00	$4.2
Totals	$20.0	$24.2	$10.0	$0.0	$20.0	$0.3	$74.5

Figure 4.10

This was a 12.1% IRR. As can be seen, even an error in expectation while reducing return still produces an impressive return for a fairly riskless investment. A note of warning, which we will discuss in more detail in the leveraged portfolio below, is the negative cumulative reserve. As can be seen in Figure 4.11, column 10, because payments from the LSP are delayed but the expenses are not, there exists a small negative cumulative reserve. This will have to be planned for. Again the negatives are small and we are not taking into consideration any interest earned on the excess cash. In addition there is always a liquid market for ripened policies, so if at any time cash flow becomes dear, some of the policies could be sold off but it is worth noting that Coventry (a major player in this market) was caught short, and when they went to the market everyone realized their situation and, as a result, beat down the price of the pools.

4.2.5 Leveraged Reinvested Pools

Next we look at a leveraged pool. There are a number of banks and financial institutions that will lend against a pool of life policies, much as they would lend against a pool of mortgages. Our assumptions concerning the construction of the LSP remain as set out in section 4.2.1, save that for this example we assume a flat 10-year LIBOR rate of 4% and the ability to borrow 50% of the invested amount of $100 or an additional $50.

Figures 4.13 and 4.14 show the cash flows from this investment and Figure 4.15 shows the additional reinvestment and runoffs.

(9) Investment	(10) Maturities of policies	(11) Total In Flows of cash	(12) Net Flows	(13) Cumulative Reserve	(14) Available for Reinvestment	(15) Life Expectancies Purchased
$100.00	$0.0	$100.0	$79.8	$79.8	$0.0	$0.0
	$0.0	$0.0	-$5.9	$73.9	$62.2	$310.8
	$0.0	$0.0	-$5.9	$5.8	$0.0	$0.0
	$0.0	$0.0	-$5.9	-$0.1	$0.0	$0.0
	$0.0	$0.0	-$5.9	-$6.0	$0.0	$0.0
	$5.0	$5.0	-$0.8	-$6.8	$0.0	$0.0
	$5.0	$5.0	-$0.6	-$7.4	$0.0	$0.0
	$10.0	$10.0	$4.7	-$2.7	$0.0	$0.0
	$10.0	$10.0	$5.0	$2.3	$0.0	$0.0
	$10.0	$10.0	$5.3	$7.5	$0.0	$0.0
	$20.0	$20.0	$15.8	$23.4	$11.7	$58.4
$100.0	$60.0	$160.0	$85.5	$23.4	$73.8	$369.2

Figure 4.11

year	(10) Maturities of new policies — Cascade										Total
	1	2	3	4	5	6	7	8	9	10	
0	$0.0										$0.0
1	$0.0										$0.0
2	$0.0	$0.0									$0.0
3	$0.0	$0.0	$0.0								$0.0
4	$0.0	$0.0	$0.0	$0.0							$0.0
5	$15.5	$0.0	$0.0	$0.0	$0.0						$15.5
6	$15.5	$0.0	$0.0	$0.0	$0.0	$0.0					$15.5
7	$31.1	$0.0	$0.0	$0.0	$0.0	$0.0	$0.0				$31.1
8	$31.1	$0.0	$0.0	$0.0	$0.0	$0.0	$0.0	$0.0			$31.1
9	$31.1	$0.0	$0.0	$0.0	$0.0	$0.0	$0.0	$0.0	$0.0		$31.1
10	$62.2	$0.0	$0.0	$0.0	$0.0	$0.0	$0.0	$0.0	$0.0	$0.0	$62.2
Totals	$186.5	$0.0	$0.0	$0.0	$0.0	$0.0	$0.0	$0.0	$0.0	$0.0	$186.5

Figure 4.12

year	(1) Life Policies	(2) Premiums on remaining active policies	Libor Loan at 4%	(3) Mgt Fee	(4) Wrap fee	(5) Custodial, Trustee, mgt, etc.	(6) Set up costs	(8) Total out flow
0	$20.0		0	$0.0	$0.0	$0.0	$0.25	$20.3
1	$0.0	$2.9	$2.00	$1.0	$0.0	$2.0	$0.00	$7.9
2	$0.0	$2.9	$2.00	$1.0	$0.0	$2.0	$0.00	$7.9
3	$0.0	$2.9	$2.00	$1.0	$0.0	$2.0	$0.00	$7.9
4	$0.0	$2.8	$2.00	$1.0	$0.0	$2.0	$0.00	$7.8
5	$0.0	$2.6	$2.00	$1.0	$0.0	$2.0	$0.00	$7.6
6	$0.0	$2.3	$2.00	$1.0	$0.0	$2.0	$0.00	$7.3
7	$0.0	$2.0	$2.00	$1.0	$0.0	$2.0	$0.00	$7.0
8	$0.0	$1.7	$2.00	$1.0	$0.0	$2.0	$0.00	$6.7
9	$0.0	$1.2	$2.00	$1.0	$0.0	$2.0	$0.00	$6.2
10	$0.0	$0.6	$52.00	$1.0	$0.0	$2.0	$0.00	$55.6
Totals	$20.0	$21.9	$70.0	$10.0	$0.0	$20.0	$0.3	$142.1

Figure 4.13

(9) Investment plus borrowed amt	(10) Maturities of policies	(11) Total In Flow of cash	(12) Net Flows	(13) Cumulative Reserve	(14) Available for Reinvestment	(15) Life Expectancies Purchased
$150.00	$0.0	$150.0	$129.8	$129.8		
	$0.0	$0.0	-$7.9	$121.9	$110.2	$550.8
	$0.0	$0.0	-$7.9	$3.8	$0.0	$0.0
	$0.0	$0.0	-$7.9	-$4.1	$0.0	$0.0
	$5.0	$5.0	-$2.8	-$6.9	$0.0	$0.0
	$5.0	$5.0	-$2.6	-$9.5	$0.0	$0.0
	$10.0	$10.0	$2.7	-$6.8	$0.0	$0.0
	$10.0	$10.0	$3.0	-$3.8	$0.0	$0.0
	$10.0	$10.0	$3.3	-$0.6	$0.0	$0.0
	$20.0	$20.0	$13.8	$13.3	$1.6	$7.9
	$20.0	$20.0	-$35.6	-$22.3	$0.0	$0.0
$150.0	$80.0	$230.0	$87.9	-$22.3	$111.7	$558.7

Figure 4.14

year	1	2	3	4	5	6	7	8	9	10	Total
0											$0.0
1	$0.0										$0.0
2	$0.0	$0.0									$0.0
3	$0.0	$0.0	$0.0								$0.0
4	$27.5	$0.0	$0.0	$0.0							$27.5
5	$27.5	$0.0	$0.0	$0.0	$0.0						$27.5
6	$55.1	$0.0	$0.0	$0.0	$0.0	$0.0					$55.1
7	$55.1	$0.0	$0.0	$0.0	$0.0	$0.0	$0.0				$55.1
8	$55.1	$0.0	$0.0	$0.0	$0.0	$0.0	$0.0	$0.0			$55.1
9	$110.2	$0.0	$0.0	$0.0	$0.0	$0.0	$0.0	$0.0	$0.0		$110.2
10	$110.2	$0.0	$0.0	$0.0	$0.0	$0.0	$0.0	$0.0	$0.0	$0.0	$110.2
Totals	$440.6	$0.0	$0.0	$0.0	$0.0	$0.0	$0.0	$0.0	$0.0	$0.0	$440.6

Figure 4.15

year	(1) Life Policies	(2) Premiums on remaining active policies	Libor Loan at 4%	(3) Mgt Fee	(4) Wrap fee	(5) Custodial, Trustee, mgt, etc.	(6) Set up costs	(8) Total out flow
0	$20.0	$0.0	0	$0.0	$0.0	$0.0	$0.25	$20.3
1	$0.0	$2.9	$2.00	$1.0	$0.0	$2.0	$0.00	$7.9
2	$0.0	$2.9	$2.00	$1.0	$0.0	$2.0	$0.00	$7.9
3	$0.0	$2.9	$2.00	$1.0	$0.0	$2.0	$0.00	$7.9
4	$0.0	$2.9	$2.00	$1.0	$0.0	$2.0	$0.00	$7.9
5	$0.0	$2.9	$2.00	$1.0	$0.0	$2.0	$0.00	$7.9
6	$0.0	$2.8	$2.00	$1.0	$0.0	$2.0	$0.00	$7.8
7	$0.0	$2.6	$2.00	$1.0	$0.0	$2.0	$0.00	$7.6
8	$0.0	$2.3	$2.00	$1.0	$0.0	$2.0	$0.00	$7.3
9	$0.0	$2.0	$2.00	$1.0	$0.0	$2.0	$0.00	$7.0
10	$0.0	$1.7	$52.00	$1.0	$0.0	$2.0	$0.00	$56.7
Totals	$20.0	$26.0	$70.0	$10.0	$0.0	$20.0	$0.3	$146.2

Figure 4.16

The net result after 10 years, paying all expenses, was $483 in return or $100 more than the non-leveraged pool:

- $22 in the cumulative account primarily due to the repayment in year 10 of the borrowed $50
- $12 from the initial portfolio still in force ($20) sold at 60%
- $441 in reinvested life policies that matured
- $53 in reinvested life policies that were still in force and sold at 45 cents on the dollar.

This was a 17% IRR and more than 3 percentage points higher than the non-leveraged pool.

The additional leverage allowed us to purchase additional policies which generated more runoff from the reinvested pool and generated the added return.

A note of caution here. The added leverage inserted added expense. Overall, the investment had to cover an additional $20 of expenses. This added risk should be modelled and monitored closely. If the life expectancies given by the actuaries are 2 standard deviations away from the actuarial expectation, the results would be different as shown in Figures 4.16, 4.17 and 4.18. Here we look at a two standard errors in life expectancies.

Figure 4.16 remains the same – the expenses will not change – but Figures 4.17 and 4.18 will be substantially different.

(9) Investment plus borrowed amt	(10) Maturities of policies	(11) Total In Flow of cash	(12) Net Flows	(13) Cumulative Reserve	(14) Available for Reinvestment	(15) Life Expectancies Purchased
$150.00	$0.0	$150.0	$129.8	$129.8		
	$0.0	$0.0	-$7.9	$121.9	$110.2	$550.8
	$0.0	$0.0	-$7.9	$3.8	$0.0	$0.0
	$0.0	$0.0	-$7.9	-$4.1	$0.0	$0.0
	$0.0	$0.0	-$7.9	-$12.0	$0.0	$0.0
	$0.0	$0.0	-$7.9	-$19.9	$0.0	$0.0
	$5.0	$5.0	-$2.8	-$22.7	$0.0	$0.0
	$5.0	$5.0	-$2.6	-$25.3	$0.0	$0.0
	$10.0	$10.0	$2.7	-$22.6	$0.0	$0.0
	$10.0	$10.0	$3.0	-$19.6	$0.0	$0.0
	$10.0	$10.0	-$46.7	-$66.4	$0.0	$0.0
$150.0	$40.0	$190.0	$43.8	-$66.4	$110.2	$550.8

Figure 4.17

year	1	2	3	4	5	6	7	8	9	10	Total
0											$0.0
1	$0.0										$0.0
2	$0.0	$0.0									$0.0
3	$0.0	$0.0	$0.0								$0.0
4	$0.0	$0.0	$0.0	$0.0							$0.0
5	$0.0	$0.0	$0.0	$0.0	$0.0						$0.0
6	$27.5	$0.0	$0.0	$0.0	$0.0	$0.0					$27.5
7	$27.5	$0.0	$0.0	$0.0	$0.0	$0.0	$0.0				$27.5
8	$55.1	$0.0	$0.0	$0.0	$0.0	$0.0	$0.0	$0.0			$55.1
9	$55.1	$0.0	$0.0	$0.0	$0.0	$0.0	$0.0	$0.0	$0.0		$55.1
10	$55.1	$0.0	$0.0	$0.0	$0.0	$0.0	$0.0	$0.0	$0.0	$0.0	$55.1
Totals	$220.3	$0.0	$0.0	$0.0	$0.0	$0.0	$0.0	$0.0	$0.0	$0.0	$220.3

Figure 4.18

The delay in the payout reduced the all-in total return to $314 from $483 and dropped the IRR down to 12%:

- $66 in the cumulative account primarily due to the repayment in year 10 of the borrowed $50
- $12 from the initial portfolio still in force ($20) sold at 60%
- $149 in reinvested life policies that matured
- $220 in reinvested life policies that were still in force and sold at 45 cents on the dollar.

But the major problem with this error in the runoff from the life policies shows up in the reserve account. Starting in year 3 there is a negative cumulative account that continues to grow throughout the life of the structure and generally could shut the process down.

4.3 GROUP POLICIES

In the appendix to this chapter there is an example of a group policy programme that was presented to a large church in the United States. It is a variation on a theme of how LSPs can be used. The policies were all originated under the assumption that the church and individuals would benefit along with the originator of the securitization. While falling within regulatory limits (see Chapter 1), a programme such as this is on the border of a STOLI and should be looked at closely before entering. It is settled law that an insurable interest exists between a church and its congregation, but it is important to ensure that a genuine benefit is being afforded at the time of issue of the policy. It should be noted that several life insurance companies were consulted and participated in the programme below thereby giving their blessing to the procedure. The major reason for this was due to the fact that the church was located in a depressed area of town and the programme would be beneficial to the people living in and around the church. Other programmes may be structured differently and may not have been prepared in consultation with the issuing carriers – prospective investors should consult with their professional advisers on any STOLI or insurable interest issues with such programmes.

4.4 CONCLUSION

4.4.1 Administration

As mentioned above, to ensure compliance with insurable interest laws, more than likely a trust will have to be established and the purchaser of the life insurance policy will have to have an interest in the trust. The only grey area of late is the idea that the owner of the policy purchased the policy with the express intent of selling it on. STOLI programmes fall into this category, although in the above example there was intent of insurable interest to the term of the programme.

Once the trust or fund is established it will have to have an administrator. This is usually a custodial agent or a bank. Today there are many custodial departments in large banks who have the experience and knowledge to handle these types of securities. As with any trust set up the custodial agent has to maintain the security of the fund. This includes all payment of expenses to include premiums and admin expense. Tracking agents can be used for notification of the payout at the term of the policy and either a separate agency can be used or the custodial agent of a bank may have this ability. Most custodial departments familiar with this type of security have the ability of tapping into the social security system and tracking notification of death through the social security number of the policy holder. There are large and onerous penalties for insurance companies if they do not pay out within a certain period of time after notification of death. As a result most insurance companies will also track death notification and this can be used as a backup.

In addition the custodial agent may have the responsibility of investing excess funds in a money market account until such time as new policies are purchased and taken into the trust. All this is done under the direction of the trust but administered via the custodial department much the same as with any security.

4.4.2   Modelling

Any institution investing in a pool of LSPs will have a reporting problem. Unlike the pricing of an MBS which are actively traded on exchanges the market value of a specific LSP is not openly traded on an exchange. As a result like many instruments purchased by institutions such as CDO tranches, the pricing of this security for reporting purposes will have to be done via mark-to-model and verified periodically by a second source. Given the lack of volatility in the product, the main reason for the purchase of the product in the first place, modelling the product using certain assumptions is not difficult.

Only in cases of trying to determine residual value over and above actuarial estimates will the modelling become more difficult. There are models available which can be purchased, see Chapter 2, which have this capability. Most of these models were developed out of CDO modelling where the ability to handle multiple asset classes to include LSPs were needed. In addition the pricing needed had to be able to distinguish the bid/asked spread so they drilled down into what was actually going on within the pricing area. Models used in this chapter and in subsequent chapters are for illustrative purposes only. A far more detailed system will be required to manage these pools.

In this chapter we looked at simple securitization. Because of a liquidity problem initially, reserves had to be established. If expectations were wrong the securitization could default.

In the next chapter we look at combining LSPs with capital markets structured products. This alleviates to some extent the liquidity problem and generates added returns from the capital markets product. And remember the advantage to this new asset class being a reduced volatility and little correlation to any other variable in the investment world.

APPENDIX: SAMPLE PRODUCT DESCRIPTION OUTLINE

Product Definition Statement

This document describes the proposed investment concept for the group insurance portfolio.

A4.1   INTRODUCTION

Group life policies have been a part of the US culture for many years. What we propose and have indeed set up is a structure whereby we purchase group life policies in an asset-backed structure. The terms of the policies state that the beneficiary of the policy is a specified trust. Because the insuree is a member of the trust there is an insurable interest established and the trust can be designated a beneficiary.

Upon the exercise of the life policy the contract states that a specified portion of the policy will go to the group, a specified portion of the policy will go to the designated family member and the remainder of the life policy will go to the trust. For that service the trust agrees to pay in full all expenses associated with the cost of the life policy to include all administrative cost and premium payments. The trust will take possession of the life policies and maintain and administer the programme.

Associations with five major insurance companies have been established and this programme has been given their blessing. All life companies have an A S&P or Moody's rating or better.

The process has been refined over a 3-year period where today the sign-up procedures require the prospective insuree to fill out a simple one-page form. All legal sign offs to include family and group member blessings have been streamlined and the entire process is fast, simple and legally blessed.

Our models suggest that by the third year there is a cross-over and that the runoffs will cover any premium payment by that year. This should then cover all cost as the runoff of the policy will increase through time. Because this is a group policy the premium is a blend, thus reducing the cost of the life policies.

Because we can do this in size, we are proposing $45 million investment in the first phase, and because we have established strong working relationships with both the insurance companies and the targeted groups we can purchase these policies for a substantial discount to face death benefit. Upon exercising the policy the returns generated after all administrative expense and payouts to group and family members are in the 15% range per year.

We want to establish a hedge fund with the express purpose of purchasing LSPs. This will require an initial investment of $45 million. We feel that a cash flow equivalent to 15% a year on the initial investment should be do-able. Administration fees for this type of investment are high due to the collections and administration of the insurance policies and the added administration of the hedge fund. Therefore a $1 million fee, while excessive given typical hedge funds, would be needed.

A4.2   PRODUCT DESCRIPTION

(a)   Description of product

Generally speaking the most brilliant of ideas are the simplest and this system is no exception. The product is simply purchasing group policies from specified corporate structures and holding the policies until term. There is, in the insurance industry, a random death statistic that suggests that as the numbers get large there will be a percentage of random deaths. These will have nothing to do with the actuarial life expectancy of the policy holder. These deaths are the result of unexpected disease, accidents, random violence or acts of nature. As a result it is expected that within the first year a $300 million pool will throw off approximately $3 million in benefits before fees in the early years.

Because the policies are from selected group members the age distribution will run from 20-year-olds to 70-year-olds. This has two advantages. First, the premiums quoted by the insurance companies are a blended rate. Averaging a 20-year-old with a 70-year-old will lower the overall cost of the premiums. Second, it creates a long tail, the payouts from the policies could run 40 years or more creating an annuity for the fund, although the highest payouts will occur within the first 15 years using even the most conservative of life expectancy runoffs. If at any time the fund would like to liquidate the policies, they can be sold on, again at a substantial profit.

We have even set up a Patent for the system of collecting policies. This system provides for the following:

1. a system and method of generating asset-backed and insurance-backed funding facilities in support of business transactions and charitable organizations which provides future cash payments through utilization of life insurance policies within a tax advantaged system;
2. maintaining policy premium payments by a system and method of guarantee which also assures that the designated beneficiaries, the sponsoring business entity, the 501c3 Charitable Insurance Plan sponsor, the Business and/or Charitable Trust and the premium provider are maintained as payees/beneficiaries of policy/endowment proceeds, therein providing;
3. final needs benefits to the insured and his/her designated family beneficiaries;
4. funding for the Business entity and/or Charitable Organizations as Plan Sponsors;
5. operating revenues sufficient for maintenance of the Trust;
6. payments sufficient to compensate a funds provider, which can exceed limits on interest imposed by state lending and/or insurance regulations and tax regulations;
7. while at the same time securing absolute guarantee of repayment of investment capital with better than market return; and
8. utilizing life insurance policies issued by insurance companies rated A or better by A.M. Best or Standard & Poor's.

(b) Cash flow diagrams

Below is the cash flow for a $45 million tranche. The $45 million will initially purchase 1,250 policies with a face value of $275,000. Of the $275,000, $35,000 will go to the family and church, the remaining $240,000 will go to the trust upon term. Remember there are no expenses for the purchaser of the policy or the church. Because of this all analysis is done off a $240 face value. We include a 1% random death statistic. Random deaths are a factor life insurance companies deal with on a daily basis. For all the actuarial analysis on life expectancies, every year people die due to events outside any actuarial model such as accidents, acts of nature, wars or disease. Further assumptions include the first life expectancy runoff to occur in the third year and that being 1% of face. From these very conservative estimates for life expectancies, coupled with random deaths payout, $141 million of the $300 million should runoff within the 10-year period.

In the analysis we took the difference between those policies that had runoff at the end of 10 years and the $300 million face and sold off that difference for an estimated 60% of value. See Figures A.1 and A.2.

Through the 10 years approximately $67 million of face value has run off or 25% of the total pool. If we then take the remainder of the portfolio and sell it off we are comfortable we can get 60% for the residual. That equates to $141 million.

(c) Advantages over related products, payout profiles and exit strategies

The returns on this product are substantial. A 10% return over a 10-year period is targeted with a 50% participation in any upside. Because of the liquidity in the portfolio and the fact that the portfolio will only gain in value over time, we can sell into the market at any time thus allowing us to create an investment of any maturity. It is thought a 10-year note would be the optimal, given the acceptance of 10-year time frames in the market and the maximum

year	year 1	year 2	year 3	year 4	year 5
Policies	1,250	1,238	1,225	1,200	1,175
Face Value	$300,000,000	$297,000,000	$294,000,000	$288,000,000	$282,000,000
Cost	$3,000,000	$2,970,000	$2,940,000	$2,880,000	$2,820,000
Random Death	1.0%	1.0%	1.0%	1.0%	1.0%
LE Runoff	0.0%	0.0%	1.0%	1.0%	2.0%
Total Runoff	1.0%	1.0%	2.0%	2.0%	3.0%
Cash Flow from Runoffs	$3,000,000	$2,970,000	$5,880,000	$5,760,000	$8,460,000
Fees + Premiums	$4,000,000	$3,970,000	$3,940,000	$3,880,000	$3,820,000
$ return	-$1,000,000	-$1,000,000	$1,940,000	$1,880,000	$4,640,000
reserve	$15,000,000	$14,000,000	$12,000,000	$11,940,000	$11,940,000
Cumulative P&L	-$1,000,000	-$2,000,000	-$60,000	$1,820,000	$6,460,000
Cumulative %	-4.0%	-8.0%	-0.2%	7.3%	25.8%
In force policies	99.0%	98.0%	96.0%	94.0%	91.0%
Cumulative Runoffs	$3,000,000	$5,970,000	$11,850,000	$17,610,000	$26,070,000
% Runoffs	1.0%	2.0%	4.0%	6.1%	9.2%

Figure A.1

year 6	year 7	year 8	year 9	year 10	Totals
1,138	1,100	1,063	1,025	981	
$273,000,000	$264,000,000	$255,000,000	$246,000,000	$235,500,000	$235,500,000
$2,730,000	$2,640,000	$2,550,000	$2,460,000	$2,355,000	$27,345,000
1.0%	1.0%	1.0%	1.0%	1.0%	%
2.0%	2.0%	2.0%	2.5%	2.5%	%
3.0%	3.0%	3.0%	3.5%	3.5%	25.0%
$8,190,000	$7,920,000	$7,650,000	$8,610,000	$8,242,500	$66,682,500
$3,730,000	$3,640,000	$3,550,000	$3,460,000	$3,355,000	$37,345,000
$4,460,000	$4,280,000	$4,100,000	$5,150,000	$4,887,500	$29,337,500
$11,940,000	$11,940,000	$11,940,000	$11,940,000	$11,940,000	$11,940,000
$10,920,000	$15,200,000	$19,300,000	$24,450,000	$29,337,500	$58,675,000
43.7%	60.8%	77.2%	97.8%	117.4%	234.7%
88.0%	85.0%	82.0%	78.5%	75.0%	50.0%
$34,260,000	$42,180,000	$49,830,000	$58,440,000	$66,682,500	$133,365,000
12.5%	16.0%	19.5%	23.8%	28.3%	56.6%

Figure A.2

appreciation of the portfolio at that time. However, a structure with any term can be created. In addition, the residual value in the pool will still have approximately 75% of the original pool. This can be rolled over and a new programme started with a seasoned pool.

Given that 10-year Treasuries are yielding 3.5% and that credit-bond funds and even long-short equity funds do not reach a double-digit yield with substantially more risk, there is nothing in the market to compete with this type of investment.

As stated in (b) above, the payouts are pretty much guaranteed, the only question being "when?".

As stated in this term sheet elsewhere, time is an ally. The longer you hold the policies the more value they accrue. If liquidation becomes necessary these policies can always be sold on in the market at a profit. The returns will be reduced but will still be positive.

A4.3   MARKETING ASSESSMENT

(a)   Liquidity

There are over 5,000 life companies providing life insurance products to both groups and individuals in the USA. Some of these companies have been in business for over 100 years. As a result, the life business is a trillion dollar business with no lack of product and a ready market to sell into. At this time there are limited buyers of secondary life products and no one purchasing group policies that we know. As a result we can dictate price at this time. As stated elsewhere in this document, we have a substantial number of policies in the pipeline and feel strongly that we can generate $300 million face value per quarter for the next several years. That would be over $7 billion face value with no price compression. As the programme grows and other firms enter the market, price compression will take place and policies will become more expensive and reduce returns, but we feel that that is at least 3 years in the future, by which time we could control the market.

(b) Competition

We are trying to keep this process under the radar so to speak. We do not want this process to hit the street, and that gives us a great advantage in the market. We are aware that as the programme grows this structure will become known and, as with any other structure that is financially sound, other firms will "pile on". One of the members of this management team was involved with one of the original interest rate swaps. At that time the bid/asked spread was between 90 and 120 basis points. Today the bid/asked spread is only 2 basis points and in fact they can be traded on organized exchanges if 2 basis points is too expensive.

That said, because the idea is so simple in its concept it is not at all simple in its logistics. It took part of this team over 3 years to set up the process. Insurance companies have to be contacted and sign-offs have to be obtained that requires legal review which, as anyone who has worked in that area knows, is not a fast process. The structure of the trust has to be established, group relationships have to be developed, etc. If an organization started out today to set this process up it would take them the better part of a year to put it in place.

We are at the beginning of what we think is a process that will grow into a major industry.

A4.4   MODELLING AND PRICING

(a) Description of model used and calibration

A pool of insurance products can be modelled using standard and acceptable securitizations techniques already in place in the market. A newer structure that mirrors what we will call a Collateralized Insurance Obligation (CIO) is the standard Collateralized Debt Obligation. The stochastic nature of default equates very nicely to the probability of death. Actuaries use a standard normal probability measure, given the large number of entries and the fact that they hold to the law of large numbers theories. From this measure a contingent payoff can be forced out using the standard:

$$R = \int \lambda \eta \varepsilon^{-rt}$$

where R is the contingent payoff or the life expectancy

$$\lambda = Mortality\ Rate$$
$$\eta = Survival\ Probability$$
$$\varepsilon^{-rt} = Discount\ Function$$

This is the well-known survival probability curve. Taking a page from the financial markets we convert the probability density functions from a survival density function to a forward density function called a hazard rate within the CDO community. From here we can combine density functions using copulas and Monte Carlo simulation to come up with a real-time value for the CIO. This will then allow us to mark-to-market on a real-time basis (or in this case mark-to-model that has recently been approved by the regulators and all accounting firms for non-traded securities). Given this ability, detailed financial statements can be provided on line.

Optimization techniques are used to form the portfolio. Running excess policies through the model allows us to select a portfolio that will optimize a low premium cost against the maximum face value of the portfolio.

(b)   Sensitivities and risks

Once pricing methodologies have been established, derivative calculations on the important variables can be done to allow for sensitivities. These sensitivities then give risk measures.

There are, however, few risks that could affect the price of the product. Liquidity is the most important risk factor. However, time is an ally. These are life insurance policies and the closer to the life expectancy the individual gets the more likely is the payoff of the policy. Hence liquidity can be hedged if absolutely necessary with the sale of the policy in a liquid market at ever-increasing prices.

The credit rating of the insurance companies would be the only other risk factor. Close evaluations of the credit derivative markets should give hints of problems and if necessary default swaps or options could be purchased before any credit event at little cost. That said, the US insurance industry is a doubly regulated industry, being scrutinized by both the State regulators and the Federal regulators. Any problems and a merger or acquisition would probably be forced upon the insurance firm.

Other statistical risks such as correlation intra portfolio are virtually non-existent. The deaths of one individual in normal circumstances will not affect the death of another within the pool.

Correlations inter portfolio can be high and un-hedgeable. However, the probability of these occurrences is very remote and can move the returns of the fund in both directions. A sudden cure for cancer will extend the life expectancies and hence the payouts from the portfolio. But a sudden new flu epidemic, major unpredicted acts of nature, or a terrorist act within a major city could reduce the life expectancies and hence the returns.

Variance, a common risk measure in the financial community can push back payouts, but in an analysis already eluded to, a 3 standard deviation move against the portfolio still produces outstanding results.

In no circumstances, using modern risk techniques, should this portfolio lose money and in fact the statement can be more dynamic: *in no circumstances, using modern risk techniques, should the returns from this portfolio not beat comparable risk-adjusted returns in the market.*

A4.5   ADMINISTRATION AND ACCOUNTING

Because of the insurable interest all insurance policies and administration of the benefits should be kept within the trust structure. Because of this the hedge fund will have to own an interest in the trust. All administration of the hedge fund will then be provided by the trust.

Marking to model can be done on an as-needed basis. The portfolio can be tracked via the internet. Close cooperation will be needed between the reporting administration of the trust and the hedge fund, but this is by no means an unusual circumstance. Most hedge funds have the fund registered off shore and the management of the fund on shore. This structure would not be very different.

Those with a need can be given a user name and password that will allow entry into the portfolio at different levels. The internet information can be updated in real time if necessary.

A4.6   CONCLUSION

Several important points should be made about this product in conclusion:

- Time is a factor that only increases the value of the policy. As the policy holder gets older the value of his/her policy grows.

- Payoffs are 100% sure. Death and Taxes are certain.
- The insurance companies selected are A-rated or better, and if at any time there is some concern about the credit quality of the insurance company, a credit derivative can be purchased, usually for a few basis points.
- The portfolio can always be sold in the market. Again because time is an increasing variable the portfolio will only gain in value over time.
- The returns that can be made are substantially above market yields with similar risk parameters.

5

Capital Markets Products: Principal Protection

INTRODUCTION

This chapter is simply an extension of Chapter 4. Additionally we use LSPs to wrap capital market products and structures instead of simple stand-alone securitizations. This is an efficient method of using these products given that the cash flow from life settlements in the initial years is non-existent. By combining life settlements with products sold into the markets an initial and usually large cash flow can be put in place. In addition, the structure then has in place a principal guarantee which in these markets today is invaluable.

This idea is not new. It has been around for some time. In the mid to late 1980s Chase Manhattan bank had a product called a bull or bear CD. The investor had the option of (1) choosing the direction of the market and (2) choosing the risk they were willing to take. As an example, the investor could purchase a bull CD with an 20% floor. That meant that the investor thought the market, in this case represented by the S&P 500, was going up. If it did indeed go up over the term of the CD the investor received a percentage of that increase, the percentage of increase depending upon the level of the floor. In this case the 80% CD guaranteed that the investor could lose no more than 20% of his investment. Again the investor could choose the direction, a bear CD or a bull CD and the level of protection.

This was a hugely successful product. It was also a profitable product for Chase because at the time Chase could simply take a portion of the investment and invest in a government zero coupon bond which, at term, would equal the par value of the CD. The remainder of the investment was placed in the index. This worked well because at the time the returns on the zero were substantial and the portion of the funds needed to be invested in the zero was not very much. Again the amounts invested in the index and the zero and the exit strategies depended upon the choice of the investor.

Today even a 5% zero with a 5-year maturity would have a discount of only approximately 75%. This means that only 25% of the funds would be put to work in whatever investment you had. What we have today with LSPs is simply the ability to invest a small percentage in the protection part of the investment and a large part of the investment elsewhere. While the LSP is not a federal government guaranteed investment we have shown that it is a very creditworthy investment with state guarantees.

An advantage of combining resources is the ability to fund the project from outside investments. Because the variations on a theme are endless, we concentrate on just a few examples but recognize that the process is only limited to imagination. An analogy would be the use of toy building blocks – you can plug and play in an almost endless variety. The benefits to this process using LSPs, as opposed to other instruments, is the correlation and volatility dampening, and the above market returns on the principal protection alone. If in fact the structure does make money the overall returns are increased by the return on the protection pool.

Below are several examples of the almost infinite possibilities. As mentioned in previous chapters we were weaned on the "building block" approach to derivatives: simply plug different securities together in different formats to accomplish whatever results you desire. We were involved in some brilliant examples and some complete busts.

Because of regulations in Japan, institutional investors were not allowed to invest in non-yen-denominated securities. Using a building block approach, structured around an off-shore trust, we were able to develop a power reverse dual currency bond which allowed Japanese investors to take advantage of off-shore higher yields converted back into yen at a time when Japan actually had negative interest rates. This was a hugely successful product.

However, the other side of that was a yield enhancement bond that was a complete bust. This bond yielded fully 300 basis points through the curve of a comparable rated bond. This involved purchasing a look-back option from the investor and paying them 300 basis points in premium for that option. The products were subsequently known as precipice bonds or granny busters because they were sold to pensioner widows. While it was a brilliant idea from a financial engineering standpoint, it was totally lacking in common sense. The reason being that there were only two outcomes to this investment: (1) the look-back option was never exercised by the issuing firm, in which case the firm's borrowing costs increased by 300 basis points needlessly; (2) the look-back option were exercised, in which case the issuing firm did not have to pay back some or any of the principal. This was a bond sold to an 80-year-old widow with the understanding that she understood a partial look-back option. In the end none of the options were exercised, not because they were not in the money, as some were, but because of threats of law suits and threats from the central banks.

Below are some, certainly in no way conclusive, bond structures wrapped by life settlements. We have chosen examples that might be of most interest in the markets today. Examples are:

1. A zero coupon bond
2. A coupon bond
3. A convertible bond
4. A longevity bond
5. An inverse longevity bond
6. Barrier bonds to include
   (a) PAC (Planned Amortization Class)
   (b) TAC (Target Amortization Class)
   (c) VADAM (Very Accurately Defined Maturity) with a Z bond
7. A Sharia compliant bond
8. Dual currency bonds
9. Power bonds
10. An equity-linked note.

5.1 BOND CONSTRUCTIONS

We use the same basic assumptions that were used in Chapter 4 for the LSPs. Additional assumptions are added for each specific debt issue. The major difference in all these programmes being the security sold into the street is a registered and hopefully rated security backed by a pool of life settlements. Therefore, return of principal is not dependent upon the performance of the debt issue. The LSP will pay back the principal at maturity. The descriptions below will show the cash flow of the entire structure with the payout of the bond being only part of the cash flow.

Please note that in most examples below the cumulative reserve account will show a sometimes large, negative balance in the last year of the programme. This should not be a problem given that the structure is being unwound in the last year and all principal is being paid with the proceeds of the sale of the LSP. Again, note the risks inherent in this process – the life settlements have not all paid out and we are left with a deficit between the principal owed and the value of the remaining life settlements. We cover hedging techniques for this risk in detail in Chapter 8.

Another extremely important point to mention is the leverage of the debt. If, for example, the debt is leveraged, i.e. placed in pork belly futures, the loss on the pork belly futures can be greater than the initial investment, in which case the LSP will not cover the entire loss. This is an extreme example, and although we do not touch upon it here it should be considered if the funds from the sale of the security are to be heavily leveraged.

5.2   A ZERO COUPON BOND

Assumptions

- It is assumed that we are issuing a zero coupon bond valued at $100 at term. The discount will be a straight 5% flat for 10 years. This equates to a discount factor of 61% or a purchase price on the zero of $61.
- The $61 will be invested in a pool of life policies with a cost of 20 cents on the dollar.
- In this example we purchase policies from only A-rated or better life companies.
- These policies are only non-contestable policies (using contestable policies and over-collateralizing will greatly improve yields but will not be shown here) and are either Whole Life or Universal Life policies (again programmes using term or variable life could be structured to yield better returns, but we defer those examples also).
- The average life of the pool is 10 years, which has been determined by a New York Stock exchange-listed actuarial firm, and the life expectancies are adjusted life expectancies. By that we mean that the life expectancies are calculated as of the time of purchase into the trust, not when originally issued.
- The runoff schedule (see Figure 5.1) was taken from the life expectancies of the pool. This is the same runoff schedule that was used in Chapter 4. As mentioned previously, simulating this

Year	80% runoff Normal	1 std extension	2 std extension
0	0	0	0
1	0	0	0
2	0	0	0
3	0	0	0
4	0.05	0	0
5	0.05	0.05	0
6	0.1	0.05	0.05
7	0.1	0.1	0.05
8	0.1	0.1	0.1
9	0.2	0.1	0.1
10	0.2	0.2	0.1
	0.8	0.6	0.4

Figure 5.1   Runoff schedule

year	(1) Life Policies	(2) Premiums on remaining active policies	(3) Mgt Fee	(4) Wrap fee	(5) Custodial, Trustee, mgt, etc.	(6) Set up costs	(7) Investment Payout	(8) Total out flow
0	$20.0	$0.0	$0.0	$0.0	$0.0	$0.25		$20.3
1	$0.0	$2.9	$0.6	$0.0	$1.2	$0.00		$4.7
2	$0.0	$2.9	$0.6	$0.0	$1.2	$0.00		$4.7
3	$0.0	$2.9	$0.6	$0.0	$1.2	$0.00		$4.7
4	$0.0	$2.8	$0.6	$0.0	$1.2	$0.00		$4.6
5	$0.0	$2.6	$0.6	$0.0	$1.2	$0.00		$4.5
6	$0.0	$2.3	$0.6	$0.0	$1.2	$0.00		$4.2
7	$0.0	$2.0	$0.6	$0.0	$1.2	$0.00		$3.9
8	$0.0	$1.7	$0.6	$0.0	$1.2	$0.00		$3.6
9	$0.0	$1.2	$0.6	$0.0	$1.2	$0.00		$3.0
10	$0.0	$0.6	$0.6	$0.0	$1.2	$0.00	$100.0	$102.4
Totals	$20.0	$21.9	$6.1	$0.0	$12.3	$0.3	$100.0	$160.6

Figure 5.2

runoff schedule will generate risk parameters as to residual values and longevity/extension risk.

- Because the pool has an average expected life of 10 years, only 80% of the pool matures on or before the 10-year term.
- Any policies still in force at the end of term (10 years) can be sold back into the market at 60% of face value. This should be a very conservative assumption given that there is a secondary market for these policies which is becoming more and more liquid, and the value of the policy grows almost linearly as each day the policy holder lives brings the policies closer to term, and time is very much a linear function.
- Insurance premiums (2.9% of face) have to be maintained to keep the policies in force. Also, a management fee (1% of investment) and custodial fees (2% of investment) have to be paid in addition to set-up costs and other miscellaneous fees.
- Because, for at least 3 years, there is little or no cash flow from the portfolio, 3 years of expenses will be maintained in a reserve account.
- Any and all excess cash will be invested at a 4% rate.
- Any cash excess over and above the 3-year reserve requirement will be invested in new life policies.
- Excess cash reinvested into new life policies will be priced at the same rate as the original policies. The expenses for the new policies will also be the same.

(9) Investment	(10) Maturities of policies	(11) Total In Flows of cash	(12) Net Flows	(13) Cumulative Reserve	(14) Excess cash reinvested in LS
$61.39	$0.0	$61.4	$41.1	$41.1	$21.1
	$0.0	$0.0	-$4.7	$15.3	$0.0
	$0.0	$0.0	-$4.7	$10.5	$0.0
	$0.0	$0.0	-$4.7	$5.8	$5.8
	$5.0	$5.0	$0.4	$0.4	$0.4
	$5.0	$5.0	$0.5	$0.5	$0.5
	$10.0	$10.0	$5.8	$5.8	$5.8
	$10.0	$10.0	$6.1	$6.1	$6.1
	$10.0	$10.0	$6.4	$6.4	$6.4
	$20.0	$20.0	$17.0	$17.0	$17.0
	$20.0	$20.0	-$82.4	-$82.4	$0.0
$61.4	$80.0	$141.4	-$19.2	-$82.4	$63.3

Figure 5.3

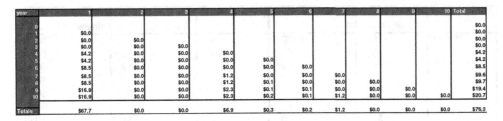

year	1	2	3	4	5	6	7	8	9	10	Total
0											$0.0
1	$0.0										$0.0
2	$0.0	$0.0									$0.0
3	$0.0	$0.0	$0.0								$0.0
4	$4.2	$0.0	$0.0	$0.0							$4.2
5	$4.2	$0.0	$0.0	$0.0	$0.0						$4.2
6	$8.5	$0.0	$0.0	$0.0	$0.0	$0.0					$8.5
7	$8.5	$0.0	$0.0	$1.2	$0.0	$0.0	$0.0				$9.6
8	$8.5	$0.0	$0.0	$1.2	$0.1	$0.0	$0.0	$0.0			$9.7
9	$16.9	$0.0	$0.0	$2.3	$0.1	$0.1	$0.0	$0.0	$0.0		$19.4
10	$16.9	$0.0	$0.0	$2.3	$0.2	$0.1	$1.2	$0.0	$0.0	$0.0	$20.7
Totals	$67.7	$0.0	$0.0	$6.9	$0.3	$0.2	$1.2	$0.0	$0.0	$0.0	$76.3

Figure 5.4

Using the runoff schedule we used for the other examples we have the cash flows shown in Figures 5.1 to 5.4.

The net result after 10 years, paying all expenses was $113 in return

- $82 in the cumulative account
- $12 from the initial portfolio still in force ($20) sold at 60%
- $76 in reinvested life policies that matured
- $107 in reinvested life policies that were still in force and sold at 45 cents on the dollar.

While this is only a 1.2% return, it is on top of a 5% IRR zero and a management fee of 1% per year – with one important factor stated at the beginning: this is done with funding from the market. In trading speak: with OPM (other people's money).

We will also show later how to improve the return by using less COI (cost of insurance).

5.3   A COUPON BOND

The coupon bond will result in a lot more risk initially, given that a coupon is being paid in addition to the costs of the life settlement portfolio. However, we receive the full value from the investment as opposed to the discounted value of a zero.

Assumptions

- It is assumed that we are issuing a 10-year coupon paying bond with a 7% coupon selling at par.
- Again, a reserve has to be established to pay for the coupon payment in addition to the life policy costs.
- All other assumptions are the same as above.

Figures 5.5–5.7 show the cash flow for this security.

The net result after 10 years, paying all expenses, was $74 in return.

year	(1) Life Policies	(2) Premiums on remaining active policies	Coupon Payment on Bond	(3) Mgt Fee	(4) Wrap fee	(5) Custodial, Trustee, mgt, etc.	(6) Set up costs	(7) Investment Payout	(8) Total out flow
0	$20.0	$0.0	$0.0	$0.0	$0.0	$0.0	$0.25		$20.3
1	$0.0	$2.9	$7.0	$0.2	$0.0	$0.4	$0.00		$10.5
2	$0.0	$2.9	$7.0	$0.2	$0.0	$0.4	$0.00		$10.5
3	$0.0	$2.9	$7.0	$0.2	$0.0	$0.4	$0.00		$10.5
4	$0.0	$2.8	$7.0	$0.2	$0.0	$0.4	$0.00		$10.4
5	$0.0	$2.6	$7.0	$0.2	$0.0	$0.4	$0.00		$10.2
6	$0.0	$2.3	$7.0	$0.2	$0.0	$0.4	$0.00		$9.9
7	$0.0	$2.0	$7.0	$0.2	$0.0	$0.4	$0.00		$9.6
8	$0.0	$1.7	$7.0	$0.2	$0.0	$0.4	$0.00		$9.3
9	$0.0	$1.2	$7.0	$0.2	$0.0	$0.4	$0.00		$8.8
10	$0.0	$0.6	$7.0	$0.2	$0.0	$0.4	$0.00	$100.0	$108.2
Totals	$20.0	$21.9	$70.0	$2.0	$0.0	$4.0	$0.25	$100.0	$218.1

Figure 5.5

(9) Investment	(10) Maturities of policies	(11) Total In Flows of cash	(12) Net Flows	(13) Cumulative Reserve	(14) Excess cash reinvested in LS
$100.00	$0.0	$100.0	$79.8	$79.8	$39.4
	$0.0	$0.0	-$10.5	$29.9	$0.0
	$0.0	$0.0	-$10.5	$19.4	$0.0
	$0.0	$0.0	-$10.5	$8.9	$0.0
	$5.0	$5.0	-$5.4	$3.5	$0.0
	$5.0	$5.0	-$5.2	-$1.7	$0.0
	$10.0	$10.0	$0.1	-$1.6	$0.0
	$10.0	$10.0	$0.4	-$1.2	$0.0
	$10.0	$10.0	$0.7	-$0.6	$0.0
	$20.0	$20.0	$11.2	$10.7	$0.0
	$20.0	$20.0	-$88.2	-$77.5	$0.0
$100.0	$80.0	$180.0	-$38.1	-$77.5	$39.4
					$157.4

Figure 5.6

- $78 in the cumulative account
- $12 from the initial portfolio still in force ($20) sold at 60%
- $126 in reinvested life policies that matured
- $14 in reinvested life policies that were still in force and sold at 45 cents on the dollar.

Again this is a low IRR, only 1%, but that is on top of a 7% coupon and a management fee of 1% per year. Without being too repetitive we will demonstrate how these returns can be improved later. We are just setting the stage for the present.

5.4   A CONVERTIBLE BOND

In this example we look at a XYZ convertible bond. This bond will have a lockout period of 5 years after which it can be converted to one share of XYZ stock.

Assumptions

- This is a 10-year convertible bond with a 1.5% coupon
- It is convertible into XYZ stock after a 5-year lockout period at $100 a share. XYZ stock is now selling at $80 a share and has 40% volatility.
- To hedge the conversion, assuming no ownership of the stock at present, a 5-year LEAP with a strike of $80 was used. The price on the LEAP was $41.

year	1	2	3	4	5	6	7	8	9	10	Total
0											$0.0
1	$0.0										$0.0
2	$0.0	$0.0									$0.0
3	$0.0	$0.0	$0.0								$0.0
4	$7.9	$0.0	$0.0	$0.0							$7.9
5	$7.9	$0.0	$0.0	$0.0	$0.0						$7.9
6	$15.7	$0.0	$0.0	$0.0	$0.0	$0.0					$15.7
7	$15.7	$0.0	$0.0	$0.0	$0.0	$0.0	$0.0				$15.7
8	$15.7	$0.0	$0.0	$0.0	$0.0	$0.0	$0.0	$0.0			$15.7
9	$31.5	$0.0	$0.0	$0.0	$0.0	$0.0	$0.0	$0.0	$0.0		$31.5
10	$31.5	$0.0	$0.0	$0.0	$0.0	$0.0	$0.0	$0.0	$0.0	$0.0	$31.5
Totals	$125.9	$0.0	$0.0	$0.0	$0.0	$0.0	$0.0	$0.0	$0.0	$0.0	$125.9

Figure 5.7

Years	Coupon 1.5% flat	Life settlement Purchase	Bond Piece		Premiums 2.9% Face	Bond Payback	Insurance Wrapper	Capital set-up Fees .025%	Cash Out Flows Bond
			Management Fee 1%	Hedging Cost 5 Yr LEAP					
0	$0.00	$20.00	$0.00	$40.00	$0.00			$2.50	$62.50
1	$1.50	$0.00	$1.00	$0.00	$2.90				$5.40
2	$1.50	$0.00	$1.00	$0.00	$2.90				$5.40
3	$1.50	$0.00	$1.00	$0.00	$2.90				$5.40
4	$1.50	$0.00	$1.00	$0.00	$2.90				$5.40
5	$1.50	$0.00	$1.00	$0.00	$2.90				$5.40
6	$0.00	$0.00	$0.00	$0.00	$0.00				$0.00
7	$0.00	$0.00	$0.00	$0.00	$0.00				$0.00
8	$0.00	$0.00	$0.00	$0.00	$0.00				$0.00
9	$0.00	$0.00	$0.00	$0.00	$0.00				$0.00
10	$0.00	$0.00	$0.00	$0.00	$0.00	$0.00			$0.00
Totals	$7.50	$20.00	$5.00	$40.00	$14.50	$0.00	$0.00	$2.50	$89.50

Figure 5.8

- We sold the bond at $106 using a Convertible Bond Pricing model
- Two distinct paths were analysed
  1. the conversion into stock at 5 years (with the price of the conversion only 20 points out of the money and a 40% volatility conversion is almost guaranteed);
  2. no conversion and the payoff of the bond at year 10.

Again all assumptions, other than the above, are the same as before for the LSP.

5.4.1   The Convertible is Exercised

Figures 5.8–5.12 show the cash flow of this bond given that the 40% volatility holds and the bond is converted to stock at year 6.

By year 5 the price of the stock has grown to $307 and conversion is obvious. The LEAP hedge allows us to purchase the stock for $80 thus generating a $227 profit in the LEAP to offset the $307 cost of the stock for a net cost of $80.

Years	XYZ Growth in value at 40% per year	Equity Piece Convertible Worth	Stock Purchase	Cash Out Flow Equity
0	$0.00	$0.00	$0.00	$0.00
1	$80.00	$80.00	$0.00	$0.00
2	$112.00	$112.00	$0.00	$0.00
3	$156.80	$156.80	$0.00	$0.00
4	$219.52	$219.52	$0.00	$0.00
5	$307.33	$307.33	$307.33	$307.33
6		$0.00	$0.00	$0.00
7		$0.00	$0.00	$0.00
8		$0.00	$0.00	$0.00
9		$0.00	$0.00	$0.00
10		$0.00	$0.00	$0.00
Totals				$307.33

Figure 5.9

Years	Cash In Flows	S&P Hedge profits	Sale of the Option	Policy Flows	Net cash In flows
0	$100.00	$0.00	$0.00	$0.00	$100.00
1	$0.00	$0.00	$0.00	$0.00	$0.00
2	$0.00	$32.00	$0.00	$0.00	$0.00
3	$0.00	$76.80	$0.00	$0.00	$0.00
4	$0.00	$139.52	$0.00	$5.00	$5.00
5	$0.00	$227.33	$227.33	$57.00	$284.33
6	$0.00	$0.00	$0.00	$0.00	$0.00
7	$0.00	$0.00	$0.00	$0.00	$0.00
8	$0.00	$0.00	$0.00	$0.00	$0.00
9	$0.00	$0.00	$0.00	$0.00	$0.00
10	$0.00	$0.00	$0.00	$0.00	$0.00
Totals	$100.00	$227.33	$227.33	$62.00	$389.33

Figure 5.10

year	Net Flows Gross	Cumulative Reserve Account	Reinvested Flows
0	$37.50	$37.50	$17.50
1	-$5.40	$14.60	$0.00
2	-$5.40	$9.20	$0.00
3	-$5.40	$3.80	$0.00
4	-$0.40	$3.40	$0.00
5	-$28.40	-$25.00	$0.00
6	$0.00	$0.00	$0.00
7	$0.00	$0.00	$0.00
8	$0.00	$0.00	$0.00
9	$0.00	$0.00	$0.00
10	$0.00	$0.00	$0.00
Totals	-$7.50	-$25.00	$17.50
			$87.50

Figure 5.11

year	1	2	3	4	5	6	7	8	9	10	Total
0	$0.00										$0.00
1	$0.00	$0.00									$0.00
2	$0.00	$0.00	$0.00								$0.00
3	$0.00	$0.00	$0.00	$0.00							$0.00
4	$4.38	$0.00	$0.00	$0.00	$0.00						$4.38
5	$4.38	$0.00	$0.00	$0.00	$0.00	$0.00					$4.38
6	$8.75	$0.00	$0.00	$0.00	$0.00	$0.00	$0.00				$8.75
7	$8.75	$0.00	$0.00	$0.00	$0.00	$0.00	$0.00	$0.00			$8.75
8	$8.75	$0.00	$0.00	$0.00	$0.00	$0.00	$0.00	$0.00	$0.00		$8.75
9	$17.50	$0.00	$0.00	$0.00	$0.00	$0.00	$0.00	$0.00	$0.00	$0.00	$17.50
10	$17.50	$0.00	$0.00	$0.00	$0.00	$0.00	$0.00	$0.00	$0.00	$0.00	$17.50
Totals	$70.00	$0.00	$0.00	$0.00	$0.00	$0.00	$0.00	$0.00	$0.00	$0.00	$70.00

Figure 5.12

Policy flows from the LSPs are almost non-existent given that we are only 5 years into the programme. Therefore only approximately $62 is generated from the original pool.

The net result after 5 years, paying all expenses, was $36 in return.

- $25 in the cumulative account
- $12 from the initial portfolio still in force ($20) sold at 60%
- $18 in reinvested life policies that matured
- $32 in reinvested life policies that were still in force and sold at 45 cents on the dollar.

Any calculations on the IRR will be dependent upon the entity. There is only $36 in residual value after 5 years but the investor now owns a stock worth $307 and the management team keeps the residual value on no investment plus a management fee.

5.4.2   The Convertible is Not Exercised

Figures 5.13–5.16 show the cash flow if the conversion is not exercised. If the historical growth in the shares is not realized and the bond is not converted, this convertible bond "converts" to a straightforward coupon bond, and a low-paying coupon bond at that. But because of the cost of the hedge, the $40 LEAP, an added expense is incurred. A residual value of $22 results because the LSPs initial and reinvested, are allowed to mature.

The net result after 10 years, paying all expenses, was $22 in return.

- $85 in the cumulative account
- $12 from the initial portfolio still in force ($20) sold at 60%
- $85 in reinvested life policies that matured
- $10 in reinvested life policies that were still in force and sold at 45 cents on the dollar.

Several things should be noted. First we had chosen to look at the extremes, an exercise after the lockout period and no exercise at all. In reality, by the way the bond is structured, exercise can occur at any time after the lockout period. Second, the cost of the life settlement policy is high as a LEAP must also be purchased. If the programme were allowed to use other less expensive policies such as "contestables", the returns would be higher. For example, the residual value would be $206 on the non-exercised bond and $141 on the exercised bond. Finally, a LEAP

Years	Coupon 1.5% flat	Life settlement Purchase	Management Fee 1%	Hedging Cost 5 Yr LEAP	Premiums 2.9% Face	Bond Payback	Insurance Wrapper	Capital set-up Fees .025%	Cash Out Flows Bond
0	$0.00	$20.00	$0.00	$40.00	$0.00			$2.50	$62.50
1	$1.50	$0.00	$1.00	$0.00	$2.90				$5.40
2	$1.50	$0.00	$0.00	$0.00	$2.90				$5.40
3	$1.50	$0.00	$1.00	$0.00	$2.90				$5.40
4	$1.50	$0.00	$1.00	$0.00	$2.76				$5.26
5	$1.50	$0.00	$1.00	$0.00	$2.61				$5.11
6	$1.50	$1.00	$1.00	$1.00	$2.32				$6.82
7	$1.50	$2.00	$1.00	$2.00	$2.03				$8.53
8	$1.50	$3.00	$1.00	$3.00	$1.74				$10.24
9	$1.50	$4.00	$1.00	$4.00	$1.16				$11.66
10	$1.50	$5.00	$1.00	$5.00	$0.58	$100.00			$113.08
Totals	$15.00	$35.00	$10.00	$55.00	$21.90	$100.00	$0.00	$2.50	$239.40

Figure 5.13

		Equity Piece			
	XYZ Growth in value at 0% per year	Convertible Worth	XYZ Hedge Value @ two to one	Stock Purchase	Cash Out Flow Equity
Years					
0	$0.00	$0.00	$0.00	$0.00	$0.00
1	$80.00	$80.00	$0.00	$0.00	$0.00
2	$80.00	$80.00	$0.00	$0.00	$0.00
3	$80.00	$80.00	$0.00	$0.00	$0.00
4	$80.00	$80.00	$0.00	$0.00	$0.00
5	$80.00	$80.00	$0.00	$0.00	$0.00
6		$0.00	$0.00	$0.00	$0.00
7		$0.00	$0.00	$0.00	$0.00
8		$0.00	$0.00	$0.00	$0.00
9		$0.00	$0.00	$0.00	$0.00
10		$0.00	$0.00	$0.00	$0.00
Totals					$0.00

Figure 5.14

	Cash In Flows	S&P Hedge profits	Sale of the Option	Policy Flows	Net In flows	Net Flows Gross	Cumulative Reserve Account	Reinvested Flows
Years								
0	$100.00	$0.00	$0.00	$0.00	$100.00	$37.50	$37.50	$21.30
1	$0.00	$0.00	$0.00	$0.00	$0.00	-$5.40	$10.80	$0.00
2	$0.00	$0.00	$0.00	$0.00	$0.00	-$5.40	$5.40	$0.00
3	$0.00	$0.00	$0.00	$0.00	$0.00	-$5.40	$0.00	$0.00
4	$0.00	$0.00	$0.00	$5.00	$5.00	-$0.26	-$0.25	$0.00
5	$0.00	$0.00	$0.00	$5.00	$5.00	-$0.11	-$0.36	$0.00
6	$0.00	$0.00	$0.00	$10.00	$10.00	$3.18	$2.82	$0.00
7	$0.00	$0.00	$0.00	$10.00	$10.00	$1.47	$0.00	$0.00
8	$0.00	$0.00	$0.00	$10.00	$10.00	-$0.24	-$0.24	$0.00
9	$0.00	$0.00	$0.00	$20.00	$20.00	$8.34	$8.10	$0.00
10	$0.00	$0.00	$0.00	$20.00	$20.00	-$93.08	-$84.98	$0.00
Totals	$100.00	$0.00	$0.00	$80.00	$180.00	-$59.40	-$84.98	$21.30
								$106.50

Figure 5.15

				Reinvested Runoffs							
year	1	2	3	4	5	6	7	8	9	10	Total
Years											
0	$0.00										$0.00
1	$0.00	$0.00									$0.00
2	$0.00	$0.00	$0.00								$0.00
3	$0.00	$0.00	$0.00	$0.00							$0.00
4	$5.33	$0.00	$0.00	$0.00	$0.00						$5.33
5	$5.33	$0.00	$0.00	$0.00	$0.00	$0.00					$5.33
6	$10.65	$0.00	$0.00	$0.00	$0.00	$0.00	$0.00				$10.65
7	$10.65	$0.00	$0.00	$0.00	$0.00	$0.00	$0.00	$0.00			$10.65
8	$10.65	$0.00	$0.00	$0.00	$0.00	$0.00	$0.00	$0.00	$0.00		$10.65
9	$21.30	$0.00	$0.00	$0.00	$0.00	$0.00	$0.00	$0.00	$0.00	$0.00	$21.30
10	$21.30	$0.00	$0.00	$0.00	$0.00	$0.00	$0.00	$0.00	$0.00	$0.00	$21.30
Totals	$85.20	$0.00	$0.00	$0.00	$0.00	$0.00	$0.00	$0.00	$0.00	$0.00	$85.20

Figure 5.16

year	(1) Life Policies	(2) Premiums on remaining active policies	(3) Mgt Fee	(4) Wrap fee	(5) Custodial, Trustee, mgt, etc.	(6) Set up costs	(7) Investment Payout	(8) Total out flow
0	$10.0	$0.0	$0.0	$0.0	$0.0	$0.25		$10.3
1	$0.0	$1.5	$0.5	$0.0	$0.6	$0.00		$2.6
2	$0.0	$1.5	$0.5	$0.0	$0.6	$0.00		$2.6
3	$0.0	$1.5	$0.5	$0.0	$0.6	$0.00		$2.6
4	$0.0	$1.4	$0.5	$0.0	$0.6	$0.00		$2.5
5	$0.0	$1.3	$0.5	$0.0	$0.6	$0.00		$2.4
6	$0.0	$1.2	$0.5	$0.0	$0.6	$0.00		$2.3
7	$0.0	$1.0	$0.5	$0.0	$0.6	$0.00		$2.1
8	$0.0	$0.9	$0.5	$0.0	$0.6	$0.00		$2.0
9	$0.0	$0.6	$0.5	$0.0	$0.6	$0.00		$1.7
10	$0.0	$0.3	$0.5	$0.0	$0.6	$0.00	$50.0	$51.4
Totals	$10.0	$10.9	$5.0	$0.0	$6.1	$0.3	$50.0	$82.3

Figure 5.17

is an expensive way to hedge a long-term stock price, and was only used for demonstration purposes. Equity traders can hedge a stock price for long periods of time much cheaper than LEAP pricing, and in fact some proprietary desks specialize in the arbitrage process between LEAPs and the underlying.

5.5   PRINCIPAL PROTECTION

In the above examples we simply issued a security into the market and managed the proceeds. We swept the excess funds and purchased more life settlements as the funds were available. Next we look at taking this security and applying the proceeds to a special project while at the same time managing the LSP as a principal guarantee pool.

In this example we take in $100 and split up the investment into a $50 LSP and $50 into the project. We leave the project to the reader's imagination. By that we mean it could be used as a merger or acquisition engine, to purchase machinery, or as a start-up fund. As can be seen in Figures 5.17 to 5.19 the $50 in LSPs will in 10 years return $109, which will pay for the initial investment no matter what the other $50 was used for. If the other investment did in fact return enough to pay for the principal, the result would be a principal free loan. One point to note is that the interest on the loan, assumed to be 7%, is not taken into consideration here. By that we mean that if the loan or bond structure required a 7% interest payment year on year, the project is assumed to carry that expense in this example. This programme will guarantee the principal only, not the interest and principal. If 50% of the interest were built into the LSP pool as an expense, then the overall return under these assumptions would only be $40 or only guarantee

(9) Investment	(10) Maturities of policies	(11) Total In Flows of cash	(12) Net Flows	(13) Cumulative Reserve	(14) Excess cash reinvested in LS
$50.00	$0.0	$50.0	$39.8	$39.8	$19.8
	$0.0	$0.0	-$2.6	$17.4	$0.0
	$0.0	$0.0	-$2.6	$14.9	$0.0
	$0.0	$0.0	-$2.6	$12.3	$12.3
	$2.5	$2.5	$0.0	$0.0	$0.0
	$2.5	$2.5	$0.1	$0.1	$0.1
	$5.0	$5.0	$2.7	$2.7	$2.7
	$5.0	$5.0	$2.9	$2.9	$2.9
	$5.0	$5.0	$3.0	$3.0	$3.0
	$10.0	$10.0	$8.3	$8.3	$8.3
	$10.0	$10.0	-$41.4	-$41.4	$0.0
$50.0	$40.0	$90.0	$7.7	-$41.4	$49.1

Figure 5.18

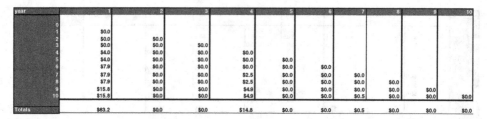

year		1	2	3	4	5	6	7	8	9	10
	0										
	1	$0.0									
	2	$0.0	$0.0								
	3	$0.0	$0.0	$0.0							
	4	$4.0	$0.0	$0.0	$0.0						
	5	$4.0	$0.0	$0.0	$0.0	$0.0					
	6	$7.9	$0.0	$0.0	$0.0	$0.0	$0.0				
	7	$7.9	$0.0	$0.0	$2.5	$0.0	$0.0	$0.0			
	8	$7.9	$0.0	$0.0	$2.5	$0.0	$0.0	$0.0	$0.0		
	9	$15.8	$0.0	$0.0	$4.9	$0.0	$0.0	$0.0	$0.0	$0.0	
	10	$15.8	$0.0	$0.0	$4.9	$0.0	$0.0	$0.5	$0.0	$0.0	$0.0
Totals		$63.2	$0.0	$0.0	$14.8	$0.0	$0.0	$0.5	$0.0	$0.0	$0.0

Figure 5.19

40% of the loan. The project would have to come up with the remaining 60% principal. Finally, as stated above, reducing the COI would allow the LSP to carry the interest expense for its part of the loan.

5.6   LONGEVITY BONDS

In 2003 Swiss Re offered a mortality-linked note. It was a 3-year note designed to hedge mortality risk. The coupon was a floating rate coupon tied to LIBOR but the principal payout was tied to the mortality rate of the underlying index. If the mortality rate exceeded the index mortality rate by a certain percent, then the principal was reduced by a calculated factor. If the mortality rate did not exceed the expectation, then the principal was paid in full.

In 2004 EIB and BNP came out with a longevity bond of 25 years. This was an amortizing bond with the coupons linked to an index.

To date there are not a lot of longevity bonds in the market but because of their functions longevity bonds can come in a variety of sizes and shapes. Below we give examples of several simple structures. Again the variations on a theme are endless.

The main purpose of the bond is as a hedge against mortality risk. We will cover hedging techniques in more detail in Chapter 8, but because this is issued as a capital market product it has a dual role and we will look at it here.

There are generally two major categories of longevity bonds: those with the principal at risk, and those with the coupon at risk. The bond can also be structured as an inverse longevity bond. Tables 5.1 and 5.2 show the advantages/disadvantages of an extension/reduction in mortality. For example, if the mortality rate is extended a life insurance company may receive more premium payment and extend out the time to payout on the policy. An annuity has the opposite effect if mortality is extended as payment has to be made over a longer period of time. Note that longevity and extension, and mortality and survival, are used interchangeably in this document.

Tables 5.1 and 5.2 give a brief summary of the type of longevity bonds that are either out in the market today or can be constructed.

Table 5.1   Mortality

	Lengthened	Shortened
Life Insurance Companies	Good	Bad
Annuities	Bad	Good
Pensions	Good	Bad
Structured LSPs	Bad	Good

Table 5.2 Mortality

	Lengthened		Shortened		
Coupon at Risk longevity bond	To the Investor – Less coupon	To the Issuer – Less payout of coupon	To the Investor – More coupon	To the Issuer – More coupon payout, higher cost of funds	Coupon tied to the mortality rate
Principal at Risk longevity bond	To the Investor – Less principal	To the Issuer – Less principal repayment and less interest on reduced principal	To the Investor – Principal in full	To the Investor – Principal paid in full, higher cost of funds	Principal payback tied to mortality rate
Inverse longevity bond	To the Investor – More coupon payout	To the Issuer – more coupon, higher cost of funds	To the Investor – Less coupon payout lower cost of funds		Coupon inversely tied to mortality rate

5.6.1   The Longevity Bonds: Principal at Risk

As mentioned above, longevity bonds are a hedge against a reduction in the mortality rate. Life insurance companies and pensions can use this instrument as a hedge against mortality reductions. The longer the Life/Pension Company has funds coming in via premiums and payments, or the longer the firm has the cash to invest, the more profitable the firm will be. If there is a reduction in mortality rate, payouts will have to be made and there will be a reduction in cash flow and returns.

In the example below, the coupon payout is fixed for 10 years at 7% of the par bond. However, the principal paid at term is a function of the mortality rate. There are a number of ways to fix that rate but in the example below we looked at the actuarial expectation or run off schedule (Figure 5.1) and used that as our base rate. If the mortality rate fell below our expected base rate, the principal payout could be reduced.

Using the portfolio given in this book and the base assumptions, we will look at a 10-year longevity bond. Generally speaking the coupon payment will be through the curve, given the downside risk of the principal with no offset to the upside. Again there are many ways this could be constructed but we are simply looking at the general concept here.

Figure 5.20 shows the expected mortality curve for this portfolio.

Figures 5.21 to 5.23 show the cash flow of this bond given it performs to expectation.

The net result after 10 years, paying the coupon of 7% and all expenses save the principal, was $141. That netted the bond a $41 profit while at the same time acting like a hedge against mortality risk.

- $73 in the cumulative account
- $12 from the initial portfolio still in force ($60) sold at 60%
- $129 in reinvested life policies that matured
- $73 in reinvested life policies that were still in force and sold at 45 cents on the dollar.

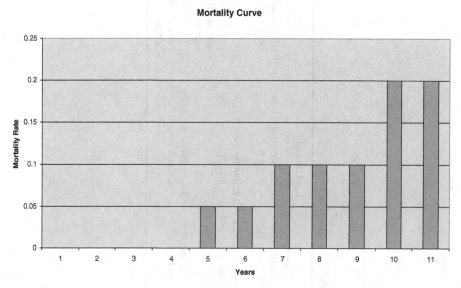

Figure 5.20

year	(1) Life Policies	(2) Premiums on remaining active policies	(3) Mgt Fee	(4) Wrap fee	(5) Custodial, Trustee, mgt, etc.	(6) Set up costs	(7) Bond coupon	(8) Total out flow
0	$25.0	$0.0	$0.0	$0.0	$0.0	$0.25	$0.0	$25.3
1	$0.0	$2.9	$1.0	$0.0	$0.0	$0.00	$7.0	$10.9
2	$0.0	$2.9	$1.0	$0.0	$0.0	$0.00	$7.0	$10.9
3	$0.0	$2.9	$1.0	$0.0	$0.0	$0.00	$7.0	$10.9
4	$0.0	$2.8	$1.0	$0.0	$0.0	$0.00	$7.0	$10.8
5	$0.0	$2.6	$1.0	$0.0	$0.0	$0.00	$7.0	$10.6
6	$0.0	$2.3	$1.0	$0.0	$0.0	$0.00	$7.0	$10.3
7	$0.0	$2.0	$1.0	$0.0	$0.0	$0.00	$7.0	$10.1
8	$0.0	$1.7	$1.0	$0.0	$0.0	$0.00	$7.0	$9.8
9	$0.0	$1.2	$1.0	$0.0	$0.0	$0.00	$7.0	$9.2
10	$0.0	$0.6	$1.0	$0.0	$0.0	$0.00	$7.0	$8.6
Totals	$25.0	$21.9	$10.0	$0.0	$0.2	$0.3	$70.0	$127.3

Figure 5.21

Figures 5.24 to 5.27 show a 2 standard deviation move in the mortality rate to the downside. This would be hugely profitable to the life insurance and pension industry. However, for this bond it will reduce the principal payout at term.

The net result after 10 years, paying the coupon of 7% and all expenses save the principal was $95. The investor under these severe conditions would have lost principal in the amount of $5.

- $117 in the cumulative account
- $36 from the initial portfolio still in force ($60) sold at 60%
- $64 in reinvested life policies that matured
- $112 in reinvested life policies that were still in force and sold at 45 cents on the dollar.

This is an extreme example and would hopefully never be accepted but demonstrates that a principal-at-risk bond can and does lose principal.

5.6.2 Longevity Bonds: Coupons at Risk

In this instance the principal is fixed but the coupon is floating and calculated off the mortality rate. A fall in the mortality rate will reduce the coupon payment, as can be seen in Figure 5.28.

In the example below, the coupon is simply LIBOR plus 100 basis points minus the difference between the expected runoff (mortality rate) and the actual runoff. Here we assume a flat 5% LIBOR rate. In Chapters 7 and 8 we go into much more detail as to how to bootstrap this mortality curve, we calculate spot and forward rates and apply a number of option pricing

(9) Investment	(10) Maturities of policies	(11) Total In Flows of cash	(12) Net Flows	(13) Cumulative Reserve	(14) Excess cash reinvested additional LSP	(15)Sale of Policies Still in Force
$100.00	$0.0	$100.0	$74.8	$74.8	$0.0	
	$0.0	$0.0	-$10.9	$63.8	$35.8	
	$0.0	$0.0	-$10.9	$10.1	$27.1	
	$0.0	$0.0	-$10.9	-$34.9	$0.0	
	$5.0	$5.0	-$5.8	-$47.6	$0.0	
	$5.0	$5.0	-$5.6	-$60.3	$0.0	
	$10.0	$10.0	-$0.3	-$67.6	$0.0	
	$10.0	$10.0	-$0.1	-$74.7	$0.0	
	$10.0	$10.0	$0.2	-$81.4	$0.0	
	$20.0	$20.0	$10.8	-$77.6	$0.0	
	$20.0	$20.0	$11.4	-$73.2	$0.0	$12.0
$100.0	$80.0	$180.0	$52.7	-$73.2	$62.9	$12.0
					$251.5	

Figure 5.22

year	1	2	3	4	5	6	7	8	9	10
0	$0.0									
1	$0.0									
2	$0.0	$0.0								
3	$0.0	$0.0	$0.0							
4	$0.0	$0.0	$0.0	$0.0						
5	$0.0	$7.2	$0.0	$0.0	$0.0					
6	$0.0	$7.2	$5.4	$0.0	$0.0	$0.0				
7	$0.0	$14.3	$5.4	$0.0	$0.0	$0.0	$0.0			
8	$0.0	$14.3	$10.8	$0.0	$0.0	$0.0	$0.0	$0.0		
9	$0.0	$14.3	$10.8	$0.0	$0.0	$0.0	$0.0	$0.0	$0.0	
10	$0.0	$28.6	$10.8	$0.0	$0.0	$0.0	$0.0	$0.0	$0.0	$0.0
Totals	$0.0	$85.9	$43.3	$0.0	$0.0	$0.0	$0.0	$0.0	$0.0	$0.0

Figure 5.23

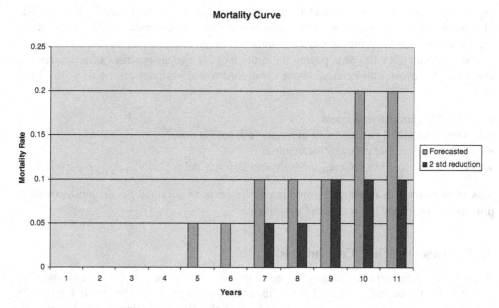

Figure 5.24

year	(1) Life Policies	(2) Premiums on remaining active policies	(3) Mgt Fee	(4) Wrap fee	(5) Custodial, Trustee, mgt. etc.	(6) Set up costs	Bond coupon	(8) Total out flow
0	$25.0	$0.0	$0.0	$0.0	$0.0	$0.25	$0.0	$25.3
1	$0.0	$2.9	$1.0	$0.0	$0.0	$0.00	$7.0	$10.9
2	$0.0	$2.9	$1.0	$0.0	$0.0	$0.00	$7.0	$10.9
3	$0.0	$2.9	$1.0	$0.0	$0.0	$0.00	$7.0	$10.9
4	$0.0	$2.9	$1.0	$0.0	$0.0	$0.00	$7.0	$10.9
5	$0.0	$2.9	$1.0	$0.0	$0.0	$0.00	$7.0	$10.9
6	$0.0	$2.8	$1.0	$0.0	$0.0	$0.00	$7.0	$10.8
7	$0.0	$2.6	$1.0	$0.0	$0.0	$0.00	$7.0	$10.6
8	$0.0	$2.3	$1.0	$0.0	$0.0	$0.00	$7.0	$10.3
9	$0.0	$2.0	$1.0	$0.0	$0.0	$0.00	$7.0	$10.1
10	$0.0	$1.7	$1.0	$0.0	$0.0	$0.00	$7.0	$9.8
Totals	$25.0	$26.0	$10.0	$0.0	$0.2	$0.3	$70.0	$131.4

Figure 5.25

(9) Investment	(10) Maturities of policies	(11) Total In Flows of cash	(12) Net Flows	(13) Cumulative Reserve	(14) Excess cash reinvested additional LSP	(15)Sale of Policies Still in Force
$100.00	$0.0	$100.0	$74.8	$74.8	$0.0	
	$0.0	$0.0	-$10.9	$63.8	$35.8	
	$0.0	$0.0	-$10.9	$10.1	$27.1	
	$0.0	$0.0	-$10.9	-$34.9	$0.0	
	$0.0	$0.0	-$10.9	-$52.8	$0.0	
	$0.0	$0.0	-$10.9	-$70.7	$0.0	
	$5.0	$5.0	-$5.8	-$83.5	$0.0	
	$5.0	$5.0	-$5.6	-$96.1	$0.0	
	$10.0	$10.0	-$0.3	-$103.5	$0.0	
	$10.0	$10.0	-$0.1	-$110.5	$0.0	
	$10.0	$10.0	$0.2	-$117.3	$0.0	$36.0
$100.0	$40.0	$140.0	$8.6	-$117.3	$62.9	$36.0

Figure 5.26

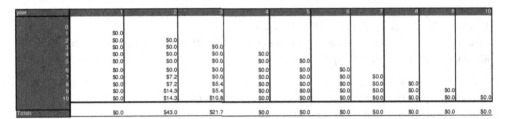

Figure 5.27

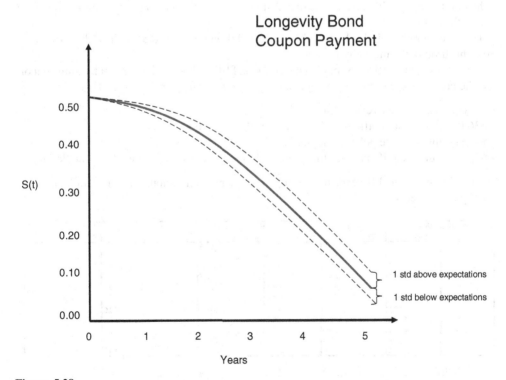

Figure 5.28

year	(1) Life Policies	(2) Premiums on remaining active policies	(3) Mgt Fee	(4) Wrap fee	(5) Custodial, Trustee, mgt, etc.	(6) Set up costs	Bond coupon	(8) Total out flow
0	$20.0	$0.0	$0.0	$0.0	$0.0	$0.25	$0.0	$20.3
1	$0.0	$2.9	$1.0	$0.0	$0.0	$0.00	$6.0	$9.9
2	$0.0	$2.9	$1.0	$0.0	$0.0	$0.00	$6.0	$9.9
3	$0.0	$2.9	$1.0	$0.0	$0.0	$0.00	$6.0	$9.9
4	$0.0	$2.8	$1.0	$0.0	$0.0	$0.00	$6.0	$9.8
5	$0.0	$2.6	$1.0	$0.0	$0.0	$0.00	$6.0	$9.6
6	$0.0	$2.3	$1.0	$0.0	$0.0	$0.00	$6.0	$9.3
7	$0.0	$2.0	$1.0	$0.0	$0.0	$0.00	$6.0	$9.1
8	$0.0	$1.7	$1.0	$0.0	$0.0	$0.00	$6.0	$8.8
9	$0.0	$1.2	$1.0	$0.0	$0.0	$0.00	$6.0	$8.2
10	$0.0	$0.6	$1.0	$0.0	$0.0	$0.00	$6.0	$7.6
Totals	$20.0	$21.9	$10.0	$0.0	$0.2	$0.3	$60.0	$112.3

Figure 5.29

models to the curve. The difficulty with pricing comes with the difference between realized values and expected values. For now we keep it fairly simplistic. As can be seen in Figures 5.29 to 5.31 the coupon is a flat 6% because the expected mortality rate is the realized mortality rate and we held LIBOR flat plus 100 basis points

The net result after 10 years, paying the coupon of LIBOR + 100 basis point floating coupon and all expenses save the principal, was $194.

- −$42 in the cumulative account
- $12 from the initial portfolio still in force ($60) sold at 60%
- $143 in reinvested life policies that matured
- $81 in reinvested life policies that were still in force and sold at 45 cents on the dollar.

If, however, the mortality rate comes in at 2 standard deviations below expectations, you have the result shown in Table 5.3.

The coupon rate will also be less than expected. Figures 5.32 to 5.34 show the cash flows from this drop in the mortality rate.

The net result after 10 years, paying the coupon of LIBOR + 100 basis point floating coupon less the fall off in the mortality rate and all expenses save the principal, was $149.

- −$83 in the cumulative account
- $36 from the initial portfolio still in force ($60) sold at 60%
- $72 in reinvested life policies that matured
- $124 in reinvested life policies that were still in force and sold at 45 cents on the dollar.

Figure 5.35 shows the difference in the coupon payments. This amounts to an overall reduction in coupon payments of 3%.

(9) Investment	(10) Maturities of policies	(11) Total In Flows of cash	(12) Net Flows	(13) Cumulative Reserve	(14) Excess cash reinvested additional LSP	(15) Sale of Policies Still in Force
$100.00	$0.0	$100.0	$79.8	$79.8	$0.0	
	$0.0	$0.0	-$9.9	$69.8	$31.8	
	$0.0	$0.0	-$9.9	$22.1	$23.9	
	$0.0	$0.0	-$9.9	-$17.7	$0.0	
	$5.0	$5.0	-$4.8	-$28.4	$0.0	
	$5.0	$5.0	-$4.6	-$39.1	$0.0	
	$10.0	$10.0	$0.7	-$44.4	$0.0	
	$10.0	$10.0	$0.9	-$49.5	$0.0	
	$10.0	$10.0	$1.2	-$54.2	$0.0	
	$20.0	$20.0	$11.8	-$48.4	$0.0	
	$20.0	$20.0	$12.4	-$42.0	$0.0	$12.0
$100.0	$80.0	$180.0	$67.7	-$42.0	$55.7	$12.0

Figure 5.30

Table 5.3

Year	LIBOR Curve + 100bps	Expected	Realizes	% Difference
0	6.00%	0	0	0.00%
1	6.00%	0	0	0.00%
2	6.00%	0	0	0.00%
3	6.00%	0	0	0.00%
4	6.00%	0.05	0	5.00%
5	6.00%	0.05	0	5.00%
6	6.00%	0.1	0.05	5.00%
7	6.00%	0.1	0.05	5.00%
8	6.00%	0.1	0.1	0.00%
9	6.00%	0.2	0.1	10.00%
10	6.00%	0.2	0.1	10.00%

year	1	2	3	4	5	6	7	8	9	10	Total
0											$0.0
1	$0.0										$0.0
2	$0.0	$0.0									$0.0
3	$0.0	$0.0	$0.0								$0.0
4	$0.0	$0.0	$0.0	$0.0							$0.0
5	$0.0	$8.0	$0.0	$0.0	$0.0						$8.0
6	$0.0	$8.0	$6.0	$0.0	$0.0	$0.0					$13.9
7	$0.0	$15.9	$6.0	$0.0	$0.0	$0.0	$0.0				$21.9
8	$0.0	$15.9	$11.9	$0.0	$0.0	$0.0	$0.0	$0.0			$27.8
9	$0.0	$15.9	$11.9	$0.0	$0.0	$0.0	$0.0	$0.0	$0.0		$27.8
10	$0.0	$31.8	$11.9	$0.0	$0.0	$0.0	$0.0	$0.0	$0.0	$0.0	$43.7
Totals	$0.0	$95.4	$47.7	$0.0	$0.0	$0.0	$0.0	$0.0	$0.0	$0.0	$143.1

Figure 5.31

year	(1) Life Policies	(2) Premiums on remaining active policies	(3) Mgt Fee	(4) Wrap fee	(5) Custodial, Trustee, mgt, etc.	(6) Set up costs	(7) Bond coupon	(8) Total out flow
0	$20.0	$0.0	$0.0	$0.0	$0.0	$0.25	$0.0	$20.3
1	$0.0	$2.9	$1.0	$0.0	$0.0	$0.00	$6.0	$9.9
2	$0.0	$2.9	$1.0	$0.0	$0.0	$0.00	$6.0	$9.9
3	$0.0	$2.9	$1.0	$0.0	$0.0	$0.00	$6.0	$9.9
4	$0.0	$2.9	$1.0	$0.0	$0.0	$0.00	$6.0	$9.9
5	$0.0	$2.9	$1.0	$0.0	$0.0	$0.00	$5.7	$9.6
6	$0.0	$2.8	$1.0	$0.0	$0.0	$0.00	$5.7	$9.5
7	$0.0	$2.6	$1.0	$0.0	$0.0	$0.00	$5.7	$9.3
8	$0.0	$2.3	$1.0	$0.0	$0.0	$0.00	$5.7	$9.0
9	$0.0	$2.0	$1.0	$0.0	$0.0	$0.00	$6.0	$9.1
10	$0.0	$1.7	$1.0	$0.0	$0.0	$0.00	$5.4	$8.2
Totals	$20.0	$26.0	$10.0	$0.0	$0.2	$0.3	$58.2	$114.6

Figure 5.32

(9) Investment	(10) Maturities of policies	(11) Total In Flows of cash	(12) Net Flows	(13) Cumulative Reserve	(14) Excess cash reinvested additional LSP	(15) Sale of Policies Still in Force
$100.00	$0.0	$100.0	$79.8	$79.8	$0.0	
	$0.0	$0.0	-$9.9	$69.8	$31.8	
	$0.0	$0.0	-$9.9	$22.1	$23.9	
	$0.0	$0.0	-$9.9	-$17.7	$0.0	
	$0.0	$0.0	-$9.9	-$33.6	$0.0	
	$0.0	$0.0	-$9.6	-$49.2	$0.0	
	$5.0	$5.0	-$4.5	-$59.4	$0.0	
	$5.0	$5.0	-$4.3	-$69.4	$0.0	
	$10.0	$10.0	$1.0	-$74.2	$0.0	
	$10.0	$10.0	$0.9	-$78.9	$0.0	
	$10.0	$10.0	$1.8	-$83.1	$0.0	$36.0
$100.0	$40.0	$140.0	$25.4	-$83.1	$55.7	$36.0

Figure 5.33

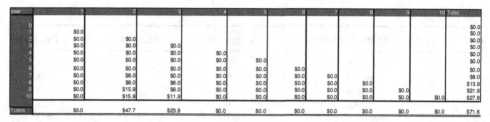

Figure 5.34

5.6.3 The Inverse Longevity Bond

The inverse longevity bond can be used to hedge extension risk from the standpoint of a hedge fund with a fixed term or the residual risk of a fixed term bond wrapped with life settlements. For example, if the fund or bond has a fixed 10-year payout with that payout backed by the pool of life settlements, an inverse longevity bond can hedge extension risk, i.e. the risk that the pool of life settlements will not sufficiently pay off the principal on the bond.

In the simple example below, it is just a rate minus the payout on the LSPs. As the payout on the LSPs is extended, the fixed payout on the bond remains in place for a longer period of time – a higher payout than would normally be received for a like rated bond.

One of the requirements of an inverse longevity bond is the establishment of a liquidity provider. As can be seen in Figure 5.37, column 13, a negative cash flow is generated in the 4th year and carries on throughout the life of the structure. The net result is positive but you will have to carry the negative results in the middle of the programme (Figures 5.36 to 5.38).

Assumptions

- It is assumed that we are purchasing a $100 face value pool of life policies. The coupon on the bond will be a simple 70% of the runoffs from the pool.
- In this example we purchase policies from only A-rated or better life companies.

year	Bond coupon	Bond coupon
0	$0.0	$0.0
1	$6.0	$6.0
2	$6.0	$6.0
3	$6.0	$6.0
4	$6.0	$5.7
5	$6.0	$5.7
6	$6.0	$5.7
7	$6.0	$5.7
8	$6.0	$6.0
9	$6.0	$5.4
10	$6.0	$0.0
	60	58.2

Figure 5.35

year	(1) Life Policies	(2) Premiums on remaining active policies	(3) Mgt Fee	(4) Wrap fee	(5) Custodial, Trustee, mgt, etc.	(6) Set up costs	Bond coupon	(8) Total out flow
0	$20.0	$0.0	$0.0	$0.0	$0.0	$0.25	$0.0	$20.3
1	$0.0	$2.9	$1.0	$0.0	$0.0	$0.00	$10.0	$13.9
2	$0.0	$2.9	$1.0	$0.0	$0.0	$0.00	$10.0	$13.9
3	$0.0	$2.9	$1.0	$0.0	$0.0	$0.00	$10.0	$13.9
4	$0.0	$2.8	$1.0	$0.0	$0.0	$0.00	$6.5	$10.3
5	$0.0	$2.6	$1.0	$0.0	$0.0	$0.00	$6.5	$10.1
6	$0.0	$2.3	$1.0	$0.0	$0.0	$0.00	$3.0	$6.3
7	$0.0	$2.0	$1.0	$0.0	$0.0	$0.00	$3.0	$6.1
8	$0.0	$1.7	$1.0	$0.0	$0.0	$0.00	$3.0	$5.8
9	$0.0	$1.2	$1.0	$0.0	$0.0	$0.00	$0.0	$2.2
10	$0.0	$0.6	$1.0	$0.0	$0.0	$0.00	$0.0	$1.6
Totals	$20.0	$21.9	$10.0	$0.0	$0.2	$0.3	$52.0	$104.3

Figure 5.36

- These are only non-contestable policies (using contestable policies and over-collateralizing will greatly improve yields but will not be shown here) and are either Whole Life or Universal Life policies (again programmes using term or variable life could be structured to yield better returns, but we defer those examples also).
- The average life of the pool is 10 years, which has been determined by a New York Stock exchange-listed actuarial firm and the life expectancies are adjusted life expectancies. By that we mean that the life expectancies are calculated as of the time of purchase into the trust, and not when originally issued.
- The runoff schedule was taken from the life expectancies of the pool. This is the same runoff schedule as used in Chapter 4. As mentioned in an earlier chapter, simulating this runoff schedule will generate risk parameters as to residual values and extension risk.
- Because the pool has an average expected life of 10 years only it is assumed that only 80% of the pool matures on or before the 10-year term.
- Any policies still in force at the end of the 10-year term can be sold back into the market at 60% of face value. This should be a very conservative assumption given that there is a secondary market for these policies which is becoming more and more liquid, and the value of the policy grows almost linearly as each day the policy holder lives brings the policies closer to term, and time is very much a linear function.
- Insurance premiums (2.9% of face) have to be maintained to keep the policies in force. In addition, a management fee (1% of investment) and custodial fees (2% of investment) have to be paid in addition to set-up costs and other miscellaneous fees.
- Because, for at least 3 years, there is little or no cash flow from the portfolio, 3 years of expenses will be maintained in a reserve account.

(9) Investment	(10) Maturities of policies	(11) Total In Flows of cash	(12) Net Flows	(13) Cumulative Reserve	(14) Excess cash reinvested additional LSP	(15) Sale of Policies Still in Force
$100.00	$0.0	$100.0	$79.8	$79.8	$0.0	
	$0.0	$0.0	-$13.9	$65.8	$31.8	
	$0.0	$0.0	-$13.9	$10.1	$20.7	
	$0.0	$0.0	-$13.9	-$34.5	$0.0	
	$5.0	$5.0	-$5.3	-$49.7	$0.0	
	$5.0	$5.0	-$5.1	-$61.4	$0.0	
	$10.0	$10.0	$3.7	-$64.2	$0.0	
	$10.0	$10.0	$4.0	-$63.3	$0.0	
	$10.0	$10.0	$4.2	-$62.0	$0.0	
	$20.0	$20.0	$17.8	-$47.2	$0.0	
-$100.0	$20.0	-$80.0	-$81.6	-$128.8	$0.0	$12.0
$0.0	$80.0	$80.0	-$24.3	-$128.8	$52.5	$12.0
						$262.3

Figure 5.37

year	1	2	3	4	5	6	7	8	9	10	Total
0											$0.0
1	$0.0										$0.0
2	$0.0	$0.0									$0.0
3	$0.0	$0.0	$0.0								$0.0
4	$0.0	$0.0	$0.0	$0.0							$0.0
5	$0.0	$8.0	$0.0	$0.0	$0.0						$8.0
6	$0.0	$8.0	$5.2	$0.0	$0.0	$0.0					$13.1
7	$0.0	$15.9	$5.2	$0.0	$0.0	$0.0	$0.0				$21.1
8	$0.0	$15.9	$10.3	$0.0	$0.0	$0.0	$0.0	$0.0			$26.2
9	$0.0	$15.9	$10.3	$0.0	$0.0	$0.0	$0.0	$0.0	$0.0		$26.2
10	$0.0	$31.8	$10.3	$0.0	$0.0	$0.0	$0.0	$0.0	$0.0	$0.0	$42.1
Totals	$0.0	$95.4	$41.3	$0.0	$0.0	$0.0	$0.0	$0.0	$0.0	$0.0	$136.7

Figure 5.38

- Any and all excess cash will be invested at a 4% rate.
- Any cash excess over and above the 3-year reserve requirement will be invested in new life policies.

The net residual value after 10 years, paying all expenses to include the principal in this case was $140 in return. Again this was on little investment in addition to collecting a management fee, this with a bond yield of approximately 5.2% per year (Figure 5.39).

- −$128 in the cumulative account due to paying out the principal on the bond
- $7 from the initial portfolio still in force ($12) sold at 60%
- $137 in reinvested life policies that matured
- $124 in reinvested life policies that were still in force and sold at 45 cents on the dollar.

Again by using less expensive pools or longer terms the returns on this programme can be increased substantially while at the same time offering a hedge against extension risk.

To show how this bond hedges extension risk, assume that the life expectancies were fully 2 standard deviations away from the mean. The coupon payout would then be as shown in Figure 5.40.

This is a $20 increase in the coupon payment or an overall 2% increase in return for an extension in the longevity of the pool of life settlements backing this bond. Further examples of longevity bonds could be:

- Zero coupon longevity bonds
- Spread longevity bonds

Bond coupon
$0.0
$10.0
$10.0
$10.0
$6.5
$6.5
$3.0
$3.0
$3.0
$0.0
$0.0
$52.0

Figure 5.39

Bond coupon
$0.0
$10.0
$10.0
$10.0
$10.0
$10.0
$6.5
$6.5
$3.0
$3.0
$3.0
$72.0

Figure 5.40

- Deferred longevity bonds – extension forwards
- Tranched longevity bonds
- Equity tranched inverse longevity bonds

5.7 SHARIA COMPLIANT BONDS

Sharia compliant bonds are simply bonds that have no interest. The payouts are based upon capital appreciation. As a result, payouts from the life settlements should be perfectly acceptable given that they are not a form of interest. The exception here may be the liquidity account, as cash placed in an interest-bearing account violates the letter of the law and therefore other means of providing liquidity have to be found.

One possible means would be to purchase a put option from a hedge fund or investment bank. In the event that cash is needed, the put option could be exercised and taken down. The price of the put option would reflect the fact that any excess cash used to purchase more put options could alternatively, in normal circumstances, be earning interest.

The approval process for investments that purport to comply with Sharia law is beyond the scope of this book, but readers should note that it is not a "one size fits all" approach and that approval may be required from several bodies before a transaction can proceed to closing.

Because the cash flows from a Sharia bond are identical to other cash flows shown here, it is not necessary to produce examples. The costs, returns, etc., will be very similar to that which has already been presented.

5.8 POWER BONDS

Power bonds are a good match with life settlement bonds. These are bonds that are married with a power option. The payoff on a power option is raised to a power greater than 1. In the case where a power bond backed by a pool of life settlements is in play, the power option will not kick in unless the runoffs from the LSP are within specific parameters. The set up is much like a PAC (see below) with the addition of added payouts.

In the bond below we use our standard assumptions for the LSP and structure a bond with a power option that pays out a coupon of 1.5 times the stipulated rate if the LSP has a runoff

Table 5.4

| | Percent Runoff | | |
	80%	100%	120%
Ten Year Coupon	$70	$105	$140
All in return after payout	$75	$131	$96

of between 90% of face to 110% of face after 10 years. Otherwise the payout remains fixed. If the payout is over 110% of face the options move up to twice the stipulated rate.

5.9   CIOs AND PACs, TACs AND VADAMs

We spent a great deal of time in Chapter 3 on mortgaged-backed securities and their derivatives. There was a method to our madness. Most mortgage-backed products and derivatives can be duplicated with life settlements, again with the added benefit of no correlation and little volatility. This is a major problem with mortgage-backed products in that the risk parameters of a mortgage form an S curve. We discuss this in Section 3.9.3. While mortgage derivatives were all designed to reduce this risk, as shown in Chapter 3, they were not entirely successful due to their boundary limitations. LSPs do not have this problem and as a result the tranching can be used to hedge longevity risk without fear of other correlated risk.

5.9.1   A Collateralized Insurance Obligation

Let's first look at more vanilla CIO structures which we discussed in Chapter 2. Again we use the assumptions we have been using all along, with the breakout of the tranches below.

Assumptions

- In this structure $100 is initially invested in the following proportion: 70% in the AA tranche paying a coupon of 8%; 20% in the Mezzanine tranche paying a coupon of 10%; and 10% in the equity tranche with all residual value going to the equity tranche. It is here that any excess cash flow will be reinvested in LSPs.
- This is a waterfall structure with all payments going towards the AA tranche before any payments are made to the Mezzanine tranche, and all remaining payment going to the Mezzanine tranche before any payments are made to the equity tranche.

In this example we purchase an insurance policy from an S&P AA-rated insurance company which will guarantee payout of the principal and interest on the AA tranche should the pool not cover all obligations at term. The cost of this insurance policy is 7% of the invested amount. This is an up-front cost in year zero.

Figures 5.41 and 5.42 show the cash flows for the AA tranche, which is nothing more than the equivalent of a coupon bond with the added insurance premium. Figures 5.43 and 5.44 are the cash flows for the mezzanine tranche and Figures 5.45 to 5.47 are the cash flows for the equity piece with any excess cash flow reinvested in LSPs and all residual value proceeds going to the equity piece.

year	Purchase of policies 70% tranche	(1) Interest on Note 8%	(3) Management Fee	(4) Premium Payment	Custodial and Trust Fees	Setup Costs	Insurance Premium	AA Tranche Bond Repayment	(5) Cash Out Flow
0	$14.00	$0.00	$0.00	$0.00	$0.00	$2.50	$4.90		$21.40
1		$5.60	$1.40	$2.03	$0.50				$9.53
2		$5.60	$1.40	$2.03	$0.50				$9.53
3		$5.60	$1.40	$2.03	$0.50				$9.53
4		$5.60	$1.40	$1.96	$0.50				$9.46
5		$5.60	$1.40	$1.89	$0.50				$9.39
6		$5.60	$1.40	$1.75	$0.50				$9.25
7		$5.60	$1.40	$1.60	$0.50				$9.10
8		$5.60	$1.40	$1.46	$0.50				$8.96
9		$5.60	$1.40	$1.18	$0.50				$8.88
10		$5.60	$1.40	$0.89	$0.50			$70.00	$78.39
Totals	$14.00	$56.00	$14.00	$16.82	$5.00	$2.50	$4.90	$70.00	$183.22

Figure 5.41   AA tranche

(7) Policy Flows	Investment	(8) Cash In Flows	(9) Net Flow
$0.00	$70.00	$70.00	$48.60
$0.00	$0.00	$0.00	-$9.53
$0.00	$0.00	$0.00	-$9.53
$0.00	$0.00	$0.00	-$9.53
$3.50	$0.00	$3.50	-$5.96
$3.50	$0.00	$3.50	-$5.89
$7.00	$0.00	$7.00	-$2.25
$7.00	$0.00	$7.00	-$2.10
$7.00	$0.00	$7.00	-$1.96
$14.00	$0.00	$14.00	$5.32
$14.00	$0.00	$14.00	-$64.39
$56.00	$70.00	$91.00	-$64.39

Figure 5.42   AA tranche

year	Purchase of policies 20% tranche	(1) Interest on Note 10%	(3) Management Fee	(4) Premium Payment	Bond Repayment	(5) Cash Out Flow
	$4.00					$4.00
1		$2.00	$0.2 0	$058		$2.78
2		$2.00	$0.2 0	$058		$2.78
3		$2.00	$0.2 0	$058		$2.78
4		$2.00	$0.2 0	$055		$2.75
5		$2.00	$0.2 0	$052		$2.72
6		$2.00	$0.2 0	$046		$2.66
7		$2.00	$0.2 0	$041		$2.61
8		$2.00	$0.2 0	$035		$2.55
9		$2.00	$0.2 0	$023		$2.43
10		$2.00	$0.2 0	$012	$20.00	$22.32
Total	$4.00	$20.00	$2.0 0	$438	$20.00	$50.38

Figure 5.43   Mezzanine tranche

(7) Policy Flows	Investment	(8) Cash In Flows	(9) Net Flow Mezz	Net Flow AA	Net Flow AA and Mezz tranches
$0.00	$20.00	$20.00	$16.00	$70.00	$86.00
$0.00	$0.00	$0.00	-$2.78	$0.00	-$2.78
$0.00	$0.00	$0.00	-$2.78	$0.00	-$2.78
$0.00	$0.00	$0.00	-$2.78	$0.00	-$2.78
$1.00	$0.00	$1.00	-$1.75	$3.50	$1.75
$1.00	$0.00	$1.00	-$1.72	$3.50	$1.78
$2.00	$0.00	$2.00	-$0.66	$7.00	$6.34
$2.00	$0.00	$2.00	-$0.61	$7.00	$6.39
$2.00	$0.00	$2.00	-$0.55	$7.00	$6.45
$4.00	$0.00	$4.00	$1.57	$14.00	$15.57
$4.00	$0.00	$4.00	-$18.32	$14.00	-$4.32
$16.00	$20.00	$36.00	-$14.38	$126.00	$111.62

Figure 5.44 Mezzanine tranche

year	Purchase of policies 10% Equity tranche	(2) Management Fee	(3) Premium Payment	(4) Cash Out Flow
	$2.00	$0.00		$2.00
1		$0.20	$0.29	$0.49
2		$0.20	$0.29	$0.49
3		$0.20	$0.29	$0.49
4		$0.20	$0.28	$0.48
5		$0.20	$0.26	$0.46
6		$0.20	$0.23	$0.43
7		$0.20	$0.20	$0.40
8		$0.20	$0.17	$0.37
9		$0.20	$0.12	$0.32
10		$0.20	$0.06	$0.26
Totals	$2.00	$2.00	$2.19	$6.19

Figure 5.45 Equity tranche

(6) Policy Flows	Equity Investment	(7) Cash In Flows	(8) Net Flow Equity	Net Flow AA and Mezz	Total Net Flow	Total Cumulative Reserve	Reinvested in Life Policies
$0.00	$10.00	$10.00	$8.00	$8.00	$16.00	$16.00	
$0.00	$0.00	$0.00	-$0.49	$7.51	$7.02	$23.02	
$0.00	$0.00	$0.00	-$0.49	$7.02	$6.53	$29.55	$0.00
$0.00	$0.00	$0.00	-$0.49	$6.53	$6.04	$35.59	$0.00
$0.50	$0.00	$0.50	$0.02	$6.55	$6.58	$42.17	$3.49
$0.50	$0.00	$0.50	$0.04	$6.59	$6.63	$48.80	$10.07
$1.00	$0.00	$1.00	$0.57	$7.16	$7.73	$56.53	$16.70
$1.00	$0.00	$1.00	$0.60	$7.76	$8.36	$64.89	$24.43
$1.00	$0.00	$1.00	$0.63	$8.38	$9.01	$73.90	$32.79
$2.00	$0.00	$2.00	$1.68	$10.07	$11.75	$85.65	$41.80
$2.00	$0.00	$2.00	$1.74	$11.81	$13.55	$99.20	$53.55
$8.00	$10.00	$18.00	$11.81	$87.39	$99.20	$99.20	$182.82
							$914.12

Figure 5.46 Equity tranche

year	1	2	3	4	5	6	7	8	9	10	Total
0											$0.00
1	$0.00										$0.00
2	$0.00	$0.00									$0.00
3	$0.00	$0.00	$0.00								$0.00
4	$0.00	$0.00	$0.00	$0.00							$0.00
5	$0.00	$0.00	$0.00	$0.00	$0.00						$0.00
6	$0.00	$0.00	$0.00	$0.00	$0.00	$0.00					$0.00
7	$0.00	$0.00	$0.00	$0.87	$0.00	$0.00	$0.00				$0.87
8	$0.00	$0.00	$0.00	$0.87	$2.52	$0.00	$0.00	$0.00			$3.39
9	$0.00	$0.00	$0.00	$1.75	$2.52	$4.18	$0.00	$0.00	$0.00		$8.44
10	$0.00	$0.00	$0.00	$1.75	$5.03	$4.18	$6.11	$0.00	$0.00	$0.00	$17.06
Totals	$0.00	$0.00	$0.00	$5.23	$10.07	$8.35	$6.11	$0.00	$0.00	$0.00	$29.76

Figure 5.47 Equity tranche runoff

Given our assumptions, the coupons and the payout of the principal are easily met. The AA tranche is such because it has an AA-rated insurance wrap guaranteeing principal and interest should the bond writer fail to pay. Under the conditions set out above, the equity holder receives the following payout.

The net results for the equity holder after 10 years were enormous. After paying off the first two tranches completely the equity holder was left with $482.71 on a $10 investment.

- $99.20 in the cumulative reserve account
- $12 from the initial portfolio still in force ($20) sold at 60%
- $353.74 in reinvested life policies that were still in force sold at 45 cents on the dollar
- $29.76 in reinvested life policies that have runoff.

This equates to approximately a 32% IRR.

While the equity holder is exposed to the bulk of the risks the returns can be substantial even if projections are not met. For example, if expected lives fall 2 standard deviations below expectations, the returns for the equity holder are still above 20% using our assumptions.

Again there are variations on a theme. In Chapter 2 we talked about a tranched life settlement CDO with the payouts from the CDO tranched. The [0–3] tranche will be paid first from the runoff from the pool after all expenses are paid. The runoffs will continue to pay the [0–3] tranche until all principal and interest have been paid back. Next the runoffs will start to pay down the [4–7] tranche, etc., until the remainder of the pool goes to the equity tranche.

5.9.2   PAC

In the mortgage market a PAC is a Planned Amortization Class. It is a tranche within a CMO structure. Because a mortgage could lose value no matter which direction interest rates moved, certain boundary level structures were designed. We named a few of the many in Chapter 3. For example, if you hold a mortgage-backed security and interest rates rise, your structure would lose in value because of the reduction in return given comparable structures. This is a standard fixed income risk. However, in the mortgage market in the USA, if interest rates fall the owner of the mortgage has the option of paying off the mortgage and refinancing at a lower rate. As a result the holder of a mortgage-backed security would lose in value in the event of a fall in rates because he would end up holding cash which would now have to be invested at a lower rate.

For that reason boundary products were developed in the mortgage derivatives market. A PAC is just such a product. As long as the prepayment rates – as measured by an acceptable standard such as a PSA – held within certain boundaries, the coupon on the structure was guaranteed. Only if rates broke the boundaries could the coupon be adjusted.

A mirror product within the life settlement industry could guarantee a fixed coupon as long as runoffs within the pool held within certain percentages. Because a faster runoff would not actually hurt the return of a life settlement structure but increase it, this could be a one-sided boundary. In the example below we use both boundaries using the short side as an enhancement to the yield if the runoff is fast enough.

Again we start with the same assumptions, except that the mezzanine tranche is an 8% PAC as long as the runoffs fall above 80%. If in fact runoffs are in excess of 100%, the added return will be shared equally between the PAC holder and the equity holder.

In essence, this is very similar to the CDO life settlement product in that the tranche is bounded to reduce the risk of a shortfall with the equity tranche taking all the risk.

Figures 5.48 to 5.54 show the cash flows of this product given the expected runoffs.

year	Purchase of policies 70% tranche	(1) Interest on Note 8%	(3) Management Fee	(4) Premium Payment	Custodial and Trust Fees	Setup Costs	Insurance Premium	AA Tranche Bond Repayment
0	$14.00	$0.00	$0.00	$0.00	$0.00	$2.50	$4.90	
1		$5.60	$1.40	$2.03	$0.50			
2		$5.60	$1.40	$2.03	$0.50			
3		$5.60	$1.40	$2.03	$0.50			
4		$5.60	$1.40	$1.96	$0.50			
5		$5.60	$1.40	$1.89	$0.50			
6		$5.60	$1.40	$1.75	$0.50			
7		$5.60	$1.40	$1.60	$0.50			
8		$5.60	$1.40	$1.46	$0.50			
9		$5.60	$1.40	$1.18	$0.50			
10		$5.60	$1.40	$0.89	$0.50			$70.00
Totals	$14.00	$56.00	$14.00	$16.82	$5.00	$2.50	$4.90	$70.00

Figure 5.48

(5) Cash Out Flow	(7) Policy Flows	Investment	(8) Cash In Flows	(9) Net Flow
$21.40	$0.00	$70.00	$70.00	$48.60
$9.53	$0.00	$0.00	$0.00	-$9.53
$9.53	$0.00	$0.00	$0.00	-$9.53
$9.53	$0.00	$0.00	$0.00	-$9.53
$9.46	$3.50	$0.00	$3.50	-$5.96
$9.39	$3.50	$0.00	$3.50	-$5.89
$9.25	$7.00	$0.00	$7.00	-$2.25
$9.10	$7.00	$0.00	$7.00	-$2.10
$8.96	$7.00	$0.00	$7.00	-$1.96
$8.68	$14.00	$0.00	$14.00	$5.32
$78.39	$14.00	$0.00	$14.00	-$64.39
$183.22	$56.00	$70.00	$91.00	-$64.39

Figure 5.49

year	Purchase of policies 20% tranche	(1) Interest on Note 10%	(3) Management Fee	(4) Premium Payment	Bond Repayment	(5) Cash Out Flow PAC 8%
0	$4.00					$4.00
1		$1.60	$0.20	$0.58		$2.38
2		$1.60	$0.20	$0.58		$2.38
3		$1.60	$0.20	$0.58		$2.38
4		$1.60	$0.20	$0.55		$2.35
5		$1.60	$0.20	$0.52		$2.32
6		$1.60	$0.20	$0.46		$2.26
7		$1.60	$0.20	$0.41		$2.21
8		$1.60	$0.20	$0.35		$2.15
9		$1.60	$0.20	$0.23		$2.03
10		$1.60	$0.20	$0.12	$20.00	$21.92
Total	$4.00	$16.00	$2.00	$4.38	$20.00	$46.38

Figure 5.50

(7) Policy Flows	Investment	(8) Cash In Flows	(9) Net Flow Mezz	Net Flow AA	Net Flow AA and Mezz tranches
$0.00	$20.00	$20.00	$16.00	$48.60	$64.60
$0.00	$0.00	$0.00	-$2.38	-$9.53	-$11.91
$0.00	$0.00	$0.00	-$2.38	-$9.53	-$11.91
$0.00	$0.00	$0.00	-$2.38	-$9.53	-$11.91
$1.00	$0.00	$1.00	-$1.35	-$5.96	-$7.31
$1.00	$0.00	$1.00	-$1.32	-$5.89	-$7.21
$2.00	$0.00	$2.00	-$0.26	-$2.25	-$2.51
$2.00	$0.00	$2.00	-$0.21	-$2.10	-$2.31
$2.00	$0.00	$2.00	-$0.15	-$1.96	-$2.11
$4.00	$0.00	$4.00	$1.97	$5.32	$7.29
$4.00	$0.00	$4.00	-$17.92	-$64.39	-$82.31
$16.00	$20.00	$36.00	-$10.38	-$57.22	-$67.60

Figure 5.51   The reinvested portfolio runoff

The equity tranche will be responsible for all negative cash flow from the AA tranche and PAC bond and receive payment only after the AA tranche and PAC bond have been paid, assuming that the boundary of the PAC bond has not been breached. The net results for the equity holder after 10 years were as follows. After paying off the first two tranches completely, the equity holder was left with $277.44 on a $10 investment.

- −59.79 in the cumulative reserve account
- $12 from the initial portfolio still in force ($20) sold at 60%
- +$59.18 in reinvested life policies that were still in force sold at 45 cents on the dollar
- +278.05 in reinvested life policies that have runoff.

5.9.3   PAC Bond – Breaching the Boundaries by 40%

If the PAC bond breached the boundaries then the 8% coupon will be reduced by a previously agreed amount. In this instance the coupon is reduced by the percent over/under mortality rate. In this example the boundary was 80% to 120%. With a 2 standard deviation reduction in the mortality rate, the reduction in coupon will be 40% and in this example fixed at the time of the breach. From Figure 5.54 we see that in year 7 the coupon is reduced by 40%. Also note that the equity holders have a reduction in payout.

year	Purchase of policies 10% Equity tranch	(2) Management Fee	(3) Premium Payment	(4) Cash Out Flow
	$2.00	$0.00		$2.00
1		$0.20	$0.29	$0.49
2		$0.20	$0.29	$0.49
3		$0.20	$0.29	$0.49
4		$0.20	$0.28	$0.48
5		$0.20	$0.26	$0.46
6		$0.20	$0.23	$0.43
7		$0.20	$0.20	$0.40
8		$0.20	$0.17	$0.37
9		$0.20	$0.12	$0.32
10		$0.20	$0.06	$0.26
Totals	$2.00	$2.00	$2.19	$6.19

Figure 5.52

(6) Policy Flows	Equity Investment	(7) Cash In Flows	(8) Net Flow Equity	Net Flow AA and Mezz	Total Net Flow	Total Cumulative Reserve	Reinvested in Life Policies
$0.00	$10.00	$10.00	$8.00	$64.60	$72.60	$72.60	
$0.00	$0.00	$0.00	-$0.49	-$11.91	-$12.40	$60.20	$41.70
$0.00	$0.00	$0.00	-$0.49	-$11.91	-$12.40	$47.80	$29.30
$0.00	$0.00	$0.00	-$0.49	-$11.91	-$12.40	$35.40	$16.90
$0.50	$0.00	$0.50	$0.02	-$7.31	-$7.29	$28.11	$4.50
$0.50	$0.00	$0.50	$0.04	-$7.21	-$7.17	$20.94	$0.00
$1.00	$0.00	$1.00	$0.57	-$2.51	-$1.94	$19.00	$0.00
$1.00	$0.00	$1.00	$0.60	-$2.31	-$1.71	$17.29	$0.00
$1.00	$0.00	$1.00	$0.63	-$2.11	-$1.48	$15.81	$0.00
$2.00	$0.00	$2.00	$1.68	$7.29	$8.97	$24.78	$0.00
$2.00	$0.00	$2.00	$1.74	-$82.31	-$80.57	-$55.79	$0.00
$8.00	$10.00	$18.00	$11.81	-$67.60	-$55.79	-$55.79	$92.40
							$462.00

Figure 5.53

Figure 5.55 shows the adjusted payout for the PAC bond under a shortfall in the mortality runoff. Figure 5.56 shows the adjusted equity payout with the 2 standard deviation move.

The net results for the equity holder after 10 years were as follows. After paying off the first two tranches completely the equity holders were left with $180.50 on a $10 investment.

- −$92.19 in the cumulative reserve account
- $12 from the initial portfolio still in force ($20) sold at 60%
- +$126.20 in reinvested life policies that were still in force sold at 45 cents on the dollar
- +$146.50 in reinvested life policies that have runoff.

5.10   EQUITY-LINKED NOTES

An Equity-Linked Note (ELN) is a debt instrument, usually a note that differs from a standard fixed income security in that the final payout is based on the return of the underlying equity. This equity can be a single stock or a basket of stocks to include an equity index.

In the late 1980s the then Chase Manhattan bank had a certificate of deposit which they called a bull or bear CD. The investors could choose the direction they thought the market was going and also the payouts they wanted based upon some guarantee. For example, if investors thought the market was going to rise, they could choose a bull CD. In addition, they could choose the level of risk they were willing to take by choosing the percentage of that rise they wanted. If the investors wanted security they could purchase a bull CD with a 2% floor

year	1	2	3	4	5	6	7	8	9	10	Total
0											$0.00
1	$0.00										$0.00
2	$0.00	$0.00									$0.00
3	$0.00	$0.00	$0.00								$0.00
4	$10.43	$0.00	$0.00	$0.00							$10.43
5	$10.43	$7.33	$0.00	$0.00	$0.00						$17.75
6	$20.85	$7.33	$4.23	$0.00	$0.00	$0.00					$32.40
7	$20.85	$14.65	$4.23	$1.13	$0.00	$0.00	$0.00				$40.85
8	$20.85	$14.65	$8.45	$1.13	$0.00	$0.00	$0.00	$0.00			$45.08
9	$41.70	$14.65	$8.45	$2.25	$0.00	$0.00	$0.00	$0.00	$0.00		$67.05
10	$41.70	$29.30	$8.45	$2.25	$0.00	$0.00	$0.00	$0.00	$0.00	$0.00	$81.70
Totals	$166.80	$87.90	$33.80	$6.75	$0.00	$0.00	$0.00	$0.00	$0.00	$0.00	$295.25

Figure 5.54

(1) Interest on Note 8%	(1) Interest on Note 8%
$1.60	$1.60
$1.60	$1.60
$1.60	$1.60
$1.60	$1.60
$1.60	$1.60
$1.60	$0.60
$1.60	$0.60
$1.60	$0.00
$1.60	$0.00
$1.60	$0.00
$16.00	$9.20

Figure 5.55

with a 75% appreciation. That meant that no matter what happened in the market they were guaranteed a 2% return on the CD. However, if the index rose 10% they would receive a 7.5% return on the CD. If the index fell they would still receive their 2%. They could as indicated take the opposite position if they thought the market would fall with the same floor. If the investors wanted more risk, they could take a bull or bear CD with no floor and receive 100% of the move.

An added advantage to this programme was the fact that these were bank CDs. This was a programme that had FDIC insurance, giving a government guarantee to the principal.

While the maturity on these CDs could be short term, the longer the CD term the better the payout. These programmes were hugely successful as the bank could hedge the product successfully. This was done with a simple zero strip and an equity option. As rates declined and the zero became more expensive, the programme became more and more difficult to hedge and was stopped.

Usually, the final payout is the amount invested, times the gain in the underlying stock or index times a note-specific *participation rate*, which can be more or less than 100%. For example, if the underlying equity gains 50% during the investment period, and the participation rate is 80%, the investor receives $1.40 for each dollar invested. If the equity remains unchanged or declines, the investor still receives $1 per dollar invested (as long as the issuer does not default). Generally, the participation rate is better in longer maturity notes, since the total amount of interest given up by the investor is higher.

An equity-linked note can be thought of as a combination of a zero-coupon bond and an equity option. Indeed, the issuer of the note usually covers the equity payout liability by

	Purchase of policies 10% Equity tranche	(2) Management Fee	(3) Premium Payment	(4) Cash Out Flow	(6) Policy Flows	Equity Investment	(7) Cash In Flows	(8) Net Flow Equity	Net Flow AA and Mezz	Total Net Flow
year	$2.50	$0.00		$2.50	$0.00	$10.00	$10.00	$7.50	$60.10	$67.60
1		$0.20	$0.29	$0.49	$0.00	$0.00	$0.00	-$0.49	-$12.31	-$12.80
2		$0.20	$0.29	$0.49	$0.00	$0.00	$0.00	-$0.49	-$12.31	-$12.80
3		$0.20	$0.29	$0.49	$0.00	$0.00	$0.00	-$0.49	-$12.31	-$12.80
4		$0.20	$0.28	$0.48	$0.50	$0.00	$0.50	$0.02	-$7.71	-$7.69
5		$0.20	$0.26	$0.46	$0.50	$0.00	$0.50	$0.04	-$7.61	-$7.57
6		$0.20	$0.23	$0.43	$1.00	$0.00	$1.00	$0.57	-$2.91	-$2.34
7		$0.20	$0.20	$0.40	$1.00	$0.00	$1.00	$0.60	-$2.71	-$2.11
8		$0.20	$0.17	$0.37	$1.00	$0.00	$1.00	$0.63	-$2.51	-$1.88
9		$0.20	$0.12	$0.32	$2.00	$0.00	$2.00	$1.68	$6.89	$8.57
10		$0.20	$0.06	$0.26	$2.00	$0.00	$2.00	$1.74	-$82.71	-$80.97
Totals	$2.50	$2.00	$2.19	$6.69	$8.00	$10.00	$18.00	$11.31	-$76.10	-$64.79

Figure 5.56

purchasing an identical option. In some equity-linked notes, the payout structure is more complicated, resembling an exotic option.

Most equity-linked notes are not actively traded on the secondary market and are designed to be kept to maturity. However, the issuer or arranger of the notes may offer to buy back the notes. Unlike the maturity payout, the buy-back price before maturity may be below the amount invested in first place.

With the evolution of the life settlement market the programme can be restarted. Two caveats, however: (1) the term of the programme would have to be at least 5 years, hence the note not CD and the government guarantee is not in place but replaced with the credit of the underlying pool which will guarantee payout.

5.11 CONCLUSION

Above we looked at a number of capital markets structures that can be modelled using LSPs. In most cases the expected returns were substantial with less volatility and correlation risk than like products using vanilla securities. In addition, the returns can be substantial and certainly through the curve. While these examples are simple illustrations, it definitely shows what can be done.

Note that in all of the above cases we looked at expected cash flows. Assuming that these cash flows come to fruition, the pricing of these instruments is easy. In all cases above we priced everything off par. We will discuss the much more difficult problem of pricing these products when cash flows are not known for certain and delve into hedging the variations that can come from expectations. Remember these products are all stochastic in nature and parameterizing the product is therefore a difficult process.

6

Structured Financing: Guaranteed
Loan Repayment

INTRODUCTION

In this chapter we look at using LSPs to wrap both commercial and industrial loans, retail loans, their use in asset financing, balance sheet restructuring, asset swaps and in floors in asset funds. We also show how LSPs can be used for credit enhancements for both poor credit in the retail and commercial markets. These are just some of the many examples for which LSPs can be used in structured finance. LSPs have been used in or, considered for use in, the following – and this is just a partial list.

- Euro Tunnel
- Ports in Eastern Europe
- Hotel construction and purchases
- Apartment complexes
- Resurrection of Chapter 11 businesses and putting them back on solid ground.

6.1 PROJECT FINANCING: COMMERCIAL AND INDUSTRIAL USES

6.1.1 Purchase of a Restaurant Chain

Below is a term sheet for the purchase of a large restaurant chain. The purchase price for the chain was $1.3 billion. A hedge fund was ready to lend funding for this project (or any project) up to $3 billion but wanted a guarantee on the funds. Guarantees could be obtained in a number of ways but by far the cheapest wrap, if accepted, would be the life settlement wrap if for no other reason than the LSPs at term would pay off 80% (in this situation) of the principal on the loan (and if managed properly, potentially much more) at a substantially reduced price when compared with other types of insurance.

The analysis below shows the project cost of $1.3 billion. For confidentiality reasons the detail surrounding the restaurant chain is not divulged. We look at only the life settlement side of the trade ignoring the profitability or lack of it on the restaurant side.

Figure 6.1 shows the term sheet for the loan. It was decided initially that contestable life policies could be used to reduce the cost of the protection.

In the term sheet the loan is a 10-year loan. The cost of the LSPs to guarantee the entire loan of $2.5 billion is $240 million, which is an average price of 12 cents on the dollar. As explained above, these policies are much cheaper than whole life hence the 12 cent cost.

This is an 80% guarantee. In other words, the $240 million in life settlement policies will pay out $2 billion ($240/12) on or before the term of the loan. The remainder of the loan is assumed to be covered by the profits of the restaurant chain initially, but as will be shown, a managed pool will more than cover all costs.

Restaurant Loan (billions)		
Purchase Price of Restaurant Chain	$1.300	
Life Settlement Pool costs using contestable life policies	$0.240	
Reserve requirement 3 years expense	$0.750	
Fees	$0.017	
Total amount of the Loan	$2.307	
Reserve hedge	$0.193	
Yearly Expenses		
Debt Service on Loan at 7.5%	$0.175	
Other Loan Expense	$0.050	
Total		$0.225
Expense Cover Assuming no Income for Restaurants		
Debt Service cover (years)		4.29 years
Total Expense cover (years)		3.33 years

Figure 6.1

In addition there were approximately $17 million in start-up fees, bringing the total loan to $2.33 billion. For conservatism we also set up an approximately $200 million reserve, bringing the total loan up to $2.5 billion.

Figures 6.2 and 6.3 show the cash out flows for the LSP on this structure. The restaurant financial statements are not included in this write up for confidential reasons. Suffice to say, the returns generated by the restaurant chain were substantial enough to merit a $1.3 billion price tag.

Figure 6.4 shows the cash in flow for this project.

year	(1) Life Policies	(2) Premium on remaining active policies	(3) Mgt Fee	(4) Underwriting Fee	(5) Admin and Legal
0	$240,000,000	$0	$0	$9,000,000	$8,000,000
1	$0	$40,000,000	$12,500,000		
2	$0	$40,000,000	$12,500,000		
3	$0	$40,000,000	$12,500,000		
4	$0	$38,000,000	$12,500,000		
5	$0	$36,000,000	$12,500,000		
6	$0	$34,000,000	$12,500,000		
7	$0	$30,000,000	$12,500,000		
8	$0	$24,000,000	$12,500,000		
9	$0	$16,000,000	$12,500,000		
10	$0	$8,000,000	$12,500,000		
Totals	$240,000,000	$306,000,000	$125,000,000		

Figure 6.2

(6) Purchase Price of Restaurant Chain	(7) Interest Payment	Wrap Fee	(11) Total out flow
$1,300,000,000	$0	$24,000,000	$1,581,000,000
	$187,500,000		$240,000,000
	$187,500,000		$240,000,000
	$187,500,000		$240,000,000
	$187,500,000		$238,000,000
	$187,500,000		$236,000,000
	$187,500,000		$234,000,000
	$187,500,000		$230,000,000
	$187,500,000		$224,000,000
	$187,500,000		$216,000,000
	$187,500,000		$208,000,000
	$1,875,000,000	$24,000,000	$3,887,000,000

Figure 6.3

In this example there is an additional up-front fee. This is the "wrap fee", which, in this case, is $24 million or approximately 10% of the invested amount in the LSP.

This is the insurance on the LSP guaranteeing the face value of the pool. We referred to this insurance package in Chapter 5. It was required by the hedge fund but because of this guarantee on the face value the borrower was allowed to use contestable policies. There is always a trade-off between the insurance guarantee and the over/under-collateralization and the type of policy allowed.

Figure 6.5 gives a matrix of possible results. Across the top we use the 1 and 2 standard deviation test we have used in previous chapters to test the error in the life expectancy calculations. Down the side we looked at over/under-collateralization of the pool; 100% collateral would represent a pool of life settlement policies with a face value equal to the loan amount, in this case $2.5 billion; 80% would be less than the $2.5 billion or a face value in

(12) Investment (Loan Amount)	(13) Maturities of policies	(14) Total In Flows of cash	(15) Net Flows	(16) Cumulative Reserve	(17) Excess cash reinvested in LS
$2,500,000,000	$0	$2,500,000,000	$919,000,000	$919,000,000	$0
	$0	$0	-$240,000,000	$679,000,000	$281,500,000
	$0	$0	-$240,000,000	$157,500,000	$0
	$0	$0	-$240,000,000	-$82,500,000	$0
	$100,000,000	$100,000,000	-$138,000,000	-$220,500,000	$0
	$100,000,000	$100,000,000	-$136,000,000	-$356,500,000	$0
	$100,000,000	$100,000,000	-$134,000,000	-$490,500,000	$0
	$200,000,000	$200,000,000	-$30,000,000	-$520,500,000	$0
	$300,000,000	$300,000,000	$76,000,000	-$444,500,000	$0
	$400,000,000	$400,000,000	$184,000,000	-$260,500,000	$0
	$400,000,000	$400,000,000	$192,000,000	-$68,500,000	$0
$2,500,000,000	$1,600,000,000	$4,100,000,000	$213,000,000	-$68,500,000	$281,500,000

Figure 6.4

	Most Likely	1 Std Down	2 Std Down
80% collateralize	$2,445,833,333	$1,831,625,000	$1,235,416,667
100% collateralized	$4,101,166,667	$1,422,125,000	$785,583,333
120% over collateralized	$5,633,333,333	$201,762,500	-$321,906,250

Figure 6.5

the pool of $2 billion. Finally 120% collateral would represent a face value in the pool of $3 billion.

Again because of the insurance policy and the return forecast by the restaurant chain we were allowed to under-collateralize and use contestable policies.

Figure 6.5 shows the fact that over-collateralization hurts the revenue stream if in fact the life expectancy estimate is overestimated.

Because the lender in this example will have access to both the LSP and the restaurant chain in the event of default, the loan was considered to be very secure and the 80% collateral was agreed.

The net result for this programme was the fact that the borrowers could borrow $2.5 billion in a secured loan guaranteeing the payback of the principal and use $1.3 billion to purchase the loan and not have to worry about the principal being paid back by the restaurant chain.

6.1.2 Leasing

Like the financing project described above, life settlements can be used to wrap leasing projects. In the simplest form the lessee would have to put down funding. A partial payment would be used to purchase a pool of life settlements. If the lessor defaulted on the lease the funder of the lease would repossess the underlying asset and still maintain the pool of life settlements.

The major drawback to this programme is the time frame involved. Most leased assets are short term; by which we mean 5 years or less. Autos are the most commonly leased product, but there are multiple chain stores that lease all sorts of appliances, all shorter term.

There are leasing programmes that do extend out in years. The leasing of tankers, for example, is usually a 10-year programme, and in these circumstances the life settlement guarantee would be ideal.

We will not go into detail about the lease programme as it is much the same as the financing arrangement just described. Suffice to say, any programme that would benefit from a longer term guarantee would be an ideal candidate for a life settlement wrap guaranteeing the principal.

6.1.3 Balance Sheet Restructuring

LSPs can be used in restructuring a balance sheet, provided that the organization does not want to dilute the equity position with the injection of equity capital. This is the case in many banks today but, unfortunately, this possibility may be coming to little too late. The simple process would be to borrow $100 from the street. With $40, purchase a pool of life settlements which would grow to $100 in 7 years. Invest the rest trying to clean up the balance sheet, perhaps by trying to increase the tier capital of the assets. The LSP would grow to pay off the loan while the reinvested assets would help to clean up the asset side of the balance sheet. In 7 years the LSP would pay back the $100 loan without having to dilute any equity position.

6.2   RETAIL PRODUCT

6.2.1   Principal Reduced Mortgages

As an example of a LSP used in the retail venue let us look at a simple retail mortgage product. Figure 6.6 shows the monthly stream of payments of a simple 30-year 6% fixed rate mortgage payout with the consumer borrowing $100. As is typically the case, the principal is paid down slowly at first while the interest payout as a percentage of total payment is high initially. As the payments progresses the principal is paid down and the interest payments on that principal are reduced. As a result, the amount of principal paid in a fixed payment stream grows and the interest decreases. Figure 6.7 shows the full payout stream for both the principal and interest over a 30-year period.

In this example we assume a $100 mortgage where the borrower pays out a 20% down payment and borrows the remaining $80. The bank will pay out $100 for the purchase price of the house but will have $20 in down payments, thus only needing an $80 payout on the loan. With $20 the bank purchases a $10 LSP and uses the remaining $10 for expenses.

Figure 6.8 shows the yearly mortgage payments to the bank, both principal and interest, along with the payout of the LSP. Figure 6.9 shows the cumulative payback of the loan including the life settlement payout. As can be seen, by the end of the 7th year the $80 loan

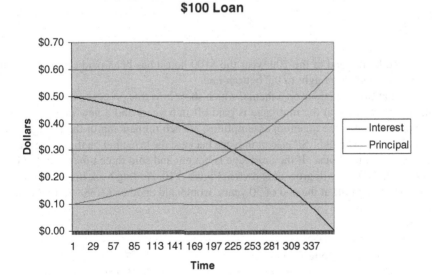

Figure 6.6

year	Total Payouts	Mortgage Payouts
0	$13.61	$5.81
1	$13.02	$5.81
2	$6.39	$5.81
3	$5.80	$5.81
4	$7.24	$5.81
5	$8.64	$5.81
6	$11.94	$5.81
7	$13.43	$5.81
8	$13.50	$5.81
9	$18.10	$5.81
10	$22.45	$5.81
11	$16.63	$5.81
12	$14.07	$5.81
13	$18.95	$5.81
14	$25.41	$5.81
15	$32.47	$5.81
16	$37.21	$5.81
17	$37.30	$5.81
18	$36.73	$5.81
19	$36.19	$5.81
20	$28.00	$5.81
21	$16.40	$5.81
22	$13.84	$5.81
23	$18.72	$5.81
24	$25.19	$5.81
25	$32.27	$5.81
26	$37.04	$5.81
27	$37.15	$5.81
28	$36.62	$5.81
29	$36.14	$5.81
30	$22.19	$0.00
Totals	$692.59	$174.36

Figure 6.7

is paid off and by the end of the 10th year the $100 house has been paid off. The remaining 20 years of payouts fall straight to the bottom line.

Let us look at two variations on a theme, which show how this process can be pushed to the extreme. First assume that the mortgage is paid off in 5 years and a new mortgage takes its place. Again making some quantum assumptions, at each refinancing of the mortgage a new LSP is put in place. The old LSP is kept in place because the principal on the mortgage is paid off with the sale of the house. If the mortgage is bought and sold three times over the life of a 30-year period, the LSP will grow as shown in Figure 6.10. Adding back in any residual value from these LSPs sold off at the end of 30 years, would add another $1,388.75 to the return or $2,748.71

Mortgage payout	$ 174.36
LSP runoff	$1,185.60
Life Settlement Residual (60%)	$1,388.75

year	Total Payouts	Mortgage Payouts	LS Payouts
0	$13.61	$5.81	$7.80
1	$13.02	$5.81	$7.21
2	$6.39	$5.81	$0.58
3	$5.80	$5.81	-$0.01
4	$7.24	$5.81	$1.42
5	$8.64	$5.81	$2.83
6	$11.94	$5.81	$6.12
7	$13.43	$5.81	$7.62
8	$13.50	$5.81	$7.69
9	$18.10	$5.81	$12.28
10	$22.45	$5.81	$16.64
11	$16.63	$5.81	$10.82
12	$14.07	$5.81	$8.26
13	$18.95	$5.81	$13.14
14	$25.41	$5.81	$19.59
15	$32.47	$5.81	$26.66
16	$37.21	$5.81	$31.40
17	$37.30	$5.81	$31.48
18	$36.73	$5.81	$30.92
19	$36.19	$5.81	$30.38
20	$28.00	$5.81	$22.19
21	$16.40	$5.81	$10.58
22	$13.84	$5.81	$8.02
23	$18.72	$5.81	$12.90
24	$25.19	$5.81	$19.38
25	$32.27	$5.81	$26.45
26	$37.04	$5.81	$31.22
27	$37.15	$5.81	$31.34
28	$36.62	$5.81	$30.80
29	$36.14	$5.81	$30.32
30	$22.19	$0.00	$22.19
Totals	$692.59	$174.36	$518.23

Figure 6.8

A second variation would be to sweep the mortgage payments and purchase more life settlements with the proceeds. In Figure 6.11 50% of the mortgage payments went to purchasing more life policies. This resulted in a LSP at the end of 30 years of $11,828. Again in both examples we are investing $100 in a single mortgage. Many of the assumptions are questionable, not the least of which is the price of life settlements as they become more and more popular. Today, with redemptions among hedge funds, seniors needing cash, and lack of capital at financial institutions being the plague of the first part of the twenty-first century, LSPs are relatively cheap.

6.2.2   Credit Enhancement for the Retail Borrower

With the large amounts of foreclosures many people wanting to purchase a home will be hampered by poor credit. One programme might be to use life settlements to enhance credit. An individual with poor credit would be required to put down an amount of payment larger than

Cumulative	Loan paid back in X years
$13.61	$66.39
$26.63	$53.37
$33.03	$46.97
$38.83	$41.17
$46.06	$33.94
$54.71	$25.29
$66.64	$13.36
$80.07	$0.00
$93.57	$0.00
$111.67	$0.00
$134.12	$0.00
$150.74	$0.00
$164.81	$0.00
$183.76	$0.00
$209.16	$0.00
$241.63	$0.00
$278.84	$0.00
$316.14	$0.00
$352.87	$0.00
$389.07	$0.00
$417.06	$0.00
$433.46	$0.00
$447.30	$0.00
$466.01	$0.00
$491.20	$0.00
$523.47	$0.00
$560.50	$0.00
$597.65	$0.00
$634.27	$0.00
$670.40	$0.00
$692.59	$0.00

Figure 6.9

a standard mortgage. A portion of that payment would go towards purchasing a contestable insurance policy which would jump in value at the end of the contestability period (usually 2 years). If the individual had remained current for that trial period, then the mortgage will revert to the traditional mortgage described above and the 2-year trial period will be applied to the period required to build principal paydowns. However the jump in value of the contestable pool would be reflected in the increase in the asset value.

6.3   REVERSE MORTGAGE OR EQUITY REVERSAL PROGRAMME

A programme that has been in existence for some time is known as a reverse mortgage in the USA and an equity release scheme in the UK. As this programme has been abused in the past, we propose a fairer structure. Simply stated, a buyer of a pool of assets would offer to purchase a home usually from an elderly couple while allowing them to stay in the home rent

year	LS Payout 1st Loan	LS Payout 2nd Loan	LS Payout 3rd Loan	Total	Cumulative Total
0	$7.80			$7.80	$7.80
1	$7.21			$7.21	$15.01
2	$0.58			$0.58	$15.59
3	-$0.01			-$0.01	$15.58
4	$1.42			$1.42	$17.00
5	$2.83	$7.80		$10.63	$27.63
6	$6.12	$7.21		$13.33	$40.97
7	$7.62	$0.58		$8.20	$49.17
8	$7.69	-$0.01		$7.68	$56.84
9	$12.28	$1.42		$13.71	$70.55
10	$16.64	$2.83	$7.80	$27.27	$97.82
11	$10.82	$6.12	$7.21	$24.15	$121.97
12	$8.26	$7.62	$0.58	$16.45	$138.42
13	$13.14	$7.69	-$0.01	$20.81	$159.24
14	$19.59	$12.28	$1.42	$33.30	$192.54
15	$26.66	$16.64	$2.83	$46.13	$238.66
16	$31.40	$10.82	$6.12	$48.34	$287.00
17	$31.48	$8.26	$7.62	$47.36	$334.36
18	$30.92	$13.14	$7.69	$51.74	$386.10
19	$30.38	$19.59	$12.28	$62.26	$448.36
20	$22.19	$26.66	$16.64	$65.48	$513.84
21	$10.58	$31.40	$10.82	$52.80	$566.64
22	$8.02	$31.48	$8.26	$47.76	$614.40
23	$12.90	$30.92	$13.14	$56.96	$671.36
24	$19.38	$30.38	$19.59	$69.35	$740.71
25	$26.45	$22.19	$26.66	$75.30	$816.01
26	$31.22	$10.58	$31.40	$73.21	$889.22
27	$31.34	$8.02	$31.48	$70.85	$960.07
28	$30.80	$12.90	$30.92	$74.63	$1,034.69
29	$30.32	$19.38	$30.38	$80.08	$1,114.77
30	$22.19	$26.45	$22.19	$70.83	$1,185.60

Figure 6.10

year	Cumulative Total	year	Cumulative Total	year	Cumulative Total
0	$8	11	$122	21	$567
1	$15	12	$138	22	$614
2	$16	13	$159	23	$671
3	$16	14	$193	24	$741
4	$17	15	$239	25	$816
5	$28	16	$287	26	$889
6	$41	17	$334	27	$960
7	$49	18	$386	28	$1,035
8	$57	19	$448	29	$1,115
9	$71	20	$514	30	$1,186
10	$98			Total	$11,828

Figure 6.11

and mortgage free provided that they maintained the home and paid all living expenses, such as heating, etc., associated with the home. Maintenance will be performed by the buyer of the home. This gives the couple the ability to take out a large cash position while still allowing them to stay in the home they have known all their lives. The purchaser of the home, usually a hedge fund or asset fund, will then take possession of the home upon the death or relocation of the couple.

Modelling this type of programme offers several problems. First, the fund has to evaluate the value of the home today. Given the volatility in the housing markets this is not as easy as it once was. The second problem is the estimation of the years the couple will remain in the home. This could, however, be estimated on a conservative basis as a second-to-die life policy. Any move into a nursing home or in with family rather than death will only improve returns. The final risk is the value of the home when the fund takes possession. Neighbourhoods can deteriorate, populations can change, and any number of things can happen to reduce the value of the home in x years.

Using life settlements we can wrap a reverse mortgage programme. We can offer the couple an amount for the home and then try to re-mortgage. If we are a mortgage firm we can carry the mortgage ourselves. Using the equity built up in the home we can then purchase a life settlement plan which we can use to guarantee the value of the home at term. If the home does deteriorate in price, the LSP will hold the value of the overall investment with the value of the house just being added equity. If the value of the home does in fact increase, then the return on the investment will be at least doubled.

Again, because of the life settlement wrap, we do not need to be mercenary with the pricing we give the retirement couple, and can allow them to walk away with more cash in their pocket.

6.3.1 Home Lease Programme

Similar to a traditional balloon mortgage, the home lease allows the customer to plan on interest-only payments for 5-year periods. At the end of a 5-year term, there are three options: (a) renew the home lease for another 5-year term; (b) purchases the home with a conventional mortgage (which includes the aforementioned principal forgiveness benefits); or (c) turn it in and find something new.

Again, with a guarantee date within the 5-year term, remaining monthly payments are pure profit, before the borrower either decides to pay 60 additional months of profit (through renewing their home lease), pay 22 to 30 more years of profit (through refinancing with a conventional mortgage), or give back the property to put back into the cycle itself. Legal terms of the contract will make customers responsible for any possible devaluation of the property at turn-in, should that ever be the case.

Given that most lease programmes require a first and last month lease, and some a first, last and security deposit, a portion of that money can go into a LSP which will be used to improve the return and guarantee property value at a 5-year term or a 30-year term and any point in between.

6.4 ASSET SWAPS

6.4.1 Simple Review

Before we discuss the asset swap let us review a simple buy and hold LSP. Figures 6.12 to 6.14 are examples of a simple cash flow diagram of the purchase of a pool of life settlement

Run Off Schedule	Years	Purchase of Life Settlements	Face value of the pool at 20 cents	Premium Expense	Management fee	Underwriting Legal Admin fees	Set up fees	Total Costs
0	0	$20	$80	$0	$0.0		$0	$1	$21
0	1			$2	$0.2				$3
0	2			$2	$0.2				$3
0.05	3			$2	$0.2				$2
0.05	4			$2	$0.2				$2
0.05	5			$2	$0.2				$2
0.05	6			$2	$0.2				$2
0.1	7			$2	$0.2				$2
0.1	8			$1	$0.2				$2
0.1	9			$1	$0.2				$1
0.2	10			$1	$0.2				$1
0.2	11			$0	$0.2				$0
0.05	12			$0	$0.2				$0
Totals		$20	$80	$18	$2	$0	$1	$42

Figure 6.12

policies. It is assumed these policies are all universal or whole life and that the purchase price on average is 20 cents on the dollar, thus creating a portfolio with a face value of $100 with a $20 investment. Because this is assumed to be a straightforward purchase through a broker and not a structure with other cash flows embedded, the costs are simply: (1) the premium needed to keep the policies in force; (2) the management fee to maintain the management of the portfolio; and (3) the brokerage fee for the sale of the portfolio.

Because of liquidity reasons reviewed in detail in other chapters, an additional $25 is required to be held in reserve for a total investment of $45.

All other assumptions are the same as those set out in Chapter 4 section 4.2.1

Figures 6.12 to 6.14 show the cash flows from this simple pool.

Swapped In discounted plus cash	Run off schedule	Total In Flow	Net Flows	Cumulative	Reinvested in Life Settlement Pools
$25	$0	$25	$4	$4	$0
$0	$0	$0	-$3	$1	$0
$0	$5	$5	$2	$3	$0
$0	$5	$5	$2	$5	$0
$0	$5	$5	$2	$7	$0
$0	$5	$5	$2	$10	$0
$0	$10	$10	$8	$17	$8
$0	$10	$10	$8	$17	$8
$0	$10	$10	$8	$18	$8
$0	$20	$20	$19	$28	$19
$0	$20	$20	$20	$29	$20
$0	$10	$10	$10	$19	$10
$0	$0	$0	$0	$9	$0
$25	$100	$125	$82	$9	$73

Figure 6.13

Run Off of reinvested pool												Totals
1	2	3	4	5	6	7	8	9	10	11	12	
												$0
$0												$0
$0	$0											$0
$0	$0	$0										$0
$0	$0	$0	$0									$0
$0	$0	$0	$0	$0								$0
$0	$0	$0	$0	$0	$0							$0
$0	$0	$0	$0	$0	$2	$0						$2
$0	$0	$0	$0	$0	$2	$2	$0					$4
$0	$0	$0	$0	$0	$2	$2	$2	$0				$6
$0	$0	$0	$0	$0	$2	$2	$2	$5	$0			$11
$0	$0	$0	$0	$0	$4	$2	$2	$5	$5	$0		$18
$0	$0	$0	$0	$0	$4	$4	$2	$5	$5	$2	$0	$22
$0	$0	$0	$0	$1	$16	$12	$8	$14	$10	$2	$0	$64

Figure 6.14

As can be seen, this construction yields a $22 return in 12 years.

- $ 9 in the cumulative account
- $12 from the initial portfolio still in force ($20) sold at 60%
- $64 in reinvested life policies that matured
- $135 in reinvested life policies that were still in force and sold at 60 cents on the dollar.

In this example we use a 12-year runoff (unlike all other examples in the book). There are a number of reasons, but the most prominent is the cost of a 12-year average life compared to a 10-year average life. By continually reinvesting in life policies, the term of this structure is in reality perpetual. As a result, we arbitrarily pick a cutoff point.

Also note that any excess cash not reinvested in life policies will be held in a cash account which should yield an interest payment. We have not considered that in this analysis.

This yields an IRR of 13.5% over the life of the pool.

6.4.2   The sub-prime swap

What we propose is a sub-prime mortgage swap designed to act like any other asset swap with the benefit of moving off the balance sheet an underwater asset in exchange for a hard asset of like value (in reality this can be used with any underwater assets such as CDOs, CLOs, bonds, etc.).

The advantages to the holders of the underwater asset are that they get the asset off the books at little or no loss to the asset side of the balance sheet, and can sell the swapped asset on in the market at full value if liquidity is needed.

The advantages to the swap counter party are that the cash requirement on their side of the trade is small, no cash infusion is needed from the swapping party, and a nice return can be made in the process.

The key is the structure that backs the swapped hard asset.

Figure 6.15 is a flow chart showing how this structure will work.

Asset Swap

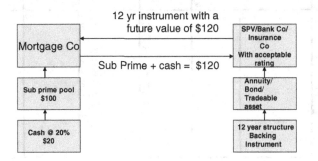

Figure 6.15

Example 6.1. *The Vanilla Swap: The purchase of life policies at 20 cents for 12 years*

As an example, Mortgage Co. holds a $100 portfolio of sub-prime loans. Bank Co. is an established bank or other established entity that can easily set up an SPV or has a credit rating of its own. The credit rating of the counterparty in the swap is of vital importance. It is needed to allow the swapped-in asset to have true value. Mortgage Co. swaps-out the $100 sub-prime portfolio to Bank Co. In addition, Mortgage Co. swaps-out $20 dollars in cash. In total, Mortgage Co. has swapped-out $120.

For the $120 Bank Co. swaps a 12-year rated bond/annuity/asset. The asset will be worth the future value of $120 compounded using the LIBOR curve or some other form of future valuing. If we assume a 5% flat LIBOR curve, $120 compounded at 5% for 12 years would be worth $215. Bank Co. swaps a very real investment grade asset worth $215 in 12 years.

If Mortgage Co. wishes, they can hold the asset earning LIBOR and carry the asset on the books at $120 today without fear of an underwater asset being marked to market, or they can simply sell the asset on to gain liquidity.

Bank Co. would do the deal because they put no cash into the deal. Much of the $215 required payout in 12 years can be funded with the cash from Mortgage Co. and some of the value from the "swapped-in" sub-prime pool. Any and all value above what is needed to fund the $215 is pure profit.

In this example, Figures 6.16 to 6.18 show that what is required from the sub-prime portfolio is $75 plus the $20 cash.

As can be seen, $20 of the $120 is used to purchase a life settlement pool with $80 in death benefit. That leaves $100 of the mortgage pool to be used elsewhere. Because the LSPs don't throw off any cash in the first few years, a reserve cash account is needed. In Figure 6.17 the heading titled "cumulative" shows the cumulative cash account throughout the life of the structure. We assume that the cash account has to cover at least 3 years of expenses at the start and should never let the cumulative account go into the red.

For that reason we need to bring in at least $75 from the sub-prime pool. As shown in Figures 6.16 to 6.18 this structure produces the approximate $215 needed in year 12 to fund the bond, including the LIBOR flat coupon and all expenses.

However a 75% payout on the mortgage pool is probably at the top end of the real market value of that pool. It is not beyond the realm of reason, but certainly at the top end of

Run Off Schedule	Years	Purchase of Life Settlements	Face value of the pool at 20 cents	Premium Expense	Management fee	Underwriting Legal Admin fees	Set up fees	Total Costs
0	0	$20	$80	$0	$0.0	$0	$1	$21
0	1			$2	$0.2			$3
0	2			$2	$0.2			$3
0.05	3			$2	$0.2			$2
0.05	4			$2	$0.2			$2
0.05	5			$2	$0.2			$2
0.05	6			$2	$0.2			$2
0.1	7			$2	$0.2			$2
0.1	8			$1	$0.2			$2
0.1	9			$1	$0.2			$1
0.2	10			$1	$0.2			$1
0.2	11			$0	$0.2			$0
0.05	12			$0	$0.2			$0
Totals		$20	$80	$18	$2	$0	$1	$42

Figure 6.16

expectations and if any assumptions used in this example miss on the downside, the $215 payout at year 12 might be missed.

All assumptions used above are extremely conservative as already stated, and there are a number of ways of making this structure much more profitable. For example:

1. The assumption of swapping-in full value for the sub-prime pool. Most holders of a sub-prime pool would be happy to receive a discount for their pools. This could greatly reduce the $215 value needed in year 12 of the security swapped-out.
2. Using a longer term will enhance the yield on the LSP by allowing the reinvested pools to mature. Remember, in Example 6.1 we are using a 5 to 1 leverage with little risk of

Swapped In discounted plus cash	Run off schedule	Total In Flow	Net Flows	Cumulative	Reinvested in Life Settlement Pools
$75	$0	$75	$54	$54	$0
$0	$0	$0	-$9	$45	$29
$0	$5	$5	-$4	$12	$0
$0	$5	$5	-$4	$8	$0
$0	$5	$5	-$4	$4	$0
$0	$5	$5	-$4	$1	$0
$0	$10	$10	$2	$2	$0
$0	$10	$10	$2	$4	$0
$0	$10	$10	$2	$7	$0
$0	$20	$20	$13	$20	$4
$0	$20	$20	$14	$29	$14
$0	$10	$10	$4	$19	$4
$0	$0	$0	-$6	$9	$0
$75	$100	$175	$60	$9	$51

Figure 6.17

Run Off of reinvested pool													Totals
1	2	3	4	5	6	7	8	9	10	11	12		
$0													$0
$7	$0												$0
$7	$0	$0											$7
$7	$0	$0	$0										$7
$7	$0	$0	$0	$0									$7
$15	$0	$0	$0	$0	$0								$7
$15	$0	$0	$0	$0	$0	$0							$15
$15	$0	$0	$0	$0	$0	$0	$0						$15
$29	$0	$0	$0	$0	$0	$0	$0	$0					$15
$29	$0	$0	$0	$0	$0	$0	$0	$1	$0				$29
$15	$0	$0	$0	$0	$0	$0	$0	$1	$3	$0			$30
$0	$0	$0	$0	$0	$0	$0	$0	$1	$3	$1	$0		$19
													$5
$146	$0	$0	$0	$0	$0	$0	$0	$3	$7	$1	$0		$157

Figure 6.18

loss. The more we can use this leverage, the more return we can generate. Also the most sought-after term within this structure seems to be a 10-year term. As a result, moving the term out to 12, 15, 20+ years reduces the costs of the policies and increases the riskless leverage.

3. Using pools of life policies that are not the most sought after will be priced much lower. Policies such as variable life policies or contestable policies have a much lower cost basis.

4. Using leverage, i.e. borrowing funds to generate this structure, give an added return in that it uses a double leverage, the leverage of the borrowing costs to the return on the structure and the leverage in the purchase price of the life policies.

In Example 6.2 below, we use contestable policies. As explained below, because these policies may be cancellable by the issuing insurance company at any time over the next one to two years, there is an added risk and a reduced cost. Many of these policies can be purchased in the 10–12 cent range for a 10-year life, and lower for an extended life. We use a 10 cent value below.

Example 6.2. *The Vanilla Swap: The purchase of life policies at 10 cent costs for 12 years*

This example is the same as Example 6.1, with the exception that here we substitute contestable policies for non-contestable policies. Figures 6.19 to 6.21 show the results of using the contestable policies costing only 12 cents.

Using the assumptions above, swapping-in $100 of sub-prime pools and $20 of cash can be invested in life settlement pools which will generate $215 (actually $256) in 12 years with only $5 of the sub-prime pool needed. Any and all amounts above that on the sale or management of the sub-prime pool are pure profit. But notice once again the "cumulative" column.

6.4.3 Risks of this Transaction

One risk that is very obvious. In Figure 6.20, under the heading of "cumulative", the cash flows in the first year are substantially negative if we bring in only $5 from the sub-prime portfolio. In the end this portfolio will generate a residual value of approximately $256 to pay

Run Off Schedule	Years	Purchase of Life Settlements	Face value of the pool at 10 cents	Premium Expense	Management fee	Set up fees	Paid out Asset	Total Out Flow
0	0	$20	$200	$0	$0.0	$1	$0	$21
0	1	$0	$0	$6	$0.2	$0	$0	$6
0.05	2	$0	$0	$6	$0.2	$0	$0	$6
0.05	3	$0	$0	$5	$0.2	$0	$0	$5
0.05	4	$0	$0	$5	$0.2	$0	$0	$5
0.05	5	$0	$0	$5	$0.2	$0	$0	$5
0.1	6	$0	$0	$4	$0.2	$0	$0	$4
0.1	7	$0	$0	$3	$0.2	$0	$0	$4
0.1	8	$0	$0	$3	$0.2	$0	$0	$3
0.2	9	$0	$0	$2	$0.2	$0	$0	$2
0.2	10	$0	$0	$1	$0.2	$0	$0	$1
0.1	11	$0	$0	$0	$0.2	$0	$0	$0
0	12	$0	$0	$0	$0.2	$0	$0	$0
Totals		$20	$200	$39	$2	$1	$0	$62

Figure 6.19

out the required $215 or 21% IRR, but – like most optimization programmes getting from A to B – you go out of business.

Again, because LSPs generate no cash flows initially you have to set up a cash reserve to cover this shortfall. Using optimizations to maximize the residual value, and yet show no substantial negative cumulative cash flows, produces the need to bring in $40 from the sub-prime portfolio. However, this produces a residual value of $440 with which to pay the $215, leaving a residual value profit of $225: All this on no investment. As they say in the mortgage business, "the bank has no skin in the game".

Another risk to consider would be the volatility to the earnings stream. Marking the sub-prime portfolio to market will create a problem. Valuation models are all over the board as far as acceptable calculations are concerned. Taking the high road and simply marking the

Swapped In discounted plus cash	Run off schedule	Total In Flow	Net Flows	Cumulative	Reinvested in Life Settlement Pools
$5	$0	$5	-$16	-$16	$0
$0	$0	$0	-$12	-$28	$0
$0	$10	$10	-$2	-$30	$0
$0	$10	$10	-$1	-$31	$0
$0	$10	$10	-$1	-$32	$0
$0	$10	$10	-$1	-$33	$0
$0	$20	$20	$10	-$24	$0
$0	$20	$20	$10	-$13	$0
$0	$20	$20	$11	-$2	$0
$0	$40	$40	$32	$30	$0
$0	$40	$40	$33	$63	$33
$0	$20	$20	$14	$44	$14
$0	$0	$0	-$6	$24	$0
$5	$200	$205	$71	$24	$47

Figure 6.20

Run Off of reinvested pool												Totals
1	2	3	4	5	6	7	8	9	10	11	12	
$0												$0
$0	$0											$0
$0	$0	$0										$0
$0	$0	$0	$0									$0
$0	$0	$0	$0	$0								$0
$0	$0	$0	$0	$0	$0							$0
$0	$0	$0	$0	$0	$0	$0						$0
$0	$0	$0	$0	$0	$0	$0	$0					$0
$0	$0	$0	$0	$0	$0	$0	$0	$0				$0
$0	$0	$0	$0	$0	$0	$0	$0	$0	$0			$0
$0	$0	$0	$0	$0	$0	$0	$0	$0	$16	$0		$16
$0	$0	$0	$0	$0	$0	$0	$0	$0	$16	$7	$0	$23
$0	$0	$0	$0	$0	$0	$0	$0	$0	$33	$7	$0	$40

Figure 6.21

pools down upon purchase doesn't offer much help. The minute you sell the asset there is a good chance that the value will be marked back up again, causing large swings to earnings. Remember that these sub-prime portfolios have real estate behind them and the possibility of being marked down substantially is low, since, in the last resort, there is still land to consider.

The volatility issue is a theoretical argument we would love to debate. Using a Sharpe Ratio, a portfolio that has a volatility of +5% to –5% is supposedly less volatile (less risk) than a portfolio that moves from +50% to +100%. There should, however, be no question of what the investor would prefer, even with the high volatility.

The other risk is yet to play out. There are law suits in the courts regarding the treatments of the resale of contestable insurance policies. However, given the benefit to the consumer and holder of the policy, we feel that there should always be a way around any objection and, as yet, no decisions have been made and should not be grandfathered in allowing anything in place to continue.

6.5   THE PENSION SWAP

The asset swap for pensions is almost identical to the sub-prime mortgage swap and can in fact be used for any underwater asset (see Figure 6.22). The extension to the process is not rocket science, as even an investment in a treasury bond will yield a 1.6 times return in 10 years at a 5% compounded rate. Given a 5% compounded return, a $1 investment will yield $1.60 in 10 years, and on a $2 loan, taking $1 and putting it into a reserve will guarantee 80% of the loan in 10 years. In fact there are a number of lending programmes in place at present that do almost that, or are a variation on that theme.

If it is a managed programme, the LSP programme offers the advantage of a potential return in double digits with little risk, as shown above. The main difference with the pension swap is the legal challenges to overcome; pensions are heavily regulated and exactly how funds can be invested and what firms can and cannot do with the pensions are very controlled.

An added advantage to this process is that it has already been put in place in London and blessed by the regulators. It was put in place by a major law firm acting on behalf of their client. The client had recently been resurrected from bankruptcy and now was in the process of a merger, the problem with the merger being the underwater pension the company controlled.

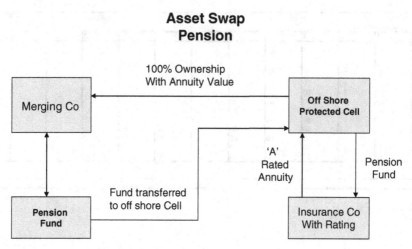

Figure 6.22

By moving the pension to an off-shore protected cell and then allowing the firm to own 100% of the cell, the firm could then swap the pension portfolio for an A-rated annuity which would pay full value for the pension in 10 years. The annuity was backed by a pool of life settlement policies with a face value in excess of the pension value in 10 years. The pool was then insured, guaranteeing the principal payment of the face value, in 10 years. This guaranteed annuity could then be swapped-in and placed on the books at full value negating the underwater pension fund and allowing the value placed on the merger to increase substantially.

6.6   A NEW CPPI PRODUCT

Below we look at a CPPI study done for a major London bank. The process had three different sets of asset classes: a riskless asset (Treasury bonds); a risky asset (Equity index); and cash. We review the process, without going into the actual testing of the system review. Much of the study concerned itself with the simulation process and the correlation between bonds and stocks. We then substitute a new asset class, a low-risk asset class (life settlements) and review the outcome. As will be seen, much of the simulation needs will be eliminated due to the low correlation and volatility risk of the life settlement asset class as opposed to the sensitivities of both the Treasuries and Equities to variables within the market.

6.6.1   The Initial CPPI Study

With the irrational exuberance seen in the markets during the 1990s portfolio insurance fell out of favour, but with the downturn in the markets over the last few years there has been a resurgence in portfolio protection. Because of the turmoil in the markets over the last several years' downside, protections with regard to investments has become very popular and a number of firms have engaged in the practice of insuring funds and investments. Even the hedge fund industry has brought to the market insurance protection. Underwriters such as the Lloyds group have provided wrappers around funds for a number of years now.

The original concept, introduced by Leland and Rubinstein, was Option Based Portfolio Insurance (OBPI). The OBPI was extended about a decade later by several authors – Penrod, Sharpe, Black and Jones among them – to include Constant Proportionality Portfolio Insurance (CPPI). The CPPI product synthetically replicates the option in OBPI and is generally cheaper than the OBPI.

The CPPI fund guarantees the investor that a predetermined percentage of the entire fund is invested in equity (the risky asset) while the remaining funds are kept in a risk-free asset like a zero coupon Treasury bond. This percentage is keyed off the clean price of the underlying risk-free investment. Should the fund fall in value, the percentage of equity is reduced and eventually converted entirely into the Treasury bond. To keep the transaction costs small, the adjustments are only done if the realized equity component deviates from the target percentage by a certain percentage. Once the equity percentage of the fund is below a predetermined level, the entire equity holdings are converted into the Treasury bond (plus cash and an equity option). At all times a small percentage of the fund is kept in cash.

6.6.2 Allocation Process

The Guaranteed Investment Fund allocates a specific proportion of the assets to equity. Specifically, the equity value of the fund *Equity(t)* at time *t* equals

$$Equity(t) = 3.3\,NAV(t)\left(1 - \frac{B_t(t)}{NAV(t)}\right), \tag{6.1}$$

where

Equity(t) = equity value of the fund
NAV = the combined value of the fund or Cash + Equity
$B_t(t)$ = the Clean Bond at time t

NAV is the Net Asset Value of the fund, assumed to be 100% initially but then changes as the bond and equity part of the fund starts to return value. The Treasury bond here has a coupon, which will equal all or part of the fee extracted from the fund, depending on the coupon size. The multiplier 3.3 is applied for initial leverage and a number of papers have been written exploring the optimal multiplier (see below).

A cash reserve is kept at all times and accrues continually while the non-equity part of the fund is kept in the riskless asset.

The Bond Fund manager (riskless asset) simply agrees to a floor value at the end of the term equal to 100%, so the investor has been provided with a put option guaranteeing the notional of their investment.

On a daily basis, as time goes on, the portfolio is adjusted until the actual equity percentage of the portfolio deviates by more than 5% from the target weight introduced above. Hence, the change in the *Equity* component is zero unless:

$$Abs\left(\frac{Actual\ Equity(t)}{Equity(t)} - 1.0\right) > 5\%. \tag{6.2}$$

Once the *Actual Equity(t)/NAV(t)* becomes less than 3%, the entire equity holding is converted into the Treasury bond.

	Initial %		Initial $
NAV(0)	100%	NAV(0)	$330.00
Treasury	60%	Treasury	$198.00
Equity	40%	Equity	$132.00
Multiplier	3.3	Multiplier	

Figure 6.23

Given a 5% flat 10-year rate on the Treasury bond, the zero would cost around 60%. Therefore, given the equation above, the equity portion of the CPPI initially would be:

$$Equity = 3.3 \times \left(1 - \frac{60}{100}\right)$$
$$Equity = \$132$$

Figure 6.23 shows the set up of the programme.

Figure 6.24 shows the liquidation prospects for a 5-year exit strategy if there is a 1 standard deviation fall in the equity value and a 2 standard deviation fall in value. Under a 1 standard deviation fall in equity value the fund would still be in force after 5 years, but would have lost $34 or 10% of its value, although the floor would still be in place. If the fall in equity prices were more along the lines of what we have experienced in 2008, the equity fund would have been liquidated and the entire fund would be in Treasuries. The loss in the fund would be $76 or 23% of its value. After 10 years the Treasuries would have grown to the initial $330 and the fund would have returned principal.

$$Actual\ Equity(t)/NAV(t) < 3\%$$

If, instead of Treasuries, the fund invested in Life Settlements as the riskless asset (a less risky asset although not completely riskless), the fund would not be liquidated even under the extreme conditions of 2008 (see Figures 6.25 and 6.26).

In fact the fund would still be up 4% under a 1 standard deviation move down in equities and up 2% in a 2 standard deviation move in equities.

Again much of the study was done to determine the volatility and correlation risk in this programme using Treasuries. As interest rates moved, the value of the Treasuries moved and the floor was in essence a moving target. Equities exhibit a jump diffusion process. As a result, any simulation testing has to include this process. With the Life Settlement process the equity movement is dampened and interest rates are not a problem.

	Liquidation 5 yr exit	
	1 std down	2 std down
NAV(t)	$295.96	$253.68
Treasury	$252.70	$252.70
Equity	$43.25	$0.98

Figure 6.24

	Initial %		Initial $
NAV(0)	100%	NAV(0)	$330.00
Life Settlements	60%	Life Settlements	$198.00
Equity	40%	Equity	$132.00

Figure 6.25

	Liquidation	5 yr exit
	1 std down	2 std down
NAV(t)	$343.96	$336.60
Life Settlements	$289.89	$318.88
Equity	$54.07	$17.72

Figure 6.26

6.7 CONCLUSION

This has been a catch-all chapter grouping many of the non-traditional uses for life settlements. The basic theory is quite simple. Any time we can purchase an asset for cents on the dollar, and be certain that the dollar will be there in x years, the calculation of worth is straightforward. And if the purchase price is a small percentage of the final value, we can combine that process in many ways to produce exciting and profitable products.

Life settlements have been shown to be of low risk with a certainty of payout; the only major risks involved being those of longevity and liquidity. We address these two risks in more detail in the next two chapters.

7

Life Settlement Derivatives

INTRODUCTION

The standard definition of a derivative is that it is a financial contract whose value changes in response to changes in an underlying instrument. The main types of derivatives are futures, forwards, options and swaps. Most, if not all, derivatives were developed to manage risk. The price of a derivative is usually, but not always, low relative to the underlying. In some cases such as an interest rate swap, fair pricing at inception for the exchange of future interest payments would give this derivative contract a value of zero. With option type contracts, it is also important to distinguish between the buyer of the option and the writer of it; the buyer's exposure is limited to the acquisition cost but the writer's may be unlimited. There is an effective leverage inherent in many derivative structures, but this brings the benefit of improved market liquidity for traded contracts. Most of the derivatives covered in this chapter, however, have significant costs and are limited in effective leverage. Further, many of those discussed below do not yet have established trading markets.

Chapter 5 introduced derivatives. Longevity bonds, inverse longevity bonds, and barrier products like PACs, are all forms of derivatives generating their value from an underlying instrument. This can itself be financial in nature, or more general such as accident occurrence; in this latter case the derivative needs to specify the financial consequence of the underlying event. Though the structures above are covered in passing, the main focus of this chapter is upon more advanced, perhaps exotic instruments. The purpose of such developments is, of course, increasingly specific risk management.

7.1 LONGEVITY BONDS

Chapter 5 considered longevity, inverse longevity and barrier bonds. These structures are combinations of vanilla instruments and derivatives; all have application in risk management.

Initially developed in 2003 by Swiss Re, this bond offered a LIBOR + 135 bps coupon but the repayment of principal was dependent upon the performance the mortality rate of the standardized index established at the time of inception of the bond. The principal would be repaid in full provided that the rate of this chosen mortality index did not exceed 1.3 times the base rate; and this type of arrangement is often referred to as a "parametric trigger". The principal would reduce by 5% for every 0.01% increase in the mortality index above the base rate.

If the mortality rate fell, causing longevity or extension risk, the bond would continue to pay a healthy coupon and the principal in full. If the mortality increased above the trigger level, the issuer (a re-insurer) would benefit through lower principal repayment and also lower interest payments on the reduced principal. In the case of failure to trigger lower principal repayments, Swiss Re, the issuer, would benefit from the extension of premium payments on the underlying insurance contracts that this security was used to hedge. The term of the bond was only 3 years, which is a very short time frame for mortality or extension risk.

In 2004 another issue entered the market, a longer term longevity bond. This bond had a substantially longer term of 25 years and linked the coupon payments to a survivor index, a coupon at risk structure.

The coupon on the bond started with a payout 1 times a fixed coupon, year on $S(0)$. Each year the death rate was calculated and multiplied by the previous year's death rate, commencing from the starting point of $S(0) = 1$. If the death rates increased year over year, the coupon decreased. The principal, however, was guaranteed by a re-insurer and a major European Bank.

As can be seen from these examples, the market in traded mortality linked securities is relatively young, but opportunities exist as the need to hedge mortality increases.

7.2 ASSET SWAP

Asset swaps have been used in the past to hedge longevity risk. While few in nature, the idea is growing, save for the fact that more efficient methods discussed below may overtake the volume of asset swap trading in the future.

The idea is simple. An annuity provider will swap a portfolio of annuities for a portfolio of life insurance policies issued by a life insurance carrier. For the annuity provider an extension of mortality causes returns to fall, as the annuitant will receive payment from the provider for a longer period of time. For the life carrier, however, an extension of mortality is a benefit. The life provider receives cash flow for an extended period of time and pushes back the payment on the life policy. As a result, exchanging or swapping assets would cause a natural hedge diversifying mortality risk.

These products have to be custom set-ups and have large basis risk. A shock to the mortality of either side of the trade will cause what initially was a matched trade to be off. Given this, it is still a preferable hedge against extension risk as opposed to carrying the risk un-hedged. We will talk more about the asset swap in the next chapter and give some examples.

7.2.1 Deterministic Mortality Swap

We can see from the above that natural hedging will help to lower risk and therefore prices. However, natural hedging is very expensive in itself and may force the insurer to realign his business. Of late, several investment banks have established a mortality index. These constructs are very new and as yet have not become the vanilla product used in hedging longevity, but newer innovation in financial products may be the way to reduce risk and improve balance sheet efficiency and therefore profit.

Financial indices have been in use for almost 100 years in America, with the Dow Jones Index the best-known example. Indices in Europe can be traced back to the fourteenth century. The design and calculation of indices varies significantly with their use and function. The types we will be considering are usually referred to as "tracker" indices and their primary use is as a benchmark against which other portfolios or indices can be compared and measured.

Population statistics or indices for mortality or longevity have therefore two forms of basis risk: the usual statistical sampling risk, that the population insured differs in material ways from the overall population; and also a weighting risk, that the weights due to policy size or value bias the insured population yet further. We consider these issues later.

7.2.2   Mortality Swap: Single payment

In this example we look at mortality swaps which exchanges payments of "anticipated for actual" at term, the actual payment being the random event. As stated, this derivative bears a resemblance to a reinsurance product. However, as it is not an insurance product it is not affected by the legal features of an insurance contract. If there is no insurable interest, the contract is generally a legal contract between parties and any risks associated with the transactions are risks associated with the counterparties. Insurance contracts have insurable interest and allow for an exit, given that the insured somehow misrepresents their position.

To date there have been few single pay mortality swaps and all have been "over the counter" customized trades. Because of the specificity of the trade no liquidity of a market is needed and the only real risk, other than the basis risk in the trade, is counterparty risk.

At the inception the two parties agree to exchange a single payment at term. As such, at time t the two parties agree to exchange payments $K(t)$, a preset amount, for $S(t)$, an unknown amount, at time T. The contract is almost exactly like a Forward Rate Agreement where one counterparty agrees to pay a fixed rate at the end of a term and receive a floating rate at term, whatever that floating rate may be. Here counterparty A would agree to pay $K(t)$ at the onset, which would be a mortality rate based on a reference curve, and receive from counterparty B a mortality rate $S(t)$ at time T based on a realized rate from B's portfolio. If at term T, $K(T) > S(T)$ then B pays $(K(T) - S(T))$ times the notional amount. If $S(T) > K(T)$, then A pays B $(S(T) - K(T))$ times the notional amount. The notional here can be the size of the reference portfolio. We discuss later the possibility of establishing a reference mortality index replicating the LIBOR curve in the interest rate environment. Several firms are moving in this direction.

Also note that $K(t)$ can be a fixed rate or the rate of a referenced portfolio in which case we would have a floating to floating exchange, both over a single period.

7.2.3   Mortality Swap: Multiple Periods

If we let t reset over a period of time then $t = 1, 2, 3, \ldots, T$ and what evolves is a vanilla interest rate swap using mortality. To limit counterparty risk the exchange of cash flows is done at each time t. Again this can be a fixed vs floating or a floating vs floating.

Figure 7.1 illustrates a basic mortality curve, the younger the individual the less chance of mortality.

Figure 7.2 represents a simple mortality swap at term. Here the reference curve is compared to the realized curve and exchanges of payments are made. The payment being the difference in the mortality rate times the notional amount of the swap agreed to at the initiation of the contract.

Figure 7.3 is an example of a fixed rate swap. Here we establish a fixed mortality rate at the onset of the contract. At term this fixed rate is compared to the fixed rate of the customer portfolio over the life of the investment, or payment can be exchanged over time.

A variation to this would be the equivalent of a default swap. While called a swap it is really an option because the purchaser of the protection has the option as to whether or not to exercise the contract. If there is no default there would be no reason to exercise the default swap.

The mortality swap modelled after the default swap would allow the purchaser of the mortality swap the option of exercising the swap. If, at term, the mortality rate of the standardized

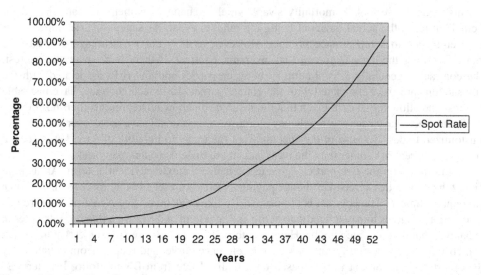

Figure 7.1 Spot mortality rate.

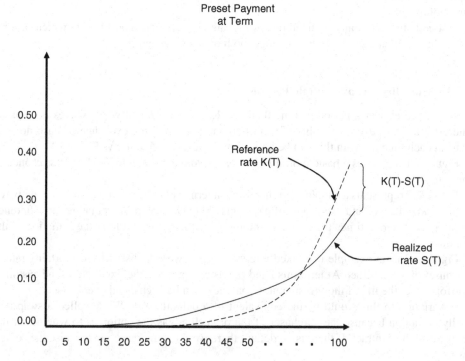

Figure 7.2 Mortality swap.

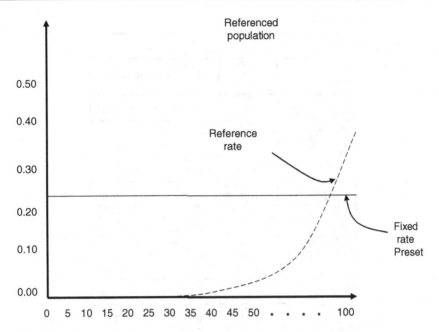

Figure 7.3 Mortality rate.

base was lower than the portfolio, the purchaser would walk away, given that they were trying to protect against extension risk. If, however, the mortality rate of the standardized base rate were higher, the purchaser of the swap could exercise the swap and obtain the pool of life settlements with the higher mortality rate.

We looked at default swaps and their relationship to mortality swaps in Chapter 2 when we discussed the stochastic process.

7.3 MORTALITY CURVES

Table 7.1 below shows the mortality rate for males and females age 65 in the USA.

From the information in Table 7.1 we can create a spot mortality curve by bootstrapping. Letting $S(0)$ equal year 0 with no mortality we have:

$$S(0) = 1$$
$$S(1) = S(0) \times (1 - (d(t + 1)))$$
$$S(2) = S(0) \times (1 - d(t + 1)) \times (1 - d(t + 2))$$
$$S(t) = S(0) \times (1 - d(t + 1)) \times (1 - d(t + 2)) \times \wedge \times (1 - d(t + n))$$

where $(1 - d(t))$ is the death rate at time t.

In our initial calculation we are forced to use a survival curve, starting with year 0 equal to 100% survival, because forcing out a calculation using a mortality curve will start with a year 0 of 0, and any calculation from that curve will not make sense. Here we look at a survival curve and then assume a calculation of 1 minus the survival rate will equate to a mortality

Table 7.1

Year	Exact Age	Probability of Death within 1 year	Number of Lifes	Life Expectancy
			Males	
1	65	0.017976	79,190	16.67
2	66	0.019564	77,766	15.96
3	67	0.021291	76,245	15.27
4	68	0.023162	74,621	14.59
5	69	0.025217	72,893	13.93
6	70	0.027533	71,055	13.27
7	71	0.030131	69,098	12.64
8	72	0.032978	67,016	12.01
9	73	0.036086	64,806	11.41
10	74	0.039506	62,468	10.81
11	75	0.043415	60,000	10.24
12	76	0.047789	57,395	9.68
13	77	0.052464	54,652	9.14
14	78	0.057413	51,785	8.62
15	79	0.062789	48,812	8.11
16	80	0.068836	45,747	7.62
17	81	0.075724	42,598	7.15
18	82	0.083466	39,372	6.7
19	83	0.092144	36,086	6.26
20	84	0.101803	32,761	5.84
21	85	0.112468	29,426	5.45
22	86	0.124164	26,116	5.08
23	87	0.136917	22,874	4.73
24	88	0.150754	19,742	4.4
25	89	0.165704	16,766	4.09
26	90	0.181789	13,988	3.8
27	91	0.199019	11,445	3.54
28	92	0.217396	9,167	3.29
29	93	0.236906	7,174	3.06
30	94	0.257525	5,475	2.86
31	95	0.278031	4,065	2.68
32	96	0.298111	2,935	2.52
33	97	0.317432	2,060	2.38
34	98	0.335655	1,406	2.25
35	99	0.352438	934	2.13
36	100	0.37006	605	2.02
37	101	0.388563	381	1.91
38	102	0.407991	233	1.81
39	103	0.42839	138	1.71
40	104	0.44981	79	1.61
41	105	0.4723	43	1.52
42	106	0.495915	23	1.43
43	107	0.520711	12	1.35
44	108	0.546747	6	1.26
45	109	0.574084	3	1.19
46	110	0.602788	1	1.11
47	111	0.632928	0	1.04
48	112	0.664574	0	0.97
49	113	0.697803	0	0.91
50	114	0.732693	0	0.84
51	115	0.769327	0	0.78
52	116	0.807794	0	0.72
53	117	0.848183	0	0.67
54	118	0.890592	0	0.62
55	119	0.935122	0	0.57

(Continued)

Table 7.1 (*Continued*)

| Year | Females | | | | |
	Probability of Death within 1 year	Number of Lifes	Life Expectancy	Total Population Prob of Dying Within 1 Year	Spot Rate $R_s(t,T)$
1	0.011511	87,031	19.5	2.95%	
2	0.012572	86,029	18.72	3.21%	0.26%
3	0.013772	84,947	17.95	3.51%	0.29%
4	0.01513	83,777	17.19	3.83%	0.32%
5	0.016651	82,510	16.45	4.19%	0.36%
6	0.018406	81,136	15.72	4.59%	0.41%
7	0.020342	79,643	15.01	5.05%	0.45%
8	0.022346	78,023	14.31	5.53%	0.49%
9	0.024382	76,279	13.62	6.05%	0.51%
10	0.026551	74,419	12.95	6.61%	0.56%
11	0.029073	72,443	12.29	7.25%	0.64%
12	0.032023	70,337	11.64	7.98%	0.73%
13	0.035307	68,085	11.01	8.78%	0.80%
14	0.038949	65,681	10.4	9.64%	0.86%
15	0.043047	63,123	9.8	10.58%	0.95%
16	0.047769	60,405	9.22	11.66%	1.08%
17	0.05319	57,520	8.65	12.89%	1.23%
18	0.059279	54,460	8.11	14.27%	1.38%
19	0.06608	51,232	7.59	15.82%	1.55%
20	0.073685	47,847	7.09	17.55%	1.73%
21	0.082199	44,321	6.62	19.47%	1.92%
22	0.091712	40,678	6.17	21.59%	2.12%
23	0.102294	36,947	5.74	23.92%	2.33%
24	0.11399	33,168	5.33	26.47%	2.55%
25	0.12682	29,387	4.96	29.25%	2.78%
26	0.140793	25,660	4.6	32.26%	3.01%
27	0.155906	22,047	4.28	35.49%	3.23%
28	0.172147	18,610	3.97	38.95%	3.46%
29	0.189496	15,406	3.7	42.64%	3.69%
30	0.207925	12,487	3.44	46.55%	3.90%
31	0.226597	9,891	3.22	50.46%	3.92%
32	0.245258	7,649	3.01	54.34%	3.87%
33	0.263628	5,773	2.83	58.11%	3.77%
34	0.28141	4,251	2.66	61.71%	3.60%
35	0.298294	3,055	2.5	65.07%	3.37%
36	0.316192	2,144	2.36	68.63%	3.55%
37	0.335163	1,466	2.22	72.37%	3.75%
38	0.355273	975	2.08	76.33%	3.95%
39	0.37659	628	1.95	80.50%	4.17%
40	0.399185	392	1.83	84.90%	4.40%
41	0.423136	235	1.71	89.54%	4.64%
42	0.448524	136	1.6	94.44%	4.90%
43	0.475436	75	1.49	99.61%	5.17%
44	0.503962	39	1.39	105.07%	5.46%
45	0.534199	19	1.29	110.83%	5.76%
46	0.566251	9	1.2	116.90%	6.08%
47	0.600226	4	1.11	123.32%	6.41%
48	0.63624	2	1.03	130.08%	6.77%
49	0.674414	1	0.95	137.22%	7.14%
50	0.714879	0	0.87	144.76%	7.54%
51	0.757772	0	0.8	152.71%	7.95%
52	0.803238	0	0.73	161.10%	8.39%
53	0.848183	0	0.67	169.64%	8.53%
54	0.890592	0	0.62	178.12%	8.48%
55	0.935122			187.02%	8.91%

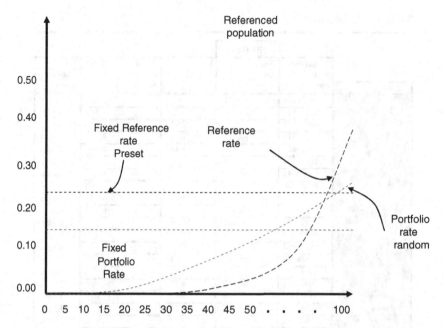

Figure 7.4   Mortality rate.

rate. Again, like many assumptions in this book, this could be argued but we are just trying to demonstrate the possibilities without going into the minutia of the calculations.

Here $S(0)$ is the start of the process. In the example above, where the coupon was at risk, the issuer took the underlying central death rates of the population as a whole. The process could be established for any cohort population. At $S(0)$ the population is healthy with 100% survival rate. At $S(1)$ we multiply the initial survival rate (100%) times the death rate that occurred in our population in year 1. At $S(2)$ we carry this out one step further, looking at the death rate in year 2. This process is bootstrapped until term, the end of the investment, $d(t + n)$. In this way we establish a survival curve for our specific population. Figure 7.5 shows the graphs of both the survival curve from Table 7.1 and the mortality curve. When we expand our analysis into forward rates and option pricing it will be the mortality curve that we need to force out forward rates, as explained later in this chapter.

The rest of this chapter is very hypothetical – the products described are in a very early stage of development, at best. However, progress is being made and the "building blocks" are in place with which to develop. As we know, "necessity is the mother of invention", and as these markets grow so will products to hedge longevity risks. In a few short years the credit derivative markets went from a theory to a $42 trillion industry simply because it fulfilled a huge need. We feel the life settlement industry has the potential to grow likewise. Given the lack of product at present, this is just a very summary discussion.

7.3.1   The Forward Mortality Rate

Through most of this text we have been looking at a deterministic world. We have assumed that the expectations used were real and realized. As such we could look at the cash flows thrown

Percentage

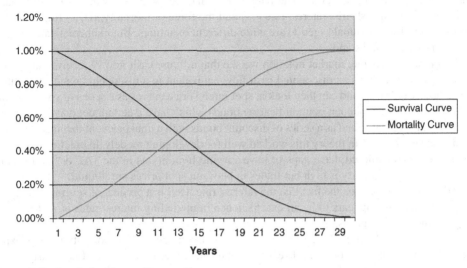

Figure 7.5 Survival and mortality curves.

off and calculate returns. In the above examples we were modelling what was in essence a one-term asset swap. At each term we viewed the actual mortality rate between each asset and settled up payment. Pricing could be based upon life expectancies provided by the actuaries, and forward expectations were not all that necessary as we were settling up using realized rates of mortality.

Moving forward into the capital markets, a better forward pricing methodology was needed to price derivative products such as caps and floors and swaps. It wasn't enough to wait till $t + 1$ time frame to see what the realized mortality rates were to price a derivative product. We needed to price the product from the start. Taking our queue from the interest rate markets, we saw that there was an arbitrage that could be established between the fixed rate and the floating rate in a swap, given a lack of equilibrium in the forward rate. For that reason, over the next few pages, we will review the forward rate pricing methodology within the interest rate market using Rebonato methods and then port this methodology over to the mortality rate. The methodologies are almost the same, except for the problem with the cohort population, which we will explain below.

All derivative products were designed to hedge risks in one way or another. Derivative development in the mortality world is no different. Longevity risk is the major risk with any instrument that is exposed to mortality. Mortality risk, like equity risk, can be broken down into two distinct parts: unsystematic risk and systematic risk.

Like equity risk, unsystematic risk can be diversified away. As shown in Chapter 4, a standard deviation around the expected mean can be measured using the formula: $\frac{\mu}{\sqrt{N}}$ where μ is the mean life expectancy of the pool and $\sqrt{N}$ is the square root of the number of life policies in the pool. As $N \Rightarrow \infty$ the variance around the mean μ goes to zero.

However, the systematic risk, $p =$ expected life, cannot be diversified and this is the problem in pricing both a life policy and a pool of life policies.

What was needed was a process that would allow expectations to be tied down and allow the forward pricing of mortality. The interest rate markets offered a wide variety of models but the underlying risk-free interest rate $r(s)$ and the force of mortality $u(t, x)$ (the mortality rate at time t for individuals aged x) are quite different quantities. But mathematically we can represent them as the same.

From the interest rate market notation we see that a future cash flow N received at term T, when looked at today, is a discounted cash flow equivalent to a discounted bond. We denote these bonds as $P(t, T)$ and can then look at spot interest rate curves as a series of spot discount bond prices. In like manner, coupon-bearing bonds which have a certain coupon at a specific term can also be described as a series of discount bonds with a final payment that includes both principal and interest. In theory this worked well for developing models. In practice many rate curves are either illiquid, have gaps or have varying liquidity as in the TAP or "on the run" bonds where the liquidity is high but trades in between spot prices are illiquid.

Add to those problems the fact that the interest rate itself is a product of several underlying variables and what appears to be an exact science in modelling interest rates is, in fact, only slightly more than a guess.

As difficult as the modelling of interest rates is, the modelling of mortality rates is exponentially more difficult for several reasons. First, there are actively traded and fairly liquid interest rate curves that allow us to at least benchmark less actively traded interest rate curves. To date there are no actively traded mortality curves, although, as we will mention below, there are several firms that are starting what could be called benchmark curves. Second, where there are a number of factors underlying the movements of interest rates, there is only one rate associated with each spot rate at time t. With mortality rates each rate is associated with a specific t and a specific cohort population x.

7.3.2   Interest Rates

Over the next few pages we review interest rate theory, the purpose being the review of the large body of modelling and methodology that allow us to price interest rate product correctly. We then port this methodology over to the mortality rate environment and show how it can be used to price mortality products. There are two main problems with this transportation: (1) the calculation of the forward rates and the lack of actual tradable forward rates to keep prices at equilibrium; and (2) the change of numeraire needed to keep the discount functions at equilibrium. We can show, in theory, how they should work but without an actively traded market this process is difficult.

Given the above, what was needed was a way to tie together these two disparate quantities and, to start, let us look at the interest rate environment. We reference Rebonato, *Interest-Rate Models,* second edition.

1. Let's start with a time t continuously compounded discrete spot rate maturing at time T, $R_c(t, T)$

$$P(t, T) = e^{[-R_c(t,T)(T-t)]}$$
$$\Rightarrow R_c(t, T) = \frac{\ln[P(t, T)]}{T - t} \tag{7.1}$$

where $P(t, T)$ is the price of a discount bond continuously compounded using R_c.

2. Then the time t continuously compounded forward rate $[T, T + \Delta t]$, $f(t, T, T + \Delta t)$

$$\frac{P(t, T + \Delta t)}{P(t, T)} = e^{[-f(t,T,T+\Delta t)\Delta t]} \tag{7.2}$$

or

$$f(t, T, T + \Delta t) = -\frac{\ln[P(t, T + \Delta t) - \ln(P(t, T)]}{\Delta t} \tag{7.3}$$

3. As $T \to t$, $\Delta t \to 0$ in (7.2) and (7.3) we have the instantaneous short rate $r(t)$ and the instantaneous forward rate $f(t, T, T + \Delta t)$

4. If we rearrange terms we have

$$\int_t^T d \ln P(t, s) = -\int_t^T f(t, s)ds = \ln[P(t, T)] - \ln[P(t, t)] \tag{7.4}$$

But since $P(t, t) = 1$ we have

$$-\int_t^T f(t, s)ds = \ln P(t, T) \Rightarrow P(t, T) = e^{(-\int_t^T f(t,s)ds} \tag{7.5}$$

Therefore

$$R_s(t, T) = \frac{1/P(t, T) - 1}{T - t} \tag{7.6}$$

which is the simply compounded spot rate and

$$F(t_1, T_1, T_2) = \frac{P(t, T_1)/P(t, T_2) - 1}{T - t} \tag{7.7}$$

the simply compounded forward rate, which is the price of a time t discount bond maturing at time T or the price of the integral over maturities of the instantaneous forward rates as seen from time t.

This then allows us to price today a series of cash flows occurring over time, maturing at time T. The idea then is to port this methodology over to the mortality rate.

7.3.3   Interest Rate Swap

Let us first look at a simple interest rate swap and then port that methodology over to the mortality swap.

In an interest rate swap the fixed leg is

$$V_i = N_i X \tau_i \tag{7.8}$$

where

$V_i = $ *fixed leg*

$N_i = $ *notional principal outstanding at time* t_i

$X = $ *fixed rate*

$\tau_i = $ *frequency of payment*

$P(0, t) = $ *discount rate*

Then the present value of the fixed leg of a swap is

$$PV(B_i) = N_i X \tau_i P(0, t_{i+1}) \tag{7.9}$$

The floating leg is

$$A_i = N_i f_i \tau_i \tag{7.10}$$

where

A_i = *Floating rate at time i*

$f_i = \tau_i$ *period forward rate at time t_i*

The present value of the floating leg of a swap is

$$PV(A_i) = E[N_i R_i \tau_i P(0, t_{i+1})] \tag{7.11}$$

Here there is an expectation because the τ_i period spot rates are not known. However, at time 0 all information is known.

Now let's assume that we purchase a bond maturing at time t_i and sell a bond maturing at time t_{i+1}. The portfolio would look like

$$V(t_i) = P(t_i, t_i) - P(t_i, t_{i+1}) = 1 - P(t_i, t_{i+1})$$
$$= 1 - \frac{1}{1 + R_i \tau_i} = \frac{R_i \tau_i}{1 + R_i \tau_i} \tag{7.12}$$

By (7.12) the payer of the floating leg of a swap will have to make a payment at time t_{i+1} of

$$V'(t_i) = \frac{R_i \tau_i}{1 + R_i \tau_i} \tag{7.13}$$

which implies that

$$V'(t_i) = V(t_i)$$

or that

$$P(0, t_i) - P(0, t_{i+1}) = R_i \tau_i P(0, t_{i+1}) \tag{7.14}$$

To avoid arbitrage

$$R_i = \frac{\dfrac{P(0, t_i)}{P(0, t_{i+1})} - 1}{\tau_i}$$

What is important to notice here is the absence of any of the expectation in this equation. This is simply the equation for the forward rate spanning the period $[t_i, t_{i+1}]$ or $F(0, t_i, t_{i+1})$.

Rebonato showed that the result could be duplicated using bonds with a maturity of t_{i+1} as the numeraire. When we move into the forward mortality swap we will need to use the correct numeraire.

We can now fix the swap rate with the elimination of the variance from the equation

$$\sum PV(V_i) = \sum N_i X \tau_i P(0, t_{i+1})$$
$$= \sum PV(A_i) = \sum N_i F_i \tau_i P(0, t_{i+1})$$

Rearranging terms

$$X = \frac{\sum N_i F_i \tau_i P(0, t_{i+1})}{\sum N_i \tau_i P(0, t_{i+1})} \tag{7.15}$$

This says that the fixed rate is nothing more than the weighted average of the forward rates, which is something that would be intuitively suspected.

$$w_i = \frac{N_i \tau_i P(0, t_{i+1})}{\sum N_i \tau_i P(0, t_{i+1})}$$

$$X = \sum F_i w_i \tag{7.16}$$

Again this shows that the initial cost is zero.

Using the forward rate formulation above it can be shown that

$$F(t_1, t_i, t_1 + \tau) = F(0, t_1, t_1 + \tau_i) \text{ with } i = 1 \tag{7.17}$$

$$F(t_1, t_1, t_1 + \tau) = R_s(t_1, \tau_1) = F(0, t_1, t_1 + \tau) \tag{7.18}$$

This means that after the initial valuation of the swap (= 0), for the swap to retain its zero value the time t_i spot rate should equal the time t_0 projected forward rate.

Using this information we can expand the swap equations

$$NPV_{swap}(t) = -\sum N_i X \tau_i P(t, t_{i+1}) + \sum N_i F_i \tau_i P(t, t_{i+1}) \tag{7.19}$$

where the $F_i's$ are the forward rates calculated at time t.

Remember that $\sum N_i F_i \tau_i P(t, t_{i+1})$ is equal to the swap rate at time t that yields a zero value. Therefore at time t

$$(x_t - X_0) \sum_i B_i = NPV_{swap}(t) \tag{7.20}$$

From equation (7.8) above we can expand the numerator to get

$$\sum_{i=1,n} N_i F_i \tau_i P(0, t_{i+1}) = \sum_{i=1,n} N_i \tau_i \left(\frac{P(0, t_i)/P(0, t_{i+1}) - 1}{\tau_i} \right) P(0, t_{i+1})$$

$$= \sum_{i=1,n} N_i [P(0, t_i) - P(0, t_{i+1})]$$

$$\Rightarrow \sum_{i=1,n} N_i F_i \tau_i P(0, t_{i+1}) = \sum_{i=1,n} P(0, t_i) - P(0, t_{i+1})$$

$$= P(0, t_1) - P(0, t_2) + P(0, t_2) - P(0, t_3) + \ldots$$

$$+ P(0, t_n) - P(0, t_{n+1})$$

$$= P(0, t_1) - P(0, t_{n+1})$$

Thus for a plain vanilla swap the present value of the floating leg of a swap is

$$\sum PV(A_i) = P(0, 0, -P(0, t_{n+1}) = 1 - P(0, t_{n+1}) \tag{7.21}$$

7.3.4 Forward Rate Agreements

A forward rate agreement is nothing more than a one-period swap. The calculation is

$$PV(FRA) = [P(0, t_i) - P(0, t_{i+1})] - XP(0, t_{i+1})\tau_i \tag{7.22}$$

Since these are one-period prices, a term swap is simply a combination of FRA agreements or what, in essence, is a set of spanning swap rates (see Figure 7.6).

This then allows us to set up the following series of spanning swap rates:

$$S_3 = (P(t_0, t_2))/(P(t_0, t_3)\tau)$$
$$S_2 = (P(t_0, t_1) - P(t_0, t_3))/((P(t_0, t_3) + P(t_0, t_2))\tau)$$
$$S_1 = (P(t_0, t_0) - P(t_0, t_3))/((P(t_0, t_3) + P(t_0, t_2) + P(t_0, t_1))\tau)$$
$$= (1 - P(t_0, t_3))/((P(t_0, t_3) + P(t_0, t_2) + P(t_0, t_1))\tau)$$

The advantage here again is that we have a series n of equation in n unknowns which will allow us to force out the discount factors that allow us to have an arbitrage-free curve. This same process can be applied to the mortality curve below.

We went through the interest rate exercise above to get to the place where the numerator above is the present value of the floating leg and the denominator is the present value of the denominator with the discount factor taken from the curve. This is key. We can then easily transfer this methodology to the mortality curve, given that the discount factor under Q' that we need to eliminate arbitrage is taken from the curve itself. This then gives us a price for the swap without any expectation in the calculation. This is a totally deterministic pricing. The key is the numeraire. Transferring this methodology to the mortality swap will eliminate all expectation there also and give us a neatly determined price for the swap.

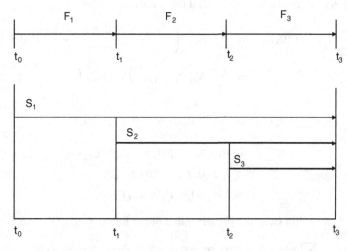

Figure 7.6 Spanning forwards.

7.3.5 Mortality Rate

Over the last several years modelling mortality rates based upon historical data plus a margin (used in the above examples) have caused problems for life carriers. High returns on investment portfolios coupled with low yields on the cash surrender value of the policy have been eroding, causing margins to slip for the insurer. This, coupled with poor cohort analyses, have forced insurance companies to look for better methods of calculating life expectancy.

Recent research has suggested that life expectancies are best modelled using a stochastic jump diffusion model with a Poisson distribution.

If we then take our spot and forward interest rates and compare them to the mortality curve we define $S(t)$ as the survival rate and $u(t, x)$ as the instantaneous rate of mortality at time t for individuals aged x. With the survival rate we are inserting an additional variable as we have to reference the survival rate to a specific cohort. We will later convert the survival rate to the mortality rate, defined as 1 minus survival rate, to allow us to treat it similarly to the forward interest rate.

We can then treat $u(t, x)$, the forward mortality rate, and $f(t, s)$, the forward interest rate, alike mathematically although they represent two different quantities.

Deterministic interest

$$P(t, T) = e^{(-\int_t^T f(t,s)ds} \qquad (7.23)$$

where $P(t, T)$ is as defined

Deterministic mortality

$$_t x_p = e^{(-\int_t^T u_{t+s}ds} \qquad (7.24)$$

where $_t x_p$ is the probability of survival from time t to T for cohort x

But deterministic pricing can allow for a mispricing of forward events through an arbitrage process. What we need is an arbitrage-free or risk-neutral pricing methodology. We do this by pricing under numeraire Q for interest rates and for Q' mortality rates. This numeraire will not allow arbitrage pricing such as borrowing/lending the spot rate/mortality rate and lending/borrowing a combination of forward rates to create a risk-free profit, and force us back to a true deterministic price.

The stochastic interest rate

$f(s, t)$

$$\int_t^T f(t, s)ds = \ln P(t, T) \Rightarrow P(t, T) =$$

$$E_Q\left[e^{(-\int_t^T f(t,s)ds}\right] \qquad (7.25)$$

The stochastic mortality rate

$u(t, x)$

$$P(t.T + \Delta t, x) = E_{Q'}\left[e^{(-\int_t^T u(s,x)ds}\right]$$

$$(7.26)$$

where both Q and Q' eliminate all possibilities of arbitrage.

From (7.26) we saw that the extension from interest rates to mortality rates required a cohort variable:

$$u(t, x)$$
$$P(t, T + \Delta t, x) = E_{Q'}\left[e^{(-\int_t^T u(s,x)ds}\right]$$

Here the x variable represented the cohort population that the mortality rate referenced. By expanding the spanning forwards above we can include the cohort factor with the correct numeraire to produce spanning forwards for the mortality swap as shown below.

$$S_3 = (P(t_0, t_2, x))/(P(t_0, t_3, x)\tau)$$
$$S_2 = (P(t_0, t_1, x) - P(t_0, t_3, x))/((P(t_0, t_3, x) + P(t_0, t_2, x))\tau)$$
$$S_1 = (P(t_0, t_0, x) - P(t_0, t_3, x))/((P(t_0, t_3, x) + P(t_0, t_2, x) + P(t_0, t_1, x))\tau)$$
$$= (1 - P(t_0, t_3, x))/((P(t_0, t_3, x) + P(t_0, t_2, x) + P(t_0, t_1, x))\tau)$$

We now have spanning forwards for this cohort population, which will be arbitrage free and discount correctly the future values of this swap at time t_0.

The next stage in the calculation of mortality swaps would be to try to hedge one set of spanning forwards from one cohort population with the spanning forwards from another cohort population. In the interest rate market the LIBOR rate can be a base rate against which everything is priced, but in the credit markets a standardized base rate mortality curve has yet to be established in the life settlements markets against which all other mortality curves can be priced. As a result most swaps will be customized, swapping one portfolio's mortality rate with that of another.

Looking at Figure 7.7 we have two forward curves from two different cohort populations. How can one curve be hedged against the other? Given that the calculations follow the standard forward rate calculations, we can use the same methodologies that were used in standard interest rate environments. Duration matching, duration and convexity matching or cash flow matching are all methods of hedging a portfolio of interest-sensitive securities against changes in interest rates. In Chapter 8 we will consider a simple duration matching and see what effect that will have on hedging a jump in the mortality curve against a base rate.

In this instance one life settlement portfolio would act as the underlying base rate and the second portfolio would be hedged against the underlying portfolio.

It is readily apparent at this time that almost each transaction would have a different base rate. Several major investment banks have mortality swap curves available that eventually could evolve into the standardized base rate curve. These are listed below.

- *Credit Suisse Longevity Index* – A standardized measure of the expected average lifetime for a general population (national statistics with US population data). Gender and age specific sub-indices (life expectancies at various attained ages).

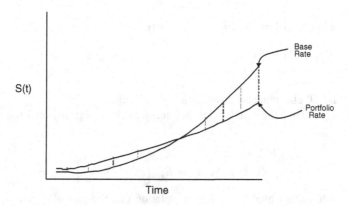

Figure 7.7   Cash flow matching or duration matching.

- *JP Morgan* – A mortality index based on the life expectancy of USA, England & Wales and the Netherlands national population data. Methodology and future longevity modelling are fully disclosed and open with software that includes various stochastic mortality models available.
- *Goldman Sachs QXX Index* – An index based on a sample of American insured population age 65 and older. As at December 2007, this was a pool of 46,290 lives. The QXX index draws its data from the portfolio of lives underwritten by AVS, one of the leading medical underwriters in the US life settlements market, and thus represents the closest available proxy to the longevity exposure in the life settlements market.

The swap construction can then be of a number of different types from a floating to floating, a fixed to floating, or an up-front payment settled at term. The construction of the swap will depend upon the needs of the customer.

Basis risks under this hedging process will be large, as the customer is hedging his pool of life policies against a reference pool above. However, the price of entry into the hedge will be zero initially, except for whatever margin requirements the counterparties may require.

7.4 FUTURES AND FORWARDS

Equations (7.1) and (7.2) above showed the relationship between spot rates and forward rates. The formal definition of a futures contract is a standardized contract, traded on a futures exchange, to buy or sell a certain underlying instrument at a certain date in the future, at a specified price basically a standardized forward contract.

A futures contract gives the holder the obligation to buy or sell, which differs from an options contract, which gives the holder the right to buy or sell, but not the obligation. In other words, the owner of an options contract may exercise the contract, but both parties of a futures contract must fulfil the contract on the settlement date. The seller delivers the commodity to the buyer, or, if it is a cash-settled future, then cash is transferred from the futures trader who sustained a loss to the one who made a profit. To exit the commitment prior to the settlement date, the holder of a futures position has to offset his position by either selling a long position or buying back a short position, effectively closing out the futures position and its contractual obligations. There are distinct advantages and disadvantages to each form of contract.

1. The futures contract is traded on an exchange and in most cases these contracts are guaranteed by the governing body standing behind the exchange. For example, in the USA the government guarantees both sides of the contract. A forward contract is an over-the-counter (OTC) product and has counterparty risk.
2. Because of the guarantee on the futures contract, a margin is usually required. This margin will grow or shrink dependent upon whether the contract is in-the-money or out-the-money. Forward contracts do not usually have this requirement, exacerbating the counterparty risk.
3. Because the forward contract is an OTC product it can be tailor made to the client's requirement. A futures contract has specific notional amounts, dates and maturities which cause basis risk.

If we expand equations (7.1) and (7.2) we have the simple compounded spot rate

$$R_s(t, T) = \frac{1/P(t, T) - 1}{T - t} \tag{7.27}$$

and the simple compounded forward rate

$$F(t, T_1, T_2) = \frac{P(t, T_1)/P(t, T_2) - 1}{T_2 - T_1} \tag{7.28}$$

Porting over to the mortality rate we have

$$B(t, T_1, T_2, x) = \frac{B(t, T_1, x)/B(t, T_2, x) - 1}{T_1 - T_2} \tag{7.29}$$

which identifies the cohort population associated with this mortality rate.

From here we can bootstrap a forward curve and have forward rates. Table 7.2 is a repeat of Table 7.1, but this time we have bootstrapped the forward rate off the spot, as shown above. Figure 7.8 shows the curves.

Once we establish a forward rate curve we can structure a futures curve because the futures curve and the forward rate curve differs only to the extent that the futures curve is discrete and somewhat linear compared to the forward curve (see Figure 7.9). Exaggerated in this example is the convexity mismatch between the futures and the forward, but this is an issue when it comes to hedging, as discussed in Chapter 8.

While futures contracts differ widely we will look at a simple future contract on the mortality curve similar to a Eurodollar future of a LIBOR future.

Let $M(t, T)$ be the mortality futures price at time t for the delivery of $X(T)$ at time T based off a standard notion contract. Here contract sizes, time of delivery and basis point values are all standardized such that at time T, the value of $X(T)$ will be clear. Initially there is no value in the trade relative to buying and holding for delivery, as all carry costs are priced into the trade. At time $t + 1$ the contract is revalued at $M(t + 1, T) - M(t)$. A holder of a long position may have a margin call if this value is positive and sufficiently large, and a holder of a short position might equally have a margin call if it is negative. At time T a final payment of $M(T, T) - M(T - 1, T)$ is made which is equal to $X(T) - M(T - 1, T)$ at the maturity of the contract, assuming that all margin calls have been met.

Forward contracts work very similarly. Initially margin was not required on a forward contract but with the recent credit collapse margin is now being required similar to the futures contract. There is a huge body of knowledge concerning counterparty risks in OTC-traded contracts.

In 2007 JP Morgan launched a mortality forward contract. It is a forward contract linked to a future mortality rate, q being the actuarial variable for mortality. At time $T + 1$ the contract exchanges a realized mortality rate given off a specific life pool versus a fixed rate priced off a life pool agreed upon at the initiation of the pool.

This forward rate can then be used to hedge a mortality swap in much the same way that forward rates and FRNs can be used to hedge an interest rate swap.

Table 7.2

Year	Exact Age	Probability of Death within a year	Number of Life's	Life Expectancy
		Males		
1	65	0.017976	79,190	16.67
2	66	0.019564	77,766	15.96
3	67	0.021291	76,245	15.27
4	68	0.023162	74,621	14.59
5	69	0.025217	72,893	13.93
6	70	0.027533	71,055	13.27
7	71	0.030131	69,098	12.64
8	72	0.032978	67,016	12.01
9	73	0.036086	64,806	11.41
10	74	0.039506	62,468	10.81
11	75	0.043415	60,000	10.24
12	76	0.047789	57,395	9.68
13	77	0.052464	54,652	9.14
14	78	0.057413	51,785	8.62
15	79	0.062789	48,812	8.11
16	80	0.068836	45,747	7.62
17	81	0.075724	42,598	7.15
18	82	0.083466	39,372	6.7
19	83	0.092144	36,086	6.26
20	84	0.101803	32,761	5.84
21	85	0.112468	29,426	5.45
22	86	0.124164	26,116	5.08
23	87	0.136917	22,874	4.73
24	88	0.150754	19,742	4.4
25	89	0.165704	16,766	4.09
26	90	0.181789	13,988	3.8
27	91	0.199019	11,445	3.54
28	92	0.217396	9,167	3.29
29	93	0.236906	7,174	3.06
30	94	0.257525	5,475	2.86
31	95	0.278031	4,065	2.68
32	96	0.298111	2,935	2.52
33	97	0.317432	2,060	2.38
34	98	0.335655	1,406	2.25
35	99	0.352438	934	2.13
36	100	0.37006	605	2.02
37	101	0.388563	381	1.91
38	102	0.407991	233	1.81
39	103	0.42839	138	1.71
40	104	0.44981	79	1.61
41	105	0.4723	43	1.52
42	106	0.495915	23	1.43
43	107	0.520711	12	1.35
44	108	0.546747	6	1.26
45	109	0.574084	3	1.19
46	110	0.602788	1	1.11
47	111	0.632928	0	1.04
48	112	0.664574	0	0.97
49	113	0.697803	0	0.91
50	114	0.732693	0	0.84
51	115	0.769327	0	0.78
52	116	0.807794	0	0.72
53	117	0.848183	0	0.67
54	118	0.890592	0	0.62
55	119	0.935122	0	0.57

(Continued)

Table 7.2   (*Continued*)

Year	Females			
	Probability of Death	Number of Life's	Life Expectancy	Total Population Prob of Dying Within 1 Year
1	0.011511	87,031	19.5	2.95%
2	0.012572	86,029	18.72	3.21%
3	0.013772	84,947	17.95	3.51%
4	0.01513	83,777	17.19	3.83%
5	0.016651	82,510	16.45	4.19%
6	0.018406	81,136	15.72	4.59%
7	0.020342	79,643	15.01	5.05%
8	0.022346	78,023	14.31	5.53%
9	0.024382	76,279	13.62	6.05%
10	0.026551	74,419	12.95	6.61%
11	0.029073	72,443	12.29	7.25%
12	0.032023	70,337	11.64	7.98%
13	0.035307	68,085	11.01	8.78%
14	0.038949	65,681	10.4	9.64%
15	0.043047	63,123	9.8	10.58%
16	0.047769	60,405	9.22	11.66%
17	0.05319	57,520	8.65	12.89%
18	0.059279	54,460	8.11	14.27%
19	0.06608	51,232	7.59	15.82%
20	0.073685	47,847	7.09	17.55%
21	0.082199	44,321	6.62	19.47%
22	0.091712	40,678	6.17	21.59%
23	0.102294	36,947	5.74	23.92%
24	0.11399	33,168	5.33	26.47%
25	0.12682	29,387	4.96	29.25%
26	0.140793	25,660	4.6	32.26%
27	0.155906	22,047	4.28	35.49%
28	0.172147	18,610	3.97	38.95%
29	0.189496	15,406	3.7	42.64%
30	0.207925	12,487	3.44	46.55%
31	0.226597	9,891	3.22	50.46%
32	0.245258	7,649	3.01	54.34%
33	0.263628	5,773	2.83	58.11%
34	0.28141	4,251	2.66	61.71%
35	0.298294	3,055	2.5	65.07%
36	0.316192	2,144	2.36	68.63%
37	0.335163	1,466	2.22	72.37%
38	0.355273	975	2.08	76.33%
39	0.37659	628	1.95	80.50%
40	0.399185	392	1.83	84.90%
41	0.423136	235	1.71	89.54%
42	0.448524	136	1.6	94.44%
43	0.475436	75	1.49	99.61%
44	0.503962	39	1.39	105.07%
45	0.534199	19	1.29	110.83%
46	0.566251	9	1.2	116.90%
47	0.600226	4	1.11	123.32%
48	0.63624	2	1.03	130.08%
49	0.674414	1	0.95	137.22%
50	0.714879	0	0.87	144.76%
51	0.757772	0	0.8	152.71%
52	0.803238	0	0.73	161.10%
53	0.848183	0	0.67	169.64%
54	0.890592	0	0.62	178.12%
55	0.935122			187.02%

Table 7.2   (*Continued*)

Survival Curve S(T) with M(0)=100	Mortality curve M(T) with M(0)=0	Forward Mortality Curve
1.00%	0.00%	
0.97%	0.03%	0.06%
0.93%	0.07%	0.13%
0.90%	0.10%	0.21%
0.86%	0.14%	0.29%
0.82%	0.18%	0.38%
0.78%	0.22%	0.47%
0.74%	0.26%	0.57%
0.69%	0.31%	0.66%
0.65%	0.35%	0.77%
0.60%	0.40%	0.87%
0.55%	0.45%	0.97%
0.50%	0.50%	1.08%
0.45%	0.55%	1.18%
0.41%	0.59%	1.27%
0.36%	0.64%	1.35%
0.31%	0.69%	1.43%
0.27%	0.73%	1.49%
0.23%	0.77%	1.54%
0.19%	0.81%	1.57%
0.15%	0.85%	1.57%
0.12%	0.88%	1.56%
0.09%	0.91%	1.53%
0.07%	0.93%	1.48%
0.05%	0.95%	1.42%
0.03%	0.97%	1.34%
0.02%	0.98%	1.27%
0.01%	0.99%	1.20%
0.01%	0.99%	1.14%
0.00%	1.00%	1.09%
0.00%	1.00%	1.06%
0.00%	1.00%	1.03%
0.00%	1.00%	1.02%
0.00%	1.00%	1.01%
0.00%	1.00%	1.00%
0.00%	1.00%	1.00%
0.00%	1.00%	1.00%
0.00%	1.00%	1.00%
0.00%	1.00%	1.00%
0.00%	1.00%	1.00%
0.00%	1.00%	1.00%
0.00%	1.00%	1.00%
0.00%	1.00%	1.00%
0.00%	1.00%	1.00%
0.00%	1.00%	1.00%
0.00%	1.00%	1.00%
0.00%	1.00%	1.00%
0.00%	1.00%	1.00%
0.00%	1.00%	1.00%
0.00%	1.00%	1.00%
0.00%	1.00%	1.00%

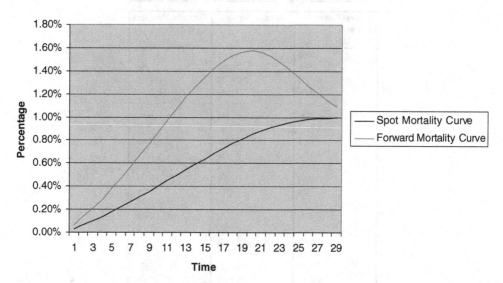

Figure 7.8   Mortality curves and spot forwards

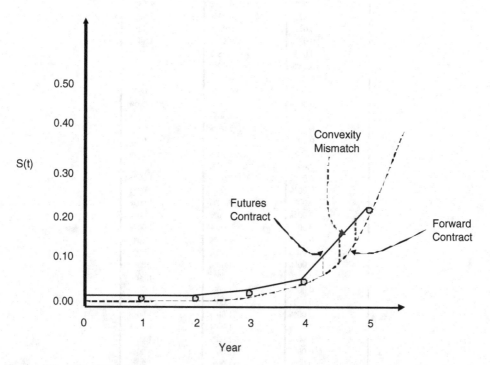

Figure 7.9   Mortality future.

7.5 OPTIONS

7.5.1 Review of Option Pricing Models used to Price Mortality Options

We now have the ability to use a stable of interest rate models to model mortality options, keeping in mind that the forward rates used in these models are the arbitrage-free forward rates and that discount functions are under the correct numeraire.

- CIR short rate model
- HJM forward rate model
- Flesaker–Hughston positive interest model
- BGM market model

The Short Rate Model

To date, short rate models have been most useful. Below is the generalized formula:

$$d_u(t, x) = a(t, x)dt + b(t, x)dW(t)$$

where

$a(t, x)$ is the drift
$b(t, x)$ is the volatility
W is the Brownian motion.

The nice part about the short rate model is that under certain conditions the model can be expressed in a closed form, which is easier to use, to calibrate to the market and faster to run. This is the main reason the short rate model has become so popular.

The Forward Mortality Model

This model follows the Heath–Jarrow–Morton (HJM) model. It is the most theoretically pure model and most other interest rate models are an extension of this generalized form. The problem with modelling mortality with this model is its intractability. It is difficult to implement and calibrate to the market.

The Market Model

The market model has taken over as the standard in interest rate modelling. The main reason being it is a subset of the generalized HJM model and most theoretically tractable. It allows the user to use a change of numeraire to model different pricing measures. In the interest rate environment the Brace–Gatarek–Musiela (BGM) model has been applied to LIBOR and swap curves and is now the standard model on the street. Unlike the HJM model, which builds the tree or simulation off the entire curve, the BGM model allows the user to target specific points along the curve. This eases the calibration and can be priced back to the market much more easily.

The advantage to the market model is that the user can use a number of tradable assets as numeraire provided that there is a tradable curve with which to reference. The main stumbling block with the use of a market model for mortality products appears to be the lack of a tradable curve. Practitioners have applied this model to the Survivor Credit Offered Rate (SCOR) curve and have had some success, but the use to date is limited.

We have already shown that the amortization of a LSP is almost linear. Options on the other hand are non-linear, and putting the two products together creates unique cash flow streams. We look at several possibilities for options. For example, the options on a longevity bond are set up much in the same way that options on Treasury bonds are traded. Finally, we discuss the plethora of possible interest rate techniques and instruments ported over to the mortality curve.

7.5.2 Options on Longevity Bond Future

In much the same way as options on the Treasury bond futures are traded at the CME, options on a standard longevity bond could be established. The calculations are very similar to any bond option calculation. A simple formula is given below:

Again working in a risk-neutral world under our measure Q' where we cannot buy at one price and simultaneously sell at a higher price, or vice versa, we see that the value of a call option with maturity T years on a bond is:

$$c = P(0, T)E_{TQ'}[\max(F_T - X, 0)]$$

Where

> $F_T =$ bond Futures price at time T
>
> $E_{TQ'} =$ expected value in forward risk neutral world
>
> $P(0, T) =$ the value of a zero coupon bond priced at time 0
>
> for delivery at time $T = $ a discount function
>
> $X = $ the strike price on the option

Assuming the bond price is log-normal with a log-normal standard distribution (Std) and Std$=\sigma\sqrt{T}$ we get

$$c = P(0, T)[E_{TQ'}(F_t)Nd_1 - XN(d_2)$$

With

$$d_1 = \frac{\ln[E_{TQ'}(F_T)/X] + \sigma^2 T/2}{\sigma\sqrt{T}}$$

$$d_2 = \frac{\ln[E_{TQ'}(F_T)/X] - \sigma^2 T/2}{\sigma\sqrt{T}} = d_1 - \sigma\sqrt{T}$$

which reduces to the standard Black model.

7.5.3 Options on the Longevity Spot Bond

To compare the price of an option on a bond futures with the price of an option on a spot bond, assume that they have the same strike and time to maturity. If we are looking at a European option the payoff from a spot option on a bond would be

$$\max(B_T - X, 0)$$

where B_t is the spot price of a bond at time T. The payoff of a future would be

$$\max(F_T - X, \ 0)$$

where F_t is the futures price of a bond at time T.

If the maturity of the two is the same time T, then the two options will be identical. If the option on the bond futures matures before the bond futures contract itself, then the option on the futures will be worth more than the option on the spot. This is the result of the fact that the futures price will generally be higher than the spot price in a normal market. Obviously the reverse will be true for the put contract.

If the option is an American option, the situation is slightly different. Because of early exercise with the American, the option on the future will be worth more than the option on the spot or the corresponding European option.

Again the construction of the option is not difficult given the underlying security either a spot bond, a bond future or an index is available and liquid.

7.5.4   Put Option on the Longevity of the Pool

At least two investment banks have issued (or offered to issue) a put option on the longevity of a pool of life settlements (in each case, to facilitate transactions structured by that invest-ment bank). The specifics of the option are not fully known to the authors but the theory is straightforward and we go through an example in Chapter 8.

Essentially the seller of the put option allows the purchaser of the option to put the portfolio back to the seller at a specific date at a specific price. In the examples we used previously, the purchaser of a put option would buy a put on the $100 portfolio for an up-front premium. In 10 years the purchaser of the put could put the life settlement portfolio back to the seller of the put option for price of $100. This would in essence guarantee the payoff of the pool of life settlements.

As with any of these products the permutations and combinations are almost endless. The put option could be for only the estimated error. In our examples only 80% of the pool ran off. That means, given standard expectations, the purchaser of the put option could put the pool back and expect the 20% shortfall to be covered. The put option could be structured to pay off 100% of the face in LE + 2 or payment is made in full only 2 years after the expected life of the pool. Payments could be made yearly with the ability to walk away at any point, much like a default swap.

The calculations of the options would not be that difficult, with the error in the life expec-tations being the major concern. For example:

$X =$ strike price (could be the face value or some portion of face value)

$r =$ the risk-free rate

$\sigma =$ the volatility (a simple calculation could be $\dfrac{\mu}{\sqrt{\text{\# of policies}}}$)

$S_0 =$ current price (this could be the purchase price plus the discount values of all expenses over the life of the pool – see Chapter 8)

$T =$ time (here we assume a 10-year option)

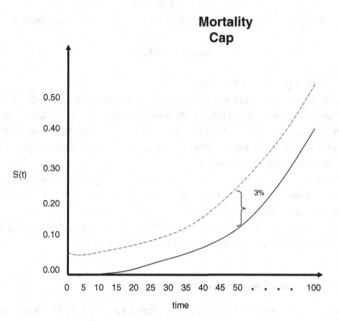

Figure 7.10   Mortality cap.

7.5.5   Mortality Caps, Floors and Swaptions

Unlike the bond option above and the swaptions that follow, caps and floors are easily constructed and can be instruments that can be used today. As we showed above, the forward mortality rate can be constructed and a series of forward captions can then be priced allowing us to price a cap or, conversely, a series of "floortions" allowing us to price the floor.

At present this would be a custom product given that we have no standardized curve but the construction is fairly easy by simply lacing a barrier on the mortality rate as shown in Figure 7.10.

7.5.6   Interest Rate Caps

Again let's first take a detour into the interest rate world. For caps and swaps in an interest rate market it is important to link the variance of the swap rates with the variance of the cap rates.

By definition, a cap is a collection of caplets. A caplet is a contract that pays the difference between the one-period spot rate and the strike price set at time t_i for payout at time t_{i+1} if positive, otherwise zero (see Figure 7.11).

$$Caplet\,(t_{i+1}) = Max[R_i - K, 0]\tau_i$$

Discounting back to time t_i

$$Caplet\,(t_{i+1}) = Max[R_i - K, 0]\frac{1}{1 + R_i\tau_i}$$

From the discussions above we determined that the resetting t_i spot rate must equal the t_i implied forward unless an arbitrage situation occurs.

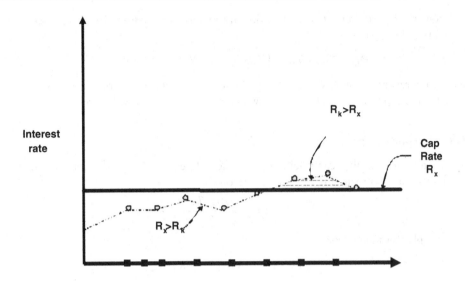

Figure 7.11 Interest rate cap.

Using the Black analogy, and assuming a log-normal distribution, we can equate a caplet with a call option on the forward rate.

$$Caplet = [F(t_0, t_i, t_{i+1})N(h_i) - K(h_2)]P(t_0, t_{i+1}) \qquad (7.30)$$

where $N(.)$ denotes the cumulative normal distribution and $h_{1,2}$ are

$$h_{1,2} = \frac{\ln\left(\frac{F}{K}\right) \pm \frac{1}{2}\sigma^2(t_1 - t_0)}{\sigma\sqrt{t_i - t_0}} \qquad (7.31)$$

where σ is the volatility of the forward rate. The two major assumptions of the Black formula are (1) a log-normal distribution and (2) an absence of drift, both of which we can justify under a mortality variance. More importantly, this terminology can be used for both the forward rates and forward bond prices, allowing us to look at options on longevity bonds.

Looking at (7.30) and (7.31) it is apparent that there is a 1-to-1 relationship between the volatility of the forward rate σ and the price of the cap. Therefore we can force out the complete volatility curve of a forward rate using the cap volatilities. We review this problem below as it applies to a mortality curve, given that the cap volatility is non-existent at this time and would apply to a cohort population.

7.5.7 Interest Rate Swaption

A European swaption gives the holder the right to enter into a swap at time t_i starting at time t_s and maturing at time t_m at a pre-known rate K:

$$Max[X - K, 0]B(payerswap)$$
$$Max[K - X, 0]B\ (receiverswap)$$
$$Where\ B = \sum_{k=1,n} P(t_i, t_{i+k})\tau_k$$

Swaption prices are driven by the expectation of forward rates, so using Black's model applied to the forward swap rate we have

$$Payer\ Swaption = [X(t_0, t_i, t_{i+1})N(h_1) - KN(h_2)]B$$

Like the interest rate market we skirt the problem of a log-normal distribution for swap rates, given that the cap rate that makes up the swap curve is log-normally distributed.

7.5.8 Mortality Caps

Moving into the mortality cap pricing we have $R(t, T)$ equal to $\frac{1/P(t,T)-1}{(T-t)}$ but we are forced here to insert a cohort variable x. This then becomes

$$R'(t, T, x) = \frac{[1/P(t, T, x) - 1]}{T - t}$$

and the caplet formula becomes

$$caplet(t_{i+1}) = Max[R'_i - K, 0]\tau_i$$

and the discounted rate becomes

$$caplet(t_{i+1}) = Max[R'_i - K, 0]\frac{1}{1 + R'_i\tau_i}$$

Stated about the volatility of the forward rate is the principal driving force in pricing caps and swaps. We deal with this problem in Chapter 8 where we build a simple pricing model, but the mainstay of this entire book has been the stability of the pricing of life settlements both as a stand-alone product and in structures. As we will see in Chapter 8 there is not a lot of volatility in the forward mortality rate in LSPs and, as such, pricing will not be that expensive.

At this point in time a standard mortality curve does not have a series of cap prices with which to force out forward volatilities. Thus, we will have to work backward using cap prices to force out volatility to be used in the swap curve.

7.6   SYNTHETIC POOLS

Referring back to the default swap we can take a position on either side of the trade. If we sell the default swap we will receive the quarterly payments but be responsible for making good on any default. We can do the same for any tradable default index or basket. If we sell the index we will receive the premium and be responsible for making payments on any default. We have in essence created a synthetic portfolio, given that we are responsible for the defaults and collecting the equivalent of a coupon.

The same idea can be said for the synthetic life settlement portfolio. By taking a position in a swap we are assuming risks as if we owned the LSP. These risks could be used to offset the risks of a portfolio we actually owned, the annuity life insurance swap being an example.

7.7   CONCLUSION

Most of this chapter has been highly speculative, but, as the saying goes, necessity is the mother of all invention. We have seen in Chapter 1 that the projected growth rate for the life settlements market is extremely rapid and the major risk with life settlements is longevity risk. We have shown that the hedging instruments available, and used quite regularly in the interest rate environment, can be ported over (albeit with some difficulty) to the mortality environment. Much more work needs to be done in this area, but there will be demand. The current risks for investing time, energy and money are great – there have been many attempts at establishing new futures products only to see them fail (the inflation rate future being one example, although that failed more out of poor construction than lack of interest). Also, the establishment as a leader in this field could prove very profitable in the near future given that, at the time of writing, markets were in turmoil with money looking for a safe haven.

8

Hedging

INTRODUCTION

Before we look at risks and methods of hedging risk we need to define basis risk in insurance securitization. Basis risk in a hedge is simply the difference between your expectation at the onset and the actual realization. In insurance basis risk is hedged via a deductible. Problems with parametric selection and non-stationary parameters can cause adverse selection problems or asymmetric information more generally. If we have a parametric trigger in an insurance securitization, there is basis for the insurer. In fact, parametric triggers can take you outside of the land of insurance, through the absence of an insurable interest, to the land of gambling. The alternative is the indemnity contract which pays the insurer's actual loss experience, but this is fraught with moral hazard since the insurer no longer has any incentive to select insurance risks carefully and may finish up with the insurance equivalent of sub-prime. We will look at hedging both problems with different types of capital market and insurance products.

The reader should also recall the difference between "assurance" and "insurance", which was explained in Chapter 1. In deciding upon a hedging programme a distinction has to be made between whether you are hedging an assurance or an insurance payout and the result of that determination will depend upon the type of hedging vehicle you use.

In Chapter 7 we looked at derivative products associated with LSPs. It has been mentioned more than once in this book that derivative products are designed to reduce risk. In exchange-traded markets, leverage lets speculators take positions for purely speculative reason, and generally this is good as it creates liquid markets and allows for the free flow of trading capital. Because of the interconnection between derivatives used for risk reduction and hedging, this chapter will, for the most part, be a repeat of Chapter 7 save the fact that we will look at examples of how these derivatives can be applied to the products discussed in this book.

The three main risks associated with any life settlement securitization are:

- Liquidity risk
- Credit risk
- Longevity/extension risk

Towards the end of the chapter we will try to develop a hedging strategy that measures hedging effectiveness across strategies. Entire libraries have been written about this topic and an exhaustive exploration of all strategies is beyond the scope of this book. We will consider a very simple strategy that can be applied easily and quickly using relatively simple technology.

8.1 HEDGING LONGEVITY OR EXTENSION RISK

For our purposes we are interested only in the fact that the life insurance policies do not runoff or mature as expected but extend out causing the cash flows to be delayed. This then puts pressure on whatever contractual obligations we have as of a specific date.

The industry as a whole has an interest not only in extension risk but in longevity risk from the standpoint of longevity shortening. Pension funds and life insurance companies are hurt by a shortening of longevity and can use many of the capital markets product discussed below to hedge their risks, but again we focus here on only unexpected residual extension risk.

Companies exposed to longevity risk have always had a choice as to how to deal with it. They could:

1. Assume it to be a business risk and hope they had priced the risk correctly.
2. Try to diversify away the risk as best they could.
3. Re-insure the risk in an attempt to remove it from their balance sheet.
4. Enter into longevity-linked instruments

The collapse of Equitable Life in 2000 has sparked concerns that assuming the business risk may not always be a choice, and has pressured the financial engineers to try to find a more acceptable way to divest the balance sheet of these risks.

In Chapter 5 we looked at longevity bonds from the standpoint of a capital market perspective and as a pure investment. However, the entire category was designed to hedge longevity risk. As a result we will touch only briefly on longevity bonds here.

This chapter concentrates more on the exotic product, much of which is either non-existent at present or still in an infancy stage with little liquidity. As the life settlement market grows, these products and many more should become commonplace.

8.1.1 Longevity Bonds

In Chapter 5 we discussed the longevity bond with both the coupon at risk and principal at risk. Figure 8.1 shows the payout of a coupon-at-risk longevity bond. If mortality $M(t)$ is increased, the coupon payment is decreased. If mortality $M(t)$ is decreased, the coupon payment is increased. A simple example of a type of calculation might be:

- Longevity bond $Coupon \times (1 - M(t))$
- Inverse longevity bond $\frac{Coupon}{(1-M(t))}$

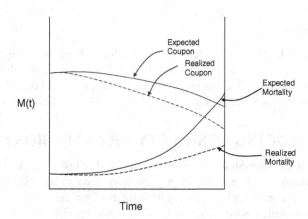

Longevity Bond
Coupon = M(t) * Principal

Figure 8.1

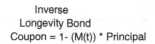

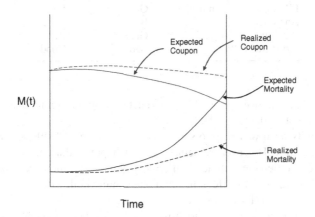

Figure 8.2

where $M(t)$ is the mortality rate at year t.

For purposes of hedging mortality extension – the main concern of the products described in this book – we would need to use an inverse longevity bond (Figure 8.2).

While this hedge moves in the right direction, the basis risk is enormous.

8.1.2   Asset Swaps

An asset swap was more or less the first attempt to divest a company of longevity risk and is still the most used process given that the idea has been expanded from single instruments to large pools of assets.

An annuity and the life insurance policy are complete complements in theory. A shortening of the longevity for an annuity will increase the return for the company because the payouts on the annuity are shortened. Extending the longevity for an annuity will do the exact opposite and cause the payouts to be extended. The shortening of longevity for a life policy will cause the returns for a life carrier to diminish because the payout on the policy will be shortened and the benefits will be paid out sooner. Lengthening the longevity of a life policy will increase the return for the company as premiums and invested cash have a longer period to work for the firm.

Below Tables 8.1 and 8.2, shown in Chapter 5, show the relationship between longevity and the product.

By putting an annuity with term x together with a life insurance policy with the same term, we create a natural hedge. This idea was not lost on the larger life carriers who quickly established an annuity business to run side by side with their life business. The problem with this programme, however, was that it carried a basis risk. We are back to the drunk and the dog. If the annuity and the life policy have differing bases both in the wrong direction, the hedge will not work. For example, the life expectancy on the annuity could be 10 years and the same for the life insurance policy. If the annuity missed the expected life by lengthening

Table 8.1   Mortality

	Lengthened	Shortened
Life Insurance Companies	Good	Bad
Annuities	Bad	Good
Pensions	Good	Bad
Structured LSPs	Bad	Good

one year and the life insurance missed the life expectancy by shortening one year, there would be a mis-match on both sides of the hedge.

Fixing the annuity term will help to some extent, but there will still be a basis risk on the upside of the life policy. However, remember from Chapter 3 that the standard deviation of the term of the life settlement policies is the mean divided by the square of the number of policies. If we are looking at one life policy and one annuity both with a 10-year expected life, the difference in terminal values could be 20 years off.

However, pooling these securities and structuring a matched term creates a natural hedge and is a practice being used today among the larger players in both markets. Again the risk to the terminal value is reduced by the number of policies in the pool, thus reducing the longevity risk to the structure.

In the above discussions we talked about users and/or providers of the product such as life insurance companies, pension funds and re-insurers. Because of the very nature of their business they had longevity risk from which they had to protect themselves. But we are looking only at hedging the residual risk, and remember, from the first part of this chapter, that we could in essence be hedging an assurance with insurance, which is never a good idea.

Table 8.2   Mortality

	Lengthened		Shortened		
Coupon at Risk longevity bond	To the Investor – Less coupon	To the Issuer – Less payout of coupon	To the Investor – More coupon	To the Issuer – More coupon payout, higher cost of funds	Coupon tied to the mortality rate
Principal at Risk longevity bond	To the Investor – Less principal	To the Issuer – Less principal repayment and less interest on reduced principal	To the Investor – Principal in full	To the Investor – Principal paid in full, higher cost of funds	Principal payback tied to mortality rate
Inverse longevity bond	To the Investor – More coupon payout	To the Issuer – more coupon, higher cost of funds	To the Investor – Less coupon payout lower cost of funds		Coupon inversely tied to mortality rate

Year	80% runoff Normal	1 std extension	2 std extension
0	0	0	0
1	0	0	0
2	0	0	0
3	0	0	0
4	0.05	0	0
5	0.05	0.05	0
6	0.1	0.05	0.05
7	0.1	0.1	0.05
8	0.1	0.1	0.1
9	0.2	0.1	0.1
10	0.2	0.2	0.1
	0.8	0.6	0.4

Figure 8.3

In this chapter, however, we will be looking solely at ways to hedge a portfolio of LSPs we have purchased either as a stand-alone portfolio or as part of a structure and not as a means to reduce the risk to our balance sheet or business as a whole.

Below we look at matching a pool of annuities with a pool of life settlements. In this example we have fixed the term of the annuity.

8.1.3 Annuity Hedging

Let us consider again the standard buy and hold LSP portfolio that we set out in Section 4.1 of Chapter 4.

Recall that our normal expectation would be for 80% of the pool to runoff by year 10. If we needed to pay out 100% by year 10, we might be in trouble. However, because of the investment of the excess cash flow in a reserve account, the un-hedged LSP will have an excess of $48, more than enough to cover our obligation.

Figure 8.3 shows the standard runoff schedule we have been using in our examples with the expectation of an 80% runoff. We also show the runoff schedules for a 1 and 2 standard deviation move away from expectations.

Figures 8.4 and 8.5 show the cash flows as discussed in Chapter 4.

year	(1) Life Policies	(2) Premiums on remaining active policies	(3) Mgt Fee	(4) Wrap fee	(5) Custodial, Trustee, mgt, etc.	(6) Set up costs	(8) Total out flow
0	$20.0	$0.0	$0.0	$0.0	$0.0	$0.25	$20.3
1	$0.0	$2.9	$1.0	$0.0	$2.0	$0.00	$5.9
2	$0.0	$2.9	$1.0	$0.0	$2.0	$0.00	$5.9
3	$0.0	$2.9	$1.0	$0.0	$2.0	$0.00	$5.9
4	$0.0	$2.8	$1.0	$0.0	$2.0	$0.00	$5.8
5	$0.0	$2.6	$1.0	$0.0	$2.0	$0.00	$5.6
6	$0.0	$2.3	$1.0	$0.0	$2.0	$0.00	$5.3
7	$0.0	$2.0	$1.0	$0.0	$2.0	$0.00	$5.0
8	$0.0	$1.7	$1.0	$0.0	$2.0	$0.00	$4.7
9	$0.0	$1.2	$1.0	$0.0	$2.0	$0.00	$4.2
10	$0.0	$0.6	$1.0	$0.0	$2.0	$0.00	$3.6
Totals	$20.0	$21.9	$10.0	$0.0	$20.0	$0.3	$72.1

Figure 8.4

(9) Investment	(10) Maturities of policies	(11) Total In Flows of cash	(12) Net Flows	(13) Cumulative Reserve	(14) Excess cash reinvested at 4%	(15) Sale of Policies Still in Force
$100.00	$0.0	$100.0	$79.8	$79.8	$0.0	
	$0.0	$0.0	-$5.9	$73.9	$3.2	
	$0.0	$0.0	-$5.9	$68.0	$3.0	
	$0.0	$0.0	-$5.9	$62.1	$2.7	
	$5.0	$5.0	-$0.8	$61.3	$2.5	
	$5.0	$5.0	-$0.6	$60.7	$2.5	
	$10.0	$10.0	$4.7	$65.4	$2.4	
	$10.0	$10.0	$5.0	$70.3	$2.6	
	$10.0	$10.0	$5.3	$75.6	$2.8	
	$20.0	$20.0	$15.8	$91.4	$3.0	
	$20.0	$20.0	$16.4	$107.9	$3.7	$12.0
$100.0	$80.0	$180.0	$107.9	$107.9	$28.3	$12.0

Figure 8.5

The net result after 10 years, paying all expenses, was $148 in return:

- $108 in the cumulative account
- $12 from the initial portfolio still in force ($20) sold at 60%
- $28 in interest earned
- In addition, if there are no further claims on the LSP the pool can be seconded and worked down adding additional protection for an investment. By that we mean instead of the $12 sell-off at term, within a very short period of time the $20 still in force could be worked off for the $20. Remember that this portfolio had an average 10-year life 10 years ago.
- The $100 obligation entered into at the inception of this structure is paid off without much problem.

This is all well and good but we have found that this is a hard sell to lenders. They are reluctant to accept the residual numbers. Their concern is they are not in the life settlement trading business. They do not have the infrastructure to trade a pool of life settlements if, at term, the principal is not met and they have to take over the pool of life settlements. In the authors' opinion, this is short sighted. Selling a residual pool of life settlements is equivalent to selling a pool of securities. There are many web pages that trade life settlements and listing the pool on the web is a simple enough process.

We will concentrate the rest of this section on hedging the residual risk to assuage the lender, and give them the comfort that they need not to end up with a pool of still-in-force life policies.

Now let us look at several hedging techniques: first, using an annuity.

8.1.4 Single Premium Annuity

Assume for the moment that your expectations are for an 80% runoff with 20% still in force at term and you want to cover your shortfall. You could purchase a single premium deferred annuity up front. Making the assumption of a 5% flat discount rate, a $20 10-year annuity (your residual value shortfall) would cost you $12.30 up front. At the end of 10 years the $12.30 annuity would mature, yielding $20 to support your shortfall. Let:

$$r = \text{the yearly nominal interest rate} = 5\%$$
$$t = \text{the number of years} = 10\,\text{years}$$

m = the number of periods per year = 1 period

i = the interest rate per period = 5%

n = the number of periods = 10 periods.

Note:

$$i = \frac{r}{m}$$
$$n = tm$$

Also let:

P = the principal (or present value).

S = the future value of an annuity.

R = the periodic payment in an annuity (the amortized payment).

That gives us

$$S_n = R \left[\frac{(1+i)^n - 1}{i} \right]$$

But we know what S_n has to be. It has to be $20. So rearranging terms we get

$$R = \frac{S_n}{\dfrac{(1+i)^n - 1}{i}}$$

$$\Rightarrow R \approx 1.50$$

In looking at an annuity that pays annually we will use 1.50 cents per period.
To get the present value for a single premium annuity we use

$$P = R \left[\frac{1 - \dfrac{1}{(1+i)^n}}{i} \right] \Rightarrow P = 12.28$$

or purchasing a single premium annuity with an up-front payment of $12.28 will yield $20 in 10 years.

Clearly, in the limit as n increases

$$n \rightarrow Lim_\infty P = \frac{R}{i}$$

Figures 8.6 and 8.7 show the cash flows for this structure.
The net result after 10 years, paying all expenses, was $151 in return:

- $20 annuity
- $96 in the cumulative accounts
- $12 from the initial portfolio still in force ($20) sold at 60%
- $23 in interest earned.

year	(1) Life Policies	(2) Premiums on remaining active policies	(3) Mgt Fee	(4) Annuity	(5) Custodial, Trustee, mgt, etc.	(6) Set up costs	(8) Total out flow
0	$20.0	$0.0	$0.0	$12.3	$0.0	$0.25	$32.5
1	$0.0	$2.9	$1.0	$0.0	$2.0	$0.00	$5.9
2	$0.0	$2.9	$1.0	$0.0	$2.0	$0.00	$5.9
3	$0.0	$2.9	$1.0	$0.0	$2.0	$0.00	$5.9
4	$0.0	$2.8	$1.0	$0.0	$2.0	$0.00	$5.8
5	$0.0	$2.6	$1.0	$0.0	$2.0	$0.00	$5.6
6	$0.0	$2.3	$1.0	$0.0	$2.0	$0.00	$5.3
7	$0.0	$2.0	$1.0	$0.0	$2.0	$0.00	$5.0
8	$0.0	$1.7	$1.0	$0.0	$2.0	$0.00	$4.7
9	$0.0	$1.2	$1.0	$0.0	$2.0	$0.00	$4.2
10	$0.0	$0.6	$1.0	$0.0	$2.0	$0.00	$3.6
Totals	$20.0	$21.9	$10.0	$12.3	$20.0	$0.3	$84.4

Figure 8.6   Single premium annuity 80% runoff

(9) Investment	(10) Maturities of policies	(11) Total In Flows of cash	(12) Net Flows	(13) Cumulative Reserve	(14) Excess cash reinvested at 4%	(15)Sale of Policies Still in Force	Single Premium Deferred Annuity
$100.00	$0.0	$100.0	$67.5	$67.5	$0.0		
	$0.0	$0.0	-$5.9	$61.6	$2.7		
	$0.0	$0.0	-$5.9	$55.7	$2.5		
	$0.0	$0.0	-$5.9	$49.8	$2.2		
	$5.0	$5.0	-$0.8	$49.0	$2.0		
	$5.0	$5.0	-$0.6	$48.4	$2.0		
	$10.0	$10.0	$4.7	$53.1	$1.9		
	$10.0	$10.0	$5.0	$58.1	$2.1		
	$10.0	$10.0	$5.3	$63.3	$2.3		
	$20.0	$20.0	$15.8	$79.2	$2.5		
	$20.0	$20.0	$16.4	$95.6	$3.2	$12.0	$20.0
$100.0	$80.0	$180.0	$95.6	$95.6	$23.4	$12.0	$20.0

Figure 8.7   Single premium annuity 80% runoff

8.1.5   80% Runoff with no Annuity vs. an Annuity

The net results above are not substantially different from no hedging at all; $148 with no hedging verses $151 with the annuity. The difference in return being excess cash for the un-hedged position is invested at 4% while in the hedged position the cash is invested in an annuity earning 5%.

The major difference to the lender is that the reserve is guaranteed by a rated annuity carrier and is separate and distinct from the pool itself. It will be there at term.

8.1.6   40% Runoff with no Annuity

If, for example, the average life expectancy of the pool was off by 2 standard deviations and the pool had 60% still in force, the results would be as follows.

The net result after 10 years, paying all expenses, was $124 in return:

- $64 in the cumulative account
- $36 from the initial portfolio still in force ($20) sold at 60%
- $24 in interest earned.

Again the reason being that the excess $40 cash is invested at 4% for 10 years. While the LSP does not yield the expected return, the excess cash investment more than covers the shortfall. This is not a guaranteed payout and, as we will see below, the annuity will produce a similar cash flow, but the shortfall will be guaranteed.

8.1.7   40% Runoff with Single Premium Annuity

The net result after 10 years, paying all expenses, was $127 in return:

- $20 annuity
- $52 in the cumulative account
- $36 from the initial portfolio still in force ($20) sold at 60%
- $19 in interest earned.

Again the reason that the results of Sections 8.1.6 and 8.1.7 are so close in value is due to the fact that the annuity payout up front reduces the reserve requirement and hence any earned interest. In this example the interest on the annuity and the cash account are about the same, hence no real difference in the outcome.

8.1.8   80% Runoff with an Annuity Payout per Year

As a final example of an annuity hedge we could pay out over time instead of a lump sum single premium. This has an advantage, given that one of the risks of a LSP is initial liquidity. Pushing off as much cash flow to the latter part of the programme increases yield and reduces risk. By rearranging the above equation we get:

$$R = \frac{S_n}{\dfrac{(1+i)^n - 1}{i}}$$

$$\Rightarrow R \approx 1.50$$

That means that we would have to pay out $1.50 every year for 9 years $(n-1)$, at the end of which we would have an annuity worth $20. Figures 8.8 and 8.9 show the cash flows followed by the summary results.

year	(1) Life Policies	(2) Premiums on remaining active policies	(3) Mgt Fee	(4) Annuity	(5) Custodial, Trustee, mgt, etc.	(6) Set up costs	(8) Total out flow
0	$30.0	$0.0	$0.0	$0.0	$0.0	$0.25	$30.3
1	$0.0	$2.9	$1.0	$1.5	$2.0	$0.00	$7.4
2	$0.0	$2.9	$1.0	$1.5	$2.0	$0.00	$7.4
3	$0.0	$2.9	$1.0	$1.5	$2.0	$0.00	$7.4
4	$0.0	$2.8	$1.0	$1.5	$2.0	$0.00	$7.3
5	$0.0	$2.6	$1.0	$1.5	$2.0	$0.00	$7.1
6	$0.0	$2.3	$1.0	$1.5	$2.0	$0.00	$6.8
7	$0.0	$2.0	$1.0	$1.5	$2.0	$0.00	$6.5
8	$0.0	$1.7	$1.0	$1.5	$2.0	$0.00	$6.2
9	$0.0	$1.2	$1.0	$1.5	$2.0	$0.00	$5.7
10	$0.0	$0.6	$1.0	$1.5	$2.0	$0.00	$5.1
Totals	$30.0	$21.9	$10.0	$15.0	$20.0	$0.3	$97.1

Figure 8.8   Yearly payout

(9) Investment	(10) Maturities of policies	(11)Total In Flows of cash	(12) Net Flows	(13) Cumulative Reserve	(14) Excess cash reinvested at 4%	(15)Sale of Policies Still in Force	Single Premium Deferred Annuity
$100.00	$0.0	$100.0	$69.8	$69.8	$0.0		
	$0.0	$0.0	-$7.4	$62.4	$2.8		
	$0.0	$0.0	-$7.4	$55.0	$2.5		
	$0.0	$0.0	-$7.4	$47.6	$2.2		
	$5.0	$5.0	-$2.3	$45.3	$1.9		
	$5.0	$5.0	-$2.1	$43.2	$1.8		
	$10.0	$10.0	$3.2	$46.4	$1.7		
	$10.0	$10.0	$3.5	$49.8	$1.9		
	$10.0	$10.0	$3.8	$53.6	$2.0		
	$20.0	$20.0	$14.3	$67.9	$2.1		
	$20.0	$20.0	$14.9	$82.9	$2.7	$12.0	$20.0
$100.0	$80.0	$180.0	$82.9	$82.9	$21.6	$12.0	$20.0

Figure 8.9   Yearly payout

The net result after 10 years, paying all expenses, was $136.5 in return:

- $20 annuity
- $82.9 in the cumulative account
- $12 from the initial portfolio still in force ($20) sold at 60%
- $21.6 in interest earned.

As can be seen, the delay of costs until the later years in this programme increases return and gives you more slippage.

8.1.9   Summary

Table 8.3 gives a summary of the possible outcomes with an annuity hedge.

This would appear to be a lot of iterations around a result that is apparent. However, below we cover what amounts to iterations of the annuity and the results are all similar to those in Table 8.3: the un-hedged position will perform as well if not better than the hedged positions and any iterations in the structure do not change the outcome substantially.

Table 8.3

		Annuity Hedge	
	No Hedge	Single Payment Up Front	Yearly Payments
Expected 80% Runoff	$148	$151	$137
Unexpected 2 Std Shortfall	$124	$127	$126

8.2   HEDGING WITH INVERSE LONGEVITY BOND

We reviewed an inverse longevity bond in Chapter 5. There we showed that the coupon on the bond was calculated as a fixed payout minus the percent runoff (above we divide the coupon by the % runoff just to show other examples of how this might be done). If, for example, the fixed payout was 12% minus the runoff and the runoff for the first few years was zero, the coupon would be a fixed 12%. It can also be seen that as the runoff is delayed, i.e. pushed back into the later years or even pushed into the residual and not matured, the return on the bond increases.

year	(1) Life Policies	(2) Premiums on remaining active policies	(3) Mgt Fee	(4) Wrap fee	(5) Custodial, Trustee, mgt, etc.	(6) Set up costs	Bond coupon	(6) Total out flow
0	$12.0	$0.0	$0.0	$0.0	$0.0	$0.25	$0.0	$12.3
1	$0.0	$1.7	$0.6	$0.0	$0.0	$0.00	$6.0	$8.4
2	$0.0	$1.7	$0.6	$0.0	$0.0	$0.00	$6.0	$8.4
3	$0.0	$1.7	$0.6	$0.0	$0.0	$0.00	$6.0	$8.4
4	$0.0	$1.7	$0.6	$0.0	$0.0	$0.00	$3.9	$6.2
5	$0.0	$1.6	$0.6	$0.0	$0.0	$0.00	$3.9	$6.1
6	$0.0	$1.4	$0.6	$0.0	$0.0	$0.00	$1.8	$3.8
7	$0.0	$1.2	$0.6	$0.0	$0.0	$0.00	$1.8	$3.6
8	$0.0	$1.0	$0.6	$0.0	$0.0	$0.00	$1.8	$3.5
9	$0.0	$0.7	$0.6	$0.0	$0.0	$0.00	$0.0	$1.3
10	$0.0	$0.3	$0.6	$0.0	$0.0	$0.00	$0.0	$1.0
Totals	$12.0	$13.1	$6.0	$0.0	$0.1	$0.3	$31.2	$62.7

Figure 8.10

Like the annuity, a use for the inverse longevity bond as a hedge against extension risk would be to purchase a bond of sufficient size to cover the extension risk.

Again, using the example we used in the annuity, we project the runoff to be 80% but are fearful that it could fall 2 standard deviations outside our projections. In that case we would want to hedge against a 60% still-in-force portfolio with only 40% of the portfolio having run off.

Ignoring the fact that we can sell off the 60% of the portfolio at an estimated 60%, we would purchase an inverse longevity bond to cover the expected exposure. The principal on the bond would then be $60.

Figures 8.10 and 8.11 show the cash flows for an inverse longevity bond backed by a pool of life settlements.

Figure 8.12 shows the coupon payout on the bond under expectation. The return on the bond would be 5.2%.

However, if the projected 80% runoff average life fell short by 2 standard deviations, this would mean that the runoff would be delayed and the coupon would be increased. Figure 8.13 shows the shortfall under our assumed 2 standard deviation drop in mortality.

This is an increase in coupon yield to 7.20% or a pick-up of 2% per year in mortality payouts. It would have to be determined if this hedge would cover the loss in return from the structure you are hedging. Again at term we would also receive our $60 investment which was designed to cover the estimated shortfall.

(9) Investment	(10) Maturities of policies	(11) Total In Flows of cash	(12) Net Flows	(13) Cumulative Reserve	(14) Excess cash reinvested additional LSP	(15) Sale of Policies Still in Force
$60.00	$0.0	$60.0	$47.8	$47.8	$0.0	
	$0.0	$0.0	-$8.4	$39.4	$17.8	
	$0.0	$0.0	-$8.4	$13.3	$9.4	
	$0.0	$0.0	-$8.4	-$4.5	$0.0	
	$3.0	$3.0	-$3.2	-$7.6	$0.0	
	$3.0	$3.0	-$3.1	-$10.7	$0.0	
	$6.0	$6.0	$2.2	-$8.5	$0.0	
	$6.0	$6.0	$2.4	-$6.1	$0.0	
	$6.0	$6.0	$2.5	-$3.6	$0.0	
	$12.0	$12.0	$10.7	$7.1	$0.0	
-$60.0	$12.0	-$48.0	-$49.0	-$41.9	$0.0	$7.2
$0.0	$48.0	$48.0	-$14.7	-$41.9	$27.1	$7.2

Figure 8.11

Bond coupon
$0.0
$6.0
$6.0
$6.0
$3.9
$3.9
$1.8
$1.8
$1.8
$0.0
$0.0
$31.2

Figure 8.12

8.2.1 Hedging with a Surety Bond

The next two hedges basically have an outside source with substantial financial backing pledged to step in and pay the principal given that we are unable to pay in full. Both have results similar to the annuity hedge above. These programmes are much preferred by the lender but are very expensive and reduce the overall returns on the structure. The two we look at here are the surety bond and an insurance wrap. We won't spend much time on them given that they are self-explanatory. We pay an upfront fee and receive a guarantee of principal and/or interest at term. The first one we look at is a surety bond.

A surety bond is a contract among at least three parties:

- *the principal* – the primary party who will be performing a contractual obligation;
- *the obligee* – the party who is the recipient of the obligation; and
- *the surety* – who ensures that the principal's obligations will be performed.

Through this agreement, the surety agrees to uphold – for the benefit of the obligee – the contractual promises (obligations) made by the principal if the principal fails to uphold its

Bond coupon
$0.0
$6.0
$6.0
$6.0
$6.0
$6.0
$3.9
$3.9
$1.8
$1.8
$1.8
$43.2

Figure 8.13

promises to the obligee. The contract is formed so as to induce the obligee to contract with the principal, i.e. to demonstrate the credibility of the principal and guarantee performance and completion per the terms of the agreement. Contract bonds guarantee a specific contract. Examples include performance, bid, supply, maintenance and subdivision bonds. Commercial bonds guarantee per the terms of the bond form. Examples include, licence and permit, union bonds, etc.

Generally speaking the surety will hold an investment grade credit rating and, as a result, the structure may receive a shadow rating given the backing of the surety. This may allow an institutional investor to purchase the structure without going through the formal process of rating the structure with a credit rating agency such as Standard and Poor's.

8.2.2 Hedging with an Insurance Wrap

The insurance wrap is almost identical to the surety bond. A highly rated insurance company will guarantee payment at the term of the structure if the structure cannot make the payment. For this guarantee the structure will have to pay an up-front premium, and this can be expensive, generally ranging from 6% to 10% of the face value of the structure.

If, in return, the insurance company or surety company has to step in and make payments, they will take control of the remaining structure. This generally means that they take control of the portfolio, in which case they will work down the remaining pool until the balance of the debt is paid off. This may include interest on the debt from the date on which the insurance/surety company takes control until the payment is "worked off". Any remaining proceeds will either be retained by the insurance/surety company or returned to the structure.

Because this is fairly new there are no standard processes and much is customized. At present there are two insurance companies insuring the residual value of the pools we are aware of. Both carry a Standard and Poor's AA rating. Because the residual value is rated by an AA-rated company the structure can carry a shadow rating of a Standard and Poor's AA rating. In many cases the shadow rating will allow institutional investors to participate in the structure.

8.2.3 Over-collateralization

Finally before diving into true derivatives we look at over-collateralization as a method of hedging residual risk. This has been a standard method of hedging in other areas for some time and is standard in the mortgage-backed and CDO markets. Within a LSP structure this is a very effective method. It simply entails purchasing $150 worth of face value to cover $100 worth of commitment. This gives you 33% excess coverage, which has two benefits. First, you should be sure that your actuarial projections are not going to be very far off so as to still have more than 33% of the pool in force when it was estimated that the entire pool would run off at term. Second, you can always sell off the still-in-force policies at term to make up any shortfall in payments or roll the excess portfolio into a new structure.

The reason this hedging technique is so effective is due to the fact that the portfolio really will not lose value over time, so your excess investment is secure and will give a nice return in addition to being a buffer. In Figures 8.14 and 8.15 we show the cash flow of a 150% over-collateralization.

As can be seen, an over-collateralization of 150% will still have a runoff of $110 in 10 years even if your projections are 2 standard deviations off.

year	(1) Life Policies	(2) Premiums on remaining active policies	(3) Mgt Fee	(4) Wrap fee	(5) Custodial, Trustee, mgt, etc.	(6) Set up costs	(8) Total out flow
0	$30.0	$0.0	$0.0	$0.0	$0.0	$0.25	$30.3
1	$0.0	$4.4	$1.0	$0.0	$2.0	$0.00	$7.4
2	$0.0	$4.4	$1.0	$0.0	$2.0	$0.00	$7.4
3	$0.0	$4.4	$1.0	$0.0	$2.0	$0.00	$7.4
4	$0.0	$4.4	$1.0	$0.0	$2.0	$0.00	$7.4
5	$0.0	$4.4	$1.0	$0.0	$2.0	$0.00	$7.4
6	$0.0	$4.1	$1.0	$0.0	$2.0	$0.00	$7.1
7	$0.0	$3.9	$1.0	$0.0	$2.0	$0.00	$6.9
8	$0.0	$3.5	$1.0	$0.0	$2.0	$0.00	$6.5
9	$0.0	$3.0	$1.0	$0.0	$2.0	$0.00	$6.0
10	$0.0	$2.6	$1.0	$0.0	$2.0	$0.00	$5.6
Totals	$30.0	$38.9	$10.0	$0.0	$20.0	$0.3	$99.2

Figure 8.14

8.2.4 Hedging with a Mortality Swap

As mentioned in Chapter 7, several mortality indices, which are now available on the market, could be used as a swap product. There are more customized swaps that have been attempted, or are today in the making, between individual LSPs.

We now make a huge leap of faith and assume that the standardized rate above will remain constant for 5 years. This is not exactly such a great a leap of faith because the CDC and others re-evaluate the mortality tables every 5 years. Let's look at a 5-year floating for floating swap.

As an example in Figures 8.16 and 8.17, we compare the realized runoff with a hypothetical standardized rate. The realized rate in year 1 is zero runoff compared to a standardized runoff of 1%. On a notional of $100 million the seller of the swap would receive $1 million from the payer of the swap in year 1.

In the fifth and final year of the swap, the reference curve has 3.5% runoff compared to a 2.5% runoff for the realized curve. The seller of the swap would have to pay the receiver of the swap $1 million. The payer has essentially hedged $1 million of extension risk against the reference curve.

But how is a swap priced at the outset? We now have the ability to look at the mortality swap in much the same way as we look at the interest rate swap and price products built off

(9) Investment	(10) Maturities of policies	(11) Total In Flows of cash	(12) Net Flows	(13) Cumulative Reserve
$150.00	$0.0	$150.0	$119.8	$119.8
	$0.0	$0.0	-$7.4	$112.4
	$0.0	$0.0	-$7.4	$105.1
	$0.0	$0.0	-$7.4	$97.7
	$0.0	$0.0	-$7.4	$90.4
	$0.0	$0.0	-$7.4	$83.0
	$7.5	$7.5	$0.4	$83.4
	$7.5	$7.5	$0.6	$84.0
	$15.0	$15.0	$8.5	$92.5
	$15.0	$15.0	$9.0	$101.4
	$15.0	$15.0	$9.4	$110.8
$150.0	$60.0	$210.0	$110.8	$110.8

Figure 8.15

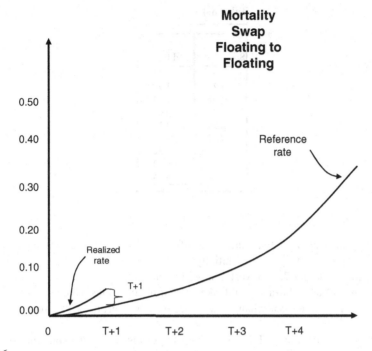

Figure 8.16

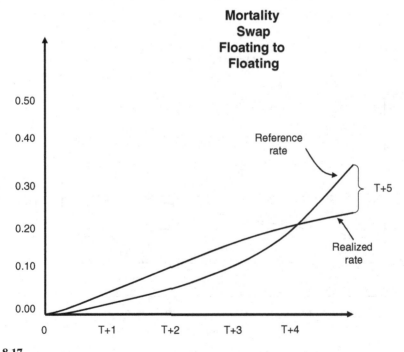

Figure 8.17

Table 8.4

Spot Rate	Fwd Rate
1.61%	
1.75%	1.90%
1.91%	2.24%
2.09%	2.63%
2.30%	3.11%
2.52%	3.66%
2.77%	4.22%
3.02%	4.82%
3.30%	5.54%

the forward mortality curve with a numeraire sufficient to eliminate arbitrage and allow us to eliminate expectation in swap pricing initially.

As explained in Chapter 7, an investor should be indifferent to the fixed or floating rate as fixed initially. A forward arbitrage could take place if the two rates were not set in such a way. However, at $t + 1$ the rates will change and there may be a profit or loss for one side of the trade.

As an example, let us look at Table 8.4 which shows the calculated spot and forward rates calculated from a pool of life settlements. Figure 8.18 shows the graph of these rates.

In Table 8.5 we have the spot and forward rates taken from Table 8.4 for a 10-year period, and using equation (8.1) below, we come up with a weighted average fixed rate for this mortality

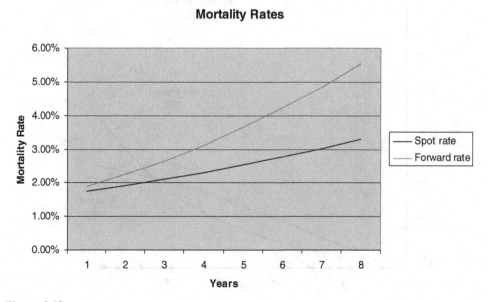

Figure 8.18

Table 8.5

Year	Spot Rate	Fwd Rate	Fixed Rate
1	1.61%		
2	1.75%	1.90%	3.51%
3	1.91%	2.24%	3.51%
4	2.09%	2.63%	3.51%
5	2.30%	3.11%	3.51%
6	2.52%	3.66%	3.51%
7	2.77%	4.22%	3.51%
8	3.02%	4.82%	3.51%
9	3.30%	5.54%	3.51%

swap (the last column).

$$X = \frac{\sum N_i f_i' \tau_i P(0, t_{i+1})}{\sum N_i \tau_i P(0, t_{i+1})} \tag{8.1}$$

Looking back from year 10 we have the actual realized rates in Table 8.6.

Figure 8.19 shows the discounted cash flows from the fixed and floating side of the swap and Figure 8.20 shows the net payouts. Figures 8.21 and 8.22 chart the cash flows.

Where f_i' is the cohort forward rate for this population (for simplicity sake we used a flat 5% rate in our discount function).

If the purpose of the initial transaction was to hedge longevity risk, the buyer of the swap would have protected 2.12% of his longevity risk with no up-front costs save margin requirements.

In any floating for floating swap there will be huge basis risk. Two life settlement portfolios, no matter how customized or similar, will have different runoffs. Portfolios with different cohort populations and standardized populations like those supported by Goldman Sachs, Credit Suisse and JP Morgan will have substantially more basis risk, as any LSP will only be a subset of the standardized pool. It will be necessary to determine the basis risk and, in some way, hedge this risk. This can be done by evaluating the two portfolios using an asset management model, preferably one with a stochastic process. In Figure 8.23 we overlay two forward mortality curves and enter into a swap.

Table 8.6

realized
1.61%
1.78%
1.98%
2.80%
3.80%
4.66%
5.00%
5.90%
6.20%

Fixed side $N_i^*f_i^*P(0,t_{i+1})$	Floating side $N_i^*f_i^*P(0,t_{i+1})$
$3.34	$1.70
$3.18	$1.80
$3.03	$2.42
$2.89	$3.13
$2.75	$3.65
$2.62	$3.73
$2.49	$4.19
$2.38	$4.20
$22.69	$24.81

Figure 8.19

Realized Payments
$1.65
$1.39
$0.61
-$0.24
-$0.90
-$1.11
-$1.70
-$1.82
-$2.12

Figure 8.20

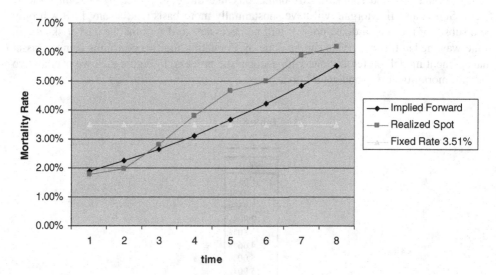

Figure 8.21

Swap Payout

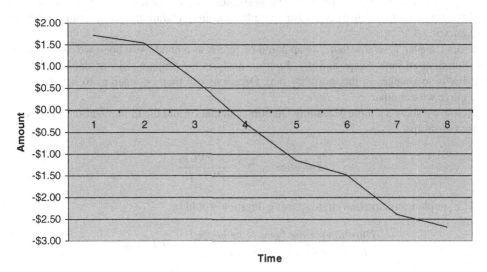

Figure 8.22

Mortality Swap

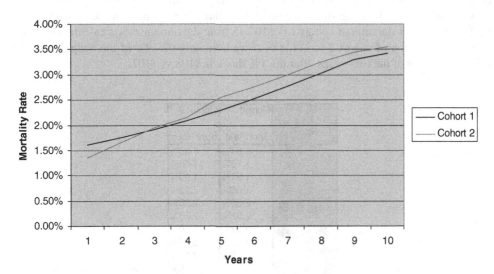

Figure 8.23

The two distributions superimposed on each other show the projected differences in the mortality rates of these two life settlement portfolios. These differences can then be overlaid and the hedge can be constructed using simple Macaulay Duration, and duration match the two curves.

From Chapter 7 we saw that a swap could be priced as a bond. As a bond we can calculate the durations of both swaps and use duration analysis to compare risks as defined by each sensitivity to changes in the mortality rate. Decisions can then be made as to how to hedge one curve with another.

Below we show a simple Macaulay Duration calculation and the immunization strategy for these two swaps:

$$Duration = \sum_{t=1}^{n} \frac{t \times PVCF_t}{PVTCF}$$

The simple immunization strategy using duration would be

$$\frac{Duration\ for\ the\ bond\ to\ be\ hedged}{Duration\ for\ the\ hedging\ vehicle} \times Yield\ beta$$

Figure 8.24 shows the spot mortality rates for the two cohort populations along with their duration calculations.

In the immunization calculation below, the yield beta would be the fixed rate of the swaps (2.60 and 2.81).

$$Immunization = \frac{107.15}{113.06} \times \frac{2.60}{2.81} = 92.79$$

The immunization strategy would say that a 1% point movement in the present value of cohort 2 would cause a 92.79% movement in the value of cohort 1 and to hedge we should hold only 92.793% of the hedging swap. We shock the mortality rates of both cohort populations by 1%. The dollar duration of cohort 1 is $107.15 from the immunization calculation above. The dollar duration of cohort 2 is $113.06. If we hold only 92.79% of the hedge swap, the change in values of the two swaps after the 1% shock is $108 vs $107

Years	Cohort 1 Spot Rate	Cohort 2 Spot Rate
1	1.61%	1.35%
2	1.75%	1.66%
3	1.91%	1.95%
4	2.09%	2.15%
5	2.30%	2.55%
6	2.52%	2.75%
7	2.77%	3.00%
8	3.02%	3.25%
9	3.30%	3.45%
10	3.42%	3.55%
Duration Yrs	5.82	5.94

Figure 8.24

While the above analysis is theoretically tractable because it mirrors interest rate analysis, it is difficult to put in place. Much research and data are available with regard to interest rate variation. Correlations intra rates, short rate movements in relation to long rates, and inter rates, AAA-rated curves versus Treasury curves or BBB-rated curves have been studied and to some extent hedging results are available. In addition, index rates like Treasury curves, supported by issuing governments and LIBOR curves, are highly liquid. The relationship between cohort curves is not known at this time and, in reality, would seem to have little or no correlation. One person's death should have no effect on another's death, save for a national catastrophe. As a result, more would be needed in this area before being useful other than to suggest a sensitivity to changes in mortality rates or as a risk measure. There are some articles on this subject, such as those written by Charles Stone of CUNY and Anne Zissu of NYU Polytechnic.

The development of a standardized forward curve to replicate the standardized LIBOR curve in the current interest rate environment is difficult and, at present, three firms have such curves although not all are tradable. Some movement has, nevertheless, developed in this direction. The Survivor Credit Offered Rate represents a bonus rate that is set one year in advance of payment, much like the forward LIBOR rate. Most bonus payouts in traditional life policies are in arrears. With the forward setting, SCORs lends itself to compare the forward LIBOR rate with $s(t, T, T + 1, x)$ as the forward mortality rate. Like the interest rates a number of derivatives can then be structured off this forward rate.

8.3   FUTURES-FORWARDS

Above we have covered forward rates to a good extent given forward rates are a major function of the pricing of a swap. There is a tradable forward rate in the market. It is JP Morgan's q-forward, utilizing the actuarial q to represent mortality rate. In essence the q-forward is a series of forward rate agreements that can be put in place to hedge a swap. In the notation to JP Morgan we have the following – but again not to confuse notation, JP Morgan is using $S(t, x)$ to denote the survival rate for ease of computation.

$$S(t, x) = (1 - q(0, x)) \times (1 - q(1, x + 1)) \times \wedge \times (1 - q(t - 1, x + t - 1))$$

We have seen this previously in Chapter 7 with respect to a single cohort.

$$S_3 = (P(t_0, t_2, x))/(P(t_0, t_3, x)\tau)$$
$$S_2 = (P(t_0, t_1, x) - P(t_0, t_3, x))/((P(t_0, t_3, x) + P(t_0, t_2, x))\tau)$$
$$S_1 = (P(t_0, t_0, x) - P(t_0, t_3, x))/((P(t_0, t_3, x) + P(t_0, t_2, x) + P(t_0, t_1, x))\tau)$$
$$\quad = (1 - P(t_0, t_3, x))/((P(t_0, t_3, x) + P(t_0, t_2, x) + P(t_0, t_1, x))\tau)$$

where $(1 - d(t))$ is the death rate at time t.

Below we have substituted the forward mortality rate q from time t_i to t_{i+1} for the spot rate $d(t + n)$.

$$S(0, x) = 1$$
$$S(1, x + 1) = S(0) \times (1 - (q(t + 1, x + 1)))$$
$$S(2, x + 2) = S(0) \times (1 - q(t + 1, x + 1)) \times (1 - q(t + 2, x + 2))$$
$$S(t, x + n) = S(0) \times (1 - q(t + 1, x + 1)) \times (1 - q(t + 2, x + 2))$$
$$\times \wedge \times (1 - q(t + n, x + n))$$

Table 8.7

		Swap Hedge		
Spot Rate	Fwd Rate	P(0, t $_{i+1}$)	% Fwd Held	S(t,x)
1.61%				
1.75%	1.90%	0.95	93.43%	$0.11
1.91%	2.24%	0.91	86.99%	$0.22
2.09%	2.63%	0.86	80.67%	-$0.14
2.30%	3.11%	0.82	74.44%	-$0.51
2.52%	3.66%	0.78	68.30%	-$0.68
2.77%	4.22%	0.75	62.30%	-$0.49
3.02%	4.82%	0.71	56.47%	-$0.61
3.30%	5.54%	0.6 8	50.80%	-$0.34
				-$2.43

By forcing out the discount factors as described in Chapter 7, we arrive at an arbitrage-free forward rate curve that can be used to hedge the swap curve where $-(1 + r)^{-(t-1)}$ is the arbitrage-free discount factor.

- $- (1+r)^{-(t-1)}S(0, x) = 1$
- $- (1+r)^{-(t-2)}S(1, x + 1) = S(0) \times (1 - (q(t + 1, x + 1)))$
- $- (1+r)^{-(t-3)}S(2, x + 2) = S(0) \times (1 - q(t + 1, x + 1)) \times (1 - q(t + 2, x + 2))$
- $- (1+r)^{-(t-n)}S(t, x + n) = S(0) \times (1 - q(t + 1, x + 1)) \times (1 - q(t + 2, x + 2))$
  $\times \wedge \times (1 - q(t + n, x + n))$

Using Table 8.4 we set up a series of forward rate hedges to hedge our swap example above. Table 8.7 shows that by weighting our forward rate using the q-forwards we have reduced the difference by over half. There are a number of factors that go into the reason the hedge is not perfect.

In general, the q-forwards or the swap will be used to hedge the mortality risk in a portfolio of life settlements.

8.4 OPTIONS

8.4.1 Bond Options

The most logical use of bond options with respect to (WRT) mortality risk would be an option on a longevity bond or inverse longevity bond. Given our problem in the extension of longevity, we will use the inverse longevity bond that was used in Section 5.6.3 of Chapter 5. From the pool of life settlements we see that the forward mortality volatility is 1.56%. To reiterate a point to *ad nausea*, one of the main purposes for using this asset class is its lack of volatility and correlation. Here we see the low volatility within the mortality rates.

From Chapter 7 we have Black's model below:

$$c = P(0, T)E_{Q'}[\max(F_T - X, 0)]$$

Bond Option	
Strike Price	$100.00
Bond Fwd Price	$97.47
Discount	0.8209
F_0	$80.01
PV Coupons	$2.53
σ	10.00%
d_1	0.49
d_2	0.39

Bond Option Price	$0.45

Figure 8.25

Where

F_T = *bond Future sprice at time T*

E_T = *expected value in forward risk neutral world*

$P(0, T)$ = *the value of a zero coupon bond priced at time 0*

where $P(0, T)$ is under Q'

for delivery at time T = a discount function

X = *the strike price on the option*

Assuming that the bond price is log-normal with a log-normal standard distribution and $\text{Std} = \sigma\sqrt{T}$ we get

$$c = P(0, T)[E_T(F_t)Nd_1 - XN(d_2)]$$

With

$$d_1 = \frac{\ln[E_T(F_T)/X] + \sigma^2 T/2}{\sigma\sqrt{T}} \tag{8.2}$$

$$d_2 = \frac{\ln[E_T(F_T)/X] - \sigma^2 T/2}{\sigma\sqrt{T}} = d_1 - \sigma\sqrt{T}$$

If we substitute in the forward price for the futures price above we can now apply Black's model to an inverse longevity bond.

Again using the expected average coupon rate we have a 6.8% coupon over the 10-year time frame.

Consider a 3-year call option on the bond (Figure 8.25) with the parameters using equation (8.2)

We get a very low price on the option of $0.45 which leads one to believe that because of the low volatility on the mortality rate, options are very stable and almost deterministic in value.

8.4.2 Put Option on the Longevity

As discussed in Chapter 7, there is at least one major bank that has sold a put option on the longevity risk – the idea being that we can put the portfolio of life settlements back to the writer of the put for the face value of the pool at term. For that option we are required to pay

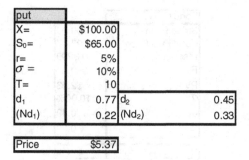

put			
X=	$100.00		
S_0=	$65.00		
r=	5%		
σ =	10%		
T=	10		
d_1	0.77	d_2	0.45
(Nd_1)	0.22	(Nd_2)	0.33

Price	$5.37

Figure 8.26

an up-front premium. This is very similar to an insurance contract except that it is a capital markets product and it would not be a large leap of faith to assume that if this option becomes popular there will be a secondary market in the option allowing the investor to enter into and exit out of the longevity risk easily, unlike an insurance contract.

Again we simplified the process for explanatory purposes and made large assumptions, but the idea is straightforward and easy to understand and replicate. Figure 8.26 shows the simple Black calculation.

Here we set the strike price X equal to the face value of the pool or $100. The risk free rate r is set at 5%, and the volatility is the same volatility that we used throughout the book, i.e. 10%. Note that this is the volatility that the life expectancy of 10 years will not be met and is calculated by the mean divided by the square root of the number of policies. Again, for clarification, this is the volatility of the average life of the pool of life settlements, which is a different volatility from the mortality forward rate volatility. Time is set at 10 years; that leaves the strike price S_0. Here we made some assumptions: (1) that the average purchase price of the pool was 25 cents; (2) that the premium payments were 3% for the full 10 years; and (3) that there was a management fee of 1% for the full 10 years, and built all that into the current price of the pool. These are all assumptions we have used throughout the book. The current price was then calculated to be $65. Plugging these figures into a simple option-pricing model gave us a put option price of $5.37. This would indicate that for $5.37 we could purchase a put option on our portfolio which, in 10 years, would allow us to put the portfolio back to the option writer and receive any and all payments needed to have a $100 balance. Generally speaking, the writer of the put option would take possession of the pool and all the runoffs to date and pay out the $100.

Like all the products discussed, the permutations and combinations are endless. Structures such as a life expectancy plus 2 years could be looked at. The possession of the pool at term could be worked down and any and all profit above the strike price and expenses could be divided up.

8.5   CAPS, FLOORS AND SWAPTIONS

8.5.1   Caps

From Chapter 7 we see that a cap is a series of caplets. Equations (8.3) to (8.5) below are the Black formula for a caplet. If we calculate the caplet price for each year and then sum, we will have the cap price of a mortality hedge for 10 years.

Table 8.8

Year	Spot Rate	Fwd Rate	Discount	h_1	h_2	$N(h_1)$	$N(h_2)$	Caplet
1	1.61%							
2	1.75%	1.90%	0.952381	-0.47	-0.49	0.32	0.31	$1.00
3	1.91%	2.24%	0.907029	-0.37	-0.37	0.36	0.36	$0.59
4	2.09%	2.63%	0.863838	-0.26	-0.26	0.40	0.40	$0.31
5	2.30%	3.11%	0.822702	-0.16	-0.16	0.44	0.44	$0.11
6	2.52%	3.66%	0.783526	-0.05	-0.05	0.48	0.48	$0.01
7	2.77%	4.22%	0.746215	0.04	0.04	0.52	0.52	$0.01
8	3.02%	4.82%	0.710681	0.13	0.13	0.55	0.55	$0.07
9	3.30%	5.54%	0.676839	0.21	0.21	0.58	0.58	$0.22
								$2.33

From above K is the strike or cap price, $F(t_0, t_i, t_{i+1}, x)$ is the forward mortality rate from t_i to t_{i+1} starting at t_0 and $h_{1,2}$ is the standard normal distribution.

Again using

$$Caplet\,(t_{i+1}) = Max[R_i - K, 0]\frac{1}{1 + R_i \tau_i} \tag{8.3}$$

$$Caplet = [F(t_0, t_i, t_{i+1})N(h_i) - K(h_2)]P(t_0, t_{i+1}) \tag{8.4}$$

$$h_{1,2} = \frac{\ln\left(\frac{F}{K}\right) \pm \frac{1}{2}\sigma^2(t_1 - t_0)}{\sigma\sqrt{t_i - t_0}} \tag{8.5}$$

we have the values shown in Table 8.8

where

K=	4%
δ=	1.56%

If the realized mortality rates come true, our cap will maintain a 4% mortality rate through the 10-year time frame (see Table 8.9 and Figures 8.27 and 8.28).

Table 8.9

realized	Cap	Payout
1.61%		
1.78%	4%	$0.00
1.98%	4%	$0.00
2.80%	4%	$0.00
3.80%	4%	$0.00
4.66%	4%	$0.66
5.00%	4%	$1.00
5.90%	4%	$1.90
6.20%	4%	$2.20
		$5.76

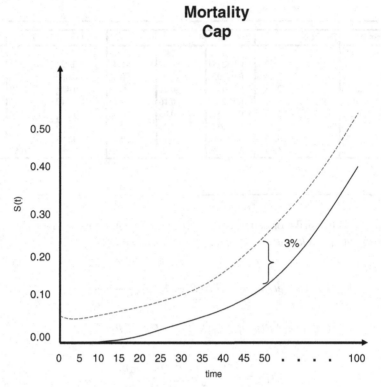

Figure 8.27

8.5.2 Swaptions

As stated in Chapter 7, the valuation of a swap is as follows:

$$Max[X - K, 0]B \textit{(payer swap)}$$
$$Max[K - X, 0]B \textit{(receiver swap)}$$
$$\textit{Where } B = \sum_{k=1,n} P(t_i, t_{i+k})\tau_k$$

The swaption calculation is expanded below.

$$\textit{Payer Swaption} = [X(t_0, t_i, t_{i+1})N(h_1) - KN(h_2)]B$$

Table 8.10 shows the calculation. We chose a 2% swaption rate, given that the average forward rate in our example is 3.87% on the forward mortality rate, and a 4% swap following the 4% cap above would prove worthless. Nevertheless the 2% swaption would cost approximately 14 cents on the 100 dollars and would allow us to maintain a 2% mortality rate until term. This is then something we can plan for and hedge effectively.

In conclusion, we want to state that the examples above were quite simple and the mathematics was kept to a minimum. For example, all terms were one year, so we did not have

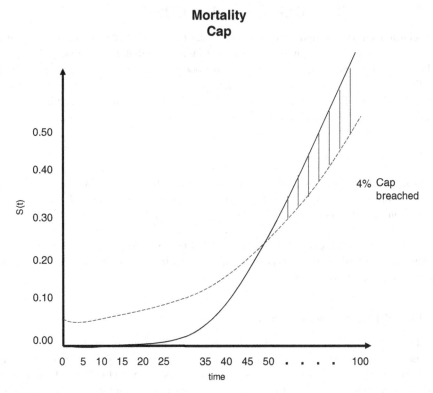

Figure 8.28

to deal with partial years in the equations. We approached the problem from a very deterministic solution rather than integrating each calculation. To do this correctly would require a lot more care and detail, but the point we want to make is that these products are achievable and will in the not too distant future become part of the lexicon of hedging longevity risk.

Table 8.10

Year	Spot Rate	Fwd Rate	Discount	h1	h2	N(h1)	N(h2)	Compounded 3yr rate	Swaption
1	1.61%							0.03	
2	1.75%	1.90%	95.24%	-0.47	-0.49	0.32	0.31	0.03	
3	1.91%	2.24%	90.70%	-0.37	-0.37	0.36	0.36	0.03	
4	2.09%	2.63%	86.38%	-0.26	-0.26	0.40	0.40		$0.00
5	2.30%	3.11%	82.27%	-0.16	-0.16	0.44	0.44		$0.01
5	2.30%	3.11%	82.27%	-0.16	-0.16	0.44	0.44		$0.01
6	2.52%	3.66%	78.35%	-0.05	-0.05	0.48	0.48		$0.02
7	2.77%	4.22%	74.62%	0.04	0.04	0.52	0.52		$0.02
8	3.02%	4.82%	71.07%	0.13	0.13	0.55	0.55		$0.03
9	3.30%	5.54%	67.68%	0.21	0.21	0.58	0.58		$0.04
		3.87%						2.00%	$0.1357

8.6   HEDGING LIQUIDITY RISK

As has been stated throughout this book, the two major risks associated with LSPs are liquidity risk and longevity risk. The liquidity risk stems from the fact that, in any pool, policies with a very short life expectancy will be expensive. Most pools have a 10-year life and, as such, there will be little to no cash flows within the first few years of a pool with the expenses of the pool starting immediately. For this reason some sort of liquidity provision is absolutely necessary and there are a number of ways that this can be established.

8.6.1   Establishing a Reserve

The easiest and most likely scenario would be to establish a reserve. In all examples in the book we set up a reserve and tried to maintain a 3-year expense cover. If the portfolio is backing a bond issue, this is not a difficult process; simply take a part of the bond proceeds and keep it in a reserve account. If, however, the programme is a fund of some sort of zero instrument, then the reserve will have to be included in the pricing of the structure.

As the reserve is built up in excess of the expense requirement the reserve can be swept and additional life policies purchased.

8.6.2   Establishing a Liquidity Provider

Many funds have established a liquidity provider they can draw upon if the liquidity in the fund should run low. With this product this is even more beneficial, given the absolute payout at some time during the life of the policies. These payouts can be in the form of lines of credit or simply a prearranged agreement to borrow up to a certain amount if the necessity occurs.

Several funds have established a Sharia compliant fund. In this instance, interest is not acceptable. There are hedge funds who will offer a put arrangement on cash drawdown that act as an option but, in reality, are lines of credit where the interest charged is simply the option premium. This should comply with Sharia law.

8.6.3   Partial Portfolio Sale

While these products are not actively traded there is a market for them. In an actively traded portfolio the manager will constantly be looking for ways to improve the yield on the portfolio. This may be accomplished by selling off a section of the pool – perhaps a cohort section or a specific rating class – and trading up to a different sector or factor. As a result, there may be constant selling and buying of pieces of the portfolio. If a liquidity need arises, the manager can simply sell off a part of the pool for cash.

However, if the market gets wind of the fact that there might be a distressed sale, they will try to beat the price down and the returns on the fund will suffer.

8.6.4   Borrow against the Portfolio

Finally, there is the ability to borrow against the portfolio. These pools are, after all, an asset and until recently many banks would lend against an asset – and this asset was no different. However, in most cases the bank would lend only against the purchase price of the asset and, as we have stated before, the growth in value of these portfolios is almost linear.

Purchasing a portfolio for 20 cents on the dollar and then borrowing just that purchase price some 8 years later would lead to the lending bank being hugely over-collateralized. Prior to the deterioration in the credit markets starting in late 2007, some banks attempted to enhance their lending capabilities by allowing some of the growth in value to count as collateral for the loan.

8.7   HEDGING CREDIT RISK

Credit risk is not a major concern with these funds. As shown in Chapters 2, 3 and 7, most pools consist of policies from carriers rated A or higher. In addition, the majority of states in the USA carry a state insurance fund that will stand behind the payout of the policy if the carrier goes into default (although note that this state support is only effective for policies of $300,000 or less).

8.7.1   Diversification

Certainly diversification is a hedge against a credit loss. By stipulating that the portfolio can have no more than 20% policies from any one carrier, the credit risk has been reduced to some extent through diversification.

8.7.2   Credit Risk

There are a number of credit wraps that you can use. We have already looked at the insurance wrap as to longevity risk but this wrap will act as a credit protection also by guaranteeing principal payout no matter what. There are also a number of other insurance products that can be purchased like the surety bond discussed above. Any programme that guarantees repayment against longevity risk will also guarantee repayment due to default.

However, there are credit-specific programmes and they usually provide less expensive protection than the other insurance products. The most common in the capital markets is the credit default swap. This is an instrument that can be purchased from an investment bank which will guarantee the repayment of principal and accrued interest in the event of a default. These products are usually set up such that payment is made quarterly in the form of basis points for the coverage. They are usually cheaper than the insurance product and offer the added advantage of being easily reversible. If at any point in time we wish to eliminate the coverage we simply sell the default swap back into the market, understanding that these are highly traded items and prices are quite volatile.

An extension of the default swap is the basket swap. The basket swap is a basket of credit default swaps that can be customized. This may include a basket of all the carriers in the pool. The payouts are also customized and may range from a first-to-default structure to the first $10 million of loss to the first 10 of 20 to default. Obviously the more coverage, the more the costs.

8.7.3   Hedging Efficiency

Finally we want to take a look at how effective all these hedges are and take a detour into the dark world of theory. While we have previously shown volatility and correlation intra-structure is low to non-existent, inter-structure is more problematic. The simplest example of this in the real world is the basis risk between the cash Treasury bond and the Treasury future. While at term the bond is exchanged for the futures contract, several factors create a longer term basis that can be quite large and volatile at times.

When looking at hundreds of bases within the LSP – the basis between each life expectancy in the pool versus the life expectancy in the hedge – a white noise is created that is difficult if not impossible to hedge.

8.8   HER (HEDGE EFFICIENCY RATIO) FOR AN INVERSE LONGEVITY BOND

Assuming that the volatility on the bond and the underlying portfolio and the correlation were close, this would still have a poor *HER* ratio because of the cost to put in place.

The resulting *HER* equation would be assuming a 60% correlation between the annuity and the portfolio and a 1% volatility in the portfolio with an equal percent volatility in the bond based upon the fact the variability of the bond is based upon the variability of the pool:

$$HER = \left[1 - \rho\left(\frac{\sigma_P}{\sigma_H}\right)\right] \times \cos t$$
$$= \left[1 - .6\left(\frac{.1}{.1}\right)\right] \times \$60$$
$$= .4 \times \$60$$
$$= 24$$

8.8.1   Theory

As with any hedging programme there is a trade-off between reducing risk and the cost of the hedge. Otherwise either a pure arbitrage can take place and, as the saying goes, "the markets abhors arbitrage" or you are forced back to the risk-free rate of return. The cost of hedging falls into two distinct categories: direct cost and opportunity costs. A simple example would be an interest rate swap. The purchaser of the fixed side of the trade reduces his risks to a rising rate environment at the cost initially of a more expensive fixed rate, but loses the opportunity cost if rates actually fall.

As a result, any hedge has to be evaluated as to the effectiveness of the hedge and the cost associated with that effectiveness, remembering that a true pure hedge will produce a risk-free return in the absence of arbitrage. Paying large fees up front for a hedge that has huge basis risk may not be a viable alternative. In order to understand this fully we come full circle, back to our co-integration problem. Hedging mortality risk becomes a problem of the longevity of the population of the LSP and the longevity of the hedge. Remember, we are looking at two or more stochastic processes which, by their very nature, are difficult to hedge unless we get exactly like for like.

8.8.2   Hedging Effectiveness

As previously observed, there are, quite literally, walls of libraries filled with treatises on hedging effectiveness. They can be quite voluminous and difficult to understand. However, the purpose of this book is not to explore the theory of hedging. For that reason we have developed a simple method of determining hedging efficiency with the understanding that it is not perfect but should give the reader some reference. We will address each risk factor individually and not worry about credit risks while we are trying to hedge longevity risk. The two examples cited above have, as an advantage, the ability to address multiple risks at once.

As a formal definition, hedging can be described as the amount of change experienced in the underlying offset by the change in the designated hedge instrument. In most cases complete hedging is difficult, if not impossible, because there will always be more than one underlying factor: like trying to herd a group of cats. The interaction of these variables in a stochastic and non-linear way makes it more useful to address each factor individually, possibly on a macro level.

8.8.3   Effectiveness of a Hedge: the Calculation

As stated above, there have been libraries written on hedging techniques and the effectiveness of a "perfect" hedge. Most hedges are less than perfect but can be measured quantitatively against a hypothetical "perfect" hedge.

We will, in this treatise, address "standardized hedges" as opposed to "customized hedges". A standardized hedge uses standard instruments in the market today. It is more liquid and, as a result, cheaper than a customized hedge. An example of a standardized hedge might be the purchase of an annuity with standard longevity measured against a customized annuity which has the longevity measure of each life policy in a pool.

Several large investment banks specializing in LSPs are more than able to measure an individual pool's longevity and match each policy, pooling that into a hedge structure like a single premium annuity.

From our experience in the equity markets, looking at α and β hedging, let U represent the underlying pool of life policies. H represents the hedging instrument. We then represent the hedged portfolio as follows:

$$P = U + \Delta H$$

where Δ is the hedge ratio.

If we let HER (no gender bias here) represent the "Hedge Equivalent Risk" to the portfolio, we can then represent HER as follows

$$HER = 1 - \frac{r_P}{r_U}$$

where r is the concurrent risk to the different securities.

In a perfect world HER would equal 1. Using this parameter we can get a metric for measuring the risks of various hedging instruments.

If we let r equal σ, the volatility of the instrument, we have

$$HER = 1 - \frac{r_P}{r_H}$$

or

$$\Rightarrow HER = 1 - \frac{\sigma_P}{\sigma_H}$$

if

$$\frac{\sigma_P}{\sigma_H} = 1 \, Or \, \sigma_P = \sigma_H \Rightarrow HER = 0$$

Realizing that σ_P and σ_H do not move in lock step, we need ρ, our leash between the drunk and the dog, to represent the correlation between the two risk factors. That then gives us Δ equal to

$$\Delta = -\rho \left(\frac{\sigma_U}{\sigma_H} \right)$$

and

$$HER = 1 - \rho \left(\frac{\sigma_U}{\sigma_H} \right)$$

One other factor has to be taken into consideration and that is the cost of the hedge. Again, from theory, if the hedge is perfect you should force the return back down to the risk-free rate. However, there are several factors working in favour of the hedge in this case. First, as stated above, it is difficult if not impossible to establish a perfect hedge. There will always be some risk, which indicates that the return should be above the risk-free rate. Second, as stated in Chapter 3, there is a regulatory arbitrage in the pricing of life settlement policies which lends itself to a hedged position with "through the curve" returns.

This results in a very simple measure for determining the effectiveness of our hedge of

$$HER = 1 - \rho \left(\frac{\sigma_U}{\sigma_H} \right) \times \cos t$$

With that we can look at *HER* to determine the efficiency of the hedge remembering that σ and ρ are parameters from an assumed normal distribution.

8.8.4 Risks

Hedging, as it relates to a LSP, is different from hedging a stock using an option or an interest rate using a cap or swap, for the reason that we are mainly looking to hedge an end result and not a day-to-day or tic-by-tic movement. The process to determine what to hedge is as difficult as the hedge itself. For example, in hedging longevity risk are we trying to hedge both the principal and interest of the fund or simply our estimate of the residual risk, realizing that runoffs occur throughout the process and cash will build up. As stated previously, policies will always pay out (absent a default on the part of the carrier), the only risk being "when". If the purpose of the hedge is to protect against a residual value much less than the expectation, then we should consider how to measure that residual. Would it be economically feasible to hedge somewhere between the estimated residual and the full principal and/or principal and interest?

These questions have to be answered in the context of the structure you are modelling and what the investors expect. Many European banks will not lend against a pool of life settlements unless there is a full "wrap" in place, by which we mean an insurance policy guaranteeing payment in full of principal and/or principal and interest as of a specific termination date.

Trying to get a relationship between σ and ρ for the number of policies within a pool (some as large as 1,000 policies) can be a daunting task. This was one of the reasons copula techniques are used in CDO pools, as discussed in Chapter 3. Copula techniques attempt to find tails in the marginal distribution of a large variable relationship, or, in other words, the estimated residual in a LSP.

Basis risk is associated with σ and ρ. We restate it here because most of the time the risk stated is basis risk, which is in reality σ and ρ risk. It is the risk that the movement in the underlying is different from the movement in the hedge instrument and this causes your hedge to break down.

8.8.5   HER for an Annuity

Given that this is a hypothetical risk, we can only make general assumptions about the parameters of the underlying and the hedging instrument. However, estimations should not be that far off, considering the nature of the instruments. The LSP, as stated previously, will have little volatility inter portfolio. An annuity chosen to hedge the pool is deterministic in nature and, as such, it has no variance.

The resulting *HER* equation would be assuming a 90% correlation between the annuity and the portfolio and a 1% volatility in the portfolio:

$$HER = \left[1 - \rho\left(\frac{\sigma_P}{\sigma_H}\right)\right] \times \cos t$$

$$= \left[1 - .9\left(\frac{.1}{0}\right)\right] \times 12$$

$$= 1 \times 12$$

$$= 12$$

As can be seen above, the conundrum being division by zero, as the hedging instrument is deterministic and has no volatility.

This will be the main problem in evaluating hedging until we get into derivative products. Any hedge instrument with a fixed outcome will be deterministic and have no volatility with respect to the payout at term, save the credit rating that we will address later, as the next instrument we want to look at is the inverse longevity bond.

8.8.6   HER for an Inverse Longevity Bond

If we look at the *HER* of a longevity bond we basically have only two different variables. As stated above, the mortality rate on an inverse longevity bond is approximately 2.56%. However, the cost of the longevity bond is the face value of the bond. In this case we will estimate the cost as the par value of the bond less the expected residual value of the portfolio we are hedging. In this case it will be $20, i.e. $100 minus the $80 dollar expected runoff.

$$HER = \left[1 - \rho\left(\frac{\sigma_P}{\sigma_H}\right)\right] \times \cos t$$

$$= \left[1 - .9\left(\frac{.02561}{.1}\right)\right] \times \$20$$

$$= \$15.39$$

8.8.7   HER for a Mortality Swap

Initially, mortality swaps are structured to be a zero-cost process. In other words, if the swap is priced correctly, the investor should not have a preference as to which side of the trade they are on. As the swap moves through time, the initial zero position is no longer in place, and it can then be determined what a swap would cost if put in place in $t + n$ years.

$$HER = \left[1 - \rho\left(\frac{\sigma_P}{\sigma_H}\right)\right] \times \cos t$$

$$= \left[1 - .9\left(\frac{.02561}{.68}\right)\right] \times \$10$$

$$= \$6.61$$

8.9 CONCLUSION

Many of the products discussed in Chapters 7 and 8 are theoretical. However, there is much interest in ways to hedge longevity risk and it will only be a matter of time before some, if not all, of the products discussed above are in place and looked upon as vanilla products. Two of the authors were involved with the first interest rate swaps when the majority of the market said they would never survive. Even the credit default swap was, apparently, not going to make it as a vanilla product because of the problems with defining a default. It is estimated that, in 2009, \$42 trillion worth of credit derivative products will trade.

The authors see the same process happening with the life settlement industry. In 2007 approximately \$12 billion in life settlements were traded, and while the exponential growth from 2005 to 2007 has slowed in 2008, a return to normality in the credit markets will undoubtedly rekindle that expansion. The product offers the advantage of little or no correlation to any of the other market parameters, exceptional returns and little risk – most of this due to the regulatory arbitrage that exists today. There is no indication that the regulatory arbitrage will soon go away; however, the life insurance companies will most likely re-evaluate their pricing policies. There is still a large lapse factor built into the carrier's pricing model for new issuance; this becomes impossible to maintain if a significant volume of policies end up in the life settlement market. However, the volume of policies traded in the life settlement market today, when seen as a percentage of the total volume of life insurance in issue in the USA, is insignificant – there is plenty of room for growth before it becomes even a sidebar concern for the life insurance community.

Appendix

Life Settlement Portfolio Projection - EXECUTIVE SUMMARY*

Stochastic Simulation Using 500 Randomly Generated Scenarios for:

Date of Death of Each Insured, Rates of Mortality Improvement, and UW Rating for Each Insured using Normal Distribution

Net Present Value of Future Cash Flows on 12/31/2006 at 10.25% Interest

Expected	**90th Percentile**	**90.00% CTE**
The Present Value of Expected Cash Flows, Consisting of Expected Revenue from Maturities, less Expected Outlays for Premiums and Expenses, discounted at an annual interest rate of 10.25% on 12/31/2006 **22,386,330**	Based on the Stochastic Projections, there is a 90.00% probability that the Net PV of Future Cash Flows on 12/31/2006 at 10.25% Interest will equal or exceed **16,428,521**	Based on the Stochastic Projections, the Net PV of the Average of the Cash Flows of Scenarios with a Net PV Less Than $16,428,521 (the 90th Percentile) (the average of all worst case scenarios) **12,663,148**

Total Internal Rate of Return

Expected	**90th Percentile**	**90.00% CTE**
The Estimated Internal Rate of Return (IRR) of Past and Future Cash Flows, Consisting of Historical and Expected Revenue from Maturities, less Historical and Expected Cash Premiums, Expenses, and Net Purchase Prices **5.90%**	Based on the Stochastic Projections, there is a 90.00% probability that the Internal Rate of Return of Historical and Expected Cash flows will equal or exceed **3.19%**	Based on the Stochastic Projections, the IRR of the Average of the Cash Flows of Scenarios with an IRR Less Than 3.19% (the 90th Percentile) (the average of all worst case scenarios) **-8.45%**

PORTFOLIO DESCRIPTION

Sample portfolio of 10 policies (including 5 LS) for Demonstration and Peer Review of Life Settlement Portfolio Model.

PORTFOLIO SUMMARY

	# Policies	
# Joint Life Policies	10	
# Unique Lives (or Joint-Life Combinations)	5	
	10	
Total DB	39,173,206	
DB per Policy	3,917,321	
DB per Life	3,917,321	
Total Net Purchase Price	24,427,676	
Average Price (as a % of DB)	62.36%	

AVERAGE AGE

	Simple Average	Face-Weighted
Average Age at UW		
Life 1	78.40	77.72
Life 2	77.20	77.60
Average Age at Valuation		
Life 1	81.81	81.01
Life 2	78.75	79.13

AVERAGE UNDERWRITING DATE

	Simple Average	Face-Weighted
Average UW Date	1/19/2004	4/10/2004

Concentration of Risk: Net DB by Insured (5 Largest)

Concentration of Risk: Net DB by Primary Diagnosis

Diabetes 24.8%
Cardio-Vascular 19.1%
None 16.8%
Cancer 39.2%

*These Results Reflect Information in the Portfolio File, related to the Insureds, Policy, Underwriting LEs and Ratings, as well as the Assumptions and Options Elected by the User. Please refer to the reports "Life Settlement Portfolio Projection - Detailed Results" and "Monthly Cash Flows" for detailed assumptions, options and results.

Notice Regarding Mortality and Volatility:

Underwriting firms commonly develop "life expectancies" for the benefit of life settlement parties. While life expectancies are provided for individuals, they are developed from expected patterns of mortality of large groups of similar individuals. No one knows exactly when any one individual will die, nor is a life expectancy intended to suggest the time until death will be near the life expectancy. For a variety of reasons (such as improvements in medical technology, unanticipated general mortality improvement misestimation of the life expectancy by underwriting firms), any one individual might live much longer than his or her estimated life expectancy. Stochastic simulation and sensitivity testing can help to quantify these risks, but such tests should not be interpreted as a guarantee of any particular financial outcome. different than predicted by any particular mortality table. With small groups of insureds, and particularly with a single insured, the actual time until death may be significantly Investors will earn less than expected on the policy of any individual who lives longer than his life expectancy.

Life Settlement Portfolio Projection - Detailed Results

(IRR excludes all cash flows on past claims and PV excludes all cash flows prior to 12/31/06)

Valuation Date: 12/31/06

User-Selected Mortality Assumption Based on:
2001 VBT 50% S&U and 50% Ult Mortality Table ANB and Supplied Life Expectancies
Past (2001–2006) Annual Improvement based on Historical Population Experience
Future Annual Improvement based on 100% Male Historical Population Experience
Future Annual Improvement based on 100% Female Historical Population Experience

Stochastic Simulation Using
500 Randomly Generated Scenarios for:
Date of Death of Each Insured
Rates of Mortality Improvement
U/W Rating for Each Insured using Normal Distribution
with Std Dev= 25.0% and Shift=0.0%

AVERAGE LIFE EXPECTANCY (LE)

	Simple Average	Face-Weighted
Average LE - Fasano^^		
Life 1	51	54
Life 2	53	56
Average LE - AVS^^		
Life 1	62	63
Life 2		
Average LE - Measured from UW Date		
Life 1	52	54
Life 2	53	56
Joint	65	67
Average LE - Measured from Valuation Date		
Joint	56	58

DIST OF PV FUTURE CASH FLOWS On 12/31/06 at 10.25%

Percentile	Present Value (000)	Contingent Tail Expectation
99%	11,373	9,422
95%	14,145	11,489
90%	16,429	12,663
75%	19,293	14,965
50%	22,417	16,998
90%	16,429	12,663

PORTFOLIO DESCRIPTION

Sample portfolio of 10 policies (including 5 LS) for Demonstration and Peer Review of Life Settlement Portfolio Model.

PORTFOLIO SUMMARY

# Policies	10
# Joint Life Policies	5
# Unique Lives (or Joint-Life Combinations)	10
Total DB	39,173,206
DB per Policy	3,917,321
DB per Life	3,917,321
Total Net Purchase Price	24,427,676
Average Price (as a % of DB)	62.36%

AVERAGE AGE

	Simple Average	Face-Weighted
Average Age at UW		
Life 1	78.40	77.72
Life 2	77.20	77.60
Average Age at Valuation		
Life 1	81.81	81.01
Life 2	78.75	79.13

AVERAGE UNDERWRITING DATE

	Simple Average	Face-Weighted
Average UW Date	1/19/2004	4/10/2004

EXPECTED RESULTS*

PV Future Cash Flow at 10.25% (000)	Internal Rate of Return^
22,386	5.90%

probabilistic projection without regard to stochastic variables

AVERAGE RATING

	Simple Average	Face-Weighted
Average Rating - Fasano^^		
Life 1	285%	267%
Life 2	361%	314%
Average Rating - AVS^^		
Life 1	358%	309%
Life 2	445%	386%
Average Rating - Projection		
Life 1	456%	434%
Life 2	798%	714%

DISTRIBUTION OF IRR* of Policies in Force On 01/01/07

Results	Avg Internal Rate of Return^	% of Scenarios
IRR < 0.00%	-75.26%	1%
IRR < 4.00%	-2.41%	20%
IRR < 8.00%	3.76%	78%
IRR < 12.00%	4.93%	97%
IRR < 16.00%	5.13%	100%
IRR < 10.25%	4.55%	92%

Percentile	IRR	Contingent Tail Expectation
99%	-60.74%	-85.62%
95%	2.44%	-19.80%
90%	3.19%	-8.45%
75%	4.39%	-1.09%
50%	5.86%	2.04%
90%	3.19%	-8.45%

Notice Regarding Mortality and Volatility:

Underwriting firms commonly develop "life expectancies" for the benefit of life settlement parties. While life expectancies are provided for individuals, they are developed from expected patterns of mortality of large groups of similar individuals. No one knows exactly when any one individual will die, nor is a life expectancy intended to suggest the time until death will be near the life expectancy. For a variety of reasons (such as improvements in medical technology, unanticipated general mortality improvement, or misestimation of the life expectancy by underwriting firms), any one individual might live much longer than his or her estimated life expectancy. With small groups of insureds, and particularly with a single insured, the actual time until death may be significantly different from the life expectancy or that predicted by any particular mortality table. Stochastic simulation and sensitivity testing can help to quantify these risks, but such tests should not be interpreted as a guarantee of any particular financial outcome.

Investors will earn less than expected on the policy of any individual who lives longer than his life expectancy.

Life Settlement Portfolio Projection - Detailed Results

(IRR excludes all cash flows on past claims and PV excludes all cash flows prior to 12/31/06)

Valuation Date: 12/31/06

Stochastic Simulation Using
500 Randomly Generated Scenarios for:
Date of Death of Each Insured
Rates of Mortality Improvement
U/W Rating for Each Insured using Normal Distribution
with Std Dev= 25.0% and Shift=0.0%

User-Selected Mortality Assumption Based on:
2001 VBT 50% S&U and 50% Ult Mortality Table ANB and Supplied Life Expectancies
Past (2001–2006) Annual Improvement based on Historical Population Experience
Future Annual Improvement based on 100% Male Historical Population Experience
Future Annual Improvement based on 100% Female Historical Population Experience

PERCENTILE DISTRIBUTION - Present Value of Future Cash Flows

Percentile	PV Future Cash Flows* on 12/31/06 0.00%	PV Future Cash Flows* on 12/31/06 4.00%	PV Future Cash Flows* on 12/31/06 8.00%	PV Future Cash Flows* on 12/31/06 12.00%	PV Future Cash Flows* on 12/31/06 16.00%	PV Future Cash Flows* on 12/31/06 10.25%	Internal Rate of Return^ (including past and future cash flows)
99%	23,800,267	18,357,933	14,164,842	9,660,014	6,803,325	11,373,378	-60.74%
95%	31,909,629	23,164,553	16,741,159	12,674,538	9,730,085	14,145,111	2.44%
90%	33,374,734	25,211,391	19,071,599	14,767,357	11,683,307	16,428,521	3.19%
75%	34,879,154	27,449,923	21,885,409	17,619,190	14,490,478	19,292,636	4.39%
50%	36,692,574	29,682,192	24,658,034	20,945,248	17,973,806	22,416,889	5.86%
25%	37,751,990	31,632,535	27,406,724	23,923,937	21,298,300	25,349,330	7.80%
10%	38,397,993	33,142,016	29,453,535	26,585,995	24,301,199	27,747,150	9.84%
90.00%	33,374,734	25,211,391	19,071,599	14,767,357	11,683,307	16,428,521	3.19%
Min	15,762,459	15,237,904	11,041,255	7,061,702	4,403,200	8,602,984	
Max	39,192,059	35,677,714	33,173,133	31,185,301	29,444,213	32,021,854	
Std Dev	2,647,072	3,339,585	4,050,002	4,507,849	4,778,350	4,335,427	
Average	36,027,999	29,314,288	24,418,002	20,742,136	17,913,032	22,227,902	
Expected**	36,274,625	29,567,106	24,615,935	20,869,004	17,970,492	22,386,330	5.90%

CUMULATIVE HISTORICAL CASH FLOWS AND PRESENT VALUE OF EXPECTED CASH FLOWS

Cumulative Historical Present Value Future	(25,868,779)	(26,660,411)	(27,447,072)	(28,229,012)	(29,006,461)	(27,887,479)	
Total at Valuation Date	10,405,846	2,906,695	(2,831,137)	(7,360,008)	(11,035,969)	(5,501,149)	5.90%

CONTINGENT TAIL EXPECTATION

Contingent Tail Expectation (CTE***)	PV Future Cash Flows* on 12/31/06 0.00%	PV Future Cash Flows* on 12/31/06 4.00%	PV Future Cash Flows* on 12/31/06 8.00%	PV Future Cash Flows* on 12/31/06 12.00%	PV Future Cash Flows* on 12/31/06 16.00%	PV Future Cash Flows* on 12/31/06 10.25%	Internal Rate of Return^
99%	21,175,278	16,424,352	12,071,852	7,728,858	4,836,579	9,421,979	-85.62%
95%	27,991,404	19,766,191	13,912,429	9,660,716	6,881,861	11,488,646	-19.80%
90%	30,373,395	21,571,040	15,245,755	11,007,896	8,085,452	12,663,148	-8.45%
75%	32,658,334	23,877,067	17,617,668	13,230,777	10,101,938	14,965,219	-1.09%
50%	34,275,621	25,730,637	19,623,711	15,262,204	12,085,342	16,997,638	2.04%
25%	35,263,415	26,989,089	21,114,124	16,989,194	13,719,896	18,565,686	3.61%
10%	35,731,231	27,680,229	21,969,323	17,807,400	14,692,400	19,474,944	4.45%
90.00%	30,373,395	21,571,040	15,245,755	11,007,896	8,085,452	12,663,148	-8.45%

	1.4%
	0.01
	1.00

Adjusted Input Distribution by UW

Underwriter	Weight
Fasano	0%
AVS	0%
	0%
	0%
	0%
Random***	100%
TOTAL	100%

Excel Random Number Generator seeded with value of 38954.

% scenarios where one or more insured survive beyond maturity without paying death benefit
Average # of policies with insured surviving beyond maturity (over all scenarios)
Average # of policies with insured surviving beyond maturity (over scenarios with 1 or more)

* This analysis is based on the following assumptions:

Policy purchase, premium, and expenses assumed to occur on the first day of each calendar month.
Premiums paid equal 100% of Input Projected Premiums.
Monthly administration expenses at annualized rate of 0.10% per In Force Death Benefits
 plus $12.50 annually per policy plus an annual portfolio fee of $15,000.00 as long as any policies are in force
Attained Age is determined based on Date of Birth and the "As of Date of LE Estimate" in Company data.
Policies assumed in force on today's date (i.e., assumed 100% survival until now) unless earlier input Claim Date
Dates, Net Purchase Price, Net Death Benefit and Projected Premiums as shown in Policy Input and Premium Input
Mortality adjustments and improvement assumption grade to 100% between attained ages 105 and 120
Claim proceeds assumed to be paid at end of each month plus 2 months from death, earning statutory interest at 0.00%

** Expected shows results of Probabilistic Approach
*** CTE equals average of results equal or less than the Percentile case.
^ Note that Scenario IRRs are based on lower and upper bounds of -100.00% and 200.00%, respectively.
^^Average of those policies for which values are available.

Life Settlement Portfolio Projection - Detailed Results

(IRR excludes all cash flows on past claims and PV excludes all cash flows prior to 12/31/06)

Valuation Date: 12/31/06

User-Selected Mortality Assumption Based on:

2001 VBT 50% S&U and 50% Ult Mortality Table ANB and Supplied Life Expectancies
Past (2001–2006) Annual Improvement based on Historical Population Experience
Future Annual Improvement based on 100% Male Historical Population Experience
Future Annual Improvement based on 100% Female Historical Population Experience

Stochastic Simulation Using
500 Randomly Generated Scenarios for:
Date of Death of Each Insured
Rates of Mortality Improvement
U/W Rating for Each Insured using Normal Distribution
with Std Dev= 25.0% and Shift=0.0%

Distribution of Net DB by State

(Including Past Claims in Portfolio)

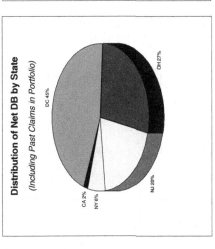

Distribution of Net DB by Primary Diagnosis

(Including Past Claims in Portfolio)

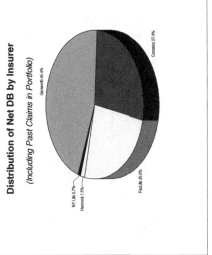

Distribution of Net DB by Insurer

(Including Past Claims in Portfolio)

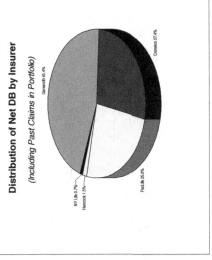

Five Largest Policies (Net DB)

Five Largest Insureds (Net DB)

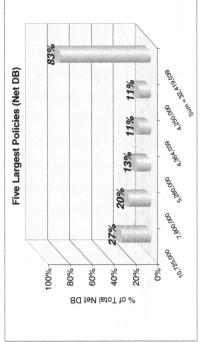

Life Settlement Portfolio Projection - Detailed Results

(IRR excludes all cash flows on past claims and PV excludes all cash flows prior to 12/31/06)

Valuation Date: 12/31/06

User-Selected Mortality Assumption Based on:

2001 VBT 50% S&U and 50% Ult Mortality Table ANB and Supplied Life Expectancies
Past (2001–2006) Annual Improvement based on Historical Population Experience
Future Annual Improvement based on 100% Male Historical Population Experience
Future Annual Improvement based on 100% Female Historical Population Experience

Stochastic Simulation Using
500 Randomly Generated Scenarios for:
Date of Death of Each Insured
Rates of Mortality Improvement
U/W Rating for Each Insured using Normal Distribution
with Std Dev= 25.0% and Shift=0.0%

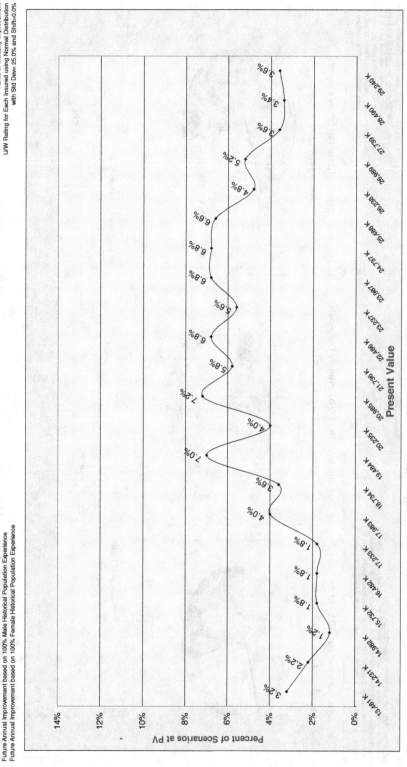

Life Settlement Portfolio Projection - Detailed Results

(IRR excludes all cash flows on past claims and PV excludes all cash flows prior to 12/31/06)

Valuation Date: 12/31/06

User-Selected Mortality Assumption Based on:
2001 VBT 50% SKU and 50% Ult Mortality Table ANB and Supplied Life Expectancies
Past (2001-2006) Annual Improvement based on Historical Population Experience
Future Annual Improvement based on 100% Male Historical Population Experience
Future Annual Improvement based on 100% Female Historical Population Experience

Stochastic Simulation Using 500 Randomly Generated Scenarios for:
Date of Death of Each Insured
Rates of Mortality Improvement
U/W Rating for Each Insured using Normal Distribution
with Std Dev= 25.0% and Shift=0.0%

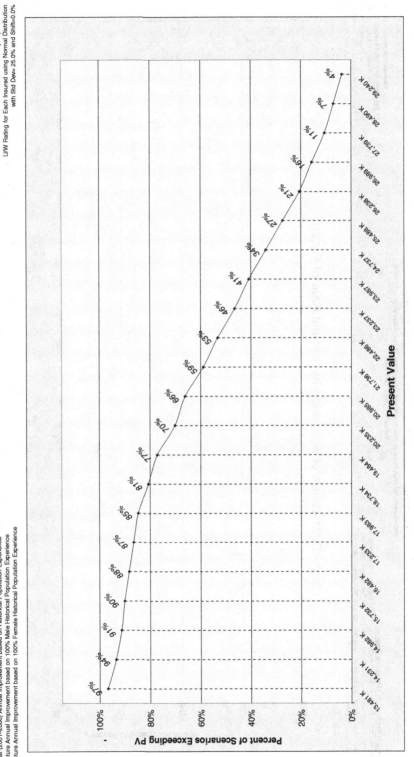

Life Settlement Portfolio Projection - Detailed Results

(IRR excludes all cash flows on past claims and PV excludes all cash flows prior to 12/31/06)

Valuation Date: 12/31/06

Stochastic Simulation Using
500 Randomly Generated Scenarios for:
Date of Death of Each Insured
Rates of Mortality Improvement
U/W Rating for Each Insured using Normal Distribution
with Std Dev= 25.0% and Shift=0.0%

User-Selected Mortality Assumption Based on:
2001 VBT 50% S&U and 50% Ult Mortality Table ANB and Supplied Life Expectancies
Past (2001-2006) Annual Improvement based on Historical Population Experience
Future Annual Improvement based on 100% Male Historical Population Experience
Future Annual Improvement based on 100% Female Historical Population Experience

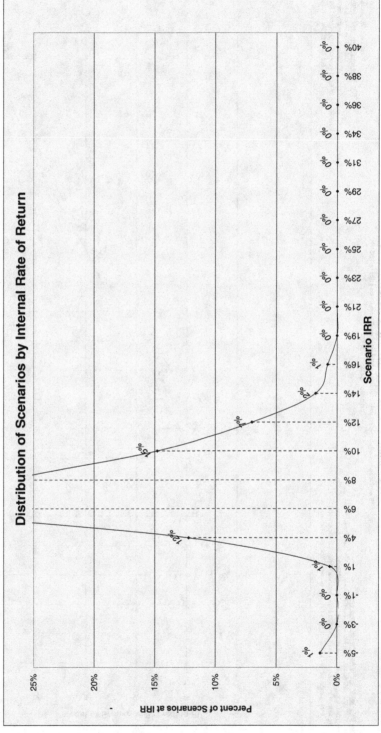

Distribution of Scenarios by Internal Rate of Return

Note that Graphs of Scenarios IRRs use lower and upper bounds of -5.00% and 40.00%, respectively.

Life Settlement Portfolio Projection - Detailed Results

(IRR excludes all cash flows on past claims and PV excludes all cash flows prior to 12/31/06)

Valuation Date: 12/31/06

User-Selected Mortality Assumption Based on:
2001 VBT 50% S&U and 50% Ult Mortality Table ANB and Supplied Life Expectancies
Past (2001–2006) Annual improvement based on Historical Population Experience
Future Annual Improvement based on 100% Male Historical Population Experience
Future Annual Improvement based on 100% Female Historical Population Experience

Stochastic Simulation Using
500 Randomly Generated Scenarios for:
Date of Death of Each Insured
Rates of Mortality Improvement
U/W Rating for Each Insured using Normal Distribution
with Std Dev= 25.0% and Shift=0.0%

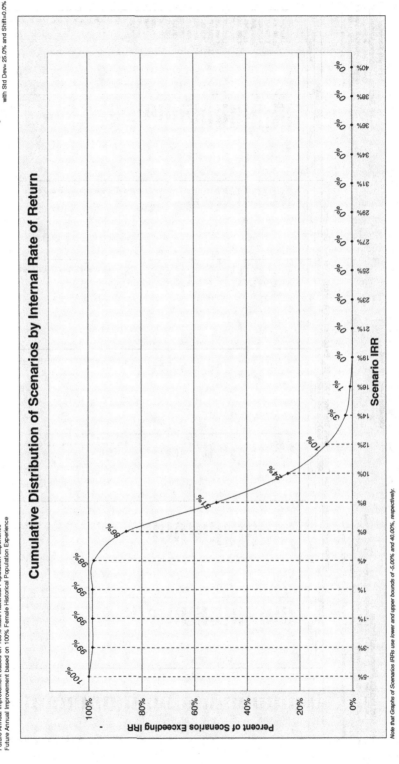

Cumulative Distribution of Scenarios by Internal Rate of Return

Note that Graphs of Scenarios IRRs use lower and upper bounds of -5.00% and 40.00%, respectively.

Life Settlement Portfolio Projection - Detailed Results

(IRR excludes all cash flows on past claims and PV excludes all cash flows prior to 12/31/06)

Valuation Date: 12/31/06

User-Selected Mortality Assumption Based on:
2001 VBT 50% S&U and 50% Ult Mortality Table ANB and Supplied Life Expectancies
Past (2001–2006) Annual Improvement based on Historical Population Experience
Future Annual Improvement based on 100% Male Historical Population Experience
Future Annual Improvement based on 100% Female Historical Population Experience

Stochastic Simulation Using
500 Randomly Generated Scenarios for:
Date of Death of Each Insured
Rates of Mortality Improvement
U/W Rating for Each Insured using Normal Distribution
with Std Dev=25.0% and Shift=0.0%

Summary of Future Annual Cash Flows Starting 12/31/06: Expected vs Average Over 500 Scenarios

Calendar Year	NET CASH FLOWS Expected	NET CASH FLOWS Average	PREMIUMS AND PURCHASE PRICE Expected	PREMIUMS AND PURCHASE PRICE Average	EXPENSES Expected	EXPENSES Average	CLAIMS Expected	CLAIMS Average
2006	0	0	0	0	0	0	0	0
2007	1,667,361	1,687,285	(1,286,504)	(1,288,753)	(53,582)	(53,567)	3,007,447	3,029,604
2008	3,505,898	3,606,304	(1,194,650)	(1,191,553)	(49,758)	(49,658)	4,750,306	4,847,515
2009	4,112,870	4,293,130	(1,067,536)	(1,059,106)	(45,244)	(44,979)	5,225,650	5,397,214
2010	4,367,307	4,091,466	(927,167)	(927,927)	(40,445)	(40,268)	5,334,919	5,059,661
2011	4,336,626	3,990,878	(768,715)	(795,659)	(35,643)	(35,892)	5,140,984	4,822,429
2012	3,991,185	3,633,191	(635,294)	(689,975)	(31,045)	(31,813)	4,657,513	4,354,980
2013	3,571,373	3,485,339	(477,005)	(517,587)	(26,554)	(27,473)	4,074,932	4,030,399
2014	3,072,964	2,987,554	(319,954)	(350,166)	(21,909)	(23,214)	3,414,827	3,360,934
2015	2,458,664	2,673,743	(220,811)	(244,474)	(17,126)	(18,391)	2,696,601	2,936,609
2016	1,839,883	1,619,386	(152,882)	(193,110)	(12,529)	(14,076)	2,005,293	1,826,572
2017	1,304,300	1,296,391	(92,828)	(139,407)	(8,538)	(10,703)	1,405,665	1,445,501
2018	839,776	678,403	(59,167)	(112,612)	(5,469)	(8,079)	904,412	799,093
2019	518,328	612,060	(33,278)	(88,958)	(3,325)	(5,774)	554,930	706,792
2020	310,819	461,671	(19,116)	(66,772)	(1,919)	(4,078)	331,854	532,520
2021	179,686	357,318	(9,942)	(49,775)	(1,046)	(2,736)	190,673	409,830
2022	99,609	151,013	(5,037)	(35,916)	(534)	(1,812)	105,179	188,742
2023	51,683	163,067	(2,409)	(15,817)	(257)	(1,225)	54,348	180,110
2024	25,971	92,426	(1,054)	(12,130)	(115)	(785)	27,140	105,341
2025	12,248	104,456	(452)	(5,185)	(47)	(463)	12,746	110,105
2026	5,346	26,407	(166)	(2,364)	(17)	(321)	5,529	29,092
2027	2,018	9,785	(49)	(1,638)	(5)	(237)	2,072	11,660
2028	586	(746)	(10)	(633)	(1)	(114)	597	0
2029	117	8,472	(0)	(206)	(0)	(50)	118	8,728
2030	11	0	(0)	0	(0)	0	11	0
2031	0	0	0	0	0	0	0	0
2032	0	0	0	0	0	0	0	0
2033	0	0	0	0	0	0	0	0
2034	0	0	0	0	0	0	0	0
2035	0	0	0	0	0	0	0	0
2036	0	0	0	0	0	0	0	0
2037	0	0	0	0	0	0	0	0
2038	0	0	0	0	0	0	0	0
2039	0	0	0	0	0	0	0	0
2040	0	0	0	0	0	0	0	0
2041	0	0	0	0	0	0	0	0
2042	0	0	0	0	0	0	0	0
2043	0	0	0	0	0	0	0	0
2044	0	0	0	0	0	0	0	0
2045	0	0	0	0	0	0	0	0
2046	0	0	0	0	0	0	0	0
2047	0	0	0	0	0	0	0	0
2048	0	0	0	0	0	0	0	0
2049	0	0	0	0	0	0	0	0
2050	0	0	0	0	0	0	0	0
2051	0	0	0	0	0	0	0	0
2052	0	0	0	0	0	0	0	0
2053	0	0	0	0	0	0	0	0
2054	0	0	0	0	0	0	0	0
2055	0	0	0	0	0	0	0	0
2056	0	0	0	0	0	0	0	0
PV at 10.25%	22,396,380	22,227,902	(7,274,015)	(5,472,587)	(365,108)	(251,103)	43,903,748	27,771,574

Life Settlement Portfolio Projection - Detailed Results

(IRR excludes all cash flows on past claims and PV excludes all cash flows prior to 12/31/06)

Valuation Date: 12/31/06

User-Selected Mortality Assumption Based on:
2001 VBT 50% S&U and 50% Ult Mortality Table ANB and Supplied Life Expectancies
Past (2001–2006) Annual Improvement based on Historical Population Experience
Future Annual Improvement based on 100% Male Historical Population Experience
Future Annual Improvement based on 100% Female Historical Population Experience

Stochastic Simulation Using
500 Randomly Generated Scenarios for:
Date of Death of Each Insured
Rates of Mortality Improvement
U/W Rating for Each Insured using Normal Distribution
with Std Dev= 25.0% and Shift=0.0%

Selected Random Future Annual Cash Flow Scenarios Starting 12/31/06 Satisfying Percentile Rank (PV on 12/31/06 at 10.25%)*

Calendar Year	Cash Flow Expected	Cash Flow Avg of All Scenarios	90.00% Percentile	50% Percentile	75% Percentile	90% Percentile	95% Percentile	99% Percentile
2006	-	-	-	-	-	-	-	-
2007	1,667,361	1,687,285	1,477,197	(1,444,796)	(816,325)	1,477,197	(1,444,086)	(1,444,796)
2008	3,505,898	3,606,304	(1,579,215)	(1,603,034)	(1,506,997)	(1,579,215)	3,929,339	5,418,546
2009	4,112,870	4,293,130	(1,682,323)	14,602,200	8,360,556	(1,682,323)	416,160	(1,487,565)
2010	4,367,307	4,091,466	4,560,977	(638,473)	5,320,234	4,560,977	1,918,076	(1,304,027)
2011	4,336,626	3,990,878	447,125	8,141,994	(1,747,799)	447,125	(1,644,326)	(1,684,259)
2012	3,991,185	3,633,191	14,667,938	7,231,037	(637,214)	14,667,938	(1,830,161)	2,489,428
2013	3,571,373	3,485,339	(810,460)	1,119,388	(2,050,211)	(810,460)	15,670,088	(1,985,312)
2014	3,072,964	2,997,554	(891,952)	4,136,890	27,508,792	(891,952)	(891,952)	541,961
2015	2,458,864	2,673,743	7,739,869	(274,882)		7,739,869	(991,287)	6,264,150
2016	1,839,883	1,619,386	(148,133)	5,211,711		(148,133)	4,295,508	(1,462,228)
2017	1,304,300	1,295,391	(178,060)			(178,060)	3,273,281	5,302,390
2018	839,776	678,403	(276,672)			(276,672)	(1,159,120)	(1,517,831)
2019	518,328	612,060	9,711,705			9,711,705	7,798,099	24,245,170
2020	310,819	461,671	-	-	-	-	-	-
2021	179,696	357,318	-	-	-	-	-	-
2022	99,609	151,013	-	-	-	-	-	-
2023	51,683	163,067	-	-	-	-	-	-
2024	25,971	92,426	-	-	-	-	-	-
2025	12,248	104,456	-	-	-	-	-	-
2026	5,346	26,407	-	-	-	-	-	-
2027	2,018	9,785	-	-	-	-	-	-
2028	586	(746)	-	-	-	-	-	-
2029	117	8,472	-	-	-	-	-	-
2030	11	-	-	-	-	-	-	-
2031	0	-	-	-	-	-	-	-
2032	-	-	-	-	-	-	-	-
2033	-	-	-	-	-	-	-	-
2034	-	-	-	-	-	-	-	-
2035	-	-	-	-	-	-	-	-
2036	-	-	-	-	-	-	-	-
2037	-	-	-	-	-	-	-	-
2038	-	-	-	-	-	-	-	-
2039	-	-	-	-	-	-	-	-
2040	-	-	-	-	-	-	-	-
2041	-	-	-	-	-	-	-	-
2042	-	-	-	-	-	-	-	-
2043	-	-	-	-	-	-	-	-
2044	-	-	-	-	-	-	-	-
2045	-	-	-	-	-	-	-	-
2046	-	-	-	-	-	-	-	-
2047	-	-	-	-	-	-	-	-
2048	-	-	-	-	-	-	-	-
2049	-	-	-	-	-	-	-	-
2050	-	-	-	-	-	-	-	-
2051	-	-	-	-	-	-	-	-
2052	-	-	-	-	-	-	-	-
2053	-	-	-	-	-	-	-	-
2054	-	-	-	-	-	-	-	-
2055	-	-	-	-	-	-	-	-
PV at 10.25%	22,386,330	22,227,902	16,428,585	22,423,366	19,299,109	16,428,585	14,149,601	11,374,148

*Note that the cash flows shown are those random scenarios that fell into the desired ranking (by PV at 10.25%).
Other cash flow patterns could achieve the same IRR and different results may appear when model is rerun with a different seed for the random number generator.

Life Settlement Portfolio Projection - Detailed Results

(IRR excludes all cash flows on past claims and PV excludes all cash flows prior to 12/31/06)

Valuation Date: 12/31/06

User-Selected Mortality Assumption Based on:
2001 VBT 50% S&U and 50% Ult Mortality Table ANB and Supplied Life Expectancies
Past (2001–2006) Annual Improvement based on Historical Population Experience
Future Annual Improvement based on 100% Male Historical Population Experience
Future Annual Improvement based on 100% Female Historical Population Experience

Stochastic Simulation Using
500 Randomly Generated Scenarios for:
Date of Death of Each Insured
Rates of Mortality Improvement
U/W Rating for Each Insured using Normal Distribution
with Std Dev= 25.0% and Shift=0.0%

Historic Annual Cash Flows plus Selected Random Future Annual Cash Flow Scenarios Starting 12/31/06 Satisfying Percentile Rank (by IRR)*

Calendar Year	Cash Flow Expected	Cash Flow Avg of All Scenarios	90.00% Percentile	50% Percentile	75% Percentile	90% Percentile	95% Percentile	99% Percentile
2006	(25,868,779)	(25,868,779)	(25,868,779)	(25,868,779)	(25,868,779)	(25,868,779)	(25,868,779)	(25,868,779)
2007	1,667,361	1,687,285	(1,444,796)	885,640	(1,428,791)	(1,444,796)	(1,444,748)	(1,444,796)
2008	3,505,698	3,606,304	6,479,701	15,759,564	13,504,862	6,479,701	1,327,161	3,690,091
2009	4,112,670	4,293,130	125,624	(773,676)	5,386,931	125,624	(1,712,196)	16,344,393
2010	4,367,307	4,091,466	(520,777)	3,078,274	(797,646)	(520,777)	(1,867,506)	(234,035)
2011	4,336,626	3,990,878	3,183,856	4,405,126	(870,529)	3,183,856	7,417,459	1,246,666
2012	3,991,185	3,633,191	8,862,621	(989,656)	(931,415)	8,862,621	3,080,320	(830,827)
2013	3,571,373	3,486,339	985,091	(997,806)	5,083,770	985,091	(685,676)	3,483,461
2014	3,072,964	2,987,554	1,418,932	7,562,706	7,314,662	1,418,932	(1,352,966)	(664,115)
2015	2,458,664	2,673,743	(1,262,597)	4,959,113	(105,296)	(1,262,597)	(1,457,698)	(1,041,001)
2016	1,839,883	1,619,986	(1,331,577)		(139,071)	(1,331,577)	19,653,807	(1,115,240)
2017	1,304,300	1,295,391	(1,420,219)		4,194,688	(1,420,219)	(289,970)	(1,223,510)
2018	839,776	678,403	(1,517,831)		(186,390)	(1,517,831)	4,032,336	20,022
2019	518,328	612,060	(1,649,903)		2,461,243	(1,649,903)	2,047,338	(1,468,932)
2020	310,819	461,671	(1,900,849)			(1,900,849)	(287,340)	(1,582,571)
2021	179,696	357,318	(2,175,413)			(2,175,413)	5,190,069	(1,573,485)
2022	99,609	151,013	(2,639,250)			(2,639,250)		(1,382,091)
2023	51,683	163,067	32,456,786			32,456,786		(20,911)
2024	25,971	92,426						7,800,000
2025	12,248	104,456						
2026	5,346	26,407						
2027	2,018	9,785						
2028	586	(746)						
2029	117	8,472						
2030	11							
2031	0							
2032								
2033								
2034								
2035								
2036								
2037								
2038								
2039								
2040								
2041								
2042								
2043								
2044								
2045								
2046								
2047								
2048								
2049								
2050								
2051								
2052								
2053								
2054								
2055								
IRR	5.90%	3.19%	3.19%	5.86%	4.39%	3.19%	2.45%	-60.57%

Note that Scenarios IRRs are based on lower and upper bounds of -100.00% and 0.00%, respectively.

*Note that the cash flows shown are those random scenarios that fell into the desired ranking (by IRR), starting from the policy purchase dates.
Other cash flow patterns could achieve the same IRR and different results may appear when model is rerun with a different seed for the random number generator.*

Life Settlement Portfolio Projection - Detailed Results

(IRR excludes all cash flows on past claims and PV excludes all cash flows prior to 12/31/06)

Valuation Date: 12/31/06

User-Selected Mortality Assumption Based on:
2001 VBT 50% S&U and 50% Ult Mortality Table ANB and Supplied Life Expectancies
Past (2001–2006) Annual Improvement based on Historical Population Experience
Future Annual Improvement based on 100% Male Historical Population Experience
Future Annual Improvement based on 100% Female Historical Population Experience

Stochastic Simulation Using
500 Randomly Generated Scenarios for:
Date of Death of Each Insured
Rates of Mortality Improvement
U/W Rating for Each Insured using Normal Distribution
with Std Dev= 25.0% and Shift=0.0%

Contingent Tail Expectation (CTE) for Future Annual Cash Flows based on PV on 12/31/06 at 10.25%*

Calendar Year	Cash Flow Expected	Cash Flow Avg of All Scenarios	90.00% CTE	50% CTE	75% CTE	90% CTE	95% CTE	99% CTE
2006	-	-	-	-	-	-	-	-
2007	1,667,361	1,687,285	1,972,046	3,589,167	2,497,116	1,972,046	1,827,177	1,713,519
2008	3,505,698	3,606,304	3,914,635	5,735,720	4,488,583	3,914,635	3,750,494	3,647,756
2009	4,112,870	4,293,130	4,650,102	6,047,122	5,229,418	4,650,102	4,469,590	4,349,118
2010	4,367,307	4,091,466	4,369,211	4,805,594	4,553,400	4,369,211	4,278,821	4,124,749
2011	4,336,626	3,990,878	4,242,040	4,370,883	4,473,746	4,242,040	4,116,652	4,023,004
2012	3,991,185	3,633,191	3,787,722	3,373,012	3,766,656	3,787,722	3,655,912	3,636,173
2013	3,571,373	3,485,339	3,656,226	2,799,939	3,452,596	3,656,226	3,694,714	3,536,844
2014	3,072,964	2,987,554	2,993,433	2,013,569	2,536,615	2,993,433	3,006,619	3,015,522
2015	2,458,664	2,673,743	2,436,791	1,677,570	2,122,048	2,436,791	2,534,549	2,646,107
2016	1,839,883	1,619,386	1,408,516	764,301	1,072,576	1,408,516	1,471,233	1,621,841
2017	1,304,300	1,295,391	1,070,459	595,964	880,898	1,070,459	1,117,650	1,193,918
2018	839,776	678,403	572,841	421,754	510,423	572,841	639,774	645,643
2019	518,328	612,060	440,706	311,982	375,178	440,706	577,681	624,907
2020	310,819	461,671	339,200	180,879	260,071	339,200	442,880	464,216
2021	179,686	357,318	259,971	338,076	278,255	259,971	300,851	281,597
2022	99,609	151,013	170,420	56,113	150,547	170,420	151,700	153,254
2023	51,683	163,067	72,039	51,227	60,712	72,039	135,124	154,103
2024	25,971	92,426	58,697	32,113	43,497	58,697	79,919	93,360
2025	12,248	104,456	20,982	21,703	25,207	20,982	28,059	105,511
2026	5,346	26,407	30,559	16,718	10,292	30,559	27,845	26,674
2027	2,018	9,785	11,889	17,257	10,607	11,889	10,348	9,884
2028	596	(746)	(783)	-	(940)	(783)	(778)	(754)
2029	117	8,472	9,414	-	11,296	9,414	8,918	8,558
2030	11	-	-	-	-	-	-	-
2031	0	-	-	-	-	-	-	-
2032	-	-	-	-	-	-	-	-
2033	-	-	-	-	-	-	-	-
2034	-	-	-	-	-	-	-	-
2035	-	-	-	-	-	-	-	-
2036	-	-	-	-	-	-	-	-
2037	-	-	-	-	-	-	-	-
2038	-	-	-	-	-	-	-	-
2039	-	-	-	-	-	-	-	-
2040	-	-	-	-	-	-	-	-
2041	-	-	-	-	-	-	-	-
2042	-	-	-	-	-	-	-	-
2043	-	-	-	-	-	-	-	-
2044	-	-	-	-	-	-	-	-
2045	-	-	-	-	-	-	-	-
2046	-	-	-	-	-	-	-	-
2047	-	-	-	-	-	-	-	-
2048	-	-	-	-	-	-	-	-
2049	-	-	-	-	-	-	-	-
2050	-	-	-	-	-	-	-	-
2051	-	-	-	-	-	-	-	-
2052	-	-	-	-	-	-	-	-
2053	-	-	-	-	-	-	-	-
2054	-	-	-	-	-	-	-	-
2055	-	-	-	-	-	-	-	-
PV at 10.25%	22,386,330	22,227,902	12,663,148	16,997,638	14,965,219	12,663,148	11,488,646	9,421,979

* Note that the cash flows shown are those random scenarios that fell into the desired ranking (by PV at 10.25%).
Other cash flow patterns could achieve the same IRR and different results may appear when model is rerun with a different seed for the random number generator.

Life Settlement Portfolio Projection - Detailed Results

(IRR excludes all cash flows on past claims and PV excludes all cash flows prior to 12/31/06)

Valuation Date: 12/31/06

User-Selected Mortality Assumption Based on:
2001 VBT 50% S&U and 50% Ult Mortality Table ANB and Supplied Life Expectancies
Past (2001-2006) Annual Improvement based on Historical Population Experience
Future Annual Improvement based on 100% Male Historical Population Experience
Future Annual Improvement based on 100% Female Historical Population Experience

Stochastic Simulation Using
500 Randomly Generated Scenarios for:
Date of Death of Each Insured
Rates of Mortality Improvement
U/W Rating for Each Insured using Normal Distribution
with Std Dev= 25.0% and Shift=0.0%

Contingent Tail Expectation (CTE) for Historic and Projected Future Annual Cash Flows based on Internal Rate of Return*

Calendar Year	Cash Flow Expected	Cash Flow Avg of All Scenarios	90.00% Percentile	50% Percentile	75% Percentile	90% Percentile	95% Percentile	99% Percentile
2006	(25,868,779)	(25,868,779)	(25,868,779)	(25,868,779)	(25,868,779)	(25,868,779)	(25,868,779)	(25,868,779)
2007	1,667,361	1,687,285	1,938,706	3,247,346	1,938,706	1,938,706	1,830,345	1,712,420
2008	3,505,898	3,606,304	3,870,045	5,715,246	5,715,246	3,870,045	3,724,079	3,627,080
2009	4,112,870	4,293,130	4,615,418	6,034,778	6,034,778	4,615,418	4,392,555	4,255,777
2010	4,367,307	4,091,466	4,376,649	4,981,524	4,981,524	4,376,649	4,247,797	4,097,287
2011	4,336,626	3,990,878	4,225,264	4,506,848	4,506,848	4,225,264	4,126,257	4,025,425
2012	3,991,185	3,633,191	3,774,189	3,424,756	3,788,587	3,774,189	3,683,506	3,653,961
2013	3,571,373	3,485,339	3,619,799	2,991,068	3,456,449	3,619,799	3,635,627	3,508,057
2014	3,072,964	2,987,554	2,998,446	1,933,316	2,535,769	2,998,446	2,952,579	3,000,831
2015	2,458,664	2,673,743	2,486,654	1,830,016	2,185,794	2,486,654	2,638,642	2,698,091
2016	1,839,883	1,619,386	1,459,349	747,179	1,219,585	1,459,349	1,643,435	1,639,215
2017	1,304,300	1,295,391	1,054,731	551,627	905,740	1,054,731	1,106,352	1,290,125
2018	839,776	678,403	552,340	384,640	519,350	552,340	604,361	685,285
2019	518,328	612,060	483,135	362,529	368,142	483,135	573,305	629,844
2020	310,819	461,671	401,230	184,465	387,444	401,230	453,495	455,954
2021	179,686	357,318	289,840	296,390	259,269	289,840	308,036	369,193
2022	99,609	151,013	152,786	57,649	136,441	152,786	158,852	146,134
2023	51,683	163,067	143,892	52,889	50,182	143,892	128,944	134,257
2024	25,971	92,426	68,271	33,782	43,905	68,271	56,235	69,674
2025	12,248	104,456	21,017	5,442	25,665	21,017	111,009	106,478
2026	5,346	26,407	30,594	-	10,784	30,594	28,951	27,735
2027	2,018	9,785	11,918	-	11,136	11,918	11,263	10,762
2028	586	(746)	(783)	-	(369)	(783)	(742)	(719)
2029	117	117	9,414	-	(40)	9,414	8,918	8,558
2030	11	11	-	-	-	-	-	-
2031	0	0	-	-	-	-	-	-
2032	-	-	-	-	-	-	-	-
2033	-	-	-	-	-	-	-	-
2034	-	-	-	-	-	-	-	-
2035	-	-	-	-	-	-	-	-
2036	-	-	-	-	-	-	-	-
2037	-	-	-	-	-	-	-	-
2038	-	-	-	-	-	-	-	-
2039	-	-	-	-	-	-	-	-
2040	-	-	-	-	-	-	-	-
2041	-	-	-	-	-	-	-	-
2042	-	-	-	-	-	-	-	-
2043	-	-	-	-	-	-	-	-
2044	-	-	-	-	-	-	-	-
2045	-	-	-	-	-	-	-	-
2046	-	-	-	-	-	-	-	-
2047	-	-	-	-	-	-	-	-
2048	-	-	-	-	-	-	-	-
2049	-	-	-	-	-	-	-	-
2050	-	-	-	-	-	-	-	-
2051	-	-	-	-	-	-	-	-
2052	-	-	-	-	-	-	-	-
2053	-	-	-	-	-	-	-	-
2054	-	-	-	-	-	-	-	-
2055	-	-	-	-	-	-	-	-

Note that Scenarios IRRs are based on lower and upper bounds of -100.00% and 0.00%, respectively.

* Note that the cash flows shown are those random scenarios that fell into the desired ranking (by IRR), starting from the policy purchase dates.
Other cash flow patterns could achieve the same IRR and different results may appear when model is rerun with a different seed for the random number generator.

Expected and Average Monthly Cash Flow

(IRR excludes all cash flows on past claims and PV excludes all cash flows prior to 12/31/06)

Date	Year	Historic Cash Flows	Expected Premiums for 10 Policies	Expected Expenses for 10 Policies	Expected Death Claims for 10 Policies	Expected Future Cash Flow For PV	Avg Future Premiums over 100 Scenarios	Avg Future Expenses over 100 Scenarios	Avg Future Death Claims over 100 Scenarios	Avg Future Cash Flow over 100 Scenarios
Jan-2006	2006	(7,644,206)	-	-	-	-	-	-	-	-
Feb-2006	2006	(1,135,308)	-	-	-	-	-	-	-	-
Mar-2006	2006	(6,830,308)	-	-	-	-	-	-	-	-
Apr-2006	2006	(2,997,007)	-	-	-	-	-	-	-	-
May-2006	2006	(122,219)	-	-	-	-	-	-	-	-
Jun-2006	2006	(1,532,536)	-	-	-	-	-	-	-	-
Jul-2006	2006	(2,790,051)	-	-	-	-	-	-	-	-
Aug-2006	2006	(75,572)	-	-	-	-	-	-	-	-
Sep-2006	2006	(2,263,695)	-	-	-	-	-	-	-	-
Oct-2006	2006	(68,607)	-	-	-	-	-	-	-	-
Nov-2006	2006	(273,518)	-	-	-	-	-	-	-	-
Dec-2006	2006	(135,753)	-	-	-	-	-	-	-	-
Jan-2007	2007	-	64,031	4,585	-	(68,616)	64,031	4,585	-	(68,616)
Feb-2007	2007	-	125,177	4,565	-	(129,742)	123,872	4,563	-	(128,435)
Mar-2007	2007	-	130,982	4,548	-	(135,530)	132,609	4,549	-	(137,158)
Apr-2007	2007	-	147,781	4,520	304,963	152,661	146,505	4,521	329,394	178,367
May-2007	2007	-	122,121	4,504	323,752	197,127	121,421	4,507	280,941	155,012
Jun-2007	2007	-	123,680	4,486	329,251	201,085	125,344	4,483	333,120	203,294
Jul-2007	2007	-	58,227	4,457	332,651	269,968	57,416	4,456	311,531	249,659
Aug-2007	2007	-	78,589	4,433	337,493	254,470	77,436	4,428	403,497	321,633
Sep-2007	2007	-	133,706	4,410	341,515	203,399	136,415	4,405	317,833	177,013
Oct-2007	2007	-	58,013	4,382	343,589	281,194	57,417	4,379	395,129	333,333
Nov-2007	2007	-	116,587	4,357	346,005	225,062	115,360	4,352	337,261	217,549
Dec-2007	2007	-	127,611	4,335	348,229	216,283	130,926	4,337	320,898	185,634
Jan-2008	2008	-	55,555	4,304	353,756	293,896	55,044	4,307	380,184	320,833
Feb-2008	2008	-	111,655	4,276	366,556	250,625	109,911	4,270	285,920	171,739
Mar-2008	2008	-	123,520	4,251	372,285	244,515	125,697	4,244	370,532	240,591
Apr-2008	2008	-	126,088	4,217	392,491	262,186	124,003	4,212	490,158	361,944
May-2008	2008	-	107,490	4,193	408,619	296,936	105,465	4,183	415,489	305,841
Jun-2008	2008	-	123,343	4,167	409,689	282,178	124,974	4,160	387,406	258,272
Jul-2008	2008	-	27,758	4,133	408,827	376,936	27,325	4,125	466,680	435,230
Aug-2008	2008	-	98,945	4,101	409,495	306,449	97,334	4,086	379,826	278,406
Sep-2008	2008	-	129,170	4,075	409,511	276,266	131,175	4,063	412,634	277,395
Oct-2008	2008	-	62,089	4,042	407,746	341,615	61,180	4,031	497,396	432,186
Nov-2008	2008	-	106,920	4,013	406,089	295,156	105,642	3,999	361,839	252,199
Dec-2008	2008	-	122,118	3,985	405,243	279,139	123,803	3,979	399,451	271,669
Jan-2009	2009	-	59,788	3,950	410,707	346,969	59,693	3,951	446,724	383,080
Feb-2009	2009	-	101,982	3,917	425,398	319,498	102,154	3,916	322,961	216,891
Mar-2009	2009	-	117,894	3,887	429,067	307,306	118,807	3,875	344,302	221,621
Apr-2009	2009	-	59,625	3,850	443,974	380,500	58,566	3,818	480,479	418,095
May-2009	2009	-	97,744	3,817	452,554	350,992	95,923	3,796	581,683	481,964
Jun-2009	2009	-	110,361	3,787	449,796	335,648	110,931	3,760	682,251	567,560
Jul-2009	2009	-	64,233	3,751	445,331	377,347	62,839	3,719	318,359	251,800
Aug-2009	2009	-	87,387	3,720	441,668	350,561	85,061	3,684	507,271	418,527
Sep-2009	2009	-	113,828	3,690	438,356	320,838	112,894	3,663	491,711	375,153
Oct-2009	2009	-	58,475	3,656	433,474	371,343	57,902	3,629	483,205	421,674
Nov-2009	2009	-	89,327	3,624	429,547	336,596	88,273	3,601	324,289	232,414
Dec-2009	2009	-	106,892	3,594	425,757	315,271	106,062	3,567	413,978	304,349
Jan-2010	2010	-	56,829	3,557	430,262	369,876	56,003	3,529	395,154	335,622
Feb-2010	2010	-	84,638	3,523	443,479	355,318	83,402	3,503	482,422	395,518
Mar-2010	2010	-	103,335	3,490	444,357	337,532	104,511	3,461	462,540	354,568
Apr-2010	2010	-	55,799	3,452	458,970	399,719	55,820	3,423	364,891	305,648
May-2010	2010	-	80,331	3,418	467,629	383,880	80,605	3,389	566,616	482,622
Jun-2010	2010	-	95,215	3,386	461,629	363,027	93,837	3,365	461,255	364,053
Jul-2010	2010	-	61,185	3,350	454,195	389,660	61,564	3,326	456,158	391,269
Aug-2010	2010	-	71,558	3,318	447,821	372,945	72,254	3,297	355,369	279,818
Sep-2010	2010	-	96,513	3,287	441,774	341,974	95,113	3,282	478,206	379,811
Oct-2010	2010	-	56,072	3,253	434,410	375,085	57,382	3,250	392,648	332,016
Nov-2010	2010	-	76,102	3,221	428,238	348,915	78,475	3,234	254,075	172,365
Dec-2010	2010	-	89,591	3,190	422,155	329,374	88,961	3,209	390,325	298,155

Expected and Average Monthly Cash Flow

(IRR excludes all cash flows on past claims and PV excludes all cash flows prior to 12/31/06)

Date	Year	Historic Cash Flows	Expected Premiums for 10 Policies	Expected Expenses for 10 Policies	Expected Death Claims for 10 Policies	Expected Future Cash Flow For PV	Avg Future Premiums over 100 Scenarios	Avg Future Expenses over 100 Scenarios	Avg Future Death Claims over 100 Scenarios	Avg Future Cash Flow over 100 Scenarios
Jan-2011	2011	-	55,055	3,153	427,046	368,838	57,384	3,171	237,579	177,024
Feb-2011	2011	-	64,549	3,120	436,416	368,747	67,285	3,133	374,134	303,716
Mar-2011	2011	-	88,462	3,087	435,744	344,196	88,241	3,096	456,478	365,141
Apr-2011	2011	-	51,718	3,049	449,627	394,859	53,922	3,062	501,077	444,093
May-2011	2011	-	60,570	3,016	453,148	389,562	62,472	3,026	502,066	436,568
Jun-2011	2011	-	83,197	2,985	445,027	358,845	83,496	2,996	409,315	322,824
Jul-2011	2011	-	54,413	2,950	435,726	378,363	57,307	2,970	480,776	420,499
Aug-2011	2011	-	53,248	2,919	427,669	371,502	56,260	2,946	416,097	356,891
Sep-2011	2011	-	81,254	2,889	419,903	335,760	83,745	2,919	313,193	226,529
Oct-2011	2011	-	49,781	2,856	411,053	358,416	52,580	2,884	335,820	280,356
Nov-2011	2011	-	51,203	2,825	403,547	349,518	53,906	2,856	372,724	315,962
Dec-2011	2011	-	75,266	2,795	396,079	318,019	79,061	2,835	423,171	341,276
Jan-2012	2012	-	52,940	2,760	401,283	345,583	57,213	2,815	388,528	328,500
Feb-2012	2012	-	47,487	2,729	405,431	355,216	51,772	2,786	306,538	251,980
Mar-2012	2012	-	72,661	2,697	403,285	327,927	77,740	2,769	238,815	158,306
Apr-2012	2012	-	53,704	2,662	409,962	353,597	60,023	2,744	394,859	332,092
May-2012	2012	-	44,046	2,631	410,901	364,224	48,514	2,691	250,516	199,310
Jun-2012	2012	-	64,605	2,601	401,857	334,651	69,310	2,658	299,910	227,943
Jul-2012	2012	-	54,313	2,568	391,921	335,040	59,013	2,623	689,485	627,849
Aug-2012	2012	-	38,150	2,539	383,515	342,825	41,680	2,601	413,924	369,643
Sep-2012	2012	-	63,121	2,510	375,093	309,462	67,957	2,571	413,676	343,149
Oct-2012	2012	-	49,404	2,479	365,849	313,966	54,753	2,541	286,569	229,275
Nov-2012	2012	-	37,789	2,450	358,161	317,923	42,263	2,522	404,380	359,594
Dec-2012	2012	-	57,064	2,420	350,254	290,770	59,738	2,493	267,780	205,550
Jan-2013	2013	-	46,871	2,386	355,090	305,833	52,581	2,459	250,360	195,320
Feb-2013	2013	-	34,642	2,355	357,269	320,271	38,799	2,429	392,529	351,301
Mar-2013	2013	-	53,247	2,323	353,077	297,507	55,725	2,392	402,943	344,826
Apr-2013	2013	-	42,507	2,289	364,155	319,359	47,441	2,357	315,847	266,049
May-2013	2013	-	31,623	2,259	362,828	328,947	34,238	2,328	484,480	447,915
Jun-2013	2013	-	47,875	2,228	353,332	303,230	51,126	2,299	389,231	335,806
Jul-2013	2013	-	40,581	2,195	343,162	300,386	45,819	2,280	390,393	342,294
Aug-2013	2013	-	28,963	2,166	334,496	303,367	31,431	2,247	373,667	339,989
Sep-2013	2013	-	45,967	2,136	325,806	277,703	51,680	2,214	134,288	80,394
Oct-2013	2013	-	37,043	2,104	316,497	277,350	42,140	2,184	293,922	249,598
Nov-2013	2013	-	26,313	2,073	308,624	280,239	30,292	2,161	328,660	296,208
Dec-2013	2013	-	41,374	2,041	300,597	257,182	36,314	2,125	274,079	235,640
Jan-2014	2014	-	34,327	2,007	307,588	271,254	40,186	2,096	199,983	157,702
Feb-2014	2014	-	23,744	1,974	306,726	281,008	27,079	2,071	394,001	364,852
Mar-2014	2014	-	32,203	1,941	301,564	267,421	31,602	2,043	231,209	197,564
Apr-2014	2014	-	30,660	1,906	308,160	275,594	37,396	2,021	306,206	266,789
May-2014	2014	-	23,224	1,874	304,971	279,873	26,611	1,983	327,321	298,727
Jun-2014	2014	-	28,816	1,841	295,637	264,980	28,328	1,952	203,153	172,873
Jul-2014	2014	-	29,687	1,808	285,866	254,372	35,098	1,921	365,066	328,046
Aug-2014	2014	-	21,229	1,777	277,428	254,422	22,875	1,883	333,483	308,705
Sep-2014	2014	-	27,253	1,745	269,014	240,016	26,013	1,859	282,887	255,014
Oct-2014	2014	-	27,085	1,712	260,199	231,403	32,418	1,836	365,909	331,656
Nov-2014	2014	-	17,445	1,679	252,659	233,535	19,644	1,792	180,285	158,848
Dec-2014	2014	-	24,283	1,646	245,014	219,086	22,916	1,757	171,450	146,777
Jan-2015	2015	-	24,494	1,611	250,397	224,293	29,635	1,730	365,700	334,336
Feb-2015	2015	-	16,701	1,577	248,474	230,196	19,000	1,694	287,832	267,138
Mar-2015	2015	-	21,822	1,542	242,518	219,153	20,505	1,659	212,559	190,396
Apr-2015	2015	-	21,475	1,507	246,646	223,664	26,766	1,623	243,499	215,110
May-2015	2015	-	17,025	1,475	241,563	223,064	19,238	1,584	254,156	233,334
Jun-2015	2015	-	18,954	1,442	233,066	212,671	16,476	1,531	254,573	236,566
Jul-2015	2015	-	20,285	1,409	224,314	202,621	24,750	1,500	247,706	221,456
Aug-2015	2015	-	14,592	1,377	216,702	200,732	16,005	1,468	323,424	305,951
Sep-2015	2015	-	17,844	1,346	209,131	189,941	16,344	1,450	223,029	205,235
Oct-2015	2015	-	18,388	1,313	201,338	181,637	23,752	1,411	219,565	194,401
Nov-2015	2015	-	13,648	1,281	194,613	179,684	16,716	1,390	139,389	121,283
Dec-2015	2015	-	15,583	1,248	187,839	171,009	15,286	1,352	165,177	148,539

Expected and Average Monthly Cash Flow

(IRR excludes all cash flows on past claims and PV excludes all cash flows prior to 12/31/06)

Date	Year	Historic Cash Flows	Expected Premiums for 10 Policies	Expected Expenses for 10 Policies	Expected Death Claims for 10 Policies	Expected Future Cash Flow For PV	Avg Future Premiums over 100 Scenarios	Avg Future Expenses over 100 Scenarios	Avg Future Death Claims over 100 Scenarios	Avg Future Cash Flow over 100 Scenarios
Jan-2016	2016	-	16,174	1,214	192,370	174,982	21,692	1,331	91,252	68,228
Feb-2016	2016	-	17,414	1,181	189,202	170,607	20,394	1,313	236,672	214,965
Mar-2016	2016	-	13,834	1,149	183,340	168,357	14,168	1,271	156,238	140,799
Apr-2016	2016	-	13,962	1,117	185,640	170,561	19,917	1,238	141,826	120,672
May-2016	2016	-	15,827	1,086	180,361	163,448	18,438	1,194	253,892	234,260
Jun-2016	2016	-	10,267	1,056	173,116	161,794	11,454	1,159	154,498	141,885
Jul-2016	2016	-	12,835	1,026	165,779	151,918	16,831	1,136	209,759	189,792
Aug-2016	2016	-	13,475	997	159,366	144,894	15,910	1,128	226,621	209,583
Sep-2016	2016	-	9,540	969	153,026	142,516	11,311	1,110	145,816	133,395
Oct-2016	2016	-	11,366	940	146,609	134,303	18,084	1,096	52,632	33,452
Nov-2016	2016	-	10,087	911	141,034	130,036	13,236	1,064	104,390	90,090
Dec-2016	2016	-	8,102	882	135,450	126,466	9,676	1,035	52,976	42,265
Jan-2017	2017	-	9,774	853	138,776	128,149	16,497	1,006	158,896	141,393
Feb-2017	2017	-	12,378	825	135,627	122,424	16,179	995	119,550	102,377
Mar-2017	2017	-	7,066	797	130,599	122,736	8,838	978	134,501	124,685
Apr-2017	2017	-	8,156	770	131,294	122,367	15,280	951	88,283	72,052
May-2017	2017	-	10,463	745	127,286	116,079	13,578	917	88,241	73,746
Jun-2017	2017	-	5,925	720	121,459	114,815	7,267	906	90,576	82,403
Jul-2017	2017	-	7,413	695	115,663	107,555	13,378	883	236,102	221,841
Aug-2017	2017	-	8,898	672	110,564	100,994	11,754	864	82,815	70,197
Sep-2017	2017	-	5,349	650	105,572	99,573	7,790	840	182,498	173,868
Oct-2017	2017	-	6,230	626	100,607	93,750	12,378	817	57,779	44,584
Nov-2017	2017	-	6,679	604	96,261	88,979	9,220	779	143,038	133,039
Dec-2017	2017	-	4,496	581	91,956	86,879	7,248	768	63,221	55,206
Jan-2018	2018	-	5,198	559	92,828	87,071	11,101	755	170,294	158,438
Feb-2018	2018	-	10,050	538	90,218	79,630	13,649	743	74,857	60,465
Mar-2018	2018	-	3,831	518	86,212	81,864	6,800	728	40,175	32,648
Apr-2018	2018	-	4,226	498	85,085	80,361	9,996	703	64,748	54,048
May-2018	2018	-	8,215	479	81,599	72,904	11,596	695	63,363	51,073
Jun-2018	2018	-	3,160	461	77,532	73,910	6,193	679	141,635	134,763
Jul-2018	2018	-	3,732	443	73,541	69,366	10,359	658	20,669	9,651
Aug-2018	2018	-	7,064	427	70,007	62,516	10,796	649	44,282	32,836
Sep-2018	2018	-	2,825	411	66,580	63,343	6,685	645	65,662	58,331
Oct-2018	2018	-	3,070	394	63,218	59,753	10,283	618	28,248	17,348
Nov-2018	2018	-	5,461	378	60,249	54,411	9,650	612	21,585	11,322
Dec-2018	2018	-	2,335	362	57,343	54,646	5,502	594	63,576	57,480
Jan-2019	2019	-	2,499	347	58,547	55,702	9,594	575	47,772	37,604
Feb-2019	2019	-	6,201	333	56,393	49,860	10,732	553	66,122	54,837
Mar-2019	2019	-	1,957	319	53,631	51,355	5,021	528	45,078	39,530
Apr-2019	2019	-	1,985	305	52,379	50,089	7,646	513	125,863	117,704
May-2019	2019	-	5,260	292	49,996	44,444	9,280	490	125,357	115,587
Jun-2019	2019	-	1,553	280	47,362	45,529	4,913	477	30,712	25,322
Jul-2019	2019	-	1,694	269	44,807	42,844	8,080	467	73,002	64,455
Aug-2019	2019	-	4,553	257	42,522	37,711	8,759	458	33,797	24,579
Sep-2019	2019	-	1,356	247	40,329	38,726	5,220	450	34,314	28,644
Oct-2019	2019	-	1,373	236	38,201	36,593	7,302	432	19,258	11,523
Nov-2019	2019	-	3,758	225	36,300	32,316	7,921	420	8,696	355
Dec-2019	2019	-	1,089	215	34,464	33,160	4,490	410	96,821	91,921
Jan-2020	2020	-	1,092	205	35,724	34,427	5,841	387	65,560	59,332
Feb-2020	2020	-	4,099	195	34,015	29,721	7,492	382	67,381	59,506
Mar-2020	2020	-	896	186	32,239	31,157	4,580	369	121,120	116,171
Apr-2020	2020	-	839	178	31,664	30,647	5,478	360	30,397	24,559
May-2020	2020	-	3,414	170	30,025	26,441	6,980	351	39,456	32,125
Jun-2020	2020	-	707	162	28,335	27,466	4,472	348	16,280	11,459
Jul-2020	2020	-	695	154	26,712	25,863	5,728	342	27,951	21,881
Aug-2020	2020	-	3,034	147	25,248	22,067	6,512	320	8,728	1,896
Sep-2020	2020	-	590	141	23,860	23,129	4,671	317	9,921	4,933
Oct-2020	2020	-	551	134	22,527	21,842	4,588	311	123,374	118,476
Nov-2020	2020	-	2,729	127	21,322	18,466	6,417	298	2,790	(3,926)
Dec-2020	2020	-	471	120	20,183	19,592	4,012	292	19,563	15,259

Expected and Average Monthly Cash Flow
(IRR excludes all cash flows on past claims and PV excludes all cash flows prior to 12/31/06)

Date	Year	Historic Cash Flows	Expected Premiums for 10 Policies	Expected Expenses for 10 Policies	Expected Death Claims for 10 Policies	Expected Future Cash Flow For PV	Avg Future Premiums over 100 Scenarios	Avg Future Expenses over 100 Scenarios	Avg Future Death Claims over 100 Scenarios	Avg Future Cash Flow over 100 Scenarios
Jan-2021	2021	-	425	114	21,173	20,634	4,577	278	28,315	23,460
Feb-2021	2021	-	2,435	108	20,101	17,557	6,153	278	19,584	13,153
Mar-2021	2021	-	378	103	18,952	18,471	4,067	258	47,896	43,571
Apr-2021	2021	-	320	98	18,165	17,747	4,044	255	-	(4,299)
May-2021	2021	-	2,008	93	17,152	15,052	4,770	243	91,362	86,349
Jun-2021	2021	-	235	88	16,144	15,821	3,230	235	10,856	7,391
Jul-2021	2021	-	253	84	15,185	14,848	4,027	224	21,971	17,719
Aug-2021	2021	-	1,735	80	14,309	12,494	4,293	211	14,340	9,836
Sep-2021	2021	-	231	76	13,486	13,180	4,039	194	38,363	34,130
Oct-2021	2021	-	203	71	12,703	12,429	2,986	188	68,996	65,822
Nov-2021	2021	-	1,548	67	11,987	10,371	3,862	188	60,469	56,419
Dec-2021	2021	-	170	64	11,315	11,081	3,727	184	7,677	3,766
Jan-2022	2022	-	153	60	11,943	11,730	2,451	177	8,728	6,100
Feb-2022	2022	-	1,354	57	11,307	9,896	3,585	170	10,877	7,122
Mar-2022	2022	-	140	53	10,617	10,423	3,279	159	25,462	22,023
Apr-2022	2022	-	113	50	10,068	9,905	2,046	159	19,605	17,400
May-2022	2022	-	1,099	48	9,462	8,315	3,315	156	44,258	40,787
Jun-2022	2022	-	113	45	8,875	8,717	3,425	152	-	(3,577)
Jul-2022	2022	-	85	42	8,320	8,193	1,855	148	10,877	8,874
Aug-2022	2022	-	935	40	7,810	6,835	3,740	139	17,482	13,603
Sep-2022	2022	-	87	38	7,334	7,210	3,425	138	17,456	13,893
Oct-2022	2022	-	69	36	6,885	6,781	1,788	138	20,287	18,362
Nov-2022	2022	-	822	33	6,471	5,616	3,543	138	13,710	10,029
Dec-2022	2022	-	68	31	6,086	5,987	3,463	138	-	(3,602)
Jan-2023	2023	-	51	30	6,336	6,256	1,790	132	-	(1,922)
Feb-2023	2023	-	699	28	5,948	5,222	3,333	122	-	(3,455)
Mar-2023	2023	-	52	26	5,559	5,482	-	115	12,092	11,977
Apr-2023	2023	-	37	24	5,223	5,162	1,191	107	33,056	31,758
May-2023	2023	-	560	23	4,887	4,304	2,238	104	24,328	21,986
Jun-2023	2023	-	41	22	4,567	4,505	-	97	66,358	66,261
Jul-2023	2023	-	31	20	4,268	4,217	1,377	97	10,898	9,424
Aug-2023	2023	-	464	19	3,992	3,509	2,424	95	19,626	17,107
Sep-2023	2023	-	31	18	3,735	3,686	-	91	-	(91)
Oct-2023	2023	-	22	17	3,495	3,456	1,293	91	2,852	1,468
Nov-2023	2023	-	404	16	3,272	2,852	2,171	88	10,898	8,639
Dec-2023	2023	-	19	15	3,065	3,032	-	85	-	(85)
Jan-2024	2024	-	16	14	3,263	3,233	1,295	85	8,728	7,349
Feb-2024	2024	-	332	13	3,040	2,696	2,109	81	15,600	13,409
Mar-2024	2024	-	14	12	2,824	2,798	-	74	-	(74)
Apr-2024	2024	-	11	11	2,630	2,608	831	70	8,728	7,827
May-2024	2024	-	261	10	2,446	2,175	2,038	68	29,307	27,201
Jun-2024	2024	-	-	10	2,273	2,263	-	65	15,600	15,535
Jul-2024	2024	-	9	9	2,112	2,094	853	61	1,193	279
Aug-2024	2024	-	210	8	1,965	1,746	2,177	61	8,728	6,490
Sep-2024	2024	-	-	8	1,828	1,820	-	58	8,728	8,670
Oct-2024	2024	-	6	7	1,701	1,687	817	58	-	(875)
Nov-2024	2024	-	195	7	1,583	1,382	2,010	52	8,728	6,666
Dec-2024	2024	-	-	6	1,475	1,468	-	52	-	(52)
Jan-2025	2025	-	5	6	1,582	1,571	817	52	17,456	16,587
Feb-2025	2025	-	151	5	1,462	1,306	2,015	52	-	(2,067)
Mar-2025	2025	-	-	5	1,349	1,344	-	43	-	(43)
Apr-2025	2025	-	3	5	1,246	1,238	184	40	-	(224)
May-2025	2025	-	117	4	1,158	1,036	597	37	79,834	79,200
Jun-2025	2025	-	-	4	1,068	1,064	-	37	1,193	1,156
Jul-2025	2025	-	3	4	985	978	245	37	8,728	8,446
Aug-2025	2025	-	92	3	908	813	597	34	-	(632)
Sep-2025	2025	-	-	3	839	835	-	34	-	(34)
Oct-2025	2025	-	2	3	774	769	172	34	2,894	2,687
Nov-2025	2025	-	78	3	715	634	558	31	-	(589)
Dec-2025	2025	-	-	2	661	659	-	31	-	(31)

Expected and Average Monthly Cash Flow

(IRR excludes all cash flows on past claims and PV excludes all cash flows prior to 12/31/06)

Date	Year	Historic Cash Flows	Expected Premiums for 10 Policies	Expected Expenses for 10 Policies	Expected Death Claims for 10 Policies	Expected Future Cash Flow For PV	Avg Future Premiums over 100 Scenarios	Avg Future Expenses over 100 Scenarios	Avg Future Death Claims over 100 Scenarios	Avg Future Cash Flow over 100 Scenarios
Jan-2026	2026	-	1	2	730	726	172	31	8,728	8,525
Feb-2026	2026	-	59	2	665	605	500	30	-	(531)
Mar-2026	2026	-	-	2	606	604	-	30	-	(30)
Apr-2026	2026	-	1	2	552	549	115	28	8,728	8,586
May-2026	2026	-	44	2	503	458	490	28	-	(518)
Jun-2026	2026	-	-	1	458	457	-	28	2,908	2,880
Jul-2026	2026	-	1	1	418	416	124	24	-	(149)
Aug-2026	2026	-	33	1	381	346	411	24	-	(435)
Sep-2026	2026	-	-	1	347	346	-	24	8,728	8,704
Oct-2026	2026	-	0	1	317	315	122	24	-	(146)
Nov-2026	2026	-	27	1	289	261	429	24	-	(453)
Dec-2026	2026	-	-	1	263	263	-	24	-	(24)
Jan-2027	2027	-	0	1	300	299	122	24	-	(146)
Feb-2027	2027	-	19	1	267	248	456	24	-	(481)
Mar-2027	2027	-	-	1	238	238	-	24	-	(24)
Apr-2027	2027	-	0	0	213	212	122	24	-	(146)
May-2027	2027	-	13	0	190	176	359	21	-	(380)
Jun-2027	2027	-	-	0	169	169	-	18	-	(18)
Jul-2027	2027	-	0	0	151	150	61	18	8,728	8,649
Aug-2027	2027	-	9	0	135	125	360	18	2,932	2,554
Sep-2027	2027	-	-	0	120	120	-	18	-	(18)
Oct-2027	2027	-	0	0	107	107	61	18	-	(79)
Nov-2027	2027	-	7	0	96	89	97	13	-	(110)
Dec-2027	2027	-	-	0	86	86	-	13	-	(13)
Jan-2028	2028	-	0	0	98	97	61	13	-	(74)
Feb-2028	2028	-	4	0	85	80	94	13	-	(107)
Mar-2028	2028	-	-	0	73	73	-	9	-	(9)
Apr-2028	2028	-	0	0	63	63	61	9	-	(70)
May-2028	2028	-	3	0	55	52	94	9	-	(104)
Jun-2028	2028	-	-	0	47	47	-	9	-	(9)
Jul-2028	2028	-	0	0	41	41	61	9	-	(70)
Aug-2028	2028	-	2	0	35	34	94	9	-	(104)
Sep-2028	2028	-	-	0	31	31	-	9	-	(9)
Oct-2028	2028	-	0	0	27	27	61	9	-	(70)
Nov-2028	2028	-	1	0	23	22	107	6	-	(113)
Dec-2028	2028	-	-	0	20	20	-	6	-	(6)
Jan-2029	2029	-	0	0	25	25	-	6	-	(6)
Feb-2029	2029	-	1	0	19	19	103	6	-	(109)
Mar-2029	2029	-	-	0	16	16	-	6	-	(6)
Apr-2029	2029	-	0	0	13	13	-	6	-	(6)
May-2029	2029	-	0	0	10	10	103	6	-	(109)
Jun-2029	2029	-	-	0	9	9	-	6	-	(6)
Jul-2029	2029	-	0	0	7	7	-	3	-	(3)
Aug-2029	2029	-	0	0	6	5	-	3	-	(3)
Sep-2029	2029	-	-	0	5	5	-	3	8,728	8,725
Oct-2029	2029	-	0	0	4	4	-	3	-	(3)
Nov-2029	2029	-	0	0	3	3	-	3	-	(3)
Dec-2029	2029	-	-	0	2	2	-	-	-	-
Jan-2030	2030	-	-	0	3	3	-	-	-	-
Feb-2030	2030	-	0	0	2	2	-	-	-	-
Mar-2030	2030	-	-	0	2	2	-	-	-	-
Apr-2030	2030	-	-	0	1	1	-	-	-	-
May-2030	2030	-	0	0	1	1	-	-	-	-
Jun-2030	2030	-	-	0	1	1	-	-	-	-
Jul-2030	2030	-	-	0	0	0	-	-	-	-
Aug-2030	2030	-	0	0	0	0	-	-	-	-
Sep-2030	2030	-	-	0	0	0	-	-	-	-
Oct-2030	2030	-	-	0	0	0	-	-	-	-
Nov-2030	2030	-	-	-	0	0	-	-	-	-
Dec-2030	2030	-	-	0	0	0	-	-	-	-

Expected and Average Monthly Cash Flow

(IRR excludes all cash flows on past claims and PV excludes all cash flows prior to 12/31/06)

Date	Year	Historic Cash Flows	Expected Premiums for 10 Policies	Expected Expenses for 10 Policies	Expected Death Claims for 10 Policies	Expected Future Cash Flow For PV	Avg Future Premiums over 100 Scenarios	Avg Future Expenses over 100 Scenarios	Avg Future Death Claims over 100 Scenarios	Avg Future Cash Flow over 100 Scenarios
Jan-2031	2031	-	-	-	0	0	-	-	-	-
Feb-2031	2031	-	-	-	-	-	-	-	-	-
Mar-2031	2031	-	-	-	-	-	-	-	-	-
Apr-2031	2031	-	-	-	-	-	-	-	-	-
May-2031	2031	-	-	-	-	-	-	-	-	-
Jun-2031	2031	-	-	-	-	-	-	-	-	-
Jul-2031	2031	-	-	-	-	-	-	-	-	-
Aug-2031	2031	-	-	-	-	-	-	-	-	-
Sep-2031	2031	-	-	-	-	-	-	-	-	-
Oct-2031	2031	-	-	-	-	-	-	-	-	-
Nov-2031	2031	-	-	-	-	-	-	-	-	-
Dec-2031	2031	-	-	-	-	-	-	-	-	-
Jan-2032	2032	-	-	-	-	-	-	-	-	-
Feb-2032	2032	-	-	-	-	-	-	-	-	-
Mar-2032	2032	-	-	-	-	-	-	-	-	-
Apr-2032	2032	-	-	-	-	-	-	-	-	-
May-2032	2032	-	-	-	-	-	-	-	-	-
Jun-2032	2032	-	-	-	-	-	-	-	-	-
Jul-2032	2032	-	-	-	-	-	-	-	-	-
Aug-2032	2032	-	-	-	-	-	-	-	-	-
Sep-2032	2032	-	-	-	-	-	-	-	-	-
Oct-2032	2032	-	-	-	-	-	-	-	-	-
Nov-2032	2032	-	-	-	-	-	-	-	-	-
Dec-2032	2032	-	-	-	-	-	-	-	-	-
Jan-2033	2033	-	-	-	-	-	-	-	-	-
Feb-2033	2033	-	-	-	-	-	-	-	-	-
Mar-2033	2033	-	-	-	-	-	-	-	-	-
Apr-2033	2033	-	-	-	-	-	-	-	-	-
May-2033	2033	-	-	-	-	-	-	-	-	-
Jun-2033	2033	-	-	-	-	-	-	-	-	-
Jul-2033	2033	-	-	-	-	-	-	-	-	-
Aug-2033	2033	-	-	-	-	-	-	-	-	-
Sep-2033	2033	-	-	-	-	-	-	-	-	-
Oct-2033	2033	-	-	-	-	-	-	-	-	-
Nov-2033	2033	-	-	-	-	-	-	-	-	-
Dec-2033	2033	-	-	-	-	-	-	-	-	-
Jan-2034	2034	-	-	-	-	-	-	-	-	-
Feb-2034	2034	-	-	-	-	-	-	-	-	-
Mar-2034	2034	-	-	-	-	-	-	-	-	-
Apr-2034	2034	-	-	-	-	-	-	-	-	-
May-2034	2034	-	-	-	-	-	-	-	-	-
Jun-2034	2034	-	-	-	-	-	-	-	-	-
Jul-2034	2034	-	-	-	-	-	-	-	-	-
Aug-2034	2034	-	-	-	-	-	-	-	-	-
Sep-2034	2034	-	-	-	-	-	-	-	-	-
Oct-2034	2034	-	-	-	-	-	-	-	-	-
Nov-2034	2034	-	-	-	-	-	-	-	-	-
Dec-2034	2034	-	-	-	-	-	-	-	-	-
Jan-2035	2035	-	-	-	-	-	-	-	-	-
Feb-2035	2035	-	-	-	-	-	-	-	-	-
Mar-2035	2035	-	-	-	-	-	-	-	-	-
Apr-2035	2035	-	-	-	-	-	-	-	-	-
May-2035	2035	-	-	-	-	-	-	-	-	-
Jun-2035	2035	-	-	-	-	-	-	-	-	-
Jul-2035	2035	-	-	-	-	-	-	-	-	-
Aug-2035	2035	-	-	-	-	-	-	-	-	-
Sep-2035	2035	-	-	-	-	-	-	-	-	-
Oct-2035	2035	-	-	-	-	-	-	-	-	-
Nov-2035	2035	-	-	-	-	-	-	-	-	-
Dec-2035	2035	-	-	-	-	-	-	-	-	-

Expected and Average Monthly Cash Flow

(IRR excludes all cash flows on past claims and PV excludes all cash flows prior to 12/31/06)

Date	Year	Historic Cash Flows	Expected Premiums for 10 Policies	Expected Expenses for 10 Policies	Expected Death Claims for 10 Policies	Expected Future Cash Flow For PV	Avg Future Premiums over 100 Scenarios	Avg Future Expenses over 100 Scenarios	Avg Future Death Claims over 100 Scenarios	Avg Future Cash Flow over 100 Scenarios
Jan-2036	2036	-	-	-	-	-	-	-	-	-
Feb-2036	2036	-	-	-	-	-	-	-	-	-
Mar-2036	2036	-	-	-	-	-	-	-	-	-
Apr-2036	2036	-	-	-	-	-	-	-	-	-
May-2036	2036	-	-	-	-	-	-	-	-	-
Jun-2036	2036	-	-	-	-	-	-	-	-	-
Jul-2036	2036	-	-	-	-	-	-	-	-	-
Aug-2036	2036	-	-	-	-	-	-	-	-	-
Sep-2036	2036	-	-	-	-	-	-	-	-	-
Oct-2036	2036	-	-	-	-	-	-	-	-	-
Nov-2036	2036	-	-	-	-	-	-	-	-	-
Dec-2036	2036	-	-	-	-	-	-	-	-	-
Jan-2037	2037	-	-	-	-	-	-	-	-	-
Feb-2037	2037	-	-	-	-	-	-	-	-	-
Mar-2037	2037	-	-	-	-	-	-	-	-	-
Apr-2037	2037	-	-	-	-	-	-	-	-	-
May-2037	2037	-	-	-	-	-	-	-	-	-
Jun-2037	2037	-	-	-	-	-	-	-	-	-
Jul-2037	2037	-	-	-	-	-	-	-	-	-
Aug-2037	2037	-	-	-	-	-	-	-	-	-
Sep-2037	2037	-	-	-	-	-	-	-	-	-
Oct-2037	2037	-	-	-	-	-	-	-	-	-
Nov-2037	2037	-	-	-	-	-	-	-	-	-
Dec-2037	2037	-	-	-	-	-	-	-	-	-
Jan-2038	2038	-	-	-	-	-	-	-	-	-
Feb-2038	2038	-	-	-	-	-	-	-	-	-
Mar-2038	2038	-	-	-	-	-	-	-	-	-
Apr-2038	2038	-	-	-	-	-	-	-	-	-
May-2038	2038	-	-	-	-	-	-	-	-	-
Jun-2038	2038	-	-	-	-	-	-	-	-	-
Jul-2038	2038	-	-	-	-	-	-	-	-	-
Aug-2038	2038	-	-	-	-	-	-	-	-	-
Sep-2038	2038	-	-	-	-	-	-	-	-	-
Oct-2038	2038	-	-	-	-	-	-	-	-	-
Nov-2038	2038	-	-	-	-	-	-	-	-	-
Dec-2038	2038	-	-	-	-	-	-	-	-	-
Jan-2039	2039	-	-	-	-	-	-	-	-	-
Feb-2039	2039	-	-	-	-	-	-	-	-	-
Mar-2039	2039	-	-	-	-	-	-	-	-	-
Apr-2039	2039	-	-	-	-	-	-	-	-	-
May-2039	2039	-	-	-	-	-	-	-	-	-
Jun-2039	2039	-	-	-	-	-	-	-	-	-
Jul-2039	2039	-	-	-	-	-	-	-	-	-
Aug-2039	2039	-	-	-	-	-	-	-	-	-
Sep-2039	2039	-	-	-	-	-	-	-	-	-
Oct-2039	2039	-	-	-	-	-	-	-	-	-
Nov-2039	2039	-	-	-	-	-	-	-	-	-
Dec-2039	2039	-	-	-	-	-	-	-	-	-
Jan-2040	2040	-	-	-	-	-	-	-	-	-
Feb-2040	2040	-	-	-	-	-	-	-	-	-
Mar-2040	2040	-	-	-	-	-	-	-	-	-
Apr-2040	2040	-	-	-	-	-	-	-	-	-
May-2040	2040	-	-	-	-	-	-	-	-	-
Jun-2040	2040	-	-	-	-	-	-	-	-	-
Jul-2040	2040	-	-	-	-	-	-	-	-	-
Aug-2040	2040	-	-	-	-	-	-	-	-	-
Sep-2040	2040	-	-	-	-	-	-	-	-	-
Oct-2040	2040	-	-	-	-	-	-	-	-	-
Nov-2040	2040	-	-	-	-	-	-	-	-	-
Dec-2040	2040	-	-	-	-	-	-	-	-	-

Expected and Average Monthly Cash Flow

(IRR excludes all cash flows on past claims and PV excludes all cash flows prior to 12/31/06)

Date	Year	Historic Cash Flows	Expected Premiums for 10 Policies	Expected Expenses for 10 Policies	Expected Death Claims for 10 Policies	Expected Future Cash Flow For PV	Avg Future Premiums over 100 Scenarios	Avg Future Expenses over 100 Scenarios	Avg Future Death Claims over 100 Scenarios	Avg Future Cash Flow over 100 Scenarios
Jan-2041	2041	-	-	-	-	-	-	-	-	-
Feb-2041	2041	-	-	-	-	-	-	-	-	-
Mar-2041	2041	-	-	-	-	-	-	-	-	-
Apr-2041	2041	-	-	-	-	-	-	-	-	-
May-2041	2041	-	-	-	-	-	-	-	-	-
Jun-2041	2041	-	-	-	-	-	-	-	-	-
Jul-2041	2041	-	-	-	-	-	-	-	-	-
Aug-2041	2041	-	-	-	-	-	-	-	-	-
Sep-2041	2041	-	-	-	-	-	-	-	-	-
Oct-2041	2041	-	-	-	-	-	-	-	-	-
Nov-2041	2041	-	-	-	-	-	-	-	-	-
Dec-2041	2041	-	-	-	-	-	-	-	-	-
Jan-2042	2042	-	-	-	-	-	-	-	-	-
Feb-2042	2042	-	-	-	-	-	-	-	-	-
Mar-2042	2042	-	-	-	-	-	-	-	-	-
Apr-2042	2042	-	-	-	-	-	-	-	-	-
May-2042	2042	-	-	-	-	-	-	-	-	-
Jun-2042	2042	-	-	-	-	-	-	-	-	-
Jul-2042	2042	-	-	-	-	-	-	-	-	-
Aug-2042	2042	-	-	-	-	-	-	-	-	-
Sep-2042	2042	-	-	-	-	-	-	-	-	-
Oct-2042	2042	-	-	-	-	-	-	-	-	-
Nov-2042	2042	-	-	-	-	-	-	-	-	-
Dec-2042	2042	-	-	-	-	-	-	-	-	-
Jan-2043	2043	-	-	-	-	-	-	-	-	-
Feb-2043	2043	-	-	-	-	-	-	-	-	-
Mar-2043	2043	-	-	-	-	-	-	-	-	-
Apr-2043	2043	-	-	-	-	-	-	-	-	-
May-2043	2043	-	-	-	-	-	-	-	-	-
Jun-2043	2043	-	-	-	-	-	-	-	-	-
Jul-2043	2043	-	-	-	-	-	-	-	-	-
Aug-2043	2043	-	-	-	-	-	-	-	-	-
Sep-2043	2043	-	-	-	-	-	-	-	-	-
Oct-2043	2043	-	-	-	-	-	-	-	-	-
Nov-2043	2043	-	-	-	-	-	-	-	-	-
Dec-2043	2043	-	-	-	-	-	-	-	-	-
Jan-2044	2044	-	-	-	-	-	-	-	-	-
Feb-2044	2044	-	-	-	-	-	-	-	-	-
Mar-2044	2044	-	-	-	-	-	-	-	-	-
Apr-2044	2044	-	-	-	-	-	-	-	-	-
May-2044	2044	-	-	-	-	-	-	-	-	-
Jun-2044	2044	-	-	-	-	-	-	-	-	-
Jul-2044	2044	-	-	-	-	-	-	-	-	-
Aug-2044	2044	-	-	-	-	-	-	-	-	-
Sep-2044	2044	-	-	-	-	-	-	-	-	-
Oct-2044	2044	-	-	-	-	-	-	-	-	-
Nov-2044	2044	-	-	-	-	-	-	-	-	-
Dec-2044	2044	-	-	-	-	-	-	-	-	-
Jan-2045	2045	-	-	-	-	-	-	-	-	-
Feb-2045	2045	-	-	-	-	-	-	-	-	-
Mar-2045	2045	-	-	-	-	-	-	-	-	-
Apr-2045	2045	-	-	-	-	-	-	-	-	-
May-2045	2045	-	-	-	-	-	-	-	-	-
Jun-2045	2045	-	-	-	-	-	-	-	-	-
Jul-2045	2045	-	-	-	-	-	-	-	-	-
Aug-2045	2045	-	-	-	-	-	-	-	-	-
Sep-2045	2045	-	-	-	-	-	-	-	-	-
Oct-2045	2045	-	-	-	-	-	-	-	-	-
Nov-2045	2045	-	-	-	-	-	-	-	-	-
Dec-2045	2045	-	-	-	-	-	-	-	-	-

Expected and Average Monthly Cash Flow
(IRR excludes all cash flows on past claims and PV excludes all cash flows prior to 12/31/06)

Date	Year	Historic Cash Flows	Expected Premiums for 10 Policies	Expected Expenses for 10 Policies	Expected Death Claims for 10 Policies	Expected Future Cash Flow For PV	Avg Future Premiums over 100 Scenarios	Avg Future Expenses over 100 Scenarios	Avg Future Death Claims over 100 Scenarios	Avg Future Cash Flow over 100 Scenarios
Jan-2046	2046	-	-	-	-	-	-	-	-	-
Feb-2046	2046	-	-	-	-	-	-	-	-	-
Mar-2046	2046	-	-	-	-	-	-	-	-	-
Apr-2046	2046	-	-	-	-	-	-	-	-	-
May-2046	2046	-	-	-	-	-	-	-	-	-
Jun-2046	2046	-	-	-	-	-	-	-	-	-
Jul-2046	2046	-	-	-	-	-	-	-	-	-
Aug-2046	2046	-	-	-	-	-	-	-	-	-
Sep-2046	2046	-	-	-	-	-	-	-	-	-
Oct-2046	2046	-	-	-	-	-	-	-	-	-
Nov-2046	2046	-	-	-	-	-	-	-	-	-
Dec-2046	2046	-	-	-	-	-	-	-	-	-
Jan-2047	2047	-	-	-	-	-	-	-	-	-
Feb-2047	2047	-	-	-	-	-	-	-	-	-
Mar-2047	2047	-	-	-	-	-	-	-	-	-
Apr-2047	2047	-	-	-	-	-	-	-	-	-
May-2047	2047	-	-	-	-	-	-	-	-	-
Jun-2047	2047	-	-	-	-	-	-	-	-	-
Jul-2047	2047	-	-	-	-	-	-	-	-	-
Aug-2047	2047	-	-	-	-	-	-	-	-	-
Sep-2047	2047	-	-	-	-	-	-	-	-	-
Oct-2047	2047	-	-	-	-	-	-	-	-	-
Nov-2047	2047	-	-	-	-	-	-	-	-	-
Dec-2047	2047	-	-	-	-	-	-	-	-	-
Jan-2048	2048	-	-	-	-	-	-	-	-	-
Feb-2048	2048	-	-	-	-	-	-	-	-	-
Mar-2048	2048	-	-	-	-	-	-	-	-	-
Apr-2048	2048	-	-	-	-	-	-	-	-	-
May-2048	2048	-	-	-	-	-	-	-	-	-
Jun-2048	2048	-	-	-	-	-	-	-	-	-
Jul-2048	2048	-	-	-	-	-	-	-	-	-
Aug-2048	2048	-	-	-	-	-	-	-	-	-
Sep-2048	2048	-	-	-	-	-	-	-	-	-
Oct-2048	2048	-	-	-	-	-	-	-	-	-
Nov-2048	2048	-	-	-	-	-	-	-	-	-
Dec-2048	2048	-	-	-	-	-	-	-	-	-
Jan-2049	2049	-	-	-	-	-	-	-	-	-
Feb-2049	2049	-	-	-	-	-	-	-	-	-
Mar-2049	2049	-	-	-	-	-	-	-	-	-
Apr-2049	2049	-	-	-	-	-	-	-	-	-
May-2049	2049	-	-	-	-	-	-	-	-	-
Jun-2049	2049	-	-	-	-	-	-	-	-	-
Jul-2049	2049	-	-	-	-	-	-	-	-	-
Aug-2049	2049	-	-	-	-	-	-	-	-	-
Sep-2049	2049	-	-	-	-	-	-	-	-	-
Oct-2049	2049	-	-	-	-	-	-	-	-	-
Nov-2049	2049	-	-	-	-	-	-	-	-	-
Dec-2049	2049	-	-	-	-	-	-	-	-	-
Jan-2050	2050	-	-	-	-	-	-	-	-	-
Feb-2050	2050	-	-	-	-	-	-	-	-	-
Mar-2050	2050	-	-	-	-	-	-	-	-	-
Apr-2050	2050	-	-	-	-	-	-	-	-	-
May-2050	2050	-	-	-	-	-	-	-	-	-
Jun-2050	2050	-	-	-	-	-	-	-	-	-
Jul-2050	2050	-	-	-	-	-	-	-	-	-
Aug-2050	2050	-	-	-	-	-	-	-	-	-
Sep-2050	2050	-	-	-	-	-	-	-	-	-
Oct-2050	2050	-	-	-	-	-	-	-	-	-
Nov-2050	2050	-	-	-	-	-	-	-	-	-
Dec-2050	2050	-	-	-	-	-	-	-	-	-

Expected and Average Monthly Cash Flow

(IRR excludes all cash flows on past claims and PV excludes all cash flows prior to 12/31/06)

Date	Year	Historic Cash Flows	Expected Premiums for 10 Policies	Expected Expenses for 10 Policies	Expected Death Claims for 10 Policies	Expected Future Cash Flow For PV	Avg Future Premiums over 100 Scenarios	Avg Future Expenses over 100 Scenarios	Avg Future Death Claims over 100 Scenarios	Avg Future Cash Flow over 100 Scenarios
Jan-2051	2051	-	-	-	-	-	-	-	-	-
Feb-2051	2051	-	-	-	-	-	-	-	-	-
Mar-2051	2051	-	-	-	-	-	-	-	-	-
Apr-2051	2051	-	-	-	-	-	-	-	-	-
May-2051	2051	-	-	-	-	-	-	-	-	-
Jun-2051	2051	-	-	-	-	-	-	-	-	-
Jul-2051	2051	-	-	-	-	-	-	-	-	-
Aug-2051	2051	-	-	-	-	-	-	-	-	-
Sep-2051	2051	-	-	-	-	-	-	-	-	-
Oct-2051	2051	-	-	-	-	-	-	-	-	-
Nov-2051	2051	-	-	-	-	-	-	-	-	-
Dec-2051	2051	-	-	-	-	-	-	-	-	-
Jan-2052	2052	-	-	-	-	-	-	-	-	-
Feb-2052	2052	-	-	-	-	-	-	-	-	-
Mar-2052	2052	-	-	-	-	-	-	-	-	-
Apr-2052	2052	-	-	-	-	-	-	-	-	-
May-2052	2052	-	-	-	-	-	-	-	-	-
Jun-2052	2052	-	-	-	-	-	-	-	-	-
Jul-2052	2052	-	-	-	-	-	-	-	-	-
Aug-2052	2052	-	-	-	-	-	-	-	-	-
Sep-2052	2052	-	-	-	-	-	-	-	-	-
Oct-2052	2052	-	-	-	-	-	-	-	-	-
Nov-2052	2052	-	-	-	-	-	-	-	-	-
Dec-2052	2052	-	-	-	-	-	-	-	-	-
Jan-2053	2053	-	-	-	-	-	-	-	-	-
Feb-2053	2053	-	-	-	-	-	-	-	-	-
Mar-2053	2053	-	-	-	-	-	-	-	-	-
Apr-2053	2053	-	-	-	-	-	-	-	-	-
May-2053	2053	-	-	-	-	-	-	-	-	-
Jun-2053	2053	-	-	-	-	-	-	-	-	-
Jul-2053	2053	-	-	-	-	-	-	-	-	-
Aug-2053	2053	-	-	-	-	-	-	-	-	-
Sep-2053	2053	-	-	-	-	-	-	-	-	-
Oct-2053	2053	-	-	-	-	-	-	-	-	-
Nov-2053	2053	-	-	-	-	-	-	-	-	-
Dec-2053	2053	-	-	-	-	-	-	-	-	-
Jan-2054	2054	-	-	-	-	-	-	-	-	-
Feb-2054	2054	-	-	-	-	-	-	-	-	-
Mar-2054	2054	-	-	-	-	-	-	-	-	-
Apr-2054	2054	-	-	-	-	-	-	-	-	-
May-2054	2054	-	-	-	-	-	-	-	-	-
Jun-2054	2054	-	-	-	-	-	-	-	-	-
Jul-2054	2054	-	-	-	-	-	-	-	-	-
Aug-2054	2054	-	-	-	-	-	-	-	-	-
Sep-2054	2054	-	-	-	-	-	-	-	-	-
Oct-2054	2054	-	-	-	-	-	-	-	-	-
Nov-2054	2054	-	-	-	-	-	-	-	-	-
Dec-2054	2054	-	-	-	-	-	-	-	-	-
Jan-2055	2055	-	-	-	-	-	-	-	-	-
Feb-2055	2055	-	-	-	-	-	-	-	-	-
Mar-2055	2055	-	-	-	-	-	-	-	-	-
Apr-2055	2055	-	-	-	-	-	-	-	-	-
May-2055	2055	-	-	-	-	-	-	-	-	-
Jun-2055	2055	-	-	-	-	-	-	-	-	-
Jul-2055	2055	-	-	-	-	-	-	-	-	-
Aug-2055	2055	-	-	-	-	-	-	-	-	-
Sep-2055	2055	-	-	-	-	-	-	-	-	-
Oct-2055	2055	-	-	-	-	-	-	-	-	-
Nov-2055	2055	-	-	-	-	-	-	-	-	-
Dec-2055	2055	-	-	-	-	-	-	-	-	-

Expected and Average Monthly Cash Flow

(IRR excludes all cash flows on past claims and PV excludes all cash flows prior to 12/31/06)

Mortality Assumption Based on:
2001 VBT 50% S&U and 50% Ult Mortality Table ANB and Supplied Life Expectancies
Past (2001–2006) Annual Improvement based on Historical Population Experience
Future Annual Improvement based on 100% Male Historical Population Experience
Future Annual Improvement based on 100% Female Historical Population Experience

* This analysis is based on the following assumptions:

Policy purchase, premium, and expenses assumed to occur on the first day of each calendar month.

Premiums paid equal 100% of input Projected Premiums.

Monthly administration expenses at annualized rate of 0.10% per Inforce Death Benefits

plus $12.50 annually per policy plus an annual portfolio fee of $15000.00 as long as any policies are inforce

Attained Age is determined based on Date of Birth and the "As of Date of LE Estimate" in Company data.

Policies assumed in force on today's date (i.e., assumed 100% survival until now) unless earlier input Claim Date

Dates, Net Purchase Price, Net Death Benefit and Projected Premiums as shown in Policy Input and Premium Input

Mortality adjustments and improvement assumption grade to 100% between attained ages 105 and 120

Claim proceeds assumed to be paid at end of each month plus 2 months from death, earning statutory interest at 0.00%

** Expected shows results of Probabilistic Approach

Notice Regarding Mortality and Volatility: Underwriting firms commonly develop "life expectancies" for the benefit of life settlement parties. While life expectancies are provided for individuals, they are developed from expected patterns of mortality of large groups of similar individuals. No one knows exactly when any one individual will die, nor is the life expectancy intended to be predictive of a "date certain". For a variety of reasons (such as improvements in medical technology, unanticipated general mortality improvement, or misestimation of the life expectancy by underwriting firms), any one individual may live much longer than his or her estimated life expectancy. With small groups of insureds, and particularly with a single insured, the actual time until death may be significantly different than the life expectancy or that predicted by any particular mortality table. Stochastic simulation and sensitivity testing can help to quantify these risks, but such tests should not be interpreted as a guarantee of any particular financial outcome. Investors will earn significantly less than expected on the policy of any individual who lives longer than his life expectancy.

Bibliography

A.M. Best (2008, 24 March) *Life Settlement Securitisation*. Available at: http://www.ambest.com/debt/
  lifesettlement.pdf.

ABI (2008) *Mortgage Endowments: A Factsheet*. Association of British Insurers, July.

ACLI (2008) *Life Insurers Fact Book 2008*. American Council of Life Insurers, October 29.

Altman, E.I., Resti, A. and Sironi, A. (2004) Default recovery rates in credit risk modeling: a review of
  the literature and empirical evidence. *Economic Notes*, 33 (No. 2, July), 183–208.

Bauer, D., Börger, M. and Zwiesler, H.J. (2008) The Volatility of Mortality. *Asia-Pacific Journal of Risk
  and Insurance*, 3, 184–211.

Bernstein Research (2005) *Life Insurance: Life Settlements Need Not Be Unsettling*, June.

Bernstein Research (2006) *Life Insurance: Life Settlements Update – What a Difference a Year Can
  Make*, May.

Bertrand, P. and Prigent, J.-L. (2001) *Portfolio insurance strategies: OBPI versus CPPI*. Thema, Universit
  de Cergy, Working Paper.

Bertrand, P. and Prigent, J.-L. (2003) Portfolio insurance strategies: A comparison of standard methods
  when the volatility of the stock is stochastic, *International Journal of Business*, 8(4).

Black, F. and Jones, R. (1987) Simplifying portfolio insurance, *Journal of Portfolio Management*. Fall.

Black, F. and Perold, A.R. (1992) Theory of constant proportion portfolio insurance, *Journal of Eco-
  nomics and Dynamics Control*, 16, 403–426.

Blake, D., Cairns, A.J.G. and Dowd, K. (2006) Living with Mortality: Longevity Bonds and Other
  Mortality-Linked Securities. *British Actuarial Journal* 12(1), 153–197.

Cairns, A., Blake, D. and Dowd, K. (2008) Modelling and Managing of Mortality Risk: A Review.
  Scandinavian Actuarial Journal, 2–3, 79–113

Cairns, A.J.G., Blake, D. and Dowd, K. (2006) Pricing Death: Framework for the Valuation and Securitization of Mortality Risk. *ASTIN Bulletin*, 36, 79–120.

Chaplin, G. (2005) *Credit Derivatives: Risk Management, Trading and Investing*. John Wiley & Sons
  Ltd.

Cherubini, U. (2007) *Structured Finance: The Object Oriented Approach*. John Wiley & Sons Ltd.

Cox, S. and Lin, Y. (2007) Natural Hedging of Life and Annuity Mortality Rates. *North American
  Actuarial Journal* 11(3), 1–15.

Culp, C.L. (2004) *Risk Transfer Derivatives in Theory and Practice*. John Wiley & Sons Inc.

Culp, C.L. (2006) *Structured Finance and Insurance: The Art of Managing Capital and Risk*. John Wiley
  & Sons Inc.

Cummins, J.D. (2004) *Securitization of Life Insurance Assets and Liabilities*. Wharton Financial Institutions Center.

Das, S. (2001) *Structured Products and Hybrid Securities* (2nd edition). John Wiley & Sons Ltd.

Davidson, A., Sanders, A., Wolfe, L.L. and Ching, A. (2003) *Securitization Structuring and Investment
  Analysis*. John Wiley & Sons Inc.

Davis, M.H. (1998) A note on the forward measure, *Finance and Stochastics*, 2, 19–28.

Dawson, P., Blake, D., Cairns, A. and Dowd, K. (2008) *Options on Normal Underlyings with an
  Application to the Pricing of Survivor Swaptions*. Pensions Institute Discussion Paper PI-0713.

Doherty, N.A. and Singer, H.J. (2002) *Life settlements.* Wharton Working Paper.

Dowd, K., Blake, D., Cairns, A. and Dawson, P. (2006) Survivor Swaps. *Journal of Risk and Insurance*, 73, 1–17.

Fabozzi, F.J., Bhattacharya, A.K. and Berliner, W.S. (2007) *Mortgage Backed Securities: Products, Structuring, and Analytical Techniques.* John Wiley & Sons, Inc.

Hailer, A.C. and Rump, S.M. (2005) Evaluation of Hedge Effectiveness Test. *Journal of Derivatives Accounting*, 2(1), 31–51.

Hull, J. and White, A. (2006) *The Perfect Copula.* Joseph L. Rotman School of Management, University of Toronto.

Kpanzou, T.A. (2007) *Copulas in Statistics.* African Institute for Mathematical Sciences (AIMS).

Leland, H.E. and Rubinstein, M. (1976) The evolution of portfolio insurance, in D.L. Luskin (ed.), *Portfolio Insurance: A Guide to Dynamic Hedging.* John Wiley & Sons Inc.

LifeMetrics – JP Morgan Technical Document.

MacMinn, R. and Richter, A. (2006) *Hedging Brevity and Longevity Risk with Mortality-Based Securities.* Munich School of Management Discussion Paper.

Modu, E. (2008) *Life settlement securitization.* A.M. Best Paper.

Mott, A.R. (2007) New Swaps to Hedge Alpha and Beta Longevity Risks of Life Settlement Pools. *The Journal of Structured Finance*, Summer.

Nelsen, R.B. (1998). *An Introduction to Copulas.* Springer-Verlag.

Palella, F.J., Delaney, K.M., Moorman, A.C., Loveless, M.O., Fuhrer, J., Satten, G.A., Aschman, D.J. and Holmberg, S.D. (1998) Declining morbidity and mortality among patients with advanced human immunodeficiency virus infection. *New England Journal of Medicine*, 338(13), 853–860.

Perera, N. and Pearson, L. (2007) An Exploration of Mortality Risk Mitigation. *The Journal of Structured Finance*, Summer.

Press, W.H., Teukolsky, S.A., Vetterling, W.T. and Flannery, B.P. (2002). *Numerical Recipes in C++.* Cambridge University Press.

Svensson, L.E.O. (1995) Estimating Forward Interest Rates with Extended Nelson and Siegel Methods. *Sveriges Riksbank, Quarterly Review*, 3, 13–26.

Sweeting, P. (2008) *Stochastic Mortality made Easy.* Pensions Institute.

The Encyclopedia of Actuarial Science (2004). John Wiley & Sons, Inc.

Xiao, L. (2006) *Estimation of Stochastic Volatility Models using Realized Volatility.* Term paper, University of Western Ontario.

Zelizer, V.A.R (1983) Morals & Markets: the Development of Life Insurance in the United States. Transaction Publishers, p. 173.

Index

Printed in the United States
By Bookmasters